World War III
Salvation of the Jew

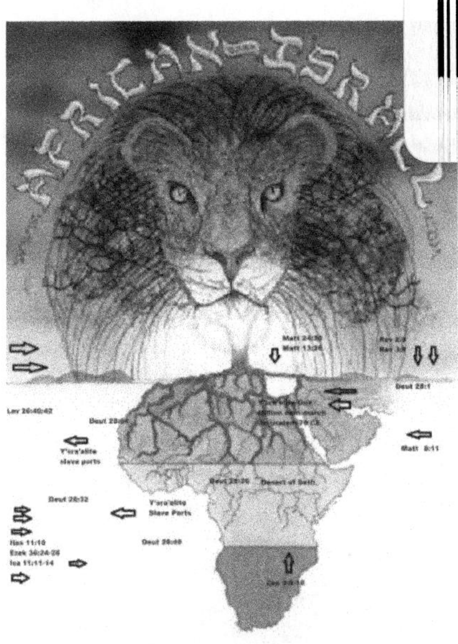

By Rabbi Simon Altaf

Third Edition

Revision: 31 March 2018.

For contacting us the USA Rabbi Lamont Clophus, Forever-Israel, 8111 Mainland, Suite 104-152, San Antonio, Texas, 78240, USA

For contacting us Rabbi Simon Altaf for forever-israel International congregations or please contact us via e-mail through foreverisrael777@yahoo.com or phone Rabbi Lamont in the USA: Tel 1-210-827-3907.

Visit our website at: www.forever-israel.com

Acknowledgments

All quotes are from the Hidden-Truths Hebraic Scrolls unless otherwise stated. We encourage you to buy these scriptures from the above website or www.amazon.com. Hardback can be obtained from www.lulu.com/simalt.

We wish to communicate that we love the Muslims as the children of Abraham and want them to come to know the true God named YHWH revealed in Master Yahushua for the increase and free gift of the salvation of their souls. This work is published with this increased hope.

Forever-Israel International Congregations

This book is dedicated in memory to my son Shujah Altaf 05/01/1994 to 31/03/2010. If it was not for my son I would not be alive today and would perhaps be dead in the 9/11 twin towers collapse. I had a job there in 1997, which I left in the US after I learnt about my son having a congenital illness from birth which took me back to England from the US. He fought to the end with his disease and passed back to the Master in March 2010 at the age of 16 the first day of the feast of Unleavened Bread and was committed to the grave the same date that Yahushua my Master was committed to the grave 2000 years ago during the festival of Passover on Nissan 14. Master Yahushua rose from the dead and He promised me 14 years ago that my family was in His hands and indeed will also be raised up. I look forward to join my son because I shall go to him and

YHWH will raise both of us up for the age to come to be restored to our Hebrew people in Israel. My son is alive with the Master Melek Yahushua. Hallelu'Yah.

It is important to say that the REAL children of Israel are the BLACK and BROWN Hebrews scattered throughout the world. One thing one can say that these are the people, the ones put down the most because of the curses in Leviticus 26 and Deuteronomy 28. The Black Hebrews were enslaved by the Jews, the apostate gentile converts to our faith who today claim to be chosen from Khazaria but are not. Please read Rev 3:9. The Sephardic Jews enslaved our people in ships and took them to the New World, these were taken from Africa to the New World and from the New World to the Caribbean's. The Jews who came from Khazaria were the largest kingdom converted to Judaism in the 8th Century CE. The Jews known as the Sephardic was the whole kingdom that was converted in Yemen in the 5th century CE. They were not the Children of Israel.

Also one other sign that I am telling you the truth is this that good men are slandered and discredited. Why? This is so that no one would believe them and the information can be passed as not credible. Look at how some have done this to me in the internet in the US, Google my name Simon Altaf polygamous and you will see slanderers typically Arab and others of gentile extraction doing the dirty deeds.

In the past one of our own brother was a rebel that has a whole parsha in his name called Korah in Numbers 16, the half brother of Moses from his father's second wife and the mixed gentiles who went up and stood against Moses. The same pattern. The Arab gentiles by the way were heavily involved in slavery and are to this day. If you ever get a chance in your life go to Abu Dhabi, Dubai and Qatar and look at the plush hotels, buildings and other structures. These were built by modern slaves. Take a guess where they came from? India, Pakistan, Bangladesh and Sri Lanka. Do not discount the South-Asian places as gentile because in these nations are our people even today who were scattered there centuries ago during the Assyrian and Babylonian expulsions of Israel. If you get a chance find out the conditions of workers in Dubai, Qatar in what squalor they live and sometimes they don't get paid for months, their passports taken away, it's a very sad affair. Yes many of these are part of the true children of Israel still living in curses due to Torah disobedience.

Let me tell you some history of Pakistan, in the ruins of Mojendaro and Harappa they found statues of Black people, a princess who was black and dancing. There was a vast advanced civilisation that lived there buried under the rubbles. Next you should look at King Solomon who was black and did trade with India in spices. India is the foremost fronted Country in spices alongside Pakistan. There was no Pakistan or Bangladesh in 1947. These were all one nation called India. Now place history, in 1947, the partition of India by the British. My family and all my families wealth was lost there, we are Persian Lewites of the tribe of Israel rom Iran of the Kohenim (True priesthood of YHWH). My great grandfather had settled in India, my mother and father were both born in Amritsar Punjab in India.

My great grandfather owned vast lands in India and was a judge and a chief. By the way this role in ancient Israel belongs to Judah but I know my lineage is not Judah but a Lewite (Kohen) but this is to show you favour that was given to our family, a Lewite can be a judge. I have proof of my lineage from Persian Israelites of my elders who were Lewites serving the Persian kings. My persian family were rich beyond measure. We lewties has suffered no slavery just as prophesied the only slavery suffered is by the twelve tribes and we are not counted in them.

The Master Yahushua told me in 2004 in Israel my background is from Moses who was Lewi and of course Aharon is my forefather. I was told in 2007 who I am, the second time by the Most High pointing to my Kohen status, I was then instructed that I should not be going to graveyards. The Lewites are not permitted to go to graveyards unless one of our very close relatives dies.

> **Leviticus 21:1-4** And YHWH said to Musa, Speak to the kohenim the sons of Aharon, and say to them, There shall none be defiled for the dead among his people: **2** But for his kin, that is near to him, that is, for his mother, and for his father, and for his son, and for his daughter, and for his brother, **3** And for his sister a virgin, that is near to him, which has had no husband; for her may he be defiled. **4** But he shall not defile himself, being a chief man among his people, to profane himself.

In my entire life to date I have only been to the graveyard for two members of my family that is my mother and my son just as YHWH instructed above. YHWH has kept me from graveyards at all other times.

We are still the priests in matters of Torah and rulings.

> **Deuteronomy 17:8** If there arise a matter too hard for you in judgment, between blood and blood, between plea and plea, and between stroke and stroke, being matters of controversy within your gates: then shall You arise, and get up into the place which

YHWH Your POWER shall choose; **9** And **<u>You shall come to the kohenim the Lewim, and to the judge that shall be in those days</u>**, and inquire; and they shall show you the sentence of judgment:

I represent the role of a Judge today with Yahudah exiled in USA, Rebbe Kefa ben Yahudah respresnet the Judge role alongside myself. If you have matters of Pidya Haben that is commanded by God you have to come to me to have it performed for your children.

We'Debar (Numbers) HTHS **18**:**2,** And your brethren also of the tribe of Lewi, the tribe of your father, bring with you, that they may be joined to you, and minister to you: but you and your sons with you shall minister before the Tent of witness.

15 Everything that opens the womb in all flesh, which they bring to YHWH, whether it be of men or beasts, shall be yours: nevertheless the Bekhor (firstborn) of man You shall redeem, and the Bekhor (firstborn) of unclean animals[1] You shall redeem.
16 And those that are to be redeemed from a month old shall You redeem, according to your estimation, for the money of five shekels, after the shekel of the sanctuary, which is twenty gerahs.

We are the Kohen to whom you are suppose to bring the offerings and tithe. The tithe only belongs to the Lewim and not to Church pastors who are swindling people out of their inheritance and eternal salvation. Salvation only belongs to Israel and those gentiles that join us and swear to uphold the contracts. If you do not swear the contracts you and your baptism are of no use, in fact most of your baptisms are at fault and of no value as you did not swear an oath and neither were you immersed in the name.

This did not just apply to Israel but also applied to wherever we were dispersed as the dispersion was by YHWH's hands. We were to manifest and magnify YHWH's name in our exile so once again we were to sit in judgment regarding matters of the Torah and be advisers to Judah as well.

The Arabs sold our people into slavery and they knew who the Hebrews were and it was certainly no James Cook English looking white man but the black Negro Hebrews alongside the lighter and darker skinned Y'sra'elites.

---

1 This law applies to unclean animals such as people owning horses and donkey's e.g. the mare giving birth to young ones.

The Master told me that I will be like Moses, since Aharon is my forefather, remember Moses was also slandered by people in his own camp and gentiles whose sole mission was to disrupt the first exodus of our people and make it fail. Read the story of the Golden Calf in Exodus 32. Then read the story of Korah in Numbers 16. What do you think? The pattern must follow.

Who do you think stood with Moses on the Day they worshipped the Calf which was the goddess Hathor, by which the Y'sra'elites rebelled? My father Aharon did not just produce the Calf it was the corrupt Egyptian preisthood in our mix that were consulted and they were the ones responsible for producing the statue of Isis in the form of a calf.

However my brothers the Lewites stood firm on YHWH's side when they were called;

> **Exodus 32:26** Then Musa stood in the entrance of the camp, and said, Whoever is on YHWH's side, come to me. And **<u>all the sons of Lewi</u>** gathered themselves together to him.

It was the Lewim who went to slay the 3000 rebels that day. In the modern world they call it a slaughter but in our world we call it YHWH's justice. Can you handle that?

> **Exodus 32:27** And he said to them, Thus says YHWH Elohim of Y'sra'el: Let every man put his sword on his side, and go in and out from entrance to entrance throughout the camp, and let every man (read Lewite) kill his brother, every man his companion, and every man his neighbour. **28** So the sons of Lewi did according to the word of Musa. And about three thousand men of the people fell that day.

If you are one of us you will turn away from whatever man-made religion you are into such as Christendom even and turn to the Torah and join back with true Y'sra'el, if you are not one of ours then you will continue in your journey away from Y'sra'el and we will say nothing further.

Now you know something of very importance of my history.

The Sephardic were heavily involved in the enslavement of our black/brown people and were the most prominent richest people in the new world, go and check your history books if you don't know this. Search for names on Google like Aaron Lopez. The famous Christopher Columbus was the first enslaver who took 600 Indians as slaves from the

Gold Coast that is Ghana to Spain in 1498 CE. His five ships expedition took these slaves distributing 200 of the Indian slaves to the Masters of the ships and the rest 400 were sold in Spain.

I would encourage that you do not hate the proselyte converts to our faith the Ashkenazim and Sephardic Jews since those that are trying to obey the Torah let it be so as they will have their reward and those that are not it's not our business to judge them. Our land of Israel is on lease to the Ashkenazim Jews, its not their land and they will be removed by the hand of YHWH himself.

The prophecy in the scroll of Genesis in 9:27 should read as follows but I am certain in all of your Bibles it is not and deliberately mistranslated by the gentiles.

Wrong translation of the KJV

> Genesis 9:27 God shall enlarge Japheth, and he shall dwell in the tents of Shem; and Canaan shall be his servant.

The word Patah has been translated on every other occurrence in the Torah "To deceive" then why translate it here as "enlarge". That translation does not line up even with the ancient Hieroglyph.

Corrected Translation in the Hidden Truths Hebraic Scrolls

> **Beresheeth (Gen) HTHS 9:27** Elohim will allow Yapet to be deceived and he will dwell in the tents of Shem; and Kanan[2] will become his servant.

From the commentary of the Hidden-Truths Hebraic Scrools
YHWH will deceive the Caucasian Europeans through the evil one that they will think they are the chosen ones when they in fact are not. They will go and take over the land of Y'sra'el as their own which has already happened. Patah means to speak evil from the heart but show a different face in other words two faced. Many European leaders will be two faced in the End of Days when they are deceived by their own minds and the people who reject YHWH will fall into lewdness see Romans chapter 1.18-32. However the door would be open for good Caucasian people to

[2] The curse only applies to Kanan's sons in the land of Y'sra'el.

join our people to serve YHWH that they may be rescued from the end-times wrath.

Today the true Y'sra'elites are not in the land of Y'sra'el but many Ashkanzim Hebrews are in fact converts from the kingdom of Khazar. They are not Semitic but in fact are the sons of Yapet. Just as YHWH had said they will occupy the tents of Shem and will look like Shem so they do today likewise. However in the future a time will come when the original Black Hebrews will be brought into Y'sra'el and Yapet removed to his proper place. According to letters sent and received by the Sephardic Yahudim the King of Khazaria who was Yosef himself said they had descended from Yapet. Note also after the breakup of the kingdom they all ended in modern Western Europe from where many of these migrated into Y'sra'el claiming to be ancient Yahudim. They are not.

The 13th Tribe p28 by Arthur Koestler
Eldad visited Spain around 880 and may or may not have visited the Khazar country. Hasdai briefly mentions him in his letter to Joseph – as if to ask what to make of him. Joseph then proceeds to provide a genealogy of his people. Though a fierce Hebrew nationalist, proud of wielding the 'sceptre of Judah", he cannot, and does not, claim for them Semitic descent; he traces their ancestry not to Shem, but to Noah's third son, Japheth; [end quote]

Very few people in ancient Y'sra'el are from the Yahudim stock that is some Sephardic, most Africans and ancient Persian Jewry alone make up that stock, while the Ashkanaz are really East European Khazar gentile converts into Judaism.

The black Hebrews did not fare better because the Jews had created the economy for the marketing, selling, buying enslaving and shipping to various countries such as North America, Latin America, and the Caribbean's. Some of us fortunate to be in Iran fared much better than these brothers of ours as we the Lewites in Iran and some clans of Yahudah did not enter into slavery but many from the tribes of Yahudah who had returned from Iran after the first exile ended up in slavery also so you see many of these in USA today or in Latin America.

The Jews today that call themselves Zionist are not the children of Israel because Abraham himself was a black man from Seno/Gambia from the tribe of fulfulbe. His children would be the people of Black and brown skins. The people need to wake up or face the music as our Master

Yahushua will punish the guilty this includes Christians who wholesale helped in the slave trade and those who ignorantly help the Zionists Europeans today who took our land as prophecy and occupy our homes calling them their homes. They are to this day killing the children of Abraham such as the Muslims in the Palestinian regions who are fallahin or people of the land that were likely Y'sra'elites. The European Jews that are sincere and obey the Torah correctly will have their reward including the Sepahrdic and Hassidic ones. The time has come to tell the truth like it is.

Naturally the question is who should return to Y'sra'el when the time comes and who will rebuild the millennial Temple. It will not be Caucasians. It will be the black children of Y'sra'el with kinky hair alongside their straight hair people of colour. Those that join us are not permitted to take part in the rebuilding but can help in other areas. The Lewites and Yahudah are strictly to oversee the affairs of the coming Temple in Tel Arad the true place of Jerusalem where we do have the Tabernacle of King David see picture taken in May 4th 2014 on Rabbi Simon's trip to Israel to pay homage to YHWH. Rabbi Amariel Howshusa from the tribe of Ephrayim a Rachby spoken about in Jeremiah 35:2. This is the site that we know that was spoken about in Amos 9:11 and Acts 15:16 that Christians are ignorant of. Rabbi Amariel can be contacted in Israel on 972 (0) 52 702 8713.

Here is the picture of the fort taken by a brother from a distance.

Which denomination are the Lewites spoken of in Ezekiel 44?

> **Ezekiel 44:15** But the kohenim the Lewim, the sons of Tzadok, that kept the charge of my sanctuary when the children of Y'sra'el went astray from me, they **shall come near to me to minister to me, and they shall stand before me to offer to me the fat and the blood**, says the Master YHWH:

The Lewites have to do the service so they must be there and guess what they are not Christians, Jews or Muslims but Y'sra'elites! This means all Lewim will remove all false religious systems around them and walk in the Torah only. The same applies to the Children of Israel this you must do.

PROLOGUE......12

CHAPTER 1......16

The Third Jihad, has it already started?......*16*

CHAPTER 2......40

The Threat Assessment......*40*

CHAPTER 3......102

What will happen to Israel how will the Yahudim be saved? *102*

CHAPTER 4 .... **146**

Objections to Yahudim being saved *146*

CHAPTER 5 .... **161**

Beheading & suicide bombings– The weapon of the beast *161*

CHAPTER 6 .... **164**

The Anti-Messiah Islamic, Turkic and Muslim *164*

CHAPTER 7 .... **204**

Pakistan and the radicalism in the region – Ten years of brutal violence now what? *204*

CHAPTER 8 .... **222**

Zechariah and the horses of Revelation *222*

CHAPTER 9 .... **234**

The Rapture, The resurrection and other questions *234*

CHAPTER 10 .... **240**

Will a 3rd Temple be rebuilt in our days or after the return of the Messiah? *240*

CHAPTER 11 .... **262**

Who is the prince and why does he give the sin offering in the 3rd Temple? *262*

CHAPTER 12 .... **275**

The return of the Messiah and the prophesies of Dani'el *275*

Conclusion *291*

'WIPED OFF THE MAP' – THE RUMOR OF THE CENTURY 324

Prologue

It has been a while since I last wrote my first book and I realised after writing Islam, Peace or Beast in 2003 followed by World War III – Unmasking the End-Times Beast in 2006 that now was the right time for the next episode of the story, which is about to unfold as all the things that I had said in both earlier titles some have come to pass and others are happening as we speak and while some are still yet to take place in the future. In this book I am not just going to look at cause and effect but also offer some solutions from what YHWH has declared about these things in scripture to allow us to see what course can help us and what can be destructive for us. Now this is the third edition in writing as I first wrote this in 2006 but now updating it in 2012 October.

This book's purpose is to highlight the ongoing fight of the Beast to conquer and to try and subdue all spheres but one thing I did not mention in my previous books is how the Jews will fit into the End-Times picture, and what role would they play. After all the Messiah Yahushua/Jesus of Nazareth did not just come for some foreign entity or the Roman government but He came for His people the genetic Yahudim (not the Khazarian converts who today occupy our land until YHWH's appointed time) and the ten tribes, which had become gentile nations. America's first president was a black man a Hebrew. England was ruled by blacks before they were expelled by the Romans. Europe had the moors ruling in many places that brought culture to these nations. The moors many of which were Hebrews who were forcefully converted into Islam in North Africa to become the foot soldiers of Islam who then conquered Spain and other countries.

Yahushua came to gather the scattered tribes of Israel, which has been ongoing since that time up to today and will continue till the very end. We are talking about the real children of Israel here and not some imaginary soap opera.

The prophecy given by Noah declared that our land would be stolen and occupied by his grandsons that would come down from the line of Japheth by deception, these are Europeans that today occupy the land and Master YHWH will free that land for us and cleanse it too.

> **Genesis 9:27** Elohim will allow Yapet to be deceived and he will dwell in the tents of Shem; and Canaan will become his servant.

The results of bad translations have caused people to be thoroughly deceived. King James who had the King James Bible named after him did a good effort, he was a black man to translate our scrolls but the translation is laced with errors. Forty Seven scholars neither of which had any understanding of the ancient Hieroglyph Hebrew text but had the Modern Hebrew to translate from and the modern Jews to ask for help. The Hidden Truths Hebraic Scrolls finally translated by a Lewite using ancient Hebrew rescued by Master Yahushua fifteen and a half years ago out of obscurity will tell you the real detail so far hidden in the pages of our Hebrew scrolls.

I am not at all surprised to see the hatred that Christians and Messianics show towards the Real black Y'sra'elites and their writings. I am amazed at the spiritual blindness in these people who call the Babylonia Talmud, which is one of our writings Satanic and who have the audacity to say that we do not believe in the Yahudim's literature outside of the Bible and is of no use to us. The Talmud has somewhat tainted by Khazarian European converts to our faith who have added another thousand laws to it that are not ours so one has to read it with care. We do not espouse to the laws of Rambam or Rashi neither of which belong to the children of Y'sra'el. I know there is a time for everything and I also know that I will lose family and friends to tell the truth so here I am sacrificing my all to serve the Master not worrying about family or friends. My testimony is available to read at www.african-israel.com under the Testimonial pages in the name of Mohammed from Lahore.

Christians on the other hand show such arrogance and ignorance that is fuelled by Church Pastors who have no understanding of our writings. The present Jews (converts) have preserved our history and our writings such as the Tanak (Old Testament) and many other writings. Judah the prince one of our real hero's wrote the Mishnah in the 2nd century CE to preserve the Oral Torah which is a fete in itself but what you get from the so called communities who love to sing songs to their Greek white Jesus but hate the very fabric from where the Messiah of Israel who is black see my book Yahushua the Black Messiah who is an Israelite arose, the very people Yahushua of Nazareth conversed with on a day to day basis.

The people that he loved are just put aside and shunned by Church hypocrisy enslaved beaten and called names today we are talking about the ancient Yahud who were people of colour and those who took our faith today referred to as Jews (converts) who are Caucasian sons of Japheth. They take the things of the Yahudim and twist them to make it sound like these things belong to Christians and put the original adherents down as Christ killers.

All the church fathers from the time of Marcion were totally anti-Semitic and hated anything of Israel. So the Messiah has been coloured as a white gentile European standing aside. We will see how that will affect the End of Days and the people who follow after Him.

This book will hopefully uncover some important truths how Israel will participate in the wars that are going to unfold in the near future and how the salvation of the genetic Yahudim, which in YHWH's eyes has already happened will be revealed to the world. The best kept secret is what YHWH has already declared in scripture but many are still struggling to see this in and out of churches because they are stuck to dogma that is out of line with our Scrolls.

How the Yahudim indeed will become a light unto the nations which was always the intended mission and how they have been and will continue to remain YHWH's appointed people and emissaries just like the twelve Yahudim disciples of the Yahudim black Messiah. In fact at a mini level the twelve did become light to the nations being Yahudim themselves and this will happen at a bigger level when the scales begin to come off from the eyes of the Church, which has become in-sync with paganism and pollutions of worldly ways rather than the ways of YHWH. This is a call for the Church, the same call that YHWH gave me fourteen years ago when I returned to my people Israel in spirit and in truth to serve Melek YHWH (The magnificent Name). If you have bought this book then welcome on this fantastic journey that started with my redemption and in which YHWH has been teaching me many truths to take back and enlighten the world for the coming events in our and other peoples' lives.

> **Jeremiah 6:16** (HTHS)Thus says YHWH: "Stand in the Ways[3] and look intently, and make inquiry for the ancient paths,[4] where the good way is, [5] and walk[6] in it; then you will find rest[7] for your souls. But they said, `**We will not walk in it**.'[8]

---

3 The 'WAY,' that Yahushua proclaimed in John 14:6 is Torah truth.

4 The idea behind the Hebrew word is these paths are tried and tested and never failed, meaning Torah is our way to freedom and salvation. The written Torah leads to the living Torah Messiah.

5 Torah

6 Keep the commandments.

7 Salvation

8 Many Christians have said they will not walk in Torah just like Israel rebelled, Christians have also rebelled.

Don't be like the Israelites and Christians who said we will not walk in it (Not to walk in Torah).

Note we will use the Hidden Truths Hebraic Scrolls (HTHS) formerly called the Abrahamic-Faith Netzarim Study Scriptures (AFNHSS) throughout, which is the near accurate translation of the Hebrew text of the scriptures, the recommended this as the Bible of your choice for study that can be ordered at www.african-israel.com or from www.lulu.com/simalt and where different will be stated to show a particular verse and its intended meaning using the KJV or an alternative Bible translation. We will use the abbreviated form HTHS to show that we are using the study Bible for its references. Where necessary I will use the sacred name of YHWH, even the title God and where possible Ha'Shem or Adoni (My Master) as it needs be. These books can also be purchased from www.amazon.com in a vareity of ways such as paperback and kindle edition.

Chapter 1
The Third Jihad, has it already started?

In 1924 the British Empire alongside the French and Australians put a temporary end to the Islamic onslaught that began from Saudi Arabia in the 7th century CE, which conquered many nations including Spain called Andalusia by the Muslims, which was later lost by Islam. The defeat of the Islamic forces at the battle of Poitiers in France in 734 CE by Charles Martel and the death of Abdal Malik did not deter Muslims from attacking other parts of Europe. The Muslims ransacked many parts of France and eventually were pushed back to leave the European lands.

When Kamal Ataturk the father of Turkey said we are dropping Sha'ria (The Islamic law) in favour of European style freedoms, the Muslims at that time accused him of being an agent of the West and a hand of the Zionists Yahudim. All the events to shut down the Ottoman Empire took place in 1924. Then just four years later in Egypt something very important took place to revive the wounded head (Rev 13:3). In 1928 the brotherhood was started by Syed Qutb who wanted to galvanise Islam to take on the forces of the West and this was the time of the beginning of the third Jihad. The first Jihad began when the Muslims pushed from Arabia to start to conquer the lands in the 7th century CE and the second Jihad began with the onset of the crusaders in the 11th century CE. The 3rd Jihad had already begun but many were asleep at the realm. Syed Qutb wrote 24 books and he is the author of magnum opus Fi Zilal al Qur'an (In the shade of the Qur'an) which is a 30 volume commentary on the Qur'an which talks about the concept of Jihad and the Muslim community as a whole and its obligation. We are now in the fourth and final jihad against the Zionists (converted Jews) and Crusaders (Christians) as Muslims understand it.

The oldest and largest political Islamic centre was started by Hassan Al Bannah an Egyptian in 1928. The goal of Hassan was that people should use the Qur'an as a reference point and the Sunnah (Hadiths) Muslim historical writings about the Islamic faith similar to the Talmud on how various practices were done and should be done. There are over 600,000 Hadiths but not all of them are considered authentic and reliable, while only about five main authors were considered the most authentic of which Al Bukhari was one of them.

What many people may not realise is that Syed Qutb took his inspiration from Syed Abu Ala Mududi from Pakistan, who actually was the inspiration behind the brotherhood. He was a prominent scholar of Islam who was born in India and later settled in Pakistan and did much work in Pakistan and touched many Islamic scholars worldwide. This is where the brotherhood came out of because Syed Qutb was a fan of Syed Abu Al Madudi and had read most of his works on Islam. While Al Madudi was reviving Islam in the south-east with a view to worldwide revival and used newspapers, journals and books to bring to the people the information on how Muslims should live and how to spread Islam through active Jihad. He was the founder of the party called Jamaat e-Islami (Assembly of Islam) in Pakistan.

His work even influenced the Shi'ites though he was from the Sunni sect the largest in Islam. Ayatollah Ruhollah Khomeini did actually meet him in 1963 and it is he who translated Madudi's work into the Persian language of (Farsi). Iran's revolution also came out of this man in Pakistan and not Egypt as incorrectly thought by many today. My birth fortunately was also in 1963 from a humble Muslim family the year I was born in Lahore in a rough and tough district called Gawal Mandi. My father is the only son with several sisters who had to leave India at the age of six when the Pakistan partition came about with India where we lost all of our lands. We are inherently Yahudim of the House of Lewi from Iran a secret even I did not know until my early forties. My family had lost all their land in India during the 1947 riots and partition of Pakistan and India when 60,000 women were raped and millions of people lost their lives during the crossover. While history was being shaped YHWH was preparing me to teach me Islam and then later to bring me back to the roots of my real Y'sra'elite faith of my forefathers the Black Hebrews.

If we start to tie up the various strands of Islam from Pakistan, Iran and Egypt and how it became radicalized all these tie back not to the brotherhood in Egypt but to Pakistan to the man named Madudi who could be called the father of modern virulent form of Islam. In all honestly Madudi himself was not a violent man but a very simple man.

Unfortunately most people who rely on the Internet for history alone do not realize that at times there is a lot of misinformation out there that needs to be sifted. I know the politics of Pakistan very well and I grew up in that milieu. Since I was born during 1963 in Lahore the south-eastern city of Pakistan well known for its rich culture and food I was being brought up in a Sunni household but amongst the Shiites' as my street neighbors so it explains when things were heating up in Iran in the 1960s that is when YHWH brought me into the world to perhaps use me as a witness through that nation to rescue our people worldwide.

I have seen Madudi many times in my younger years and read some of his articles and understand the Islamic ideology he wanted to see around himself. When I was born the world around me was very hostile and things were rapidly changing. My dad went to England in 1963 just a few months after my birth for the first time to earn a better living and we saw rising tensions with India leading up to the 1965 war, it was just during this time that my dad called us to England while our stay in England only lasted a few years and we went back to Pakistan because my family found England too cold.

We were in Oxford for a very short period where my second youngest brother was born in Churchill hospital in 1966 and my dad had bought a very nice house in Huddersfield where we stayed for just over a year. I was in England in 1967 when Israel had its famous six day war but in all honesty I do not remember anything about this event being a four year old neither remember hearing or seeing any demonstrations in England against it or for it.

At that time my mum developed what I could only describe as asthma like symptoms with difficulty of breathing which really scared my dad so much that in 1968 he bought a brand new Morris Minor in black colour for £700 UK sterling which was a lot of money at that time and sold his house in a hurry and decided to head off to Pakistan with us thinking I don't want my wife to suffer in cold and dreary England and who will look after my children if something happens to her. It was then that our car was involved in an accident and guess where YHWH had us then? Right in Turkey the nation of the Anti-Messiah to come, where a lorry deliberately hit us on a major highway that was overlooking a large hill and our car went tumbling down that hill and I still remember the spins like in a washing machine. It must have taken about twelve spins before we stopped on the ground. Thanks be to Master Yahushua we survived. I was about 5 years old and I remember Huddersfield vividly even for a child at that age and clearly remember the train bridge near our house on Fitzwilliam Street and the footpath where I used to play outside our home.

I believe that this was an attempt by Satan to kill us but praise be to Melek Yahushua that we came close to death me, my two brothers and my mum in her pregnancy with my third brother and my dad but the Almighty saved us because He had a plan for us, which He was to show me later in life when I grew up. We still have pictures of the Black Morris Minor in an album in Pakistan all dented up during the accident. This was such a beautiful sturdy and strong car that was dented all over. My dad then booked us on a ship from Turkey en-route to Pakistan he went to sort out the car through the AA the insurance company that he was with from England who sent help after which he got to Pakistan later. It was then that my Islamic education began. So from my birth to five years old I saw a lot of action and in 1967 the six day Israeli war of course. These times were very turbulent and for me as a child oblivious from all these things I was growing up in the tough streets of Lahore being prepared for future action.

Pakistan had a war with India in 1965 when the Indian army said we are going to have our lunch in Lahore after conquering it. Well Pakistan soon proved them wrong and forced the Indian soldiers to rethink their lunch strategy. Perhaps they should ask politely next time and Pakistan will invite them for a guest lunch instead.

The only people who will have lunch in Lahore are the people of Lahore very proud and very formidable in their ways but at the same time very respectful and hospitable neighbors to others. There is a saying in Pakistan that if you have not seen Lahore then you have not yet been born. What a place of tremendous historical significance with the Mughal (Mongols) kings of India. The famous Shalamar Gardens (Its famous three descending terraces) of Emperor Shah Jahan is absolutely beautiful. Lahore had seen a few dynasties of its own. The Ghaznavis of the 12th century CE, the Ghurids in the 12/13th Century CE, the Mongols in the 16th Century CE and the Sikhs in the 19th Century CE and of course Lahore was the capital of Punjab for the British Raj also so it was a place of major significance and strategic importance to Pakistan and to the British while they were ruling it.

It may not be apparent that the Lahore fort was built by the Mongols in the 16th century CE and was then much like Jerusalem in the older days with many gates into the city which could be closed off to the invading enemies. The Lahore fort had 13 gates to protect Lahore so we know what is like to live in a gated city just like the Jerusalemites the home of my forefathers who were exiled in Iran.

However India Amritsar in the Punjab was my parent's birth place and home at one time so for us the war was really pointless and waste of time. I mean my great grandfather died in the fighting that started in 1947 at the partition trying to save his family but my family did not originate from India. Most of my family came out of Iran. I found out that I had an Iranian connection when I was 45 years old through the Master Yahushua. I am connected to King Cyrus's land and the mystery gets deeper because King Cyrus was one of us the son of Queen Esther of Iran. It does not end there either. I prayed to Master Yahushua after my salvation in 1998 and asked Him who am I and why did you call me out so late? Where were you all this time? Of course He was there all along but I did not know Him until He revealed Himself. No He was not Allah but YHWH the Holy One of Israel.

I thought maybe I belong to the ten scattered tribes then I thought perhaps to Judah because my family was situated in Iran at the time of Queen Esther/Hadassah but YHWH revealed to me the origins of my family were that we were the House of Lewi, kohenim priests from Israel. He in fact hinted at this in 2004 when I was 41 years old when he told me through a pastor in Israel prophesying that I was like Moses with a rod and I will strike it in the ground and living waters will rise and open people's eyes but I did not fully understand what He meant during this revelation. The living waters by the way is referring to Torah and the revelation of it that I will teach to others to know the truth and of Messiah as well.

I fully understood that prophecy a few years later and then it made sense to me why He spoke to me in the bank in London in 1998 and told me to follow Him and why I was born in Pakistan, been to Turkey, family in Iran. Notice the Bible has much to say about these places but Western Christians don't pay much attention to them perhaps because they are not talked about in churches as most sermons are just geared toward believe in Yahushua and love but they never teach you who he came for the real genetic Israelites.

These places are very significant for the End of Days prophesies.

Madudi was not a gun toting man but a mild mannered Islamic thinker and helped give shape to today's radical Islam including that of Al-Qaeda. So the roots of the brotherhood connect to Pakistan to this man. It does not matter who funds or helps Al-Qaeda and its true the American leadership has her hands behind the fueling and training of Al-Qaeda.

Here is what Madudi said:

> "It must be evident to you from this discussion that the objective of Islamic 'Jihad' is to **eliminate the rule** of an **un-Islamic system** and establish in its stead an Islamic system of state rule. **Islam does not intend to confine this revolution to a single state, or a few countries; the aim of Islam is to bring about a universal revolution**."
>
> --Sayed Abu A'la Madudi, Jihad in Islam p 24 – (Underline emphasis mine)

According to Imam Al-Qastalani (shaafi), Imam Al-Mawardi (shaafi), Imam Al-Taftazani (hanafi) and Imam Jirjani (hanafi) schools of thought, the condition to fight the Infidels is to give victory to Islam as an aim and the intention must be to make Allah's (Islamic deity) the highest. The Muslim aim is to make Allah's faith the highest and the struggle is real and it begins with fighting and the fighting has to be begun by Muslims as a precondition after offering Islam to the infidels and their non acceptance can start this off.

Now we may begin to understand the intentions of the 4th Beast and its goals, which are very different to the previous three beasts of Daniel.

> **Daniel 7:7** (HTHS) After this I saw in the night visions, and **behold a fourth beast**, **dreadful and terrible, and strong exceedingly**; and it had great iron teeth: it devoured and broke in pieces, and stamped the residue with the feet of it: and it was diverse from all the beasts that were before it; and it had ten horns.

The Roman kingdom could not seriously qualify to be the fourth beast of Daniel simply because it was nothing more than a *Republic* conquering and installing its own governors and officials in place of what was already there.

Sir Robert Anderson one of the greatest prophecy writers of his time who unlocked Daniel's time code of the seventy weeks pointed out the following;

> Concerning the Roman Empire:
> *"While the fourth beast is unquestionably Rome, the language of the seventh and twenty-third verses leaves no doubt that it is the Roman Empire in its revived and future phase. Without endorsing the views of Maitland, Browne, etc., it must be owned that there was nothing in the history of ancient Rome to correspond with the main characteristic of this beast unless the symbolism used is to be very loosely interpreted. To "devour the earth," "tread it down and break it in pieces," is fairly descriptive of other empires, but Ancient Rome was precisely the one power which added government to conquest, and instead of treading down and breaking in pieces the nations it subdued, sought rather to mould them to its own civilization and polity. All this-and more might be added-suggests that the entire vision of the seventh chapter may have a future reference."*

Sir Robert Anderson was correct in assuming that the symbols are applied loosely and not strictly applied to Rome and concluded that the four empires come on at once. We can see this is only fulfilled in Islam and no other force in the past because when we carefully examine the regions Islam is bigger, meaner and stronger. Rome did not rule in Indonesia, neither Rome ever stepped foot inside Pakistan or Afghanistan but Islam has. Let's examine the prophecy that most prophecy teachers use for Rome.

> **Daniel 9:26** (HTHS) And after sixty and two weeks shall Messiah be cut off, but not for himself: and the people of the prince that shall come shall destroy the city and the sanctuary; and the end there shall be with a flood, and to the end of the war wastes and fighting is determined.

Many teachers who use this prophecy for Rome are correct to do so but only loosely but let me show you some symbols in this piece of text.

- Messiah shall be cut off – The timing of the Messiah Yahushua of Nazareth to arrive and die.
- People of the prince – the people of the prince to come can only be loosely applied to Rome let's assume this for now as I will show you in a minute these are Islamic.
- Destruction of the city – Jerusalem being destroyed
- Sanctuary – The Temple of YHWH
- End with a flood – A literal water flood and not an allegory of an army yet to take place.
- At the end of the war - First the war then followed by the desolation.

Most prophecy teachers stop here and this is where they have their 4th beast from which many books have been written for how it is Rome and how they are going to come and be revived etc, etc which by the way does not fit the scriptures of Daniel nor the book of Revelation.

Why is it not Rome?

Many prophecy teachers who stop here their biggest hurdle is that they do not read the Hebrew and miss a crucial point. The next verse is connected because there is a connecting WA between verses 26 and verse 27. This connecting WA is what ties verse 26 to verse 27, which is used to join the two passages together and referred to in the English language as the word "And." Let me show you in the Hebrew how this cannot be Rome.

Daniel 9:26 ואחרי השבעים ששים ושנים יכרת משיח ואין לו והעיר והקדש ישחית עם
נגיד הבא וקצו בשטף ועד קץ מלחמה נחרצת שממות:
27 והגביר ברית לרבים...

If you look at the word Shimmot V' H'Gibbor highlighted, they are both connected. This means the one that makes desolate are not the Romans but the Muslims. In fact after two centuries the Romans legalized Christianity but the Muslims have never done that in any of their lands and wood not even allow you without strict permission to expand your Churches, you are not allowed to preach the gospel openly either.

The word there is that they will not allow the place to be established by the Yahudim, they will stupefy and devastate. Well the Romans have not been doing that for the last 2000 years. Since the Muslims came to Jerusalem in 637 CE they took over the area and refused to allow the Yahudim even near the place so they continue to stupefy and devastate exactly as the scripture states. It is active in the present the Hebrew letter WA also indicates it is a sealed prophecy so it cannot change until the coming of the kingdom of YHWH.

We cannot isolate verse 26 of Daniel and write a whole book about it and forget about verse 27. Let us examine the problem.

> **Daniel 9:26** (HTHS) And after sixty and two weeks shall Messiah be cut off, but not for himself: and the people of the prince that shall come shall destroy the city and the sanctuary; and the end there shall be with a flood, and to the end of the war wastes and fighting is determined.

> **Daniel 9:27** (KJV) And he shall confirm the Contract/Agreement with many for one week: and in the midst of the week he shall cause the sacrifice and the oblation to cease, and for the overspreading of abominations he shall make it desolate, even until the consummation, and that determined shall be poured upon the desolate.

> **Daniel 9:27** (HTHS) And he shall **reconfirm** the Contract/Agreement with many for one week: and in the midst of the week he shall cause the sacrifice and the offering to cease, and for the overspreading of abominations he shall make it desolate, even until the consummation, and that determined shall be poured upon the desolate.

It is absolutely essential that the prince that came if it was Rome and let us assume that it was Titus who came to destroy the Temple then he also must make a peace treaty with Israel but we know no such thing ever happened because in 70 CE when Jerusalem was destroyed there was no peace treaty between Rome and Israel for an autonomous rule and there was no literal flood either which is required but both of these are yet future.

The other thing the text requires is the peace treaty was **reconfirmed** please see the HTHS Bible text removing the bad translation of the KJV, which would mean that this treaty had existed and allowed Israel to continue in autonomous rule. However our biggest problem is that Israel did not have autonomous rule before the destruction of the Temple either as it was ruled by Roman governors. Anybody who can read this prophecy properly will understand that this rules Rome out completely.

There was no literal flood which is also required according to the text. Many teachers try to overcome this problem by stating that the flood is an allegorical army. This is not true because it is a literal water flood yet to take place as I shall prove later.

YHWH will make an utter end of them by a flood and this is the reason why Daniel's usage is literal and not allegorical. Most of the Anti-Messiah's armies will be destroyed by a flood.

> **Nahum 1:8** (NKJV) But with **an overflowing flood** He will make an utter end of its place, and darkness will pursue His enemies.

And He shall reconfirm…

Did Titus form an alliance with Israel? No, so this rules Rome out. The prophecy teachers' who are fixated with Rome are leading many people to make wrong conclusions. This also causes people to make bad choices for the future since they think it is the European Union that is the revived Roman Empire. Frankly it's not the EU.

This means in order for this prophecy to be fulfilled then Israel must have autonomous government and that has not happened until 1948. Before this the only time Israel had its own government was in 586 BCE before Nebuchadnezzar came and destroyed Jerusalem and took away many people as slaves and carried the Temple articles away.

So unless you want to be honest and do justice to the text we know Nebuchadnezzar also had no treaty with Israel and neither did he **reconfirm** one.

Now what about the Muslims?

Let us now swiftly move past the 1948 time-line. There are two nations that have formed a treaty with Israel and these two nations are Turkey and Egypt. Turkey formalized its relations with Israel in 1949 one year after Israel was established. It was one of the few Muslim nations to recognize Israel. This is the same nation that is now mediating another peace treaty remember ***Reconfirming*** the Contract/Agreement with Israel and the rest of the Muslim nations to bring a Palestinian state. This is what the text says in Daniel 9:27 that a Contract/Agreement will be confirmed with the many? Many who? These "many" are the Islamic nations that hate Israel and do not want to accept it as a state. What many people do not recognize when 150,000 Spanish Yahudim fled the Roman Catholic inquisitions in Spain to save their lives they settled in modern day Turkey in the city of Istanbul.

Israel and Turkey have signed a free trade agreement to do business deals since 2000. Israel exports around $1.5 billion of goods annually and imports around $1 billion worth. There is also a plan to build a pipeline to supply water, electricity, gas and oil to Israel. What will happen when Israel is dependent on these things and Turkey puts a stop to this?

On October 11 2009, relations were strained when Israel was barred from Anatolian Eagle military exercises in Turkey. The aerial exercise was to consist of Turkey, Israel, the United States, and Italy. However, Turkey refused to allow Israel to attend. In response, the United States pulled out of the exercise. [9]

Israel is also in talks with India and Turkey with Russia to build an energy pipeline to supply oil direct via the pipeline through the sea to Israel.

This then makes both of these nations Israel and Turkey the prime candidates for the fulfillment of the prophecy at the end of verse 26 and verse 27.

9

http://news.yahoo.com/s/ap/20091011/ap_on_re_mi_ea/ml_israel_turkey

Israel and Egypt also signed a peace treaty on 26 March 1979. Of course Egypt has very little clout when it comes to other Islamic states so this rules Egypt out plus the fact that the End-Times Anti-Messiah will conquer (Isa 19:4) and rule Egypt for a time also which rules Egypt out as the main anti-Messiah nation.

If we apply the text of Daniel loosely as Sir Robert Anderson suggested then we can say it was Rome but we do know that the Titus was a barbarian who had brutally murdered many thousands of Yahudim and did not form any treaty with Israel. According to Josephus the historian 1,100,000 people were killed during the siege and 97,000 were enslaved. This was at least two thirds of the population of Israel, which thus brought the prophecy of Zechariah to fulfillment. Note many Black Hebrews the original Israelites fled to Africa and other nations such as India. They fled to the Atlas Mountains this has been documented by Josephus. They were not Caucasians as depicted in movies but even Yahushua was a man of colour of brown skin and Rastafarian type braided hair.

Zech 13:8 (HTHS) And it shall come to pass, that in all the land, says YHWH, two parts therein shall be cut off and die; but the third shall be left therein.

The third that were left there escaped to the other nations later.

Many see Zechariah 13:8 as a future prophecy of Jacob's trouble but in my opinion part of the prophecy is partially fulfilled but there is another fulfillment yet in the future when YHWH will act for us and remove our enemies from the land and those who falsely occupy it and claim it as their own when it is not theirs. This includes both the Muslims and Zionist Jews who are not the children of Israel.

Today those Jews who claim to be owners of the land will be removed and replaced with the real owners that is my people who will be brought back at that time of which many are still in captivity in nations around the world. They are in captivity spiritually and a few physically though many of these had ended up in the cross Atlantic slave trade.

Yes there will be a major war and YHWH will remove the godless Khazari converts who today claim to be genetic Jews when they are not.

Here is proof that most of the exiles Israelites will be brought back and will then never be uprooted but this prophecy is yet future and was not fulfilled in 1948. Today many Israelites black Hebrews are stuck in America and Europe, they were taken there through the slave trade.

> **Amos 9:14-15** (HTHS) And I will bring again the captivity of my people of Y'sra'el, and they shall rebuild the waste cities, and inhabit them; and they shall plant vineyards, and drink the wine there; they shall also make orchards, and eat the fruit of them. **15**
> And I will plant them upon their land, and they shall no more be pulled up out of their land which I have given them, says YHWH Your POWER.

This then leaves the room open for two entities one Islam and one counterfeit Israel. The only entity that hates counterfeit Israel is the Muslims so these are the ones that will form the covenant with them to try to overtake the land.

The only nation to form a treaty with Israel as explained earlier is Egypt and Turkey and it is this treaty that the text in verse 27 says will be ***Reconfirmed*** with Turkey in my opinion. The Bible tells us that the Anti-Messiah is a man from Turkey, Gog from the land of Magog (Ezek 38:2) so we can then rule out Egypt but Egypt will be a partner in the treaty also. The nation of Turkey will bring it all together. Secret talks have been taking place in Turkey in the past years about these things where even Pakistan was involved. So the treaty that Turkey will form will be with the "many" (Islamic nations) just as scripture mandates. Do not get confused with the term counterfeit Israel as this simply means that those in Israel who call themselves Jews are not the true children of Israel either but claim to be chosen when they are not chosen but converted to become Jews in the 8th century CE while most of these live anti-Torah godless lives.

Now if we look at the geo-composite beast that is mentioned in Revelation 13:2 we can see how it is the Islamic regions only that are involved and you will struggle to find Europe in this mix.

- Leopard – Grecian Empire – Ruling from Mesopotamia to Pakistan.
- Bear – Persian Empire including Afghanistan and Pakistan
- Lion – The Babylonian Empire

Today all three of these are within Islamic lands meaning the **<u>four beasts come up at once just like Daniel saw</u>** and this is now beginning to be fulfilled in Islamic regions in our time and the near future to come.

Just as Daniel the prophet had prophesied The Islamic Empire was bigger and meaner than any other Empire in history and if you had looked back at its history since its inception in the 7th century CE by Muhammad the prophet of Islam it was and is truly a global beast covering from the Western shores of Algiers all the way to Indonesia. This was indeed the Beast from the East, which now had one of its head wounded but it did not die the death.

> **Gilyah'na (Rev) 13:3** (HTHS) And I saw one of his heads as it were wounded to death...

It needs to be noted that one head was wounded and not terminated but also something else remarkable about this is that the Beast has seven heads, which many may have possibly missed that important fact that it was only one of the seven heads that was wounded. So what happened to the other six heads?

> **Gilyah'na (Rev) 13:1** (KJV) And I stood upon the sand of the sea, and saw a beast rise up out of the sea, having seven heads and ten horns, and upon his horns ten crowns, and upon his heads the name of blasphemy.

> **Gilyah'na (Rev) 13:1** (HTHS) And I stood upon the sand of the sea, and saw a beast rise up out of the sea, having **seven heads** and ten horns, and upon his horns ten crowns, and upon his heads the **names** of blasphemy.

Revelation 13:1 tells us about the seven heads of the beast. One thing which most translations of the Bible have missed is a key piece of information that the beast has blasphemous names. The term 'names,' is not singular but plural which many Bible translations have got wrong. Why is this important to us? This is because this vital information helps us piece together Islam down as the End-Times Beast.

Without this key information we would miss the fact that according to Islamic theology Allah has 99 names and not just a single name. These 99 names can be found on any Muslim Qur'an's back cover. This is important because in Revelation we were told that they were plural NAMES, which fit in with the plural names of the Beast of Islam just as Revelation 13:1 suggested, these are names of blasphemy exalted in place of the name of YHWH the sacred name of the God of Israel.

I would suggest to you that the Islamic Beast and its seven heads describe how it is divided into seven regions and this is where its powerbase is most concentrated. The book of Revelation indeed does tell the prophecy reader where the seven heads are located, once you find out this truth then it totally eliminates America and Europe from the equation, which is an incorrect theory being taught in Churches. Let us examine these most important details.

> **Gilyah'na (Rev) 13:2** (HTHS) And the beast which I saw **<u>was like a leopard</u>**, and his feet were as the **feet of a bear**, and his mouth as **<u>the mouth of a lion</u>**...

:

The seven heads of Islam are going to be active in these regions more or less depending upon how much influence YHWH has allowed for the Beast to build itself. This does not mean that Islam controls all these regions but it does mean it has increasing influence there. Let us examine the details.

> **Gilyah'na (Rev) 13:1** (HTHS) ...and upon his heads the **<u>names</u>** of blasphemy.

The "names" are plural.
Do we have the evidence to locate the seven heads?

- Feet of a Bear – Persian Empire (All Islamic)
- Like a Leopard – Grecian Empire (All Islamic)
- Mount of a Lion – The Babylonian Empire (All Islamic)

Note Verse two of Revelation is connected with verse one with the Hebrew WA translated in Hebrew as the English word "And" so the two must be seen together and they cannot be isolated outside of the 4th Beast because it describes what will be the 4th Beast of Dani'el 7:7. It is crucial to see that Daniel described these beasts up coming together and the book of Revelation in chapter 13 verses 1 and 2 confirms this and now we know these regions are all Islamic. The revived Roman Empire in its revived form is actually Islamic and not European.

Many people many not realize that the ancient Persian Empire encompassed all the way from Turkey to many of the following locations including Pakistan, Afghanistan, Uzbekistan and Tajikistan but it never ruled Western Europe. The Ancient Persian Empire was vast. The conquest started with the King of Cyrus mentioned in the Bible (Isaiah 45:1) and what a great King he was indeed the son of queen Esther of Iran who taught him the Torah. He indeed came to know the God of Israel and was called the anointed one for this very reason. Did you know that though born in Iran he was actually an Israelite? Because he was born of a Yahudi mother Esther also known as Hadassah thereby that makes him Yahudi even if he had a gentile father this is in accordance to the law of the Bible. Even the present law of Israel of the orthodox Rabbis have understood it the same therefore if you look at Israel the present law determines anyone's being a Yahudi through the mother which is correct.

The likeness of a Leopard reveals to us that the Empire of Alexander the Great started from Mesopotamia (between the two rivers of Iraq, the Tigris and Euphrates in Turkey) and it ruled all the way East to Pakistan excluding central and Southern parts of India. This is why Pakistan is inclusive part of the Beast and had to separate as an Islamic Republic in 1947. This was one year before the state of Israel became a nation again, while India as a whole did not become Islamic or as radical as the Islamic republic of Pakistan is today. Pakistan has a big part to play in the End-Times Beast. This is why we see the Allied forces battling the Taliban on the borders of Pakistan and Afghanistan right now.

By the Lion Nebuchadnezzar's Empire shows us the headquarters or the mouthpiece of the Beast.

The Mouth of a Lion

The Beast has the mouth of a Lion, which indicates to us clearly that it's headquartered in the regions of ancient Babylon only. It may come as a surprise to some of you that Nebuchadnezzar's brother Nabonidus actually took the worship of the God called sin later known as Hallah and then Allah to Arabia in the 6th Century BCE. The way this works is that the Islamic Empire had its powerbase both in Saudi Arabia and later in the regions of Iraq and Syria. The Umayyad caliphate of Islam was indeed ruling out of these regions. This means according to the book of Revelation the Beast cannot have its mouth or headquarters outside of this region hence why we see the Holy sites of Islam only exists in Saudi Arabia, Iraq and Iranian regions and no other place. This is no coincidence because this tells us the book of Revelations is indeed true.

Let us look and see if any other prophet of the Tanak helps us see this truth.

> **Zechariah 5:7-8** (HTHS) And, behold, there was lifted up a talent of lead: and this is a woman that sits in the midst of the barrel of liquid. **(8)** And he said, this is wickedness. And he cast it into the midst of the barrel of liquid; and he cast the weight of lead upon the mouth thereof.

This woman (city or a range of Islamic nations sits in the middle of the oil)! The talent is presented as the city that is controlling the economic cycles of the nations. And who do we think this could be? The nations which control the economic cycles are the Gulf nations with their oil. This woman who is symbolic for a city or cities is in the midst of this entire black liquid (oil). Note the talent the Hebrew word "kikkar" also describes a round about area near Jordan a squared region. This should help us to understand what Zechariah the prophet did was describe the exact same thing I said earlier that Islam is headquartered in these regions the area of the Beast that rises out of the desert. Once again we find Zechariah pins down the land of Shinar (Iraq) as a key site of interest, which again shows us these are parts of Iraq where once Islam was and still is very dominant. Remember the Beast is made of the geo-composite regions and the Bear, Leopard and Lion are these geo-composite regions where the seven heads <u>must</u> be found.

We cannot rush off looking for them in Russia, Europe or America.

One thing many people miss is that none of these regions occupy Western European lands so all the teachers of prophecy that say that Islam is going to rule in Europe are practically proven wrong as the bible gives no such support for the boundaries of the Beast to include Western European nations or the US including Australia or New Zealand. These areas are out however just like anything in life the Beast has influence in these regions also and that is all it is allowed to have. So for me to be blunt the United Kingdom and the United States are not going to become Muslim at any stage of prophecy in the future. One more thing the Islamic Beast did indeed conquer Spain and ruled it for eight hundred years which shows us that the Beast will try to conquer parts outside of its boundaries but will not be able to hold onto them because they are outside it's jurisdiction.

One may ask then why can't it control the UK for a time or the US for that matter? The answer is given in the Scriptures that these two nations are special End-Times warriors/shepherd nations for YHWH to use which will thrash the radical Islamists and be in bitter war with them for many generations to come...

Let me show you.

The UK was the nation that conquered India and then was involved in annexing India which became a two nation state of Pakistan and India and later into a three nation state with Bangladesh. UK had her hands in India/Pakistan split because it was meant to happen and it was of God's will. Yes many people died in that split but those deaths were tragic human endeavours but sadly human nature takes over and things get out of hand. YHWH does not delight to kill people but people want to kill people using religion as a tool. We then see historically UK was fighting the Ottoman Empire and it took over from the Ottoman the area of Jerusalem again a key piece of area that YHWH has designated for Israel. The UK helped secure that area as well. The UK helped annex Israel and it also became a three state solution. Do you see the resemblance with Pakistan and India?

It became Israel, Jordan and Palestine. Many still argue for a one state which is yet future but the reality is that Israel right now is a three state solution as I showed you. The Palestinian regions are controlled and governed by Palestinians and not Israelis though the Jews do many wrongs to the Palestinians and they try to shift blame on to the Palestinians but many times the Zionist radical Jews are to blame and Israel hostile right wing government.

Though YHWH hates Israel's land to be divided and sold or even given away but again this is part of the plan that will one day allow YHWH to manifest Himself to the whole world. If Israel had not divided into a three state solution which we know it is unless you are going to tell me that Jordan is ruled by Benjamin Netanyahu back in December 2009 I think it will be unwise to think Israel controls all its former regions which King David and Solomon had owned.

YHWH will punish nations who took away Israel's land and these are Islamic and not European. All Europe did with the US is involve herself in peace treaties to give away land to the opposite side but Europe also made sure that Europeans stay in the land such as Khazarian Jews so technically they too are stealing the land from the real children of Israel. So these Euro Jews will be punished for that endeavour.

However the Yahudim are forbidden to take the land by force more on this later. The Europeans do have their hands dirty in the Hebrew slave trade and America was also involved in this. More on this in the next series of the book World War III – The Second Exodus, Y'sra'el's return journey home.

> **Joel 3:2** (HTHS) I will also gather all nations, and will bring them down into the valley of Yahushafat, and will plead with them there for my people and for my heritage Y'sra'el, whom they have scattered among the nations, and divided my land.

All nations in this passage are the same that Zechariah references in 14:14, which is roundabout Israel meaning they are all Islamic. This has nothing to do with a European or Islamic alliance. Europe will be fighting against Islam and three key European nations are involved, the UK, Italy and Spain (Jer 50:3; 48:12).

What about Jo'el 3:3?

> **Jo'el 3:3** And they have cast lots for my people; and have given a boy for a whore, and sold a girl for wine, that they might drink.

The drash is about the crude oil, boy for a harlot, and girl for wine, ancient Hebrews were sold for prostitution to the nations. The western nations carried away many slaves who were sold to them by the Arabs. In modern times the African areas like Darfur where Hebrews were living were cleared out to make way to capture rich oil in the ground. In this both Arabs and Western nations were involved. Remembered there is also judgment on those that remain silent. When a nation kills another and other nations remain quiet that is taken by Elohim as unrighteousness. When Darfur was being cleansed what did the west do? Remain quiet so as not to upset their friends in the Gulf. This makes them complicit in unrighteous action. They also sided with Ashkenazim Jews who are not true Israel and transported the real Yahudim in ships to Europe and America so the text in Joel 3:3 sits strictly in judgment on these.

The tail of the fourth beast is the seven smaller bits of this beast, which are located in the Middle-East. You may have heard of the term sheikhdoms these are part of the beast and are the following areas Dubai, Abu Dhabi, Ajman, Fujaira, Sharjah, Umm al Quwain and Ajman. It may not appear so obvious but let me show you on the map below so you can see what I mean. [10]

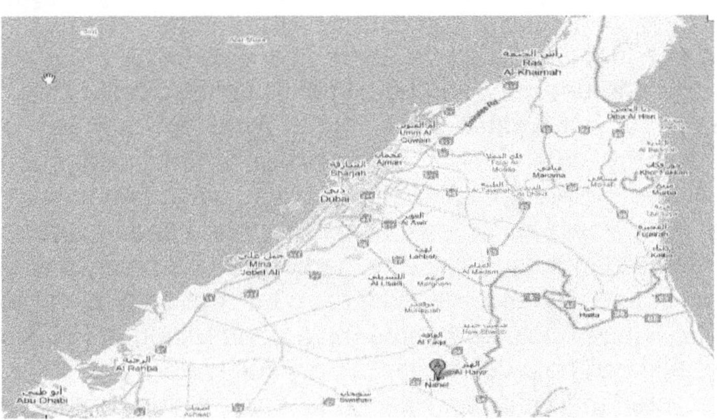

---

[10] http://maps.google.co.uk/maps?ie=UTF-8&hl=en&tab=wl

This may not be so obvious that this is the tail but let me show you a wider picture so you can see the driving part of the beast. One important thing to understand is that the USA, Europe including UK would be helping the beast initially this is how it comes to power and then it turns on these nations. Remembering that it was UK and France that jointly controlled many areas of the middle-east and then UK devised the new map of the middle-east carving out different country boundaries. This can already be seen in the way America has been putting and supporting rebels in Syria with monies alongside Europe. They also did this with Bahrain supporting the wicked government. This is all going to backfire.

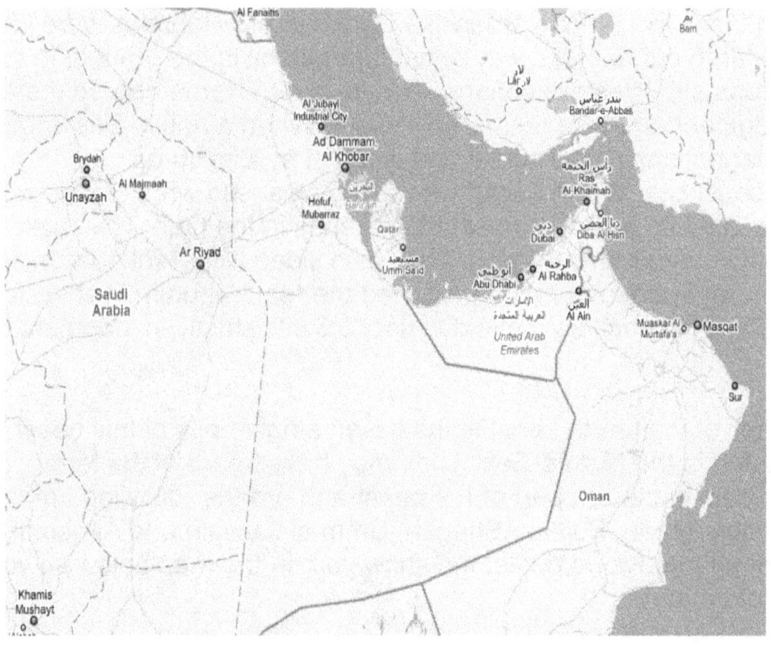

You can see that Saudi Arabia is the driving force here but what is not obvious is that the beast indeed has a tail which also drives the economies of the world, does Dubai world come to mind? In the year 2005 I warned my Indian friend not to get involved in Dubai or any of its properties when everyone was rushing to buy. I told him that Dubai was doomed and he would suffer losses so he listened and saved his money which he invested in Indian property market instead safely making much gains, while others who did not know have lost out on a lot of money in the Dubai housing bubble and some have been ruined unfortunately. Bible Prophecy can help us charter the difficult waters of our life too if we are keen to listen to YHWH and we would know where to put our assets and even in which countries that I deem safe and unsafe according to bible prophecy.

Each part of the 4th Beast is important so we must be careful what we do, where and when and what decisions we make for our children.

The 7 Heads of the Beast in Revelation 13:1

Let us think of the seven heads as seven regions and seven spiritual strongholds.

The 7 heads or strongholds in the End-Times

1. Pakistan
2. Afghanistan
3. Turkey
4. Iran
5. Iraq
6. Saudi Arabia
7. Egypt

You may wonder why I did not include countries such as Indonesia, which has the largest Muslim population. What about China with seventy-two million Muslims there and some other nations of the world.

The reason is very simple the book of Daniel and Revelation does not allow us to choose nations that were not part of the Lion, Bear and Leopard. Our seven heads fit with in the three Empires mentioned such as the Leopard (Grecian), Bear (Persian) and Lion (Babylonian). Indonesia and China were never part of any of these Empires so are ruled out! It does not mean that Muslims of these nations will not take part because some may take part but it means strictly going by what the Bible mandates the geographic regions must be adhered to by the animals mentioned with no human bias. **We must adhere to that for our seven heads or the seven strongholds of the beast.** They cannot be strongholds if they are non Islamic. Even though Indonesia is Islamic but really in the bigger picture does not have the contribution that nations such as Pakistan and Afghanistan have made to the beast. What contribution or driving factor does Indonesia have or China, none whatsoever? China in fact is a safe nation.

Pakistan is a stronghold and a head mentioned in Revelation because in the past they helped put a stop to the campaign of Alexander the great in Multan, which is ninety miles from Lahore and where Alexander almost died. Pakistan was part of the ancient Persian and Parthian Empires and the only Islamic nation with a nuclear bomb so it fits the description of the bear in revelation alongside with Iran. Turkey fits in with the Leopard.

Pakistan is the only other nation after Israel to have used its fleet of F16s to thwart enemy aircraft from Afghanistan and shoot them down. I have no doubt in my mind that one day Pakistan will take part in the war with Israel. It's also important to point out Pakistan has had successes with Israel in knocking out the Zionist planes out of the sky and Israel fears Pakistani aircraft pilots more than any other.

Flight Lieutenant A. Sittar became the first pilot to shoot down an IAF Mirage in the Yom Kippur war in direct combat while flying a Mig 21 for Syria. Pakistan pilots also engaged Israeli Phantom Jets and they did not lose a single pilot. They remained and trained Syrian pilots until 1976 that time. The only pilots that the Zionists fear are the Pakistani variety as I said earlier. The Zionist are not the chosen anyhow and YHWH is going to use other nations to get the nation of Israel cleansed and it's once again going to be Persia playing a major and not a minor role.

The Khazarian converted Jews who are not part of our people actually helped to enslave true genetic Israel. See this video on YouTube to understand why these sons of Japheth will be dealt with by YHWH one day.

Jewish role in black slavery exposed.
http://www.youtube.com/watch?v=R6r8vH8Dehw

European converting to Judaism
http://www.youtube.com/watch?v=jOcVG7zsRa4&feature=related

The battle that is called Armageddon is all about removing counterfeit Israel and bringing true Israel to the land because the Persian Empire is mentioned in Ezekiel 38:5 and Pakistan was a part of the ancient Persian Empire. It will be proven that once again I am right about this when these seven strongholds begin to align up as they already have since I am updating this book in 2012 October. New York has just been hit with a the Sandy storm while foolish Christians think this is judgement for not supporting Israel actually its judgment for supporting Israel the counterfeit while they deny and denigrate the true Hebrews who live in the land of the free called America which is not so free where the prison systems are filled with our people for cheap slave labour. When the Khazari converted gentiles destroyed the homes of Palestinians America just stood by and patted the shoulders of Netanyahu and his ilk now many homes in New York lie in ruins. YHWH is sending a reminder when a nation does not look out for the poor, the orphan and weak this is what the result is so yes it's a judgment okay but for not helping the needy and weak and poor who could not defend against gun toting Zionists with their tanks and F16 fighters. The whole thing will turn very sour for America so be prepared. It will be noting short of Sodom and Gomorrah for its wickedness since those being killed in Palestine are not just Palestinian Arabs but within these Arabs are true Israelites who were forcefully converted into Islam centuries ago. America will be judged for its behaviour towards the slaves it brought in who are the chosen people and for what it continues to do with the rest in its own country by maligning them. I have seen it how my people in America are treated and maligned, each week a person is shot because his colour is black. Those of Americans shooting these people just condemned yourself for the punishment for killing a true genetic Israelite is heavy. Your crosses and white Jesus won't be able to save you on the day of reckoning. The true Black Messiah mandates love for our true people and Torah obedience and not lawless as in the Churches.

Coming back to Turkey which has been helped by the USA as I said they would be given power has one of the best fleet of F16 fighter jets after Pakistan and is a very powerful nation. Turkey is one of the few nations to assemble its own F16 jets with courtesy of the United States. They are powering the beast thanks to American tax dollars and one day these will turn on the Americans.

Afghanistan was also part of the Medo-Persian Empire so it is part of the head according to the book of Revelation and a spiritual stronghold. What many do not know is that Afghanistan throughout its turbulent history of being conquered by the Chinese and Indians was also conquered by Turks so it's interesting that this is where it has stayed considering all the neighbouring Russian CIS states also speak Turkic languages so any wonder why the Anti-Messiah is going to be Turkic?

Alexander took six months to conquer Persia but it took him three years to conquer Afghanistan and he wrote to his mother that you produced one Alexander but the land I am in every foot-step is like walled steel for his soldiers with very brave local people and every man in this nation is like an Alexander using the term "lion like people." Just to note America with all its allies has not conquered Afghanistan so in retrospect Alexander with no drones, no ballistic missiles did very well with Afghanistan.

If we look at Bible prophecy both the British and US forces will suffer casualties in this land and continue to do so in their war on terror if one can believe that which Osama bin Laden has used to attack the US and European nations. The eventual result is that both the US and UK will not succeed in Afghanistan and will have to retreat, I wrote this in 2006 and now in 2012 my writing have been proven true! Both America and Britain pan for a withdrawal of their troops in October 2012. The year 2014 has been branded about for a pull out while some other nations there are planning a pullout in 2013. Afghanistan as I wrote in 2006 did not allow them to succeed hence I have been proven right as the Bible is my accurate measure and the direction of the Holy Spirit in my personal guidance.

This is dictated by prophecy whether we believe it or not I thank my Master Yahushua to keep me close up in His hands to teach me and show me why the lying prophets lie and make wrong predictions while I speak when I am told to speak.

Iraq was also part of the Babylonian Empire alongside Saudi Arabia so these nations are both included as strongholds. The Persians also conquered Egypt that is why Egypt is included in the seven heads or strongholds. The brotherhood movement from which many other radical Islamic movements have spun also started from Egypt influenced by Madudi's writings from Pakistan so it has to be included and part of the bear in Revelation 13:2. Some critics have noted that just like the American government has lied about the war in Vietnam where President Nixon and Johnson followed an imperialistic policy and lied to the American people and deceived them, similarly likewise president Obama and Bush governments have followed similar clandestine policies, which enrich the conglomerates in the USA but at the price of US soldiers being killed and Afghan bloodshed of many innocent people and children not to mention the bloodshed caused in Gaza that America is also complicit in when many innocents were killed and to this day are being killed thanks to American leadership and the Zionist leaders who are no part of us.

If one is brutally honest then this is true. Also on the Israeli/Palestinian warring front it is also true that some Palestinians would seriously consider a peaceful solution to the crisis but the radical elements of Islam and the dominant American/Zionist policy would rather leave things as they are to continue to put focus in the middle-east while the American Corporatocracy tries to deal in South-Asian affairs such as China, Afghanistan and the CIS nations on how to make dollars at the cost of lives lost. Remember blood of the innocent's cries out of the ground for justice and YHWH does not sleep but waits or people to repent or his wrath will be upon all these people, they are not exempt.

The prime minister of Israel Benjamin Netanyahu's new plan of going green to come up with new technologies to disarm the Arabs of oil driven wealth and terrorism by switching away from oil will also fail to offset terrorism and will ultimately fail in light of Bible prophecy, his policies which have only made the lives of real Israelites embittered by expelling the 60,000 refugees from Sudan ear marked to be flown back to their war torn nations in 2012 while some have already been flown back with giving them 1000 US dollars. The shameless European Zionist racism against the black people in Israel chanting blacks go home and destroying their shops in Tel Aviv in 2012, while the late Chief Rabbi Yosef Ovadia in Israel did not have nice words to say about the gentiles are for our use as servants and slaves. In fact Yosef Ovadia will become the servant and slave of the people he calls gentiles as many of these people he calls gentiles are true Y'sra'elites and he is not. Just by speaking Hebrew and wearing the clothes of a Jew does not make you an Y'sra'elite, yes it may make you a Yid who speaks Yiddish but is actually a European. Who has the courage to speak the truth?

These European Zionists and Yemenite converts have no part in the land since they were never there. These are European/Russian people. While the Sudanese refugees contain many people from true genetic black Israel. They should not have gone there but they have little knowledge of prophecy or about who they are. YHWH is removing them from the land through these policies to allow them safety while Zionist Israel is prepared for a cleansing and removal of the counterfeit Jews.

It's clear that Netanyahu's goals are anything but noble but he needs to take a deep look at the scriptures he reads daily and get to grip with what YHWH has already said which is a bitter pill to swallow. Israel is not exactly behaving as a holy nation right now this fact is clear even he can continue to tell the world the land is his but in reality it is not. Telling a lie numerous times does not make it true. See my next book for full answers that follows the series called World War III – Y'sra'el Return Journey home.

The Arabs will continue to use oil as a weapon to terrorise nations. The Arab success behind this is partly due to the heavy western dependence on oil but not just oil but also western greed to earn considerable revenue dollars from this trade, which do not want to give this up even if Israel produces new inventions for green energy the success of which will be limited causing the dominance of oil to continue. In fact the reality is green energy is much more expensive to produce as it requires a very heavy investment which at the end of it all is nothing but buzzwords with the output nowhere near which we get with fossil fuels but I will leave the Europeans with their deception and lies about climate control.

Chapter 2
The Threat Assessment

We know that the radical pose a threat to the Western and even Eastern nations but is it right-ruling for us to call all Muslims evil and to label them as terrorists and while they walk in the streets to be racist against them? Should one treat them with contempt when a large majority of Muslims are not involved in the radical jihad? I have seen disturbing trends in the last few years of groups rising up both in the US and Europe including individuals who claim that all Muslims are alike and so therefore should be treated the same. Some of these are Christian rightwing groups and are behaving no differently than the fascists in Germany were during the war.

I have heard even some prophecy teachers make the claim that since sixty million Germans were turned against the Jews in the holocaust therefore we have to assume that all the Muslims are also going to likewise turn against the West and the fake Jews (Zionists) including those who are moderate Muslims. This view is not only hostile but scripturally incorrect.

There is one big problem with this scenario. First only a two hundred million army emerges that enters to fight Israel for Armageddon out of the 1.6 billion population of Muslims. Well it's quite reasonable to assume that many Muslim men and women do not care about a war with Israel because they like the people in the West are trying to earn a living and are more worried about a roof over their heads than radical Jihad. There only interest is food for their children and education and likewise many other moderate Muslims who are wrongly being labelled radicals. The percentage of radicals is only about 15% at best and even then not all of these will pickup weapons to fight. It is well known that it is not poverty that drives towards Jihad but virulent Islamic teachings and many people who are the leading forefronts of Jihad are from rich backgrounds and not poor.

> **Revelation 9:16** (HTHS) And the multitude of the army of the horsemen were two hundred million: and I heard the multitude [11] of them.

So in view of present day Islamic religion there are about 1.6 billion Muslims worldwide and if we take the army above than all we have here is a 7.8% total of the entire Muslim population. Anyone who is good with

---

11 It is better translated multitude and not number.

figures can see that this is not the entire Muslim world? No, any rational man would tell you this does not fit the entire Muslim world turning against the west scenario. That is scaremongering and foolish. The Bible itself is clear that not all the nations participate so all I can say is that people who think that all of the Muslims are going to fight are creating an atmosphere of hatred against many Muslims who are both civil and peaceful.

Furthermore it is pretty foolish to say that they will attack the west not considering the fact that the western nations are the most powerful in armament, missiles, bullets and future technology, while the Muslims have only one nation with a bomb and the rest are just numbers with their people still struggling to meet basic needs. The point is that the two hundred million army will try to overwhelm Israel, which is a much smaller nation let's say 7.5 million Israelis which is understandable. Out of these seven and a half million if we consider that able bodied fighting men and women are 500,000 soldiers versus the 200 million army we arrive at odds of 400 to 1.

This shows that Israel is heavily outnumbered. However this is meant to be because it is YHWH who is about to fight hence why the odds are stacked against them. We need to ask has Israel ever faced such odds before. In fact I will prove to you that Israel has faced worst odds than this. Let me prove it to you.

In the book of Judges it talks about the account of Gideon where the Master YHWH told him to whittle down his army from 30,000 (Judges 7:3) to 300. The opposition is simply said to be as numerous as the sand of the sea (Jud 7:12).

Since we are not given a number for the army of the enemy we have no figure from the Bible but we do have a figure with the same wording in the book of Yahshar (Jasher) given in 15:17 as 800,000 men. We can therefore compare this figure to Gideon's army of 300, which is stated in Yahshar 58:17. So we can see the army is extremely large. In our case if we have an army of the enemy the size of 800,000 men then the 300 men of the army of Gideon gives us a ratio of 2667 to 1 while in Armageddon it is 400 to 1. Actually the odds in Israel's favour appear much better in the latter army but considering that we are dealing with very powerful weapons and not just swords and arrows therefore the fighting forces will be more deadly.

After hearing the reports against even secular Muslims I was most disturbed to label them all as extremists because let me state for the record that I am an ex-Muslim and know what I am about to show you is going to reveal truth that will show you how ridiculous some of the claims being made are and we will examine them one by one. I know even a Rabbi's home was attacked in California in May 2010 who advocates peace between the Muslims and the Zionist Jews.

The first claim did Hitler turn all of Germany against the Jews, all of sixty million? The answer shockingly is, No. In fact many Germans secretly helped the Ashkenazi Jews. Many of these German's names are not even recorded. This shows us some of the rightwing scaremongers are very wrong.

http://www.guardian.co.uk/world/2008/nov/02/nazi-Yahudi-hitler-schindler-holocaust

Berlin tribute to the Germans who saved the Jews

Allan Hall in Berlin

The Observer, Sunday 2 November 2008

New museum salutes the few who defied Nazis

A unique museum honouring Germans who helped persecuted Yahudim stay alive under the Nazi tyranny has opened in Berlin. The Silent Heroes Memorial Centre is the first of its kind dedicated to individuals who helped to hide, feed and care for people who otherwise would have gone to the gas chambers.

Tucked away in a tenement block on Rosenthaler Strasse, it lies in the heart of Berlin's pre-war Yahudim quarter, not far from the site of the former paintbrush factory where an anti-Nazi activist helped deaf and blind Yahudim shelter from the Gestapo round-ups.

Germany had a pre-war population of 550,000 Jews; by 1945 fewer than 15,000 were left. Many of those were saved thanks to the courage of Christians who put their own lives on the line. The names of just 3,000 'silent heroes' are officially known, but historians believe that many more cases remain unrecorded. According to some estimates 20,000 people across the country are thought to have offered their Yahudim fellow citizens some form of support and refuge.

'Compared to the number of people who allowed Nazi atrocities to happen or even took part in them, the people who shielded Yahudim were a tiny minority,' said Berlin's Mayor Klaus Wowereit. 'But it is this minority that gives us direction. By commemorating these courageous people, we are ensuring that attacks on human dignity will not be tolerated.'

On display are photographs, letters and other documents recording 250 Germans who risked their lives giving Yahudim food, shelter or a place to work from 1938 to 1945. These Yahudim were known to themselves and the authorities as 'U-boats'; like submarines, they were not to be seen.

One poignant artifact is a key that belonged to Yahudim seamstress Alice Loewenthal. It opened the door to a flat where she lived with her husband and four daughters. The family was taken by the Gestapo, but by a quirk of fate Loewenthal escaped and was given false papers by a friend in the police. Next to the key lies a doll and a small photograph album, all that remained of her family life; her daughters and husband were murdered at Auschwitz.

Another display chronicles the fate of Ilse Lewin, who was born in 1911 and grew up in Berlin. She had the chance to immigrate to England, but she did not want to leave her mother, Gretha. From September 1940 on, Lewin had to work at a Siemens factory as a forced labourer. After her mother was seized at the end of 1942, Lewin decided to evade her own impending deportation. Her friend Greta Schellwort warned her of the huge round-up planned for 27 February, 1943, in which all the Yahudim in Berlin, especially those working in armaments factories, were to be arrested and deported.

At first she was taken in by acquaintances, but after that she found no permanent shelter until mid-1944. She lived on food that Schellwort slipped to her. She was able to earn some money as a cleaner in a tailor's shop until the man took advantage of her situation to harass her sexually. Lewin's friend, Vera Freyer, provided her with forged papers and she obtained a postal identity card in Freyer's name. In the summer of 1944 another non-Yahudim friend, Ilse Glondajewski, helped her to find a hiding place in the Berlin district of Prenzlauer Berg, where she hid until the end of the war.

'There are many memorial sites dedicated to those targeted by the Nazis, but there has never been one which is solely dedicated to these heroes,' said Johannes Tuchel, director of an umbrella organisation for memorials of resistance to the Nazis which put the collection together. He now plans to work with eastern European archivists and colleagues at the Yad Vashem Holocaust memorial in Israel, to extend the project.

The museum's opening comes just days before ceremonies marking the Kristallnacht pogrom of 9 November, 1938, when the Nazis gave a foretaste of the Holocaust to come by ransacking Yahudim homes, businesses and places of worship. Hundreds died and thousands were thrown into concentration camps. The first step on the road to mass extermination had been taken.

The other shocking truth is that fascism in Germany was funded by Zionist Jews of America there is documented proof of this because they wanted to acquire the land to build a nation, they were quite happy to have German Jews killed in order to do this. Here is what Hertzel who originally came up with the plan.

> [12]You surely are aware of the words of Theodor Hertzl, who presided the first Zionist meeting: "It is essential that the sufferings of Jews....become worse....this will assist in realization of our plans....I have an excellent idea....I shall induce anti-Semites to liquidate Jewish wealth....The anti-Semites will assist us thereby in that they will strengthen the persecution and oppression of Jews. The anti-Semites shall be our best friends."

So the critics might say but is that just 3000 German Christians who helped while the majority did not. Note that the article says 20,000. I believe the real figure is a lot higher than this but is not recorded and this is what we call a remnant. What about the fact that 19,000 German Roman Catholic priests who died opposing Hitler. This does away with the myth that sixty million Germans were all part of the holocaust that is being perpetuated by some right wing Christians.

In my opinion now these same people and other folks out of fear mongering tactics and some out of personal agendas to make dollars are calling all the Muslim world wicked. Many Muslims are being labelled as terrorists when they are not terrorists. Let us examine the Catholic evidence.

> http://www.columbia.edu/cu/augustine/arch/heroes.htm
> Pinchas Lapide devotes ninety pages of Three Popes and the Yahudim to the Church's treatment of the Yahudim before the

---

12 http://www.normanfinkelstein.com/

election of Pope Pius XI. He gives much credit to the many popes who forbade persecution, but convicts the papacy in general of failing both to eradicate overt anti-Semitism and to clarify points of Catholic teaching which were taken as excusing or even supporting it.

After exhaustive research, Lapide concluded that at least 700,000 Yahudim, and more likely 860,000, owed their lives directly to the Church; he also concluded that Pius simply could not have done more than he did. The suggestion that Pius ought to have spoken more forcefully he treats with near derision; he quotes many Yahudim leaders, many of them rescued by Catholics, to the effect that more forceful speeches would certainly not have caused the Nazis to moderate the persecutions, and would most probably have induced them to intensify them.

As early as April 1935, as Vatican Secretary of State, Cardinal Pacelli addressed 250,000 pilgrims at Lourdes: "These [Nazi] ideologues are in fact only miserable plagiarizers who dress up ancient error in new tinsel. It matters little whether they rally round the flag of the social revolution...or are possessed by the superstition of race and blood." He was responsible for the final wording of Pius XI's March 1937 encyclical, Mit brennender Sorge ("With burning sorrow"), and made it more strongly antiracist. The encyclical, the first ever written in German, was read in all German churches on Palm Sunday; the Nazi Foreign Office characterized it as "a call to battle...as it calls upon Catholic citizens to rebel against the authority of the Reich."

In 1938 Italy passed its first anti-Yahudim laws. Pius XI condemned them. He took action, as well. In January 1939 he asked the ambassadors to the Vatican to procure entry visas to their countries for German and Italian Yahudim. He also called a German bishop to Rome to plan a resettlement project in Sao Paulo. Presumably his Secretary of State was involved in these initiatives (General Ludendorf wrote: "Pacelli was the live spirit which stood behind all the anti-German activities of Rome's policy"3); but he would not be Secretary of State much longer. Pius XI died in February.

Cardinal Pacelli was elected as Pius XII in March. As one of the standard first steps in the persecution, Yahudim were now banned from the learned professions. The new Pope invited many to the Vatican and offered to help them to emigrate; many accepted, and

Pius intervened with the diplomats of other countries to obtain entry visas for them. [13]

This evidence is enough to show that unlike many Christians today who label Catholics in the holocaust as evil they were not evil is pure bias on Christians who may not like Catholics.

Let me show you clear evidence that suggests many moderate Muslims will help the Yahudim. This not only has already happened in the past but this will also repeat in the future. So the claim that all the Muslims will turn against the Yahudim is false and alarmist by making people unnecessarily hate moderate Muslims while we are taught in scriptures to love our enemy. What some of the hate monger's out there or whatever they like to be known as are doing is making up assumptions based on those Muslims who have become radical. The same brush is used to paint the whole Muslim world evil. The poor woman in the village of Pakistan who goes around washing people's clothes and washing people's dishes in Muslim homes is also wicked according to these alarmist people.

The man who tends his cattle in some remote far away village in India and is Muslim is also evil if you go by the right wing haters of Muslims. Yet this man or the woman described above has very normal values and they are just trying to make ends meet and raise their family as best as they can. Do we seriously think they worry over what the Yahudim do in Israel or how the Palestinians behave in Israel? While who is going to look at the Zionist evil agenda which dictates the removal and the demolishing of Palestinian homes? Are we to assume that every Palestinian man and woman is evil and they deserve to be dead? This is the attitude of some hate mongers. All Palestinians are not evil and in fact they have a more right to living in Israel today then European Jews who are not genetic but this truth will not be told to you since the media controlled by the Zionists is continually brainwashing people the other way.

Let us examine the past how Muslims turned around and helped the Yahudim when Europeans were persecuting them.

During the Spanish inquisitions 150,000 Sephardic Yahudim fled to Turkey and established themselves in Istanbul. Turkey was the dominant Islamic force at that time and extremely powerful. The Khazarian

---

13 Pinchas Lapide, Three Popes and the Jews (New York: Hawthorne Books, 1967), p.110.

converted Jews were not only able to get protection but were offered jobs of physicians and councillors to the Sultan. While the West labelled Yahudim in England with the blood libel as blood suckers as a pretext to kick them out of England and Christian England was busy burning Yahudim Synagogues and the Bibles the Yahudim owned, and the Muslims were in fact helping them.

http://en.wikipedia.org/wiki/History_of_the_Yahudim_in_Turkey#cite_note-turkishjews.com-12

The number of native Yahudim was soon bolstered by small groups of Ashkenazi Yahudim that immigrated to the Ottoman Empire between 1421-1453.[11] Among these new Ashkenazi immigrants was Rabbi Yitzhak Sarfati, a German-born Yahudi of French descent[13] (Hebrew: צרפתי - Sarfati, meaning: "French"), who became the Chief Rabbi of Edirne and wrote a letter inviting the European Jewry to settle in the Ottoman Empire, in which he stated that: "Turkey is a land wherein nothing is lacking" and asking: "Is it not better for you to live under Muslims than under Christians?"[13][14]

The greatest influx of Yahudim into Asia Minor and the Ottoman Empire occurred during the reign of Mehmed the Conquerors' successor, Beyazid II (1481-1512), after the expulsion of the Yahudim from Spain and Portugal. The Sultan issued a formal invitation to Yahudim expelled from Spain and Portugal and they started arriving in the empire in great numbers.

The Sultan is said to have exclaimed thus at the Spanish monarch's lack of wisdom: "Ye call Ferdinand a wise king he who makes his land poor and ours rich!"[15][16] The Yahudim satisfied various needs in the Ottoman Empire: the Muslim Turks were largely uninterested in business enterprises and accordingly left commercial occupations to members of minority religions. They also distrusted the Christian subjects whose countries had only recently been conquered by the Ottomans and therefore it was natural to prefer Yahudim subjects to which this consideration did not apply. [17]

The Spanish Yahudim were allowed to settle in the wealthier cities of the empire, especially in the European provinces (cities such as: Istanbul, Sarajevo, Salonica, Adrianople and Nicopolis), Western and Northern Anatolia (Bursa, Aydın, Tokat and Amasya), but also in the Mediterranean coastal regions (for example: Jerusalem,

Safed, Damascus, Egypt). Izmir was not settled by Spanish Yahudim until later. The Yahudim population at Jerusalem increased from 70 families in 1488 to 1,500 at the beginning of the 16th century. That of Safed increased from 300 to 2,000 families and almost surpassed Jerusalem in importance. Damascus had a Sephardic congregation of 500 families. Istanbul had a Yahudim community of 30,000 individuals with 44 synagogues. Bayezid allowed the Yahudim to live on the banks of the Golden Horn. Egypt, especially Cairo, received a large number of the exiles, who soon out-numbered the native Yahudim. Gradually, the chief centre of the Sephardic Yahudim became Salonica, where the Spanish Yahudim soon outnumbered their co-religionists of other nationalities and, at one time, the original native inhabitants.

11 Avigdor Levy; The Yahudim of the Ottoman Empire, New Jersey, (1994)
12 http://www.turkishjews.com/history/letter.asp
13 B. Lewis, "The Yahudim of Islam", New York (1984), pp. 135 - 136
14 B. Lewis, "The Yahudim of Islam", New York (1984), pp. 135 - 136
15 http://binsalaam.tripod.com/
16 http://globond.blogspot.com/2009/07/what-you-may-not-know-about-turkey.html
17 H. Inalcik; The Ottoman Empire: The Classical Age 1300-1600, Phoenix Press, (2001)

I challenge anyone to look back at history and see that even while Islam was advancing yet there were many compassionate Muslim leaders who were very helpful to the Jews and allowed them not only to settle in their lands but settle in the wealthier parts of their lands. This certainly shows us that even though relations were strained at times but YHWH's hand was upon the Yahudim wherever they went since they tried to obey the Torah far more than our people the real Israelites have done in their exile. He allowed doors to be opened for them. While the Muslim prophet Muhammad drove the real Yahudim out of Saudi Arabia other Muslims welcomed them in their nation. This proves to us that we should not judge all Muslims alike. It would be very unwise and unrighteous to do that. Just like when Christians were killing the Jews in Europe and the Jews were fleeing to the East to the Islamic lands likewise I do not judge all Christians the same way and in no way suggest that all Christians are evil as this would equally be wrong because I know many are not.

What about the fact that the religion of Islam or the radical teachers teach to fight a Jihad both against the Yahudim and the west?

Let me show you something of interest, although the radicals seem to get a large slice of the media but the moderates hardly make the media and they are mostly peaceful and not violent.

My personal conviction is that Allah is not the Elohim of the Bible and Allah is not YHWH the Kadosh One of Israel however there are favourable verses in the Qur'an that speak of the Yahudim as chosen and the best race.

Let us examine the Qur'anic verses;

> **Sura Al-Bakra 2:47** Children of Israel! Call to mind the favour which I bestowed upon you, and <u>that I preferred you to all others</u>.

This verse shows that according to Allah the deity of Islam the Yahudim are favoured above all people, which according to the Qur'an at least as well shows their chosen status.

> **Surah 5:21** Remember Moses said to his people: "O my people! Call in remembrance the favour of Allah unto you, when He produced prophets among you, made you kings, and gave you what He had not given to any other among the peoples.

Prophets were given through the chosen Israelites.

> **Surah 44:30-32** We did deliver aforetime the Children of Israel from humiliating Punishment, Inflicted by Pharaoh, for he was arrogant (even) among inordinate transgressors. And we chose them aforetime above the nations, knowingly,

The chosen people were chosen according to the Qur'an to demonstrate their favour and punishment was afflicted upon them by Pharaoh to bring about the revelation of the true God of Israel to the nations.

> **Surah 45:16** We did aforetime grant to the Children of Israel the Book the Power of Command, and Prophethood; we gave them, for Sustenance, things good and pure; and we favoured them above the nations.

The critics may ask but these are all Meccan and not Medinan Suras (chapters).

The Medinan Suras were written when Muhammad migrated to Medina after being persecuted in Mecca by his own tribesman. In Medina there was a large population of the Yahudim and most of the later Medinan Suras lean towards intolerance and violence towards the unbelievers such as the Yahudim and Christians of Arabia. This fact is true however there is a caveat which the ill informed critics won't tell you and that is the following.

Just like there are a variety of Christians with differing opinions on doctrines of the Bible and likewise there are many Muslims with differing opinions on the Qur'an. While the radicals lean towards the later Medinan Suras, the moderates lean towards the Meccan Suras even though most Muslim scholars suggest that the Meccan Suras are abrogated in favour of the later ones but Muslims still debate over what is and what is not valid. Some take the whole Qur'an to be verbatim the words of Allah while others take the later Suras to be in force now. Therefore the majority of the Muslim world is not radicalized. I do not believe they will all be radicalized and neither does the Bible even suggest such a scenario that all the Islamic nations will be radicalized.

> **Isaiah 19:2** (HTHS) And I will set the Mitzrim (Egyptians) against the Mitzrim (Egyptians): and they shall fight every one against his brother, and every one against his neighbour; city against city, and kingdom against kingdom.

Even YHWH will make them fight over their doctrines and teachings. The verse above suggests that this will be a war where the radicals will kill the moderate Muslims because they will not agree with each other. Note the fighting is localised or regional and not worldwide meaning different regions will have different issues in Islamic lands. For instance in India a large portion of Muslims are Sufis, which is the peaceful side of Islam yet India has more Muslims than Pakistan. This proves my case that not all the Muslims will be radicalized. For further proof take a look at Iraq, Iran and Pakistan where Muslims are fighting each other as they do not all agree on the interpretation of the Qur'an, which is resulting in radical Muslims killing moderate Muslims. The Taliban brand of Muslims in Afghanistan are the most intolerable towards other Muslims often executing them under extra judicial killings.

Therefore all the scaremongering and hatred spreading by ultra right wing people for that matter is wrong because they are mistaken about Islam as a whole. You cannot lump everyone as a terrorist or Jihadist just because he is a Muslim! If I was to examine my Muslim family none are jihadists so that should send alarm bells to you that it is wrong to label all Muslims with this criteria simply because the statements made by right-wing groups whether Christian or otherwise are not true.

Scripture tells us that there will be a large scale problem but we will continue to see a mixture of radicals and moderates throughout the future until the return of the Messiah. Just a day ago there was a bombing in Lahore this is about one mile from where my family lives in Pakistan in the famous moon market of Lahore and my family in Lahore frequents this particular shopping bazaar quite regularly where two devices were detonated remotely. Fifty-five people were killed and many others injured. The majority of these were Muslim women, so what was their fault or were they radical too go ask the right-wing Christians?

Also the five American men who were caught in Pakistan in Sargodha on December 9th 2009 were Waqar Husain Khan, 22 (Virginia), Ahmed Abdullah Mani, 20 (Virginia), Ramay S Zamzam, 22 (Egypt), Iman Hasan Yamar, 17 (California), and Omar Farouk, 24 (Virginia). These young men are not even extremists but wanted to fight a holy war because they saw America as an aggressor nation fighting within the Muslim world. What's sad about this whole affair is this that these young men were educated to be something good in life and now they could potentially face life imprisonment in Pakistan. This also shows that if all of Pakistan wanted jihad then why would they arrest and give these people life sentences. Pakistanis in general do not want a holy jihad against the world or even Israel but the problem is media centred and mostly anti-Muslim propaganda. Muslims think America cannot bully the rest of the world into doing what they think is right hence therefore many step out to fight America as they see them as the aggressor including Zionist Israel as the finger behind America. This is a mentality issue not a religious issue. The issue is clouded by the radicals who then make this a nationalistic holy war against both America and Israel including Great Britain.

Even many of the rightwing Christians and others do not have an honest answer because I can tell you most of these Muslim women and others that are killed by Muslim bombers do not care about radical Islam and were very ordinary Muslim citizens of Pakistan just trying to live a normal life bringing up their children in their families. It's very sad that many families are without mothers and fathers and no social system to support them either. The ones who will suffer in this tragedy the most will be the children and women of the Muslim families.

What about the hundreds injured who have no help from the Pakistani government so what did they get from radical Islam? They got death and destruction but is it their fault that they were brought up Muslim and live in a Muslim land that has a number of people bent on extremism? Even in Pakistan a new comedy show was invented a few years ago based on the Taliban by Younis Butt called the Taliban T Channel. Its purpose was to make people laugh at the ideology the Taliban preach such as hiding women in Burkas (full black covering) then banning them from education, singing and from TV etc. They invented their own versions of General Musharaf, President Obama and others. It's a bit like the British comedy program The Muppet show. You can see some episodes on www.youtube.com.

This should present the evidence that moderate Pakistanis can laugh off these things and are not all trying to kill others because many moderate Muslims do seriously believe in living in peace, while the radicals drive the extremist agenda and usually are making most of the headlines with the Zionist media happy to portray them all as terrorists so it causes their goals of world domination to come one step closer but the Zionists will fail ultimately with loss of lives.

Zionist Israel is made to look bad in the Muslim eyes and through misinformation about the Palestinians anger and hatred is created in these people's hearts, which then in turn results in these kinds of Jihadi actions. It is true that much fault lays with the right wing Israeli governments for brainwashing their people and constantly suppressing any hope of peace for the Palestinians which becomes a stumbling block to all. It's clear the Zionists are not interested in peace and they keep blaming the Palestinians with misinformation spread worldwide through their controlled media. Hence why when the cleanup of Israel comes the Zionists clock is ticking and they do not have very long to go out you go.

More needs to be done by the US on why they are fighting the war and Israel needs to dig deep in its pockets to allow the true Israelites to return to the land but they will not do that and they will not allow Palestinians to have a peaceful state either so the war continues to the end.

If Israel was willing to supply proof of their actions which at times may be legitimate self defence measures then I am sure the world would pay more attention however there are many many incidents in Israel unfortunately that are contradictory to Israel's stance of self defence where innocent Palestinians have been shot and their homes illegally demolished. Israel cannot justify its policy of hatred for the sons of Abraham the Palestinian Arabs by eradicating Palestinian homes and taking away and from them by force.

Israel today is not a beacon of light this is simply because those that inhabit the land of Israel in majority are European colonists and not true chosen seed of Yaqub. While the real Yahudim in Israel who are in small numbers are looked down upon by the European Khazari converts that is the Ethiopians and the black Israelites in the south.

Israel needs to allow a bit more freedom for peaceful Muslims and Christians who want to do business in or outside Israel to have some kind of free safe travel zones rather than to be stuck in endless queues on border checkpoints which add to the daily Palestinian frustrations creating hatred and not love. This does not give Israel credibility even if Israel is right in its actions which it is not. This will cause others to see Israel as the aggressor rather than protecting her borders. However Israel can have her day today living a life of lawlessness by not obeying YHWH's laws but when YHWH's brings the real Israelites home then we will see what Israel is meant to be which today it is not.

In the 12th century famous Muslim scholars such as Ibn Rushd from Cordoba Spain fought for women's equal rights in Islam. Dr Nasaruddin Umar is also a professor in Indonesia trying to fight for women's equal rights in Islam. This proves and shows us that there is a movement in Islam to better the condition of women however how successful this has been or will be is largely dependent on the Islamic states and whether they listen to such people or not. Even in the Bible women though given equal rights were not given authority over men for the household but women in the Western world have generally over exerted the equality status and have trampled on their men to try to prove that they are superior but have only fallen flat on their faces with broken homes and fatherless children. This means their needs to be a balance and the balance is given by the law of YHWH that is if men and women are willing to obey that law written by Moses they can live in peace and harmony.

The model of the God of Israel has a proven track record in equality for both but subordination within the equality status to men in authority has always been the case and that is not about to change. When men and women remove the Islamic shackles and accept the God of Israel and His law it is that day when the Islamic women will be truly liberated and until then problems will continue both in the west and the east. The same is true for Western liberal women who will continue to reap what they sow until they submit before YHWH and accept His rule over them.

Men will need to give over the stereotype of women and allow them freedom of movement and have more trust on their actions. This is one of the key Islamic areas where men are actually afraid of women and what they might do given the freedom so the women are instead suppressed using the Islamic religion and society. The assassination of Benazir Bhutto brought that point home in Pakistan in 2007 and was a sad fact indeed when radicals were behind her assassination funded by ministers in government of Pakistan who pretend to be innocent. It is believed by many in Pakistan that she was assassinated on the orders of her husband Zardari who wanted to regain power with a sympathy vote, I have no evidence to suggest this is true as none has been provided to date but lack of evidence does not mean innocence!

Iraq and Afghanistan are prime examples of what not to do while Turkey on the other hand set the example that within the framework of Islam keeping religion away from government and allowing European freedoms could be allowed and their model has worked for over eighty years, Erdogan has proven himself as a good ruler of Turkey. While today the radicals are driving Islam towards global governance not by reason but by threat and violence this has only proved that the ancient Islamic model is but a failure.

I was speaking to my brother in law the morning of 8th December 2009 in Pakistan, he is a peaceful moderate Muslim and his exact words were that this is insanity and inhumane to kill people like this with bombs both men, women and children who have no fight. This sentiment of my brother in law is echoed by all peace loving Muslims throughout the world and it is not because they are confused and the ultra right wing people who advocate all of Islam is evil are right but this is because many Muslims still debate over how to live peacefully in a world where they feel are constantly at struggle (internal Jihad). For some this is as an internal Jihad (inner struggle) amongst the peaceful Muslims, while the radicals see this as an <u>external</u> Jihad for war with what they call the infidel west which includes both the west and Israel with three key nations in their eyes that is USA, Great Britain and Israel.

It is true that the small number of radical's pickup all the headlines but that does not make all Muslims evil. To be honest even though many Yahudim lived in a dhimma status (protected second class citizens) in times past in Muslim nations but in reality if I am totally honest with you they were better off than in anti-Semitic Europe where their synagogues and their religious books such as the Tanak (incorrectly referred to as the Old Testament) were burnt and they were taunted all the time by Christians as Christ killers and we cannot pretend that it was not the Christians but Catholics instead. The age old excuse lumbering all guilt unto the Catholics. It is quite evident that both Christians, Catholics and radical Muslims have blood on their hands including Europe especially has blood on its hands of the real genetic Israelites being made slaves and shipped to other countries that is the Black Hebrews from Africa. Muslims were involved in the trade of Black Israelites selling them off to the European Christians who pretended to go to Africa to preach the gospel treating real Israelites as beasts. I would like to see an apology from Christians in Europe and also the Khazari Jews to what atrocities they have done to the real Israelites.

The Yahudim actually fared better in Muslim lands than in Christian Europe in medieval times which gave them the holocaust after the renaissance and pogroms across the world because people thought they are the real deal when in fact they were not the real deal but only converts to our way of life and faith. Christian Euope has more Yahudim blood on its hands than radical Islam and we cannot deny it because YHWH will bring those who killed the Yahudim to book on the Day of Judgment. This includes everyone who took part in these actions. Martin Luther the hero of Christianity will be in front of the line to be judged for his vicious writings against the Yahudim and in the same queue will be the anti-Semitic church fathers of modern Christianity. Their guilt cannot be excused by simply saying they were ignorant. It is their writings which have helped to keep hatred for the Yahudim alive worldwide and even the blood libel on the Yahudim was originally brought about by Christians in England and is today used by the Muslims. So who is guilty for the blood libel charge?

Here is an excerpt:

> Martin Luther on the Yahudim and Their Lies, 154, 167, 229, cited in Michael, Robert. Holy Hatred: Christianity, Antisemitism, and the Holocaust. New York: Palgrave Macmillan, 2006, p111.
>
> **"On The Yahudim And Their Lies" (1543 CE)**
> In the treatise, Luther writes that the Yahudim are a "base, whoring people, that is, no people of God, and their boast of lineage, circumcision, and law must be accounted as filth." That they are "full of the devil's feces"... which they wallow in like swine, and the synagogue is an "incorrigible whore and an evil slut." He argues that their synagogues and schools be set on fire, their prayer books destroyed, rabbis forbidden to preach, homes razed, and property and money confiscated. They should be shown no mercy or kindness, afforded no legal protection, and these "poisonous envenomed worms" should be drafted into forced labor

or expelled for all time. He also seems to advocate their murder, writing "we are at fault in not slaying them."

[14]Massacres at London and York (1189–1190)
Richard I had taken the cross before his coronation (September 3, 1189). A number of the principal Yahudim of England presented themselves to do homage at Westminster; but there appears to have been a superstition against Yahudim being admitted to such a holy ceremony, and they were repulsed during the banquet which followed the coronation. The rumour spread from Westminster to the City of London that the king had ordered a massacre of the Yahudim; and a mob in Old Jewry, after vainly attacking throughout the day the strong stone houses of the Jews, set them on fire at night, killing those within who attempted to escape. The king was enraged at this insult to his royal dignity, but took no steps to punish the offenders, owing to their large numbers. After his departure on the crusade, riots with loss of life occurred at Lynn, where the Yahudim attempted to attack a baptised coreligionist who had taken refuge in a church. The seafaring population rose against them, fired their houses, and put them to the sword. So, too, at Stamford Fair, on March 7, 1190, many were slain, and on March 18 fifty-seven were slaughtered at Bury St. Edmunds. The Yahudim of Lincoln saved themselves only by taking refuge in a castle.

Isolated attacks on Yahudim also occurred at Colchester, Thetford, and Ospringe, but the most striking incident occurred at York on the night of March 16 (the day of the Yahudim feast of Shabbat ha-Gadol, the Shabbat before Passover) and March 17, 1190. The Yahudim of York were alarmed by the preceding massacres and by the setting on fire of several of their houses by the anti-Yahudim rioting in the wake of religious fervour during crusaders' preparations for the Third Crusade against the Saracens, led by Richard. Their leader Josce asked the warden of York Castle to receive them with their wives and children, and they were accepted into Clifford's Tower. However, the tower was besieged by the mob of crusaders, demanding that the Yahudim convert to Christianity and be baptized. Trapped in the castle, the Yahudim were advised by their religious leader, Rabbi Yomtov of Joigney, to kill themselves rather than convert; Josce began by slaying his wife Anna and his two children, and then was killed by Yomtov. The father of each family killed his wife and children, and then

---

14 http://en.wikipedia.org/wiki/History_of_the_Jews_in_England

Yomtob stabbed the men before killing himself. The handful of Yahudim who did not kill themselves surrendered to the crusaders at daybreak on March 17, leaving the castle on a promise that they would not be harmed; they were also killed. In the aftermath the wooden tower was burnt down.

With the accession of Henry III (1216) the position of the Yahudim became somewhat easier, but only for a short time. Innocent III had in the preceding year caused the Fourth Council of the Lateran to pass the law enforcing the Badge upon the Yahudim; and in 1218 Stephen Langton, Archbishop of Canterbury, brought it into operation in England, the badge taking the form of an oblong white patch of two finger-lengths by four. The action of the Church was followed by similar opposition on the part of the English boroughs.

Petitions were accordingly sent to the king in many instances to remove his Yahudim from the boroughs, and they were expelled from Bury St. Edmunds in 1190, Newcastle in 1234, Wycombe in 1235, Southampton in 1236, Berkhamsted in 1242, Newbury in 1244. Yahudim were expelled from the lands of Queen Dowager Eleanor in January 1275 (which included towns such as Guildford).

In the 1650s, Menasseh Ben Israel, a rabbi and leader of the Dutch Yahudim community, approached Oliver Cromwell with the proposition that Yahudim should at long-last be readmitted to England. Cromwell agreed, and although he could not compel a council called for the purpose in December 1655 to consent formally to readmission, he made it clear that the ban on Yahudim would no longer be enforced. In the years 1655–56, the controversy over the readmission of Yahudim was fought out in a pamphlet war. The issue divided religious radicals and more conservative elements within society. The Puritan William Prynne was vehemently opposed to permitting Yahudim to return, the Quaker Margaret Fell no less passionately in favour. In the end, Yahudim were readmitted in 1655, and, by 1690, about 3,000 Yahudim had settled in England.

Note that it was not the evangelicals that permitted the Yahudim to return to England but a Puritan Christian called Cromwell, while the Evangelicals and even some other Puritans wanted nothing to do with the Ashkenazi Jewry. Such is the history of our nation the United Kingdom and its terrible relations with the Yahudim in the past. Let us hope we never repeat this again. For once even though many of the European converts are not genetic Israel I for all practical purposes will see all those who hold fast to the Contracts/Agreements of Israel as grafted in. However we cannot say they replace the true Yahudim/Israelites but because they are Torah keeping they can be only referred to as proselytes or converted Jews.

No wonder today I see both the real sons of Abraham, Ishmael and Isaac have been thoroughly persecuted by Western nations then some pretend that they did not do it but it was someone else. All the historical reasons are there to understand why radical Islam is at war with the west and Israel. However we know this was going to happen as the Bible already declared it. The worst fared group out of these conflicts was the enslaved black Hebrews followed by European Khazari converts called Jews and then the Christians. We cannot forget the plight of the real black Israelites and they 400 year old slavery caused by converted Jews.

The radical Muslims basically took revenge on the Christians for the ills of the Western based governments throughout history.

Yes pogroms even happened in Muslim lands but if you read earlier the Jews fared the best in Turkey where the Islamic Ottoman Empire was ruling from, it not only gave them prominent positions but also settled them in good areas of their land. Apart from the incident with Haman in Iran which was real black Jews, they fared very well in Iran and Morocco and I can attest to this because my family were very wealthy land owners in Iran with whom we lost contact after the migration to India and subsequently to Pakistan in 1947.

This testimony speaks truly about YHWH's love upon the House of Judah and also the fact that we should not persecute Muslims who want to live in peace and we should give them all the room to live and present the real gospel, the Torah of Moses neglected by most of Christendom who misinterpret the New Testament according to the anti-Yahudim church fathers which then becomes a watered down social gospel parading in churches as truth in the West but the real gospel of the Messiah, which was to obey the Torah and follow the Messiah both walk hand in hand has been neglected as can be evidenced in many of our modern churches today.

Those that are redeemed by unmerited favour must walk in Torah just like father Abraham and demonstrate with Torah works such as obeying the commandments of YHWH by keeping His 7th day Sabbath sacred, keeping away from forbidden foods, not to celebrate pagan days and to celebrate His appointed seven feasts annually. This is what demonstrates that we are not only rescued but walking in favour. At the same time to show love to our enemies in this case the radicals who aspire to kill us while many of these could potentially be given the gospel to be saved but who is going to take the message that is the question? Right now what I see is some ultra orthodox right wing Christians bashing them black and blue and others joining in to support each other. This will not work and will produce an explosive mixture.

A lot of peaceful Muslims struggle with the text of the Qur'an that advocates they should go to war with the infidels and people of the book but they also debate that those verses are only incumbent if we are in war with the West and not to be taken generally. However the extremist interpretation of the Qur'an is correct that those verses can be brought to force anytime and anywhere if the neighbouring people break the treaty with the Muslims then the Muslims can effectively go to war with them.

As I suggested earlier peaceful Muslims do not get as much headlines as do the radicals, I know a Muslim man in Israel who lives on the Mount of Olives, his name is Ibrahim and he is such a nice man including his family. All his life he has struggled for peace and not only him but his forefathers too. He has opened his home in Israel to the Yahudim, the Christians and the Muslims and anyone else who cares to go there even Buddhists, he does not care what religion they are from because to him they are all welcome to come and live there as part of humanity and I had the pleasure of staying with this great man in April 2007 and what a humble man he is. He was cooking for people and feeding them and so happy to do it too a real good hearted Muslim man. Truly I thought what an example of how we should all behave and there were groups of ten or twelve people always present in the house of all nationalities. There was not an ounce of hatred or racist attitude in this Muslim man. Racist people in Israel and in Christendom can learn from this man that their racism is not within what YHWH dictates to us in His LAW the Torah.

It is people like this who are demonstrating through their works that they want a peaceful world but the media does not take notice of such people. However Ibrahim is a gem and YHWH will not look the other way for such people and will increase Him and make a way of salvation for him as he humbly listens when you tell him things. He is not the only one there but there are others like him who are not well publicised.

You cannot blame the Muslims for trying. This news was released recently by a scholar in Pakistan, Saudi Arabia and even Al Azhar in Egypt then one wonders why are all Muslims painted as terrorists and women haters?

[15]First Published 2010-04-14

Highest Saudi religious body denounces terrorism

Council of Supreme Scholars declares any act of terrorism, including providing financial support to terrorists is crime.

RIYADH - Saudi Arabia's highest religious authority issued a fatwa (edict) denouncing all acts of terrorism and criminalising its financing, Asharq al-Awsat daily reported on Tuesday.

The Council of Supreme Scholars declared "any act of terrorism, including providing financial support to terrorists, a crime," regardless of where it takes place, the London-based newspaper said.

According to the fatwa, the financier of acts of terrorism will be considered a "partner" in the crime, the newspaper said.

The council did not specify a penalty to the act of financing terrorism, leaving that decision for the Islamic courts to determine, the newspaper said. The newspaper did not say if the council prescribed a penalty for carrying out acts of terrorism.

The council described terrorism as any act that involves "targeting of public resources," "hijacking planes" or "blowing up buildings."

With this edict, the conservative body denounces all attacks carried out by Al-Qaeda cells around the world, including some against targets in the Gulf kingdom.

Since a triple suicide bomb attack in May 2003, Saudi security forces have cracked down on supporters of Saudi-born Osama bin Laden's Al-Qaeda network.

In March, the Gulf state's authorities busted three Al-Qaeda cells totalling 113 militants who it said were planning attacks inside the kingdom.

Earlier in the same month, Saudi King Abdullah said his country is determined to halt extremism.

Muslim scholar condemns terrorism

---

[15] http://www.middle-east-online.com/english/?id=38417

Friday, 03.05.2010, 11:18pm
(BBC) — An influential Muslim scholar is to issue in London a global ruling against terrorism and suicide bombing.

Dr. Tahir ul-Qadri, from Pakistan, says his 600-page judgement, known as a fatwa, completely dismantles al-Qaeda's violent ideology.
The scholar describes al-Qaeda as an "old evil with a new name" which has not been sufficiently challenged.

The scholar's movement is growing in the UK and has attracted the interest of policymakers and security chiefs.

In his religious ruling, Dr Qadri says that Islam forbids the massacre of innocent citizens and suicide bombings.

Although many scholars have made similar rulings in the past, Dr. Qadri's followers argue that the massive document being launched in London goes much further.

They say it sets out point-by-point theological arguments against the rhetoric used by al-Qaeda inspired recruiters.

The fatwa also challenges the religious motivations of would-be suicide bombers who are inspired by promises of an afterlife.

The populist scholar developed his document last year as a response to the increase in bombings across Pakistan by militants.

The basic text has been extended to 600 pages to cover global issues, in an attempt to get its theological arguments taken up by Muslims in Western nations. It will be promoted in the UK by Dr. Qadri's organization, Minhaj ul-Quran International.

Shahid Mursaleen, spokesman for Minhaj-ul-Quran in the UK, said the fatwa was hard-hitting.

"This fatwa injects doubt into the minds of potential suicide bombers," he said.

"Extremist groups based in Britain recruit the youth by brainwashing them that they will 'with certainty' are rewarded in the next life.

The document is not the first to condemn terrorism and suicide bombing to be launched in the UK.

This is good in so far as it shows that at least some Islamic scholars are beginning to see that there is a problem and it needs to be addressed. I do not think that this will go very far in combating the problem because the text is left loose. This means that unless they deal directly with the violent verses of the Qur'an and show how they cannot be construed to be for present or future violence or Jihad against non-Muslims the reformation of Islam will likely be unsuccessful. In order to make this successful they have to reinterpret the verses and teach the large body of clerics the same however to be honest this cannot be done since we cannot reinterpret to suit a modernist culture. However what could happen is a certain practice could be banned for a time such as Jihad with wording such as unless your country or family are in direct danger Jihad is forbidden but the Islamic ummah (community) does not work this way but sees oppression in any country against Muslims as a pretext to start Jihad and oppression can be interpreted in a number of ways.

This is why the radicals right now get all the attention because they see that the west is at war with Islam and causing oppression to Muslims therefore it is incumbent on them to fight back. They also feel that the West is only in particular Muslims lands because the Muslims have oil and resources there is truth to this to some extent. Many critics in the Western countries have claimed this to be true also. Now the Muslims feel that America is bullying Iran to give up nuclear weapons while it allows Israel to keep anonymity about nuclear weapons. This is seen by Muslims as a hypocritical policy. That allows Israel free reign with no questions and no sanctions and Iran to be intimidated with sanctions.

According to John Perkins an economic hit man in the past who was covertly working with a private consulting firm this is what he had to say confirming what Muslims believe.

> [16]Confessions of an Economic Hit Man is a book written by John Perkins and published in 2004. It provides Perkins' account of his career with consulting firm Chas. T. Main in Boston. Before employment with the firm, he interviewed for a job with the National Security Agency (NSA). Perkins claims that this interview effectively constituted an independent screening which led to his subsequent hiring by Einar Greve, a member of the firm (and alleged NSA liaison) to become a self-described "economic hit man". The book was

---

16 http://en.wikipedia.org/wiki/Confessions_of_an_Economic_Hit_Man

allegedly referred to in an audio tape released by Osama Bin Laden in September 2009. [1]

"Covertly recruited by the United States National Security Agency and on the payroll of an international consulting firm, he travelled the world—to Indonesia, Panama, Ecuador, Colombia, Saudi Arabia, Iran and other strategically important countries...Perkins reveals the hidden mechanics of imperial control behind some of the most dramatic events in recent history, such as the fall of the Shah of Iran, the death of Panamanian president Omar Torrijos, and the U.S. invasions of Panama and Iraq."[2]

Economic hit men (EHMs) are highly-paid professionals who cheat countries around the globe out of trillions of dollars. They funnel money from the World Bank, the U.S. Agency for International Development (USAID), and other foreign "aid" organizations into the coffers of huge corporations and the pockets of a few wealthy families who control the planet's natural resources. Their tools included fraudulent financial reports, rigged elections, payoffs, extortion, sex, and murder. They play a game as old as empire, but one that has taken on new and terrifying dimensions during this time of globalization.

"I was initially recruited while I was in business school back in the late sixties by the National Security Agency, the nation's largest and least understood spy organization; but ultimately I worked for private corporations. The first real economic hit man was back in the early 1950s, Kermit Roosevelt, Jr., the grandson of Teddy, who overthrew the government of Iran, a democratically elected government, Mossadegh's government who was Time's magazine person of the year; and he was so successful at doing this without any bloodshed—well, there was a little bloodshed, but no military intervention, just spending millions of dollars and replaced Mossadegh with the Shah of Iran.

At that point, we understood that this idea of economic hit man was an extremely good one. We didn't have to worry about the threat of war with Russia when we did it this way. The problem with that was that Roosevelt was a C.I.A. agent. He was a government employee. Had he been caught, we would have been in a lot of trouble. It would have been very embarrassing. So, at that point, the decision was made to use organizations like the C.I.A. and the N.S.A. to recruit potential economic hit men like me and then send us to work for private consulting companies, engineering firms, construction companies, so that if we were caught, there would be no connection with the government.[3] - Nov 4 '04 interview

[1] http://thelede.blogs.nytimes.com/2009/09/14/bin-ladens-reading-list-for-americans/
[2] John Perkins, author, Confessions of an Economic Hit Man
[3] Confessions of an Economic Hit Man: How the U.S. Uses Globalization to Cheat Poor Countries Out of Trillions". Democracy Now: The war and peace report. 9 Nov 04 http://www.democracynow.org/2004/11/9/confessions_of_an_economic_hit_man. Retrieved 2009-01-09

John admitted that the American government has in the last thirty-four years sent out Economic hit men to convince various nations to borrow loans to do construction projects such as building water dams, electric power plants and parks and other projects. The loans were bloated because the forecasts for electric and water were deliberately wrong, the project feasibility study were not accurately done and the men were told to draft the project report with increasing capacities of growth which was not true which would allow the IMF and World Bank to pile up a large loan on the borrowing nation and make it deliberately default the loan under heavy interest payments after which the American government would take over their resources allowing a plan of payment that suits the American government. If some leaders did not agree to this type of American imperialism they would be removed and replaced who are democratically elected leaders through assassinations. This has happened to Latin American nations and Indonesia amongst other nations where certain non cooperating leaders have been assassinated.

If you want to see evidence for this type of imperialism then go to YouTube and type economic hit man and you can see countless videos of self confessing hit man like John Perkins who confess to what they did for the US policymakers. This then allows us to see in our assessment why the Muslim nations are behaving the way they are because they are afraid of being put under the yoke but it seems the American government officials are weak on Wednesday bible readings in which YHWH himself said Ishmael shall not be subjugated and put under the yoke and will fight back with everyone. Perhaps this means that President Obama needs to do a bit more homework to bring peace between the two conflicting worlds.

> **Genesis 16:12** He shall be a wild man; his hand shall be against every man, and every man's hand against him; and he shall dwell in the presence of all his brethren.

This prophecy thanks to the West and its attitude to the poorer nations has now come to pass and we see fighting and war everywhere. So why blame the Muslims for all the troubles? This is the picture of the bigger End-Time battles yet to come. Someone needs to be the catalyst and the US has done that bit nicely!

The US policy makers have been playing a very dangerous game in the East as far as Afghanistan is concerned and using it to further their own personal goals but deceiving its own people by telling them it's a war of terror while protecting the terrorists from Saudi Arabia which should have been the first to be eliminated. The US policymakers aim was to control Afghanistan, have a good footing in Iraq this way they cover both the East side of Iran and the West side of Iran for a future attack on Iran which will allow them to take over the oil fields in these nations. The little unrest in Georgia in 2009 with Russia was also created by the American policymakers in Washington and we can rest assured that Russia will strike back by helping the Islamic terrorists covertly. The American policy makers are afraid of the rising power of Russia, China and India in the East which will give them global prominence in trade and sideline the US so in order to keep a deep footing in the East they went to war in Afghanistan to protect their interest and this is the reason why the UK was with them also for self interest and to take a slice of the pie as old colonial partners. Any honest politician will tell you that because of the unrest in Afghanistan foreign interests must be protected in other words little does anyone care about how many Afghans are killed but personal greed of nations is at work.

The American war on terror has already cost three trillion dollars with its personal debt now at sixteen trillion dollars and these are not small figures so when the bubble busts the US will come collapsing down taking many other countries with it. The American public will be funding this debt for decades. America is fast heading towards an economical meltdown if not careful about its foreign wars and spending policies and could cause it and many other nations to default on their debt which would force the poorer nations to be dependent on exporting their goods to survive while the US tries to collect payment on international debt for self survival, we are seeing some bleak times ahead. Our true Hebrew people need to get out of the US and go to another nation where their dollars will go much further to invest in local businesses would fare much better than in the US since when the economy melts and jobs are non existent, welfare programs at an all time high the people won't get very far with their welfare checks.

While if you are in a safe nation elsewhere the pinch you feel with a business is a walk in the park and you smile all the way to the bank. Think wisely how to protect your family for the coming tough times. Some safe nations are Ghana, Liberia, Gambia, Senegal, Togo, Southern Ethiopia, China, especially Northern and Western China. If you like to live amongst the Muslims and reach them then the Xinjiang province is one to look for where you can practice your faith and your lifestyle.

The US policymakers have tried to pressure China into accepting US foreign policies, China holds a lot of American debt but so far American policy has failed to succeed and will not succeed with China. If the US administration was successful then it would mean it would control Iraq, Iran, Afghanistan, Saudi Arabia and by extension it could rule the world by proxy but these ambitions of the US elitist/illuminati hierarchy are not going to succeed according to scripture and since Afghanistan turned out to be more hostile than predicted by the US policymakers, which has in the end caused more problems and less resolutions. This would result in weakening of the American government and hegemony and in turn it would mean other nations will rise up and take charge dealing with Eastern poorer states such as Russia trying to gain control over the East, which is also building its arsenal to regain power.

Everyday we hear of airstrikes in which Afghan civilians are being killed while a few radicals die but the number of civilians dying is much greater. In Feb 2, 1 2009 an air strike in an area controlled by the Dutch called Marjah was struck that killed 27 civilians and this has continued to this day in 2012. America will come out of Afghanistan pretty humiliated.

> Updated 7:27 p.m. ET Feb. 22, 2010 Associated Press
>
> KABUL, Afghanistan - A NATO airstrike killed at least 27 civilians in central Afghanistan, the third time a mistaken coalition strike has killed non-combatants since the start of a major offensive aimed at winning over the population.
>
> The top NATO commander, U.S. Gen. Stanley McChrystal, apologized to the Afghan president, NATO said.
>
> The Afghanistan Council of Ministers strongly condemned the airstrike in Uruzgan province, calling it "unjustifiable." An earlier statement issued Monday put the death toll at 33. It was not immediately clear why the figure had been revised.

Another case recently surfaced where children were killed in error reported by Media Lens.

NATO'S FIRE SALE - ONE DEAD AFGHAN CHILD, $2,000

[17]On January 11, 2010, we sent out a media alert titled, 'Were Afghan children executed by US-led forces? And why aren't the media interested?'

The alert concerned credible reports that American-led troops had dragged Afghan children from their beds and shot them during a night raid in Kunar province in eastern Afghanistan on December 27 last year. Ten people were killed, including eight schoolboys from one family. We noted that the alleged atrocity had been almost wholly ignored by the corporate media, including the BBC.

Two months after these disturbing allegations surfaced, The Times correspondent Jerome Starkey sought out two local men whose children and other relatives had been killed. ('Nato admits that deaths of 8 boys were a mistake', The Times, February 25, 2010; http://www.timesonline.co.uk/tol/news/world/afghanistan/article7040166.ece). Starkey invited the men to Kabul where:

"They provided pictures of their dead sons, a sketched map of the compound and copies of the compensation claim forms signed by local officials detailing their sons' names, relatives and positions at school. Their story was supported by Western military sources."

After its initial shameful attempts to deny culpability, NATO now asserts that the raid had been carried out on the basis of faulty intelligence and should never have been authorised:

"Knowing what we know now, it would probably not have been a justifiable attack. We don't now believe that we busted a major ring."

The Times correspondent reported the testimony of Mohammed Taleb Abdul Ajan, father of three of the boys who were killed:

---

17 http://www.medialens.org/alerts/

"'When I entered their room I saw four people lying in a heap,' said Taleb.'I shook them and shouted their names but they didn't respond. Some of them were shot in the head. Some of them were shot in the chest.

"'I was praying that in the next room maybe they were still alive but when I went in I saw everyone was dead. I saw blood on their necks. I became crazy. I don't remember what I felt.'" ('Assault force killed family by mistake in raid, claims Afghan father', The Times, February 25, 2010; http://www.timesonline.co.uk/tol/news/world/afghanistan/article7040216.ece)

However, a Times editorial on the same day managed to portray the atrocity in the required context of a "just war":

"The legitimacy of the cause in Afghanistan is called into question by civilian deaths. The conflict needs to be conducted with regard for the native population." (Editorial, 'Just War', The Times, February 25, 2010; http://www.timesonline.co.uk/tol/comment/leading_article/article7040089.ece)

The stated benign aims of Western governments have to be taken on trust; just as the Soviet government portrayed +its+ invasion of Afghanistan in 1979 as an act of humanitarian intervention initiated at the "request of the [Afghan] government". The aim of that earlier occupation, the Soviet people were reassured, was "to prevent the establishment of... a terrorist regime and to protect the Afghan people from genocide", and also to provide "aid in stabilising the situation and the repulsion of possible external aggression". (Nikolai Lanine and Media Lens, 'Invasion: A Comparison of Soviet and Western Media Performance', November 20, 2007)

The final payoff line from The Times leader could have come from a Pravda editorial of thirty years ago:

"In order to defeat our enemies we must be seen to be better than them."

Meanwhile, the rest of the corporate media averted its gaze from the bloodied remains of dead Afghan schoolchildren.

The Malodorous Myth of BBC Balance

In December, BBC news online had posted these two brief 'balanced' reports of the US-led killing of the Afghan schoolchildren:

'Afghanistan children killed "during Western operation" ', December 28, 2009; http://news.bbc.co.uk/1/hi/world/south_asia/8432653.stm

And:

'Afghan MP accuses US troops of killing schoolchildren', December 30, 2009; http://news.bbc.co.uk/1/hi/world/south_asia/8434800.stm

In the first of these reports, the BBC observed:

"NATO said it had no record of operations or deaths in the area." and

"The BBC's Peter Greste in Kabul says Kunar province is remote, snowbound and dominated by the Taliban, so the investigation into Saturday's alleged incident will be difficult."

The second report commented:

"The BBC's Peter Greste in Kabul says it is impossible to verify either account. He says it is possible that both are broadly correct - and that the victims might well have been school students, but that they helped the insurgency."

When Media Lens readers challenged the BBC's failure to report the allegations fully and responsibly, the response from the corporation was galling:

"It's worth noting that the circumstances of the incident are disputed, unlike some previous examples of civilians killed by coalition forces. The Afghan government and the UN believe that civilians were killed as the result of the US operation in Kunar. NATO still does not accept this and strongly argues that US forces killed insurgents." (Email from BBC complaints to Media Lens reader, February 19, 2010)

Evidence of a massacre is even stronger now than it was then, less than a month ago. And yet we are not aware of any subsequent BBC news reports, or any corrections or apologies.

On February 27, we contacted two senior BBC editors: Helen Boaden, director of BBC news, and Steve Herrmann, who is responsible for BBC news online. We pointed out that Jerome Starkey of The Times had now been able to verify the reports that Afghan schoolchildren had been shot dead in the December raid involving US forces. We asked the BBC editors, in light of the latest Times reporting:

"What will you and your colleagues be doing to follow up your previous reports?

"With the resources that the BBC has available, why were you apparently unable to do what Mr Starkey has done and investigate - and now indeed verify - the initial disturbing allegations of Afghan schoolchildren being shot?

"How will these latest revelations affect how you deal with NATO statements in future?" We have yet to receive any response from Helen Boaden or Steve Herrmann.

We emailed the same questions to BBC reporter Peter Greste. In an email dated March 2, he told us that he is normally based in Kenya - he had been covering Afghanistan for the Christmas and New Year period, and had left Kabul early in January. He passed on our inquiry to the BBC's Kabul bureau editor "who will get back to you in due course." Instead, a response was then sent to us by Sean Moss, a "divisional advisor" at BBC complaints, who wrote blandly:

"As I'm sure you will appreciate, it is not feasible for the Kabul bureau to enter into a dialogue with individuals. If you would like to make a complaint, you need to do so through the webform at www.bbc.co.uk/complaints." (Email, March 15, 2010)

As many of our readers will be all too aware, the BBC "complaints" procedure is a standard corporate tool for deflecting public challenges, ensuring that little of substance actually changes.

Concluding Remarks

> Meanwhile, the killing and the propaganda campaign, continue. Last week, Starkey reported that another night raid carried out by US and Afghan gunmen this month led to the deaths of two pregnant women, a teenage girl and two local officials - an atrocity which NATO then tried to cover up. ('NATO "covered up" botched night raid in Afghanistan that killed five', The Times, March 13, 2010; http://www.timesonline.co.uk/tol/news/world/afghanistan/article7060395.ece)
>
> The family were offered "American compensation" - $2,000 for each of the victims. "There's no value on human life," said Bibi Sabsparie, mother of two of the dead. "They killed our family, then they came and brought us money. Money won't bring our family back."
>
> This latest horror has again been buried by the UK media, along with its victims.
>
> BBC staff employed to manage complaints from the public are adept at robotically indicating where the latest Western crime has been 'impartially' reported - BBC radio bulletins, a paragraph or short online report, or perhaps a snippet on the BBC News Channel or the World Service. But the glaring omission is of any in-depth, headline coverage on the main BBC television news watched by millions. Nothing must question the state ideology that, while "mistakes" might happen, the aims of the government are benevolent.

This war really needs to be thought through since many civilians are needlessly dying and we cannot continue to make mistakes where our own people are needlessly dying alongside civilians in the name of corporatocracy. How many widows need be created both in the UK and the US by this war and other civilians killed in Afghanistan before it's realised the futility of war. Is it justifiable to kill civilians including innocent children like this when we know life is precious and can we just write this off as collateral damage? When one person is to be executed in the US on death row such a case can go on for years but what about these civilians in Afghanistan and Iraq who can just be shot down with a missile through a drone strike through extra judicial killings? Where is the moral fibre of leaders? This shows gentiles behave as gentiles that is why the Hebrews everywhere need to think who to align with, turn back to the Torah and do not enter into wars, if you are in military then delist and find a civilian job. We are forbidden from wars so black Hebrews take note.

The reality is that no Afghan has set foot on either European or American soil to conduct any kind of terrorist attacks therefore one cannot blame them for defending their land from foreign forces. The present way of dealing with the terrorist groups in Afghanistan has proved to be an abject failure and this needs to be reanalyzed in light of current affairs of a better way to deal with this threat. This will only cause further division in America and hatred in Afghanistan for the US and other allied forces. The end result will be that the Western nations will lose all credibility so they need to fight a constructive war and not a destructive one. Of course Muslim women's rights are very important in Afghanistan as much as they are in the UK for British women and so a method needs to be found where the radical teachings of the Qur'an could be removed from the curriculum and for people to allow for more freedom to the lower classes.

In all honesty the Judeo/Christian way of life will open up room for their freedom but in order to push for this an honest debate must be conducted on TV and radio channels to show that the present course of the radicals is doomed to eternal destruction. While peace and justice can only come when we accept the God of Israel and His laws which the Christians have yet to demonstrate since many are lawless with their so called New Testament. Israel would have to play a big part in this equation however this mission is fraught with difficulty but not impossible but present Israel is not even biological so we see the present course to destruction is what will bring construction for true biological Israel. Right now Israel cannot even be counted as a partner as the policy makers and the leading players in Israel are just serving self serving agendas and pushing for war with Iran. They are equally war mongering and in time YHWH will remove all these war mongers and liars from our given land to the true Hebrews.

We find the same issues surrounding Israel in dealing with Palestinian Muslims when certain IDF soldiers shoot up in houses they go to search, shooting through solar heater water tanks, ripping through draws, trashing Palestinian homes suspected of being radicals though it may not be the case. Deliberately making it hard for Palestinians to cross check points between Gaza and Israel so that the Palestinians know they are being harassed or put down to know who is ruling them. When twenty years old IDF kids calling themselves soldiers look into the eyes of forty year old Arab men with a scathing look one can understand why the forty year old Arab feels he is being shamefully degraded and looked down upon by a soldier holding a gun who is half his age and the Arab feels humiliated by a younger kid barely his sons age. What about the shooting of the Palestinian children one such case of the 13-year-old Udai Tantawi, during a routine operation in the Askar refugee camp when an officer got suspended. Is this the value we have placed on innocent children that they can be shot at as routine if they throw stones at soldiers? This excessive force is going to show how destructive the policies of the corrupt Israeli government and the racists' within the IDF ranks. It is clear that the IDF do not have an easy job but often times some abuse their power.

There are certain soldiers in the IDF who have abused civilians, and taken bribes at checkpoints, who deliberately fire on solar water heaters to damage them for fun, fired at street lights in PA areas. Drivers of armoured vehicles who have routinely run over Palestinian cars parked on the streets such as a tank crushing a civilian car when there is space on the road to drive the tank. Some soldiers have known to abuse corpses, and even taken photographs with them as souvenirs. The list is unfortunately very unsavoury for IDF soldiers who abuse their authority and power. I know this is not routine for all as many IDF soldiers try not to do the unsavoury things but many others do and are supported by their commanders whereby the Palestinians are seen as maggots and not human beings. It's also obvious that the IDF is at constant war with the radical elements of Islam and unless some kind of disengagement can be reached the situation will only get worse. It is highly likely that Israel's present course of actions of covert terrorism in the nations of the world where the Mossad is involved such as Iran and even Pakistan they will lead the world to a huge war which is prophesied in the bible and they will bring a cataclysmic destruction to themselves and cleansing of the land of Israel which will allow the real Israelites to return. The prophecy of Zechariah 13:8 is our evidence for this.

> **Zechar'yah 13:8-9** And it shall come to pass, that in all the land, says YHWH, two parts therein shall be cut off and die; but the third shall be left therein. **9** And I will bring the third part through the fire, and will refine them as silver is refined, and will try them as gold is tried: they shall call on my name, and I will hear them: I will say, It is my people: and they shall say, YHWH is my Elohim.

Anyone can calculate that this means two thirds of the 7.7 million people in Israel today which would have increased to whatever level will be wiped or killed. This can only happen in a huge war with bio or nuclear weapons. It can also happen through large earthquakes. The other one third people left will also be cleansed and I doubt many will come through. Clearly what YHWH is going to do is remove the so called converted Jews who are Torahless and he will only allow those to stay who are faithful to Torah and his laws. This will also create room for YHWH to bring in the real progenitor of the Jews the Black Africans and those Jews stuck in Yemen or other nations.

This should bring this prophecy to our remembrance

The last Khazari Stand

> **Leviticus 18:26-28** You shall therefore keep my statutes and my judgments, and shall not commit any of these abominations; neither any of your own nation, nor any foreigner that lives among you: **27** For all these abominations have the men of the land done, which were before you, and the land is defiled; **28** Do not make the land vomit you out also, when you defile it, as it did the nations that were before you.

Israel has used many excuses to bomb and pulverize the Palestinian areas because Udai Tantawi is not the only example of an innocent shooting. What about the shooting of Iman El-Hamas the 13 year old girl going to school who will never finish school to go to University? She was a beautiful girl who would have gone on to marry and have a family. Was it wrong for her to do this or her rights suddenly no longer relevant because she was a Palestinian Muslim? European Israel just as you have done to others and violated Torah YHWH will do to you.

The story is here:

> Chris Mcgreal / The Guardian (UK) 24 Nov 04
>
> [18]Jerusalem — An Israeli army officer who repeatedly shot a 13-year-old Palestinian girl in Gaza dismissed a warning from another soldier that she was a child by saying he would have killed her even if she was three years old. The officer, identified by the army only as Captain R, was charged this week with illegal use of his weapon, conduct unbecoming an officer and other relatively minor infractions after emptying all 10 bullets from his gun's magazine into **Imam al-Hamas** when she walked into a "security area" on the edge of Rafah refugee camp last month.

---

18 http://www.mindfully.org/Reform/2004/Imam-al-Hamas24nov04.htm

A tape recording of radio exchanges between soldiers involved in the incident, played on Israeli television, contradicts the army's account of the events and appears to show that the captain shot the girl in cold blood.

The official account claimed that Iman was shot as she walked towards an army post with her schoolbag because soldiers feared she was carrying a bomb.

But the tape recording of the radio conversation between soldiers at the scene reveals that, from the beginning, she was identified as a child and at no point was a bomb spoken about nor was she described as a threat. Iman was also at least 100 yards from any soldier.

Instead, the tape shows that the soldiers swiftly identified her as a "girl of about 10" who was "scared to death".

The tape also reveals that the soldiers said Iman was headed eastwards, away from the army post and back into the refugee camp, when she was shot.

At that point, Captain R took the unusual decision to leave the post in pursuit of the girl. He shot her dead and then "confirmed the kill" by emptying his magazine into her body.

The tape recording is of a three-way conversation between the army watchtower, the army post's operations room and the captain, who was a company commander.

The soldier in the watchtower radioed his colleagues after he saw Iman: "It's a little girl. She's running defensively eastward."

Operations room: "Are we talking about a girl under the age of 10?"

Watchtower: "A girl of about 10, she's behind the embankment, scared to death."

A few minutes later, Iman is shot in the leg from one of the army posts.

The watchtower: "I think that one of the positions took her out."

The company commander then moves in as Iman lies wounded and helpless.

Captain R: "I and another soldier ... are going in a little nearer, forward, to confirm the kill ... Receive a situation report. We fired and killed her ... I also confirmed the kill. Over."

Witnesses described how the captain shot Iman twice in the head, walked away, turned back and fired a stream of bullets into her body. Doctors at Rafah's hospital said she had been shot at least 17 times.

On the tape, the company commander then "clarifies" why he killed Iman: "This is commander. Anything that's mobile, that moves in the zone, even if it's a three-year-old, needs to be killed. Over."

The army's original account of the killing said that the soldiers only identified Iman as a child after she was first shot. But the tape shows that they were aware just how young the small, slight girl was before any shots were fired.

The case came to light after soldiers under the command of Captain R went to an Israeli newspaper to accuse the army of covering up the circumstances of the killing.

A subsequent investigation by the officer responsible for the Gaza strip, Major General Dan Harel, concluded that the captain had "not acted unethically".

However, the military police launched an investigation, which resulted in charges against the unit commander.

> Iman's parents have accused the army of whitewashing the affair by filing minor charges against Captain R. They want him prosecuted for murder.

This girl was walking towards a guard tower and was then later shot. I want to ask if this situation is different from when Hitler's Nazis shot the Jews going about their daily routine and also shooting them one by one in concentration camps. Israel really needs to behave differently with Gaza because Gaza is not a concentration camp and should not be made into one massive prison camp.

This officer who shot the girl was charged with misconduct but later acquitted. Israel's justice is not according to how YHWH would have it and this will remain a black marker on the IDF soldiers because they were guilty in this situation of cover up and of improper moral behaviour even if they give it a military slant it makes little difference.

One can see this is really uncalled for callous cruel behaviour.

These kinds of incidents only generate more hatred and bloodshed spills over in the streets of Israel by the Muslims who want to take revenge.

In the past when the IDF was accused of shooting innocent civilians such as Mohammed Al Durra at least the army went to great lengths to prove that they were innocent of that particular shooting and that boy was shot by Palestinian bullets being fired at the IDF.

I know the situation is far from perfect and sadly Muslims are being treated as less than human as other people. Sure the Israeli Defence Forces has a hard job to do but more compassion needs to be shown to non-combatants which many of these so called elites have not shown at all. When I was visiting Israel in 2007 and stopped to take some pictures near a Jewish kibbutz (settlement) a white Khazari Jewish man came out and told me to get off the land and that he would shoot me otherwise. His tone and his demeanour were totally wrong and this shows we are dealing with callous Europeans and not the chosen people of God. I have Kohenim Lewim forefathers but just because I was born in Pakistan and look Muslim is no reason to hate me for it and that is what this particular Khazari convert pretending to be my ancestor was demonstrating his hatred by his actions, arrogance and pride will bring these people down. That was completely uncalled for and unprovoked while I was not even on his area of the land because I was outside the gate on the taxpayer's road.

This type of unnecessary hatred for anyone who appears to be Muslim even though I am not reveals someone's evil heart which many of these people have hence why we cannot see peace between them and Palestinians. If the Zionist Christians want to licks Zionist boots you go ahead but both of you will be subservient to us one day the real Israelites when you realise your ills and that the kingdom gates are shut in your faces then no white Jesus or white Moses going to help you as one does not exist. Both the real Yahushua and real Musa were black and the Messiah Yahushua who is alive is returning in black colour and ethnicity and no he does not cover his face in shoe polish as we would have to do to Charleston Heston in The Ten Commandments to give him the right colour.

How do you think an Arab will feel if he is treated in such a way? Should the Arabs tolerate such behaviour if it regularly occurs in Israel against Arabs? We need to consider that not all Arabs are even Muslim. If you are to examine these causes then one can begin to understand why many Palestinian Christians began to take the side of Muslims because they are also looked down upon by the Khazari European convert pretenders. Even if I was a complete foreigner the Torah commands to treat foreigners with full dignity and respect using the same laws they would apply to the Israelites (Num 15:15).

> **Numbers 15:15** One ordinance shall be both for you of the congregation, and also for the foreigner that dwells with you, an ordinance forever in your generations: as you are, so shall the foreigner be before YHWH.

I was shocked at this east European man's behaviour and this made me realise why the Palestinians have a lot of hatred in their hearts towards the present land occupiers. In another incident three years earlier to a visit in the land I was with a Palestinian Muslim friend who was kindly taking me to show me Bethlehem from Jerusalem. We were stopped on the checkpoint and the young IDF soldier would not let him pass and said I could go but he couldn't but the stupidity of the situation was that I could not go without him since he was my driver.

My Palestinian friend Suleiman was very angry at how the young soldier was treating him because Suleiman was older in age. I calmed him down and told him to let's go back or try another checkpoint. I told him the IDF soldier had no reason to stop him but is only doing so because of some of the past actions of the suicide bombers because he was being given the treatment of a candidate of terror while I told him that you and the real Yahudim are half brothers so let it go and do not fret. The problem is that incidents like this happen in Israel daily and my friend was not a terrorist nor a suspect but a respectable businessman but was still not allowed to cross the checkpoint. Israel cannot behave this way with all the Palestinians because it is plain and simply unjust and wrong and no amount of rightwing theology can make this behaviour just. I believe only Yahushua will bring cleansing into Israel and without this cleansing we will not find a solution since America has been more than dishonest along with the European nations in not finding a peaceful solution because they are not interested.

What about when the Arabs do the same in return? Can one see why the Israelis cannot expect sympathy in return from the Muslims because unfortunately the side who thinks they have guns, bombs and tanks (Israel) then using the pages of the Qur'an against what the Muslims see as an aggressive enemy forced many Muslims to become suicide bombers with a vengeance to kill and to get even? True Israel certainly has an eternal destiny but not counterfeit Israel and right now we have the counterfeit in place. YHWH will judge all the injustices on both sides. One also needs to look which Israel has an eternal destiny. That is us we who are in the nations and those who are in minority in the land trying to keep Torah but the fake European Jewry has no eternal destiny but will one day face destruction for their evil actions.

We therefore see the politics in Israel that shape the people roundabout it and how the Islamic religion is then able to answer back with Jihad and violence. This is why we find suicide bombers amongst the rich Muslims and it's not a phenomenon for poor Muslim people. What is not understood by many is that enmity in the Islamic culture runs into generations and until blood is drawn the radical Muslim people do not feel satisfied. I mean it could be as simple as something like a checkpoint violation where an Israeli soldier spoke to an Arab man rudely and that Arab guy then takes this as an offence against himself and wants to get even.

Coming back to Afghanistan one should ask are the people of Afghanistan valued less than those on death row in America because they are Muslim? I hope not. We did see this kind of bad behaviour by the US soldiers on wikileaks.org where Iraqi journalists carrying Camera's were fired upon and indiscriminately killed at least a dozen of them and two of them were working for Reuters. They had no guns in their hands and were not firing at the US Apache gun-ships but the Pilot's in the gun-ships not only shot down the twelve innocent journalists but were heard making some unseemly remarks such as “Oh yeah, look at those dead bastards."

The pilots confused one of the journalist’s cameras for an RPG that is at least what seemed to be from the video I saw but this still seems nothing short of murder. They also deliberately targeted a man in a van that was trying to pickup the wounded men, the van also had small children inside. This is clear violation of the moral law codes that we live by and even international law may have been violated at these shootings because there were children in the van that was shot at wounding the Muslim children and killing their father who tried to help the wounded journalists. I certainly cannot condone such behaviour and simply call it justified action and brush it under the carpet in the pretext of war as collateral damage. This incident happened in 2007 in Baghdad, all the US personnel involved in this incident were cleared!!! I hope this now shows us why many Muslims are calling Israel and the US great Satan and little Satan because such injustices only help to compound the existing problem and not resolve past hatred.

The collateral murder video can be seen here on www.youtube.com released by http://www.wikileaks.org/ at the link below if it is still available.

http://www.youtube.com/watch?v=Zok8yMxXEwk&feature=fvst

Questions were raised that the journalists were amongst the terrorists and may have been a threat but this is nothing new. Journalists have in the past stood amongst fighting forces and been taking war pictures and this would not make them a threat.

In another story the following was released:

> [19]Just this morning, the *New York Times* confirmed a gruesome cover-up by U.S. forces in Afghanistan. Officials who had repeatedly denied reports by Jerome Starkey in the *Times of London* have now confirmed that American Special Operations soldiers slaughtered three women in a nighttime raid in February -- and actually dug bullets out of the bodies of the women as part of a cover-up. Starkey says U.S. and NATO forces are rarely held to account for the atrocities they commit.

By the Times newspaper of London:

---

19 http://www.huffingtonpost.com/2010/04/05/wikileaks-exposes-video-o_n_525569.html

> [20]A night raid carried out by US and Afghan gunmen led to the deaths of two pregnant women, a teenage girl and two local officials in an atrocity which NATO then tried to cover up, survivors have told The Times. The operation on Friday, February 12, was a botched pre-dawn assault on a policeman's home a few miles outside Gardez, the capital of Paktia province, eastern Afghanistan. In a statement after the raid titled "Joint force operating in Gardez makes gruesome discovery", NATO claimed that the force had found the women's bodies "tied up, gagged and killed" in a room.

Now please ask yourself the question what if the brothers and sisters of these families go after the US civilians as suicide bombers who are you going to blame? You can be certain that Muslims will go out to take revenge and this is nothing out of the ordinary as this happens in Islamic culture all the time.

YHWH tells us that innocent blood cries out from the ground and that innocent blood demands justice and if no one hears the cry of the poor than YHWH will hear them and YHWH's justice will be hard for the inhabitants of the US. The badly implemented past policies of the US did not succeed in the third world and it may leave the US with a financial debt crisis that will sadly affect millions of innocent Americans. Afghanistan and Iran are the lynchpin that are so far avoiding this scenario and even if Iran goes down Islam will not and it will fuel the insurgency even further meaning it will provoke many home grown terrorists both in the US and Europe causing a very rough response from the radical Muslims and as a result even the moderate Muslims who live abroad will then be forced to side with the radical Muslims and one can understand why this can provoke a civil war in our societies. The governments need to consider the long term impact and goals of their foreign policies. Do we want to lose the support of moderate Muslims who do not espouse terrorism?

This also shows us causes for why Muslims increasingly want to live in isolation in ghettos in western lands and create no go areas for sure where non Muslims will not be welcome. Some such areas already exist in Europe where police and others are afraid to go in such as in Sweden.

Presently because of some bad western policies what has been done is to stir the hornet's nest and now we see the consequences of that all over the world. We cannot then simply stand back and blame the Muslims,

---

20 http://www.timesonline.co.uk/tol/news/world/afghanistan/article7060395.ece

the Qur'an and do not take responsibility for our own actions when the West could do much more good and use its powers more responsibly. Perhaps this will happen in the future with good leaders in the West but right now the evil that is committed in the name of Corporatocracy is there for all to see. I see many rightwing people blaming Muslims alone but there are two sides to the conflict and both must be taken into account.

The spiritual dimension suggests this was indeed going to happen and the God of Israel has already declared this knowing the actions of men.

Such cases in which the US has helped engineer the demise of democratically elected Haitian president and other national presidents. One such case was in 2000 when Aristide became president who wanted to help his people to bring them out of poverty but this irked the White House and the then president Mr Bush then used the CIA to oust the democratically elected president with the help of Canada and France. Aristide then had to run for his life into the Central African Republic and then later to South Africa. Also many suggest the same has happened in Africa that has been raped and pillaged by the US and Western governments through setting up dictatorships which cannot be denied. They pledge to give with one hand for the country and take with the other hand and as many critics suggest the West wants to remain the slave masters that they were in the past. Now cheap slave labour has been created in the US prisons where many of our black Hebrew people have been imprisoned to use them for cheap slave labour. They get long custodial sentences for petty things. This the so called African American needs to know are the curses that are still upon them and no, no Caucasian false Jesus is going to take them away. You must turn back to the true Messiah Yahushua and renounce your worldly ways and repent for both your sins and your forefather's sins that you may be restored the Master Yahushua.

The most degrading thing that was done to the African nations by the Arabs in the old days was to make them slaves and then ship them to America and Europe in which these black Hebrew people were then treated worse than animals and no human dignity was afforded to them until good Christian men rose up to emancipate them not forgetting the whole black slave trade, the markets the ships the money came from wealthy Jews who were the finger behind the slave trade. Christians were their front men.

Today the government of Saudi Arabia funds the American national debt, prophecy makes it clear that when Saudi Arabia blows up with its oil fields in smoke as per Revelation 17/18 then the US will suffer heavy losses with many other nations going bankrupt and unfortunately this will cause much suffering for the many decent people in the US and the rest of the world who have no part in these schemes and games that are being played by some Western governments and the Zionists illuminaties' around the world who control much wealth in banks.

> **Isaiah 34:8-9** For it is the day of YHWH's vengeance, and the year of recompenses for the controversy towards Tsiyon. **9** And the streams there shall be turned into pitch, and the dust there into brimstone, and the land there shall become burning pitch.

What is the controversy of Zion?

What is the controversy about? Whose land is it? Islamists or the Khazari Jews, this matter will be settled here once and for all times before genetic Y'sra'el is brought back from exile.

This is where the Islamic nations want to split Israel to take away the land that rightly belongs to the real genetic black children of Israel and has been for the three millennium of recorded history and in turn some bad American foreign policy has only helped to further divide people and cause confusion for Israel and heartache for her people by giving patches of land that only belong to the Yahudim and ancient Israel. For this the God of Israel will destroy Saudi Arabia, which will burn as the text says the streams of it shall be turned into pitch or crude oil will burn continuously there and America will suffer for its part in the slave trade and other hostilities towards true Israelites in its own land. Once this oil burns the US economy will sink taking many other economies of the world with it!!!

If one wants to see an example of the rape and pillage of Africa where many Hebrews are landlocked then one can take a look at an American company called Anglo American mining company. They operate one of the largest gold mines in the world in Tanzania, for which the Tanzanian people receive five percent royalty, which mean for every $100 the host nation that has the wealth gets $5 and Anglo American $95 or to put it another way for every $10,000 of gold taken out Tanzania receives $500 dollars, while the US Company receives $9500 dollars. This is not helping but this is daylight robbery.

One will be hard pushed to disagree with this. Then why does one wonder at the anger of Muslims, which want to oust the US from their lands? If the scenario of Tanzania is repeated in other Muslim lands then we certainly cannot agree that this is the right-ruling way to help nations.

If the profit split was assuming 70% to Tanzania and 30% to the US then that would be fairer but at present it is extremely unfair. So these kinds of actions create reasons including past US actions and then add to this the spiritual dimension and we have ready made wars.

Yahushua our Master said to judge with right-ruling (John 7:24). If eighty nine million so called born again believers of America cannot see this because of the tailspin of the Zionist newspapers and media and are fooled by truth being suppressed its time they wake up and rise to the occasion to help Africa and other poor nations with their true heart as commanded in scripture to ease the suffering both in Africa and South-East Asia where there are still many Israelites. Yes we can all easily blame Muslims and say they are the only evil people out there but behind Muslim anger is frustration that needs to be examined openly with an honest and sincere heart to try to resolve much as we could to bring them to peace and to the truth of the Master Yahushua. Note that not all Muslims are evil and bent on destruction and likewise not all US policies are geared towards suppression but too many have become this way with different presidents. Some policies have more damaging action than others.

A US company called Trijicon, which makes the high powered US rifle sights inscribes New Testament references as codes on them such as 2COR4:6 and JN8:12. These are New Testament references because the company is owned by Christians in the US.

> **2 Corinthians 4:6** (KJV) For God, who commanded the light to shine out of darkness, hath shined in our hearts, to give the light of the knowledge of the glory of God in the face of Jesus Christ.
>
> **John 8:12** (KJV) Then spake Jesus again unto them, saying, I am the light of the world: he that followeth me shall not walk in darkness, but shall have the light of life.

Personally I do not see anything wrong with this but the radical followers of Muhammad see this as 'Jesus' rifles firing at them. Even in Pakistan and other Muslim lands there are butcher shops which have the shahada (Muslim creed) inscribed on the knife to slaughter the animals but this does not necessarily mean one can say that they are fighting a jihad against the animals but sometimes things are not what they seem and completely inaccurate meaning can be derived out of certain situations such as the rifles.

In my opinion the so called 'Jesus' rifles adds an interesting dimension to the conflict however I do not think that we can say this is counter jihad against the Muslims as they suggest since many soldiers are not believers and those that are believers know what's at stake and are only there because of country and honour without understanding all the politics and religious issues.

When Israel went to war against Lebanon in 2006 the IDF soldiers who were devout followers of Judaism would do their shachrit (Morning) prayer and wear their Teffilin and pray wearing the Tallit Shawl in the morning. I guess in this event the Muslim fighters of Hezbollah may have seen this as a holy war fought by Israel. In reality whether one calls it holy or not its clear that much is at stake for those fighting on both sides and ones faith is important to display courage and tenacity in the face of bullets and missiles. The bullets do not distinguish your religion whether you are a Muslim or a Christian but YHWH does distinguish whether you belong to Him or not and can save you from these bullets. It is my firm conviction that if you belong to the true God of Israel your chances of survival are dramatically increased and if you don't then they are dramatically decreased. Stick with the God of Israel who is the God of the Contracts/Agreements and fully able to honour those which are still true today and forever.

This type of thing plays in the hands of jihadists who see this as an opportunity to call this a crusade against them no different to the crusades of the Popes. This time around though for the Muslims the Pope is the proverbial President of the United States so to speak.

If we compare the US Corporate policy with Canada for the nation of Eritrea where a Canadian company called Nevsun will be mining gold and will be giving 40% profits to Eritrea and 60% to self. I think this is far better than the US Anglo American Mining example cited earlier but still falls short because it seems unfair that they take 60% away and only give 40% to the host nation. In order to be partners for peace and to ease poverty they should give at least 60% to the host nation and take 40%, that to me at least seems more fairer but not a 40/60 to the host nation or a 95/5 split. Also there should be visible contracts stipulating that the host nation uses the money given to help poor and jobless people which can be administered by the foreign government which then makes them not only partners for peace but also for the wellbeing of the local people leaving a lasting good impression and relationship.

This is why it is pretty clear to me that democracy is good if acted out properly with prudence but right now the western style of democracy is nothing but hypocritical corporatrocracy.

This is why the Western nations have become richer and the other nations became poorer. One cannot disagree that YHWH has increased the west but also on top they are good administrators and visionaries while in the third world there is much corruption and the nations lack vision and the true Master Yahushua whilst true Israelites live under curses haven't got off the ground. Scripture tells us where there is no vision the people perish (Proverbs 29:18). However there is more to this story but I cannot tell it all here where the West will end up because of its corruption and scandals but know this that there is a judgement day set for the west also.

We need to have right-ruling actions to prove that we exalt the name of the God of Israel and uphold the laws of YHWH with a right-ruling attitude? A Yahudim Rabbi rightly said that truth is buried in the grave. Many of us will find the truth when we enter our graves if we continue to live blindly with unrighteousness! This should help to explain when the radical Muslims kill Americans because they think they are doing a duty not only to Allah but to humanity in general, the problem is endemic and is not about to go away soon. The radicals blame their government's failings also on the West even though the problems they have at home are to do with bad politicians and corrupt greedy leaders but since they cannot do nothing to remove them from power they pin all the blame on the West and their affluence and attack the west instead.

> **Isaiah 21:2** (HTHS) A grievous vision is declared to me; the treacherous dealer deals treacherously, and the spoiler spoils. Go up, **O Elam (Iran)**: besiege, O Media (Northern Iran with Kurdistan); all the sighing there have I made to cease.

The prophecy in Isaiah 21 tells us that Iran will attack Saudi Arabia, this will cause many western businesses to collapse and many other economies alongside the US will tank and have a domino effect of going down because of severe weakness of the US and its currency. The dollar will ultimately crash taking many with it.

> **Revelation 18:9** And the Sovereigns of the earth, who have committed whoring and lived deliciously with her, **shall bewail her, and lament for her**, when they shall see the smoke of her burning,

The burning of the Saudi oil fields is not a great distance away if you read the present news and every prophecy of the Bible has been fulfilled in the past and so it shall be fulfilled for Saudi Arabia in the near future. Watch where you put your cash!!!

http://www.abc.net.au/news/stories/2010/03/25/2856260.htm?section=justin
03/25/2010
By Timothy McDonald

Dangerous: experts say Al Qaeda is well organised and should not be underestimated (Reuters)

Audio: Saudi Arabian arrests 113 suspected terrorists (The World Today) Analysts are warning Saudi Arabia not to be overly triumphant after busting Al Qaeda cells planning a major attack, because the terrorist group will not be easily defeated.

The Saudi government says it has broken up three separate Al Qaeda cells and foiled their plans for attacks on the kingdom's oil installations.

Analysts say it is a major victory for the Saudi counter-terrorism authorities, which have been attempting to dismantle the cells since October last year.

Saudi is so afraid that Iran will strike her that she is allowing even Israeli Zionist war planes to cross over skies to attack Iran which has been unheard of in the past since they hated the Jews so much.

[21]Published: 03/19/10
Report: Saudi Arabia Seeks Strike on Iran
By Maayana Miskin
Follow Israel news on Twitter and Facebook.

(IsraelNN.com) The German news magazine Der Spiegel has reported that Saudi Arabia is hoping Israel will strike Iran's nuclear facilities, and is even prepared to open its skies to Israeli warplanes to allow such an operation to take place. Similar reports were published in 2009, and denied by both Israel and Saudi Arabia.

The Der Spiegel report stated that officials in Riyadh had spoken to United States Secretary of State Hillary Clinton about the importance of stopping Iran's nuclear program, even if doing so

---

21 http://www.israelnationalnews.com/News/News.aspx/136609

requires the use of military force.

The London Sunday Times claimed in 2009 that Saudi Arabia would allow Israel to use its airspace to attack Iran. The paper quoted a former Israeli intelligence officer as saying, "The Saudis are very concerned about an Iranian nuclear bomb, even more than the Israelis."

Der Spiegel writer Bernhard Zand stated this week, "These days, the Arabs fear the terrorists of al-Qaeda and Iran's leadership, with its rabid rhetoric and nuclear program, as much as the Israelis do. Never before since the time of Israel's creation were Yahudim and Arabs as united as they are in the face of the Iranian threat."

Zand accused Prime Minister Binyamin Netanyahu of failing to take advantage of Israel's newfound common ground with the Arab world.

Iranian media dismissed the Der Spiegal report. "Der Spiegel is greatly influenced by the Israeli regime and has previously published reports that were meant to serve as an Israeli propaganda campaign or psychological warfare against the Islamic Republic," accused Iran's Press TV.

The fear of terrorist takeovers of their governments and of Iran's weaponization is the reason several Arab regimes, such as Saudi Arabia and Egypt, do not protest with U.S. military offensives against al-Kaeda and other terrorist groups in Afghanistan and Iraq, even though they are not part of the CENTCOM coalition that fights alongside the U.S.. These regimes are worried that the U.S. response to Iran will be too little and too late, according to a JINSA (the American based Yahudim Institute for National Security Affairs) analysis of the issue this week.

In fact if Egypt in the past is any indication then it is quite likely that money will also fail in the US and one can work out the consequences of this in the future so better prepare now than later whatever you do don't hoard cash but put your money into tangible goods.

Nugget from the Bible

Isaiah 34:5 (HTHS) For my sword shall be bathed in shamayim (heavens): behold, it shall come down upon Idumea, and upon the people of my curse, to right-ruling.

כי־רותה בשמים חרבי הנה על־אדום תרד ועל־עם חרמי למשפט:

When we want a deeper insight into a Hebrew text that is when we resort to Kabbalah, the word means to receive or for tradition. This has been used by the Rabbis to study elements of the Bible to get a deeper understanding of YHWH and His mysteries, it is not for the faint hearted and Kabbalah has nothing to do with the occult unless people deliberately manipulate it for such purposes as anything can be manipulated because it dates centuries back to the teachers of Israel the great men who knew how to study the Torah well. In fact I will contend even Moses knew this well because this was passed down to the priestly line and kept secret. YHWH endowed the Levitical priests of Israel to have certain wisdom on this and it passed down generation to generation until the destruction of the second Temple in 70 CE. In fact even the Essenes were of the Zadokite order that preserved these traditions who were Hassidim.

Using this technique we can see some fascinating stuff in the verses of Isaiah 34:5, which connects us back to the vision of Ezekiel in Ezekiel 1:1. Let's examine this a little bit.

> **Ezekiel 1:1** (HTHS) Now it came to pass in the thirtieth year, in the fourth month, in the fifth day of the month, as I was among the exiles by the river of Khebar, that the heavens were opened, and I saw visions of Elohim.

To the ordinary person he may say what's the big deal about this but for us Rabbis and my predecessors they have spent their lifetime understanding the visions of YHWH and the chariot (Merkabah) and its various meanings are very important. Let me now show you one side of interpretation that YHWH has revealed to me in this prophecy why because I am also of the kohenim order and many scriptures open up to me through the Spirit of YHWH and His wisdom without even trying too hard as YHWH promised us He as an inheritance therefore many secrets of the heavens belong to the Kohenim.

The thirty is significant to me in this verse because in it I see the death on the tree of Yahushua that was 30 CE April 5th in the Julian calendar. There are many others who propose for a different year but the Passover in that year was on a Wednesday evening and Yahushua was hung on the 14th of Nissan daytime which is the required day and time. Many Pharisees celebrated the Passover 15th starting Wednesday sunset and not the Friday, the theory of which did not start until 180 years after

Yahushua's death by the Roman Catholic Church. What did we see that day when He was hung on a tree? Not only did we see the amazing grace of YHWH but we also saw some dead Saints being raised Matt 27:52.

It is the fourth month (Ezek 1:1) which is the month of Tammuz our July time period. This is the month in which Israel not only sinned against YHWH by building the golden calf in idolatry out of Egypt but also the wrath of YHWH came upon Israel in the exodus so in Isaiah 34:5 we see the wrath of YHWH will come down in the future descending upon the Islamic nations and Edomites (counterfeit Jewry/Israel). His sword will bathe in their blood. This indicates to us that the glory of YHWH will be seen in the month of July and the Islamic armies will gather in July to attack Israel to attack as early as in the month of August to besiege Jerusalem on the 9th of Tisha B'Av in the future.

The visions of YHWH that appeared to Ezekiel when he was standing by the river of Chebar where he witnessed incredible presence of YHWH and the Chariot. We need to look at the passage in Isaiah mystically, which is a different type of interpretation that allows us to see and connect things otherwise not possible. The word for sword in this passage is Khereb or my sword kherebi. If we note in Hebrew the three letters for the sword are Kheth, Resh and Beth. If we switch the Beth around we arrive at a spelling of Khebar with a Kaf rather than a Kheth as it is done in the passage in Ezek 1:1 כבר. This is both interesting and important because it tells us two things. One that the judgment's starting point is the river Chebar in Iraq and two that this nation alongside Saudi Arabia is going to be judged for her sins with those Zionists (Edomites) that are playing the money game and oil game in the world. How do we know that our interpretation is correct? We look at the book of Revelation chapter 9 and see that the two hundred million army will come out of Iraq so we know that the river Chebar is the starting point.

We also look at Rev 2:9 which tells us the Jews or those converted from Europe who calls themselves Jews are part of the prophecy too so its more than one group of people who will be judged at this time in fact both the Jewry and Arab Muslims both of which helped enslave real Hebrew Israelites and ferry them across to Europe and the Americas.

> **Revelation 2:9** I know your works, and tribulation, and poverty, (but you are rich) and I know the blasphemy of them which say they are Yahudim (Hebrew people), and are not, but are the synagogue of Shaitan (Satan).

The Hebrew letter Qaf is the ancient symbol for a sling or one that is used to fight with. Remember the sling of King David. This letter has been used to spell Chebar is indicative of sins or great sins of this nation committed by their hands through warfare of killing innocent civilians. The letter resh which stands for the picture of an Eagle flying high. Note America uses eagle as a symbol as do many other nations. The letter beth for the picture of a house shows us that this place was the head and the house for all false religions of the world and we know historically that all false religions started here because this is where the single Hebrew language was scattered into many other languages. See Genesis 11:1. Nimrod was in this region who was a kushite black ruler of ancient Ethiopia and quite a great ruler in fact until he turned to idolatry while initially he paid homage to YHWH as his Master and King.

Let us assume that the US has a war with Iran before this has happened then how will Iran be in strength to attack Saudi Arabia? This indicates prophetically that all efforts of the US the eagle who is flying high to put Iran to one side or trying to sideline Iran or even pressure Iran into doing what it wants will not work and Iran will grow in strength to strength and the result will be a final assault on Saudi Arabia. Saudi Arabia is the one that underpins the US economy with oil bought with the dollars, which is reinvested back in the US stock market. Once Saudi goes up in smoke then so will many companies in the West who trade in both directions and alongside it many Americans will languish in poverty sorry to say. The attack from Iran can come in many shapes and sizes, it can be a terrorist organisation like Hezbollah or other forms that Iran can pursue and we know that it will one day succeed since this prophecy has never been fulfilled in the past. It is quite likely that UK will also involve itself with trying to protect Saudi Arabia from Iran and other hostile nations at that time because YHWH speaks about that great nation in the coastlands (UK being an Island) in Jeremiah 50:41 but neither will succeed from preventing bloodshed and the oil wells burning.

> **Jeremiah 50:41** Behold, a people shall come from the north, and a **great nation, and many Sovereigns shall be raised up** from the coasts of the earth.

If we have a true picture of Israel during King Solomon's reign, which ruled for 40 years in complete peace and if we take note that this was through peaceful means and not wars. King Solomon a Black Hebrew king acquired many wives through treaties and showed that one can live peacefully with YHWH on his side if he is honest, truthful and obedient. This was also proved by the longest African ruling monarch that is Chanoch known as Enoch who ruled over many kingdoms for over two hundred years using Torah as the rule of law with many kings/princes below him on the request of the regional kings.

However, historically the past actions of the United States in the last 40 years reveal to us that it has involved itself in many wars some legitimate and others illegitimate using false flags operations or outright lying to their public. The US administrators who want to pursue policies of cold war and covert wars with other nations then one wonders if this is the right thing to do for lasting peace? Clearly it has not brought peace so at least these policies proved to be ill founded and wrong. A nation would go to war if it was absolutely necessary because of the horrors of war but not fight first and talk later. Some wars are better fought by the pen and justice is administered through dialogue at times and I am certain that if the US shows good leadership then they can be good administrators of justice too however it shows that this is a desired thing but may not happen.

Haiti a nation in the Caribbean had the slave revolution and received its independence in 1804 from France. Note these are Hebrews but they are not all Levites while witchcraft is at an high there. At that time instead of supporting the slaves in Haiti the evidence from history suggests that the US refused to acknowledge Haiti as an independent state and continued in this dogmatic theology for another sixty years. The reason the US could not recognise Haiti was because the US was also importing slaves from Africa who were also the real Hebrew Israelites. After 1804 Haiti was levied heavy trade embargo by the French (another enslaver) and of course the US as well. The US sanctions lasted around until 1863. France levied Haiti to pay with crippling reparations for its slaves being freed, which was an amount of 150 million French francs. Compare this to the fact that the same French sold all of Louisiana for 80 million francs to the US so one wonders why the French were charging so much to poor slaves in Haiti? Clearly they were Hebrew Israelites and suffering the curses of squandered wealth and another nation seizing their land all written in the chapter of Deuteronomy 28 if one has been given the eyes to see it.

The poverty stricken Haitians had to borrow loans to pay back France, the amount, which was finally cleared by another loan from the US in 1947 for over 20 billion making the nation in debt for many more years to come. In the 80s Haiti produced its own rice and sugar but today it imports cheap US rice and sugar in spite of the fact that Haiti was known as the sugar growing capital at one time. The two corrupt entities such as the IMF (International Monetary Fund) and World Bank both run by Khazari converted Jews (counterfeit Israel) forced Haiti to open up its markets to cheap imports to kill off the farmers. This was then used by the US to dump into Haiti millions of tons of rice making the US farmers richer and Haitians even poorer. The US then forced Haiti to become the third largest importer of US rice which once again was good for the US farmers and bad for Haitian ones.

I know that the US can do good and showing the other nations when it helps out nations when they are disaster stricken such as the 2009 Haiti earthquake when the US sent an aircraft carrier equipped with nineteen helicopters, a hospital on board and assault ships. They sent in the 82nd Airborne Division with 3,500 troops alongside many medical personnel to help. President Obama pledged an initial $100 million dollars in aid. But critics argue it is true that the US has usurped out of Haiti in billons of dollars and given very little back which I have to agree with. The US owes them billions and palms off as a good steward with $100 million USD. The world then happily congratulates the US while the corrupt puppet regime of Haiti is brandished as incompetent, which it is but the irony is that it was put in place by the US, surprised not really that is what the US has been doing for over fifty years. There are many charitable organisations in the US that helped out of a genuine desire but this will not get Haiti out of debt.

While the European counterparts showed a very poor response and lacklustre attitude offering three million Euros in aid in their usual malaise. One is not surprised by this because when France was demanding reparations for no reason most of the European voices were silenced and nobody objected to this as unjust. You do not demand reparations from a country you invade enslave and occupy and then release under pressure and later demand money for doing so. So Ezekiel's prophecy which is tied to Isaiah 34 shows us clearly for those of us who can see that the US the Falcon or Eagle whichever you want to see in it alongside the Arabs and Edomites will suffer very heavy losses towards the End of Days. The signs of these are now evident with the Credit Crunch which the US will suffer under with Europe for decades since YHWH has now turned his attention to the true Hebrew Israelites the genetic black Israel. The corrupt institutions like the IMF and the World Bank will be exposed for the corruption they do as nothing but tools of the enemy to control the world.

America and Europe have to repent for what they did was terrible to genetic Israel or else they will suffer greatly for their sins, the punishment from YHWH upon these two will be both corporate and individual. So let us assume if an individual from these nations repented to YHWH and asked forgiveness for the sins committed by his forefathers towards the real Hebrews then YHWH will ease the hand of judgment upon that individual but his dead relatives will still suffer the consequences since they did and had not repented. The Hebrew Qaf is the sling in the letter Chereb shows that the high flying Falcon will be brought down because of the multitudes of its sins committed against genetic Israel. A war that is fought for ten years is not called a win but a poor loss so we can see that America has allowed itself to be bled in both Iraq (river chereb) and Afghanistan, Iran will be the next one where America and both Zionist Israel will be tested and tried. The prophecy is to run in a fuller force in the latter times which are soon to be upon us.

One country that never gets mention of its name is Cuba. Cuba also has black Hebrews in it. This was the first nation to send doctors and medical teams to the death struck Island of Haiti and alongside Haiti, Venezuela and the Dominic Republic were there too. President Hugo Chavez who is believed to be a man of the people championing poverty causes is regularly maligned by the US policy administrators and rightwing people in American with ulterior agendas, he announced to forgive all the debt of Haiti after the earthquake. Cuba was also the benevolent country to send doctors and aid to Pakistan in the 2005 earthquake and when all the other nations were gone home Cuba was still there going to treacherous mountain tops to assist Pakistani Muslims and others alike when others did not wanted to go. Yet shamefully in the western Zionist media Cuba and Venezuela regularly get bad press. The world is waking up to American hypocrisy. Some assert because they won't bow to their slave masters of the past. This shows us that much of the western Zionist media is hypocritical and not reporting on the true facts but only those that help in their political views and agendas and these need to be corrected. Many media moguls are Jews and part of these conspiracies then also adds to the frustration of the Muslims and they see Christians and the Jews as cooperating against them. There is also the spiritual dimension of psychosocial warfare.

In 2004 during the Asian Tsunami the US was there alongside India, Japan and Australia when they sent 20 ships, two Aircraft carriers with ninety helicopters. One cannot argue that the US is not good at sending armed forces and immediate help when the need arises. President Bush gave aid of up to $350 million dollars but according to John Perkins who alleges that Indonesia was also a country hit by economic hit men from the US and was raped economically for billions of dollars leaving it also in a state of poverty and incapable of paying its debt from the World Bank and IMF. Therefore if one was to take that information into consideration then even if President Bush gave $350 million it's actually not a huge amount in comparison to the billions that were made in contracts and the bloated figures produced by the economic hit men to sell the big US loans to Indonesia as indicated by John Perkins and ex economic hit man. As I said earlier those that give with one hand and take twice with another will always come back because what you sow is what you reap according to the laws of YHWH.

However in spite of the negative impression I am giving you I do believe the US has an immense capability to do good and could start undoing and easing the poverty cycle of many nations stuck in spiralling debt to the World Bank and the IMF corrupt Jewish entities run by the Rothschild's and other rich Jewish Edomite families. Will it happen or will these families go down in history as the most corrupt time will tell but their time is now very short and the hand of YHWH is not far from judging them all together as evil and corrupt.

The things I have written should help you understand why Iran does not want to cooperate with the west because of old time issues but the Bible tells us that there will be a war with Iran but the time is not yet in 2011. Now updating this book in 2012 the time is getting close for that war but we are not quite there yet.

The present US actions against Iran will lead us further into that arena. The timing will be right when we have four nations in agreement and these four nations must come from the four corners meaning at least one from the East, one from the West, one from the North and one from the South. This cannot be a Europe only alliance or America only or even an Israel only strike.

Scripture requires a four wind alliance. Note if any nation strikes alone and even if this is Israel it will not be a war according to YHWH's timing and even if it is Israel acting alone it will not be successful. If YHWH does not help Israel they cannot win any war this was made manifest in the 2006 war another unrighteous war for territorial gain disguised as a strike against the Hezbollah terrorists in which Zionist Israel miserably failed.

The vantage point is Israel so let me show you how I see this will work out:

The situation right now
Israel

- North UK and Russia – neither in full agreement
- West USA and Canada – In agreement partially.
- East – China and South Korea – Not in agreement
- South – Australia – Not in agreement yet.

These are the nations of which at least we need to have four nations in agreement and then we will have the war with Iran. Until that happens the war will Iran will have to wait. Any unilateral strike is not ordained by YHWH and hence will bring in dire consequences for those that do the striking.

So in my opinion so far proven right while many others have been proven wrong we need to have at least one nation from each region such as the US, the UK, South Korea and Australia or possibly a combination of others. Once we have this configuration then we will have the war with Iran. Do not forget other nations from the North or East can replace the configuration meaning the two key nations we need in full agreement are the US and the UK then we can add any other nations from the East and South for our alliance.

> **Jeremiah 49:35-36** Thus says YHWH of hosts; Behold, **I will break the strength of Elam (Iran)**, the chief of their might. **36**
> And upon Elam (Iran) will I bring the four winds from the four quarters of shamayim, and will scatter them toward all those winds; and there shall be no nation where the outcasts of Elam (Iran) shall not come.

We must understand whichever way America has conducted its business we already know the outcome prophetically. There was to be wars with nations and I admit that YHWH has benefited America even though America has not been always honest but nevertheless they have done many good things in the world that we should not take away from them. YHWH allowed America to be increased but if they are not careful there end will be worse than their beginning since they are the ones who also enslaved genetic black Israel.

One can ask why. Many would say because they helped Israel. However this is not accurate since Israel has only 10% of the real black Israelites present which is a minority not even recognised in the majority of the 7.1 million population which is not biological genetic Hebrews. However the reason why America was increased because it has a very large population of black Hebrews in its own land and that is the reason for its increases those that were brought in as black slaves by the gentile converted Jews as their masters. Once these Black Hebrews and other such as the Latinos in which are also many Hebrews leave then the increases will go with them. They are the prime reason for Europe and America's increase and benefit. If Europe or America persecutes these people then you will see the wrath of Elohim on these nations. It was the black Hebrews who have directly worked hard to build America and are never given the thanks. They even built the Whitehouse.

Any honest man or woman can see that to blame the Muslims for everything is foolish and not true and not all Muslims are bent on world domination or subjugating the west. However many hate mongers would like to think so because it is good policy to make $$ dollars. This is because in fact the reality is that they are greedy to make money and after a quick buck. YHWH sees all and will judge them at the End.

How serious is the threat from the Radicals?

The threat is very real and although the battle is spiritual radical Islam is trying to settle old scores but the reality is that it is YHWH who brought the judgement on the western nations in the form of radical Islam. He said when you refuse to obey Him he will bring a foreign nation whose tongue you do not understand, that also means their culture you would not understand. It really depends on whose report you want to believe, the servants that YHWH is raising up or the Pastors who propagate false peace reports.

> **Deuteronomy 28:49** YHWH shall bring a heathen nation against you from far, from the end of the earth, as swift as the eagle flies; a heathen nation whose tongue You shall not understand;

Since the Christians admit to accepting the God of Israel then they also come in the Contract/Agreement with Israel for both the increases and curses.

The radicals will continue to push and fight the allied forces in the East. They will stir trouble in the home bases in the West to cause unrest their aim is for the allies to back away from the Muslim nations and also Israel for a future attack.

Is the threat containable?

Yes. You can minimise the threat. This would mean covert monitoring of all mosques infrequently to determine if any are teaching radical Islamist teachings and if they are then actively shutting that mosque down so that sends out a clear message that we will not tolerate any radicalism here in the West by the way when I wrote this in 2006 I don't think it was common practice but now in 2012 this is becoming common practice where some mosques are being monitored. Once three or four mosques are shutdown many moderate Muslims will know that they have to teach the softer side of Islam or face their mosques being shutdown and they would police their own mosques so they are not closed. This will act as a deterrent. The second deterrent policy is to deport would be radicals who espouse to do internal Jihad attacks. This also I wrote about in 2006 is when in 2012 October when some radicals are being quietly deported and their western nationalities removed. I said these things would happen a comment I was asked to remove in my book Islam, Peace or Beast in 2002 but now as I had been shown ten years on I was right about this prophetically too.

The instant it can be proven they must be deported to their respective country and not be allowed to return. This must be swift to avoid politicising cases and avoiding publicity. This should invoke removing western nationality from people who are involved in attacks of treason.

The 3rd deterrent policy is reward for Muslims who report on those advocating attacks.

The 4th deterrent is financial rewards for Muslim nations who deter and fight Islamic radicalism by demonstrating they are working and being successful. These nations must be rewarded and encouraged to continue in these programs to keep radicalism under check.

The 5th deterrent would be to block radical websites actively through the ISPs so they will not be allowed to brainwash young individuals.

The 6th deterrent is to actively educate people on Islam and its history and the violence related to it. I believe actively teaching about the true first century biblical faith would immensely help the cause and to breakdown the advance of any false religion but because governments are secular they do not like to do this.

The 7th deterrent is to actively monitor all universities for radical activities because most youngsters are recruited here and they are active breeding grounds for the radicals.

The 8th deterrent is to actively bring programs on major TV stations to discuss Islam to explain that radical Islam does exist but is not espoused by all the Muslims and to show by Islamic scholars who say Islam is peace to teach their people that violence and murder would not lead to paradise, this is to help avoid unnecessary persecution of peaceful Muslim co-existence. Our Hebrew teachers should be there to offer an alternative peaceful solution for the redemption of the Muslims! People like me who are ex-Muslims should be encouraged to go on TV and

Radio to teach Muslims that the way of salvation is indeed attainable via the Messiah of Israel Melek Yahushua and that peace can only be achieved when we all come under the umbrella of the God of Israel and His Contracts/Agreements being fulfilled through His Messiah.

In 2012 updating during 2, November I can tell you that all of these except 6th and 8th deterrent are in affect to some measure.

These are only some important measures but many others could be adapted to help contain radicalism and it will really help if this has been done.

How to avoid beheading and to be killed in these hostilities?

First of all most of the Caucasian people should avoid hot fighting zones in Islamic nations that are actively fighting a war with the West or even adjacent nations e.g. Afghanistan and Pakistan are prime examples. If you are in these areas and you end up in a hot zone your chances of being killed are ninety percent unless the God of Israel walks with you, I know because I have been in similar situations and back safely because the God of Israel is with me, I have even had coffee with the radicals and have openly and sincerely told them who I serve that is how I know the God of Israel had opened that opportunity for me. In most of the Caucasian races please take care because even if you don't mean any harm to them they will see you as a threat and think you are a spy and would want to eliminate you perhaps with an example and that is where the most brutal form of killing comes in radical Islam which is beheading this is how Daniel Pearl was entrapped in Pakistan and brutally beheaded.

The beheading is commanded in the Qur'an to be done to those who are infidels and pose a threat especially to make an example of in war situations to deter the enemy.

> **Sura 8:12** I shall cast terror into the hearts of the infidels. Strike off their heads, maim them in every limb.

> **Revelation 20:4** And I saw thrones, and they sat upon them, and judgment was given to them: and **I saw the souls of them that were beheaded for the witness of Yahushua**, and for the **word of YHWH**, [Torah Keepers] and which had not petitioned the beast, neither his image, neither had received his mark upon their foreheads, or in their hands; and they lived and reigned with Messiah a thousand years.

Photo Above-Sadik Cufjala and his son (on the right of the first picture), a colonel in the Protection Corps of Kosovo, which is the only UCK terrorists converted by the United Nations into a civilian corps.[22]

If you look it is nothing for the radicals to kill and they will quite happily kill and behead Christians, Jews and any other person they consider as infidels. Many Serbian Christians got caught up in the fighting in the Bosnian war and many of them lost their lives. To this day no one is accountable yet Europe is foolishly bringing those to trial who rose up to defend their people while the radical perpetrators are happily living in Muslim lands and continuing in places such as Chechnya and Afghanistan.

One advice if you cannot resist to be in such places is camouflage yourself that does not mean wearing forest clothes and putting leafs and branches on your head and body but wear the clothing of the country you are in so you have more chance of looking like the locals and less chances to stand out like a sore thumb and a bulls eyes target especially if you white.

If you want to read more about this then read my book Islam, Peace or Beast or World War III – Unmasking the End-Times Beast.

If you are in the West then you want to avoid Muslim hot zones these are places where some radical may be lurking and looking out for an opportunity so do not give them this opportunity especially considering that the UK and US are still at war with Islamic radicals so this will not help. This is not to say that all the Muslims are evil but you do put yourself in considerable danger to be in areas where the tensions are high.

22 http://www.pogledi.co.yu/english/index.php

Whether we believe it or not these “No Go” zones have been created by what is going on in the Middle-East and eastern Islamic nations such as Pakistan and Afghanistan where resentment exists for the western folks. If you stay away from these places then chances of you being killed by a straying bullet looking for a western target and or radical out to kill diminish greatly. Most of all if you are a believer of the Messiah of Israel then please pray for protection before you go to these areas and don’t be foolish just to walk without any protection and I don’t’ mean a bullet proof car but protection from the Holy One of Israel, YHWH himself. He is the best protection and I can attest to it. Bullet proof cars will fail, missiles will miss their targets but YHWH never fails. Hallelu’Yah.

Chapter 3
What will happen to Israel how will the Yahudim be saved?

For a lot of the people in Christendom the people in Israel such as the Jews are not saved and going to hell however it may come as a shock to you that this is not how YHWH sees things. This is how you or your denomination may view things but I can assure you YHWH is not in the habit of compartmentalising things and looking at them in our timeline view as we do. We know Israel is going to have a 3rd Temple in Jerusalem so if it is going to have a 3rd Temple then it also has Levitical priests in the future and you will be surprised to know that those Priests are Israelites and they did not at any point in their history have to confess the four spiritual laws of Christendom, no, not even once. Those that believe that the Yahudim need to put their faith in Yahushua or become Christians really need to explain how did the following Levites and other Yahudim get into the 3rd Temple before the Christians did.

Note also that we are not talking about eastern European Zionist Jewry that is largely the converts to Judaism and the sons of Japheth but we talk about the real sons of Judah and House of Lewi. Just because you put kohen in front or behind your European name if you are Caucasian and came out of Europe or Russia it does not make you a Levite priest, sorry.

> **Ezekiel 44:15** But the **kohenim the Lewites, the sons of Tzadok**, that kept the charge of my sanctuary [Millennial Temple] when the children of Y'sra'el went astray from me, **they shall come near to me to minister to me**, and they shall stand before me to offer to me the fat and the blood, says the Master YHWH:

Note not church bells ringing, no churches allowed in Israel at that time.

Two things stand out, one that they are in the Temple in the future and there is no crosses in the Temple the symbol of Tammuz and there are no conversions to Christianity to get there, in fact the word Christianity is never even found in the Bible even once though thanks to Roman Catholicism and later translators who put the words in the book of Acts and the letter of Shimon Peter to make it appear like Christianity started in the first century the truth is it didn't.

Second these Levite priests are offering sacrifices. Now you might say hang on a minute but aren't we told that there are no sacrifices and that sacrifices stop after the final sacrifice of the Messiah? Once again let me elaborate that you will be disappointed to know that this is not how YHWH sees things. This means we must go back and re-examine the words of our Master Yahushua the Nazarene to make certain that we have not misunderstood His words and perhaps arrived at a conclusion that is not entirely scriptural? There are even marriages after the resurrection and children born to believers but it depends whether you read your KJV bible with a myopic vision or you actually bother to check the entire bible in the original language that it came in which was Hebrew and Aramaic. Or you ca n get the Hidden-Truths Hebraic Scrolls Study Scriptures from our website www.african-israel.com and it will give you very good commentary to explain things which were until recently hidden in bad translations.

First of all is the word Christian in the Bible?

Claim: The word Christian is in the Bible so I can call myself Christian!

We find most will cite you the following three Scriptural references which are given in the following verses as proof that the word "Christian" exists in the Renewed Contract/Agreement (NT) Scriptures. Now I am amazed. Like one can do anything with statistics one can also do anything with the bible especially with the English language but let's just have a closer look under the hood. Before we look at these verses in order to prove or disprove the word "Christian" it must exist in the Torah, the first five books of Moses the law of YHWH, does it, NO.

> **Acts 11:26** (NKJV) And when he had found him, he brought him unto Antioch. And it came to pass, that a whole year they assembled themselves with the church, and taught much people. And the disciples were called Christians first in Antioch.
>
> **Acts 26:28** (KJV) Then Agrippa said unto Paul, Almost thou persuadest me to be a Christian.
>
> **1 Peter 4:16** (NKJV) Yet if *any man suffer* as a Christian, let him not be ashamed; but let him glorify God on this behalf.

Now here comes the part which most are not aware of therefore the card of ignorance is played by those in the hierarchy to promote an ancient error.

None of the above words which were spoken in the Greek can be translated as the word "Christian." How do we know this?

Problem 1 – Hebrew or Greek

You would have to prove that the Messiah Yahushua came speaking Greek to the Yahudi audience, which we know He didn't since He spoke Hebrew fluently. No, Yahudi wanted to speak in the Hellenist language as they hated it. They were speaking a mixture of Hebrew/Aramaic and some of them knew some Greek but would consider it a sacrilege to call YHWH as Kurios. Most of you I know might have a hard time understanding this. There is a group of people that will help you understand this today and they are the Muslims. Why don't they call their deity Allah by using another deity's name?

Consider any Muslim today trying to call Allah by any other term such as Krishna (Hindu deity) or Gott (The old German term for a false deity), it would be a sacrilege to associate Allah with any pagan deity names for Muslims and this is proven by most Muslim translations of the Qur'an, which always write the name of their deity as Allah in every language of the world and they never use the local common words associated with Elohim for the name of their deity.

Allah (Q.1:1):

Arabic: bismi **Allaah**i arrahmaani arrahiymi.

Turkish: Rahman ve Rahim olan **Allah**'in Adiyla

English: In the name of **Allah**, Most Gracious, Most Merciful.

French: Au nom d'**Allah**, le Tout Miséricordieux, le Très Miséricordieux.

German: Im Namen **Allah**s, des Gnädigen, des Barmherzigen.

Spanish: En el nombre de **Alá**, el Compasivo, el Misericordioso!

Muslims learnt from the Arab Yahudim that they must revere the name of Allah, while the Yahudim were protecting the name of YHWH since they never spoke it in Arabia in the open, which is the four letters YHWH by obscuring it by vowel points in the 6th century CE to the 10th century by scribes known as the Masorets such as the gentile Khazari converts yes they were the scribes who ended up changing every occurrence of YHWH in the bible to Adoni which when translated in English became LORD so no gentile could pronounce the name of YHWH.

Problem 2 – Kurios or YHWH

Next, it would be blasphemy to call YHWH the term Kurios, a false pagan deity's name, the term that is translated throughout the New Testament by the Greek translations as LORD and YHWH. The Yahudim had at this time banned the sacred name being pronounced.

Problem three – Law of first occurrence

You would have to prove that this word "Christian" occurred in the Torah first five books of Moses. We find no law of first occurrence in the Hebrew Torah and it needs to occur at least once to make this a valid choice of word but it isn't ever termed or translated Christian. Even the term in Jeremiah 31:6 does not strictly speaking translate to the term Christian. The term Notzarim means "branches." It has secondary meaning to "Watch", to "Guard".

Problem four – What did Yahushua call us?

You would also have to prove when and where did the Messiah Yahushua ever say that we are called "Christians?" Frankly He didn't otherwise He would be accused of sedition and a revolt against the Father in heaven of starting a new religion. The text breaks from every angle, which says they are Christians or ever called themselves Christians in the book of Acts. Sadly most of our Bible translations are riddled with pagan titles because of bias and personal agendas of various people but most of these can be cleared up very quickly by going back to the original culture and the language which we know was Hebrew, sorry and definitely not Aramaic. Aramaic was spoken widely but religious texts of Israel were <u>always</u> written in Hebrew while the incorrect western worldview is still stuck in Greek and others in Aramaic. They do not understand how the Hebrew customs and cultures functioned and intertwined. My forefathers would never write a religious text in Aramaic and this can be proven by looking at how many extant manuscripts are written in Hebrew and not Aramaic or Greek.

Also how about if I tell you that the term has been deliberately inserted to confuse the masses and inject a brand new religion in the scriptures when one didn't exist. This was to align it with the present version of Pauline Christianity that has rejected the Law of YHWH. Note Paulos is one of the false apostles mentioned in Rev 2:2 so by definition the modern versions of Christianity which reject Torah is not of YHWH but man. To learn more about Paulos go to my website www.african-israel.com under Media and Audio Teachings where there are a number of teachings discussing this Paulos and his actions.

The Messiah refers to us as "**His sheep**." This term was mentioned both in the Torah and prophets.

> **John 10:14** (NKJV) "I am the good shepherd; and I know **My sheep**, and am known by My own.

This reference is backed up in the Torah

> **Numbers 27:17** (NKJV) "who may go out before them and go in before them, who may lead them out and bring them in, that the congregation of the LORD may not be **like sheep** which have no shepherd."

This reference is backed up by the prophets

> **Ezekiel 34:6** (NKJV) "**My sheep** wandered through all the mountains, and on every high hill; yes, My flock was scattered over the whole face of the earth, and no one was seeking or searching for them."

This reference is backed up by the Psalmists

> **Psalms 74:1** (NKJV) O God, why have You cast us off forever? Why does Your anger smoke against the sheep of Your pasture?

Now we piece together the evidence before we arrive at our conclusion.

> **Acts 24:5** (NKJV) For we have found this man *a* pestilent *fellow*, and a mover of sedition among all the Yahudim throughout the world, and a **ringleader of the sect of the Nazarenes**:

We can see that Paulos was accused of being a ringleader of the **sect of Nazarenes** so how could it be that two chapters later someone inserts the term "Christian," which is a word foreign to the disciples of Yahushua? This proves two things that Paul did have his own little group and that they were confused with another group called Kristianos.

What many people do not know is that there was a pagan deity known as Serapis whose followers were called Kristianos. The Greek term Chrestoi means "good men," which was applied to the followers of Sarapis the false god out of Egypt three centuries before Yahushua of Nazareth arrived. This term was applied by the translator of the Greek text incorrectly.

The Term Chrestos

> [23] "Krishna or Chris-na and *Christos* come from the same root. *Kris* in Sanskrit means the pure or the sacred, 'the first emanation of the invisible Godhead, manifesting itself tangibly in spirit' (*Isis Unveiled,* II, 158), it is the Spiritual Ego (Buddhi-Manas). .... 'The Spiritual, Immortal, Higher Ego in every man is an emanation, like a ray, from the Central Spiritual Sun (Paramatman), of which the visible Sun is the direct manifestation on our physical plane and its visible symbol.'"

> [24] A letter ascribed in the *Augustan History* to the Emperor Hadrian refers to the worship of Serapis by residents of Egypt who described themselves as Christians and Christian worship by those claiming to worship Serapis, suggesting a great confusion of the cults and practices:

This is how the term is confused while the believers were called either one of two terms followers of THE WAY or the Nazarenes.

The Term Notzarim, which exists in the Hebrew Renewed Contract/Agreement, was the term that had its occurrence in the Hebrew Bible, in the book of Jeremiah as a future prophecy.

> **Jeremiah 31:6** (HTHS) For there shall be a day, that the watchmen upon the Mount Ephraim shall cry, Arise you, and let us go up to Tsiyon to YHWH our Elohim.

The Hebrew word for 'watchmen' is notzarim, which means branches, or followers of the Messiah Yahushua (Christians) will go up to Jerusalem and begin to realize who they really serve and who or what they are, not a church but grafted into Israel, the ten tribes. Note original genetic Israel

---

23 teosofia.com/Mumbai/7502christmas.html

24 http://en.wikipedia.org/wiki/Serapis

was black Negroes. The Messiah was also a man of colour see my book Yahushua – The Black Messiah.

The word notzarim also means to "guard", to "keep" and for "concealed ones" so who are these concealed ones? These are the people who later started calling themselves Christians but the prophecy in Jeremiah is that the ones who call themselves believers would actually have an awakening and return unto Tsiyon both in the spiritual and physical sense on to old tried and tested Hebrew pathways. This shows us there will be a real wake up call for all Christians to drop paganism and return to their true Hebrew roots of the faith which compels us to keep the laws of YHWH numerated in the Torah of Moses and be faithful to YHWH who was revealed through Yahushua our Master. Many of these will be genetic Hebrews of black colour.

> **Acts 24:5** (HTHS) For we have found this man a troublemaker, and a stirrer of trouble among all the Yahudim (Hebrews) throughout the Roman provinces, and a ringleader of the **sect of the Nazarenes.**

First century believers were called Notzarim (Branches or watchmen) fulfilling the prophecy given in Isa 11:1, and such as Jer 31:6 and John 15:1-2. The term Nazarenes of late to some may have come to mean Christians but since many in the church system do not obey the Torah the rule of law of YHWH's people, most of the netzarim brothers and sisters today are thought to be a cult by many in churches because they obey the Torah? Most churches in the world still mix paganism into their religious practices adopted from the Roman Catholic Church. YHWH has kept the Netzarim as a separate remnant as He prophesied to grant them a greater reward in the world to come. He said He would raise us up and many will turn back to the true faith of the disciples of Yahushua leaving apostate Christianity behind.

So in conclusion, you will not find the word "Christian" even once anywhere in Scripture thus Jeremiah rightly stated the following verse which we need to read and forewarned.

> **Jeremiah 16:19** (HTHS) O YHWH, my strength, and my fortress, and my refuge in the day of affliction, the nations shall come to you from the ends of the earth, and shall say, **surely our ahvot (fathers) have inherited lies**, vanity, and things wherein there is no value.

Now after this should we should correct the error and live as YHWH wanted us to live? The choice is in our hands Truth or Tradition LIFE or DEATH? Scripture tells us that many will ignore the warnings and continue in the lies that they have been given but there is a price attached to remaining in these kind of lies and error but I won't tell you here what that price is otherwise you may get depressed about it.

Now that we have established that the word "Christian" is not in the bible we can see how that the Levites mentioned in the book of Ezekiel get into the 3rd Temple, they were not Christian nor had to convert but they remained in their true Israelite faith obeying the Torah, the law of YHWH that allowed the Father in heaven to give favour unto them for He applied His Son's sacrifice to them as much as us. For this we really have to examine the words of Yahushua more carefully and accurately praying for discernment from the heavens. Without the Father giving us wisdom we will make the wrong interpretation and live in error.

Now did Yahushua say He came for the true Yahudim? Strictly speaking the House of Judah, which comprised of three main people the Levites, the Judeans and the tribe of Benjamin. Let's see Yahushua's words.

> **Matthew 15:24** (HTHS) But he answered and said, I have been sent unto the **prostituting sheep** of the beyth (House) of Y'sra'el (Israel).

No, He does not say "I have come to rescue the lost Yahudim" because they were not lost, they were in the land and most of them were serving YHWH in the Temple. Yahushua said He came for the **lost sheep** or more accurately prostituting sheep of the House of Israel. The House of Israel is an acronym for the ten northern tribes of Israel none of which were Yahudim. This can be seen prophetically in Christendom who are even today prostituting by not behaving as the Father in heaven would like them to. Many do not keep the 7th day Sabbath, and many others do not know anything about the seven annual feasts or what is kosher food laws, what is forbidden such as pork and shell fish because they freely indulge in these unclean foods which shows they are not fit for the priesthood in the Temple.

YHWH calls shellfish an abomination but Christians continue eating it. I will be honest with you when I was a Muslim I used to eat prawns because in Sunni Islam they are not considered Haram (unlawful) to eat but when I came to faith and realised that Torah called it an abomination and unclean food I stopped eating it. I used to love shellfish and lobsters but it all had to go as YHWH did not approve and I decided to live a life pleasing to Him putting my preferences to one side. Are you willing to do that?

Then why are many Christians trying to force the Yahudim to convert if Yahushua said that He came for the disbelieving House of Israel and by the way their disbelief was that they rejected Torah and made their own? This is because of Church error as I said earlier. Error begets error.

The **House of Israel** is a clear name for the Ten Northern tribes of Israel (Ephraim) who became goy (gentiles), that is who Yahushua came for!!!

Whichever way we slice it and dice it, many of these today in the House of Israel are prophetically speaking Christians and some are unbelievers in the nations such as Muslims, Hindus and even Buddhists. Christians are both prophetically and in some case biologically connected to the House of Israel. They are clearly grafted in the natural olive tree which is Israel and that tree has the Yahudim already upon it as branches. Unfortunately not all the Yahudim were broken off as many think and it was not even a breaking off but a wounding for those who refused to obey Torah so let me show you how the bad translation of the KJV can change things around.

> **Romans 11:17** (HTHS) And if some of the branches be broken off and hanging, and you, being a wild olive etz (tree), were grafted in among them, and with them partake of the root and fatness of the olive etz (tree);

The Torah is what we measure everything with and not through the NT (Brit Chadasha) Renewed Contract/Agreement writings! We must never take a text from the New Testament and try to make something new out of it, it must fit with everything that was written by the prophets earlier and that is the test for the Renewed Contract/Agreement (NT) writings. Sadly most Bishops and Pastors out there do exactly the opposite. This includes many other laity that does not know and are not trained in a Yeshivah (house of learning) on how to interpret scriptures. They take one verse from the Renewed Contract/Agreement and try to retrofit something in the Torah. This is not how it is done. Any Orthodox Yahudi Rabbi will tell you that this type of interpretation is highly suspect and flawed and I would have to agree.

> **Deuteronomy 6:25** (HTHS) And it shall be our righteousness, if we observe to do all **these commandments** before YHWH our Elohim, as he has commanded us.

It is crystal clear that the Master will save those who obey Torah. It does not say how much right-ruling a Yahudim man or woman needs to work but clearly the ability to demonstrate obedience results in the Holy One giving them eternal life by unmerited favour what we rightly term GRACE or Favour! No Sacrifice needed! You want proof. Let me show you.

> **Psalm 51:16** For you **desire not sacrifice; else would I give it**: you delight not in burnt offering. **17** The sacrifices of Elohim are a broken ruach (spirit): a broken and a contrite heart, O Elohim, you will not despise.

The gift of YHWH was always there even in the Torah and was not something new after the death of Messiah. The death of Messiah was always veiled and only revealed once it had happened. This was to prevent Satan and his minions from obstructing YHWH's plan.

So what is your excuse now? King David could not afford a sacrifice? Did YHWH say to King David please repeat after me the four spiritual laws of Christendom, only the foolish will believe this!!!

King David said You (The kadosh YHWH) do not desire SACRIFICE else I would give it! A man after YHWH's own heart who left so much material for his son to build the first Temple could offer thousands of sacrifices as he desired but he did not need to.

What about the Messiah's death on the tree then?

That death is in fulfilment of Moses' Contract/Agreement made at Nebo and Isaiah's depicted suffering servant, the requirements for the Contract/Agreement made in Mount Nebo did require a sacrifice so the sacrifice or death of Messiah does not stand isolated or alone from the Torah. That was for all of Israel but the Yahudim the true genetic ones who obey all the Torah laws do not need to recognise their Messiah as it was prophesied by Isaiah (Isa 53:1-5). So if Isaiah is true then this shows why Christians are pursuing futile means to convert the Yahudim when Isaiah told us that they are blinded spiritually by Abbah YHWH. So do the Christians and Messianics think they can override YHWH? I don't think so.

Yes indeed a sacrifice was needed to fulfil the Contract/Agreement or to bring it to completion. There are stages, first stage was Mount Nebo, and the second stage was the death of the Messiah on the Mount of Olives. The 3rd stage is the resurrection and the worldwide re-gathering of the lost sheep of the House of Israel (Ten tribes) and a resurrection of the faithful Torah believing and obeying disciples which most Christians are not. The lie that the church teaches is that you have to keep the law of YHWH perfectly so they make out by their own foolish admission that no one can keep it perfectly. This is not true.

The fourth to the six stages are a little more complicated and requires very detailed teaching which this book is not designed to do. Also as a punishment the House of Israel or many Black Hebrews were taken as slaves to the western Isles from where they were prophesied to return. Many of them are stuck in African churches from which also they will come out when they realise who they are. Israelites were not white Caucasians but Black Negroes from which my present ancestors descended with our brown shade.

> **Deuteronomy 29:1** (HTHS) These are the words of the Contract/Agreement, which YHWH commanded Musa (Moses) to make with the children of Y'sra'el in the land of Moab, **beside** the Contract/Agreement which He made with them in Horeb.

Note this Contract/Agreement is an additional New Contract/Agreement beside the Ten Commandments made at Mount Sinai. The New Contract/Agreement did not arise out of Jeremiah 31:31 contrary to Pastors saying this.

Just because the Pastor said it does not necessarily make it true. My brother in law said to me in Pakistan before I became a believer that one and a half billion people can't be wrong going to Mecca! I said they can all be wrong!!! Likewise the 38,000 denominations of Christendom and the millions of churches are wrong on the law of YHWH including the wrong teachings regarding the Yahudim question of salvation. Look back and see if Peter or John thought that they needed to be converted into Christendom and leave Judaism the answer is no. No disciple of the master ever converted to any denomination because none existed. There was no Christianity in the first century till the later part of it. The church corrupted itself in the late first century after the death of Jacob the brother of Yahushua who is incorrectly labeled James. The early Netzarim hated all forms of Christianity and would not have anything to do with it and there is evidence of that.

> **Acts 10:28** (KJV) And he said unto them, Ye know how that it is an unlawful thing for a man that is a Jew...

Did Peter (Kefa) say that he is a Yahudi Christian or just Christian? No. He is a Yahudi only and no need to add Christian to him.

So what answer do you give to those who were massacred in the holocaust by the German Christians, yes many were Christians? What about German Christians massacring other German Christians who opposed the Yahudim holocaust? Who was right? Is YHWH going to forgive both the Christian groups and throw the Yahudim into the lake of fire for rejecting Jesus of the Germans? This kind of theology has been popular throughout the ages like in Germany at the time of the holocaust or may be popular in churches today but this is not how the Father in heaven sees it. The holocaust was for very different reasons, a holocaust that was put upon the true Hebrews to displace a hundred million of them by the Khazari Jews brought the punishment later upon them. What you sow you reap.

Likewise I will demonstrate that two billion Christians whatever you care to call them are not right about the salvation of the Yahudim either!!!! How many of the people have the guts to say that openly? I do and I say it publicly and not in a secret room and I show theologically why. This is important as this question is not only tied to many other people's redemption but also this is tied to the End of Days which we shall examine in this book.

Even the leading converted Jewish sages Rambam and Rashi agree that the New Contract/Agreement after Israel's sin at Mount Horeb of not obeying the Ten Commandments was made at Nebo and was not made with Jeremiah in 31:31, which was repeated from Deut 29:1. It would make no sense to isolate this with Jeremiah alone. Christendom would do well not to isolate one piece of text and derive new doctrines out of it. Typical bad habits very similar to what Jeroboam did in the North of Israel by erecting a new priesthood and a new Temple. Just look around and Christendom has it all the same way and even their own feasts. If Jeroboam was punished then what about Christianity? There is a real need to repent and return to the ancient path of our Torah faith, read Jeremiah 6:16 again and I can assure you many Christians will say no to YHWH's commandments therefore they have no part with us true Israelites.

> **Jeremiah 6:16** Thus says YHWH: "Stand in the Ways and look intently, and make inquiry for the ancient paths, where the good

way is, and walk in it; then you will find rest[25] for your souls. But they said, `We will not walk in it.'

Who are the "they?" In the ancient times Northern Israel and in the modern times Christendom. Many Christians will be standing outside the gates if they continue to behave like this.

It's a sorry tale that you have been led into all sorts of error. If the Messiah Yahushua is the King of Israel and if He is the same one who walked with Israel as the cloud and the pillar then Deuteronomy 6:25 and Deuteronomy 29:1 makes perfect sense to me as that statement comes from Him. Why would He change and then tell people to follow another way or another religion? Christendom pay heed! The death of the Messiah is to reconcile the allegorical adulterous wife (Ephraim/Christendom), northern Israel but Judah is not divorced so she did not need reconciling. The sacrifice of the Messiah already covers Judah and her sins and the blood will be applied retrospectively when the time comes. You are not going to make Isaiah into a liar just because your denomination insists to convert genetic Jews to Christianity, while YHWH says no they are My lawgivers. YHWH's Judges do not need to be converted.

This is hard to understand for most of you but it is easy to understand for me and let me demonstrate why I say that. Prior to September 1998 I was a Muslim so at that time I did not obey the Torah fully only the things I was taught as a child as I do now do because I did not know about it however did I ever realise that I would be blood washed in 1998 September? No. But did the Father in heaven know when I was given the new birth/rescue and restoration that He was going to apply the blood of His Son to me retrospectively so all my sins would be purged? The answer is Yes, Abbah YHWH knew this long before I accepted the Messiah as my Master.

Now this may help you to understand this a little. The genetic Yahudim question is similar but slightly different. If we apply the text of Deuteronomy 6:25 they are already saved because they are Torah obedient. Unmerited favour called grace by Christians was merited to these by YHWH long ago long before anyone heard the name Jesus in the Western lands in the 17th century since His name was not and never 'Jesus' and grace was always applied in response to the obedience to His Contracts/Agreements such as at Mount Sinai and Mount Nebo etc. Did

---

25 Rescue

Noah have to wait for the Western Jesus to be known in the 17th century to receive unmerited favour? No.

The test was Torah obedience and many genetic Yahudim in Africa have been Torah obedient for centuries, look towards Ethiopia, while Christians have not been Torah obedient at all in their majorities. This is what sets people apart and not what church or denomination you belong to! The idea of belonging to a church was started by the Catholic Church and later adopted by cults like scientology making similar claims of belonging to an organisation to have salvation.

The Messiah of Israel is not man-made, He is everlasting so unless He is YHWH revealed in the flesh which He is, we cannot have our faith in a Messiah who breaks Torah and tells people its OKAY now go ahead and break the Sabbath, stop eating kosher, do not keep the feasts because they are only for the genetic Yahudim.

This type of messiah does not know the difference between clean and unclean, holy and unholy and therefore would be classed as a false messiah. This was one of the sins of Israel of not knowing clean from unclean and also breaking the Sabbath. We find many members in the church continue in the same sin, they do not know the difference between clean and unclean, holy and unholy and I doubt many people fully understand what I am even saying here. In short anyone who refuses to keep Torah is strictly speaking has no part in the Contracts/Agreements of YHWH which means he or she is putting their salvation/rescue and kingdom coming rule at risk of losing it entirely. At best you lose the 1000 years reign and at worst you have no hope of salvation to enter the kingdom that is what we are dealing with and the fairytale of everyone goes to heaven does not apply to true believers because when we die we descend down to Sheol just like the Messiah did and we go to Paradise downstairs and not upstairs.

Any man made messiah that teaches doctrines of non Torah compliance is at best a fraud and a false messiah and a false prophet!!! This is why the genetic and even converted Yahudim reject Yahushua of Nazareth. Not that He is a false messiah but because He is portrayed like a false messiah doing the things I stated earlier because His adherents today teach law breaking and abrogating. Only some of the Messianics, 7th day Adventists and Nazarenes including the Church of God keep the law while the rest do not. The more strict Torah keepers are some of the Nazarenes and returning Israelites who do all the principles of Torah that are applicable outside the land, which include food laws, plural marriage, festivals and weekly Sabbaths etc.

Hence one can understand why the genetic Yahudim would not recognise him therefore Isaiah is correct. While Isaiah says they will not recognise Him many of you are adamant that the Christian gospel has to be forced down their throats but the reality is it does not and I stand to one side and will not teach that the genetic Yahudim need to convert to anything. In fact most of you will have to convert back to Judaism the ancient path one day when the Messiah returns!!!

> **Zechar'yah 8:23** (HTHS) Thus says YHWH of hosts; In those days it shall come to pass, **that ten men** shall take hold out of all languages of the nations, even shall take **hold of the tzitzit** of him that is a Yahudi, saying, We will go with you: for we have heard that Elohim is with you.

So if genetic Yahudim need the gospel according to Christianity, Messianics and misguided Nazarenes, then why are these nations and people that the prophet Zechariah mention, who we know are from the tribes and other gentiles going up to hold the **tzitzits (fringes)** of a genetic Yahudi? This particular text does not imply in anyway or shape or form that this particular Yahudi believed in Yahushua of Nazareth? It actually shows that he is Torah obedient because he wears the tzitzits, the four corner fringes on his garment, likewise we should too but who will teach you the proper law of YHWH unless you have a willing heart. The very word **nations/gentiles** sets Israel apart, but here the only bit of Israel that is set-apart are the genetic Yahudim, Benjamin, Judah and Levi. The text does not say these are Christians and bowing before a cross, praising the western lily white 'Jesus' or the statue of Mary as Catholics do or the statute of Jesus in Rio de Janeiro where they go to pay homage!!! The text does not say they are redeemed in the Age to come at that time. Some may come to this conclusion but albeit an erroneous one, there are no crosses or churches there in the picture of Zechariah in fact all strongholds of Tammuz will be broken down.

So how do we understand this and how do we reconcile a clear cut biblical passage that says a Torah observant genetic Yahudi is leading the nations to the God of Israel? Fantastic isn't it? The genetic Torah observant Yahudim enter the Kingdom of Heaven (The world to come) and lead others which is the clearest indication that they do not have to become Christians as we have been told. Let us analyze this further.

Now I bet you have so many questions. What about John 3:3, what about Roman 1:16? This was the same one posed by a similar Rabbi. I will answer this here.

Let me explain Romans 1:16 first.

> **Romans 1:16** (HTHS) For I am not ashamed of the besorah: for it is the power of Elohim to Rescue to every one that believes; to the Yahudi (Hebrew) person first, and also to the Greek.[26]

First, Paulos's letters need to be treated as letters and not words out of the mouth of the God of Israel they were addressed to the various messianic assemblies that were struggling in Halacha (Torah way of life) hence why we see many idiomatic expressions being used by Paulos and also he has no inspired writings and neither was he a true apostle but I will leave that bit here for the moment while you can learn about this from our site www.african-israel.com under Media – Audio Teachings. His letters applied to particular situations and cannot all be applied to us the same way today. His letters cannot be qualified scripture and were never held as sacred writ.

Yes some situations in his time may be the same but we all have different circumstances. For one we do not have the Temple of Diana near by with the whole city worshipping in it so its irrelevant however we have other types of idolatries applicable.

So why is Paulos saying this to the messianic believers at Rome? Is he saying that the Yahudim must be saved first then it's the turn of the gentiles or is he proclaiming an eternal truth stated way back in the Torah?

Note this is often misunderstood by many teachers that to the Yahudi first then the Greeks. The Messiah did not send Paulos to the genetic Jews or to anyone else but let us presuppose that he did but the reality is Paulos's message is conflicting with the Messiah's message but will people learn that he is the false apostle mentioned alongside two others in Asia minor in Ephesus in Revelation 2:2?

Paulos called himself the apostle of the gentiles (Rom 11:13) so it was

---

26 Note this often misunderstood and misconstructed doctrine by many teachers that to the Hebrew man first then to the Greek. The Messiah did not send Paulos to the Hebrew people first, in fact He told him to go to the gentiles, the lost sheep of the house of Y'sra'el so it was Paulos' own idea to go to the Yahudim first as he would have thought that it would help him if they joined him to reach other lost sheep but in reality this was a desire in Paulos' own heart so we must not mix up his desire with what he was commanded to do. See Romans 11:13, Romans 15:16 and Romans 10:1. This verse simply ranks Hebrew people in the order of truth, they have Torah, while the gentiles need to receive it.

Paulos' own idea to go to the Yahudim first as he would have thought that it would help him if they joined him to reach other lost sheep because they knew Torah well but in reality this was his own idea. So we must not mix up his desire with real truth. See Romans 11:13, Romans 15:16 and Romans 10:1. This verse simply ranks Yahudim in the order of truth, they have **Torah truth first** and the gentiles need to receive the Torah next and they do not have it yet. This is why the gentile world is in paganism. The problem with people who look at this one verse and devise their errant doctrines is that they fail to take the whole chapter into consideration. Let us see what the next verse says.

> **Romans 1:17** (HTHS) For therein is the right-ruling of Elohim revealed from faith to faith: as it is written, the right-ruling shall live by his faithfulness.

Paulos quotes from Habakkuk 2:4, the text says the right-ruling shall live by His faithfulness meaning we are relying on YHWH's trust and faithfulness. Once again you cannot isolate and break scripture because the meaning is clear to those who understand.

Let us examine the truth now under the hood.

The biological Yahudim were **NEVER EVER** counted in the nations.

Who is the Yahudi in Zechariah 8:23, who will be wearing the tzitzits? We know he is not Christian because Christians traditionally or historically do not wear tzitzits! They wear crosses.

Do we understand what the text reveals in Zechariah 8:23?

It reveals that this Yahudi is not a Marxist or an atheist; he is actually wearing tzitzits, which means he is Torah observant according to his local halacha set by his Rabbis/teachers. It is highly likely that he is following a form of traditional Judaism and the Holy One is not sending him to the Lake of Fire that is what matters. In fact he is leading the gentiles (nations) including Christians to Jerusalem as long as he is Torah obedient hence wearing the tzitzits.

Many need to wake up as they have believed whatever they have been taught without careful examination of the text of scripture regarding the Yahudim. **The Messiah is not meant to reveal Himself to His brothers (Judah) until the very end**. This is what your Pastors did not tell you since they do not understand this point themselves as they carry the party line of lawlessness. How can they teach what they know not?

Knowing that Yahushua is the Son of YHWH is a revelation and not theology. The point can be proven very easily friends.

> **Matthew 16:15-17** (HTHS) He said to them, but whom do you say that I am? **16** And Shimon Kefa (Peter) answered and said, **You are the Messiah, the Son of the living Elohim**. **17** And Yahushua answered and said to him, Benefited are you, Shimon Bar-Yonah: (Simon son of Jonah) for flesh and blood has not revealed it to you, but my Ab which is in the shamayim.

So if Peter who was an eye witness disciple of the Master did not know that Yahushua is the Son of YHWH (Ben Elohim) and he had to have a revelation from the Holy Spirit then how can anyone condemn the Yahudim who are not meant to know this truth yet according to the prophet Isaiah?

Many Messianic/Nazarene Rabbis even struggle with the text of Zechariah 8:23 trying to add the words that this Yahudi could be redeemed from the nations. However it is clear in the Hebrew that He is already saved by obeying Torah meaning being part of the Contract/Agreement given in the Torah is all you need not religious creeds of Christendom or Rome.

Here is something more that may help you to understand:

Torah = Messiah
Messiah = Torah
Torah = Grace
Messiah = Grace
Messiah = Torah and Grace intertwined
Torah = Messiah and Grace both as Akhad (One)

The Messiah was to come and redeem the whole of Israel not just Christians in fact Christianity as a religion has its roots late in the first century. However His first and foremost duty was/is to gather the true genetic Israelite exiles, while Judah was at that time in home in Israel but later also dispersed after 70 CE and further dispersion occurred in 132 CE. Even those of Judah in the nations are in the hands of our loving heavenly Father. They will be resurrected in the millennium reign even if they die in the nations. Note many of this original tribe of Yahudah are Black and not the Caucasian variety you find. Unfortunately many people have failed to observe the text of the Torah carefully to see that Abraham was a man of black Negro descent whose family had links in West Africa. See the Hidden Truths Hebraic Scrolls bible for further study on this.

The story is the same as when black Yosef was in Egypt he helped his brothers but did not tell them who he was until the very end when he had to. The TYPE and SHADOW is the same for the Messiah. The Messiah's blood shed at the tree already covers the genetic Yahudim based on the Contract/Agreement made with the forefathers on Mount Nebu Deuteronomy 29:1, which is termed the Renewed Contract/Agreement. So what is important, the Contract/Agreement or the Blood? To most Christians, the blood but to us who have some understanding of Torah it is most definitely the Contract/Agreement. Without the **Renewed Contract/Agreement** formed at Mount Nebo there is no shedding of blood pure and simple! Blood is never shed in isolation unless a Contract/Agreement is put in place first by Elohim. Christians would do well to learn this truth rather than to bark up the wrong tree with erroneous Pauline doctrines.

Also for those who think there is no salvation apart from the blood of an animal by misquoting scripture let me show you what our scrolls says on this subject:

> **Matthew 19:16-17** (KJV) **16** Now behold, one came and said to Him, "Good Teacher, what good thing shall I do that I may have eternal life**?" 17** So He said to him, "Why do you call Me good? No one is good but One, that is, *God*. But if you want to enter into life, **keep the commandments**." 18 He saith unto him, Which? Jesus said, Thou shalt do no murder, Thou shalt not commit adultery, Thou shalt not steal, Thou shalt not bear false witness,

Hear it from the horse's own mouth. So there is life in the Torah by keeping the commandments as I said earlier Abbah YHWH clothes you with His right-ruling as a gift but the King James Version translation is wrong though commendable effort by the way and here is the more accurate one from the Hidden-Truths Hebraic Scrolls bible.

> **Matthew 19:16-17 (HTHS) 16** And, behold, one came and said to him, Rebbe, what Good mitzvoth (deeds) shall I do, that I may have eternal life? **17** And he said to him, Why ask me concerning the good? There is indeed one good, if you want to enter into Life, Guard and Do the commandments. **18** He said to him which ones? Yahushua said, you shall do no murder, You shall not commit adultery, You shall not steal, You shall not bear false witness,

The word "GOOD" here is the idiomatic expression for Torah taken from the book of Proverbs 4:2.

> **Proverbs 4:2** For I give you **GOOD** teaching, forsake not my **TORAH**.

The term "good" is the idiomatic expression for the Torah and not for just God as it has been translated incorrectly in the KJV and NKJV and many other faulty translations. In fact the word God is not even present in the text and has been inserted instead by the translators. Yahushua here had repeated the Ten Commandments which somehow got missed from Matthew one wonders how? Typical gentile behaviour.

In affect by being in the Contract/Agreement and accepting YHWH's rule of law He grants you eternal life that is simply the way it works.

Did Yahushua say at anytime or give us a clear allegory of Torah applying to a fundamental commandment in the Torah?

Yes He absolutely did.

Let me show you the most misquoted passage in Christendom and the least understood.

> **John 14:6** (HTHS) Yahushua said to him, I am the way, the truth, and the life: no man comes to the Ab, but through me.

I guess it is not clear right. Let me first show you the Torah passage that this points to:

> **Deuteronomy 30:19** (KJV) I call heaven and earth as witnesses today against you, that I have set before you life [Torah with eternal life] and death,[eternal death] blessing (if you believe in the truth and act upon it) and cursing(if you reject it); therefore choose life (Salvation), that both you and your descendants may live;(To have eternity).

The key references in John 14:6;

The Way: 'The way' here means living Torah pointing back to the written Torah in Genesis 24:40, Psalm 1:6, Psalm 2:12 and Psalm 18:13. Yahushua was declaring Himself to be the middle-pillar and the way to enter the Kingdom. The middle-pillar is an esoteric term which both the modern converted Jews and our forefathers understood to be the one which connects the heaven and the earth and repairs the breech. The Way is a Yahudim idiom frequently used in the first century amongst the Rabbis for the Torah only.

The Truth: First century Yahudim idiom for Torah found in Psalm 119:142 and Psalm 40:10 among many references.

The Life: 'The life,' is also a first century Israelite idiom for the Torah taken directly from Deuteronomy 30:19, Deuteronomy 32:47 and Proverbs 6:23. This also means eternal life not just physical life.

No Man come to the Abbah: The term 'man' here is incorrectly applied to every man, woman and child in the whole world by Christendom but this is not how the first century Hebrews including the Messiah saw this statement. This is a loaded statement!!!

Whenever we apply scripture we need to be careful not to apply it incorrectly as many have erred over this one. We need to understand the terms because behind these terms are hidden expressions that many today do not realize nor understand because they are not living in the ancient rabbinical culture. First of all: the term 'man' is a first century midrash term that the Rabbis understood and was only applicable to goyim (gentiles), therefore by definition this only applied to the Ten Northern tribes of Israel, who for all practical purposes had become many gentile nations. The Rabbis knew this fact very well and had communicated this truth orally until it was penned in the Mishnah and Gemorah in the 3rd century CE.

So when the Messiah uses this term he is not saying that the Hebrews need to come through me because the fact of the matter is that they already have the written Torah which is the idiomatic Messiah because what would be the purpose of the Torah if the Messiah was not on the scene for another 4000 years? We need to wake up to the real truth that the Messiah came proclaiming the same Torah but they did not fully understand that truth, because the written Torah is the outer garment of the Messiah. If the Torah is the Messiah then if you have the written Torah and believe in it then by definition you have the inward Torah which is the Messiah but yet concealed to the Hebrew nation by YHWH's own hand. To be frank the Torah is a feminine word originally applied to the feminine Holy Spirit and from there handed to the Messiah since he is he Son of the heavenly Mother and Father.

This truth is not always evident and many today still do not understand this. Note the preceding three references in John 14:6 to 'the Way, the

Truth and the Life' are all Torah references out of the Torah and for the Torah, which the Hebrews have but they are all personified in the living Messiah. Yahudah is not meant to understand this truth yet because it is hidden for deliberate reasons to bring in the multitude of gentiles from the nations. So by definition right-ruling Torah keeping Yahudah is saved through the same Messiah (one door) but He is not yet revealing this truth just as Yosef fed his brothers in Egypt and gave them the rich abundance of Egypt for his family to take home but did not reveal the truth to them. He made the truth known to them at the end.

This likewise is the same ancient pattern applied here. However the Messiah himself tells us that Judah the elder brother is with Abbah YHWH in Luke 15:31. Similarly, when we fail to understand terms as many do, we end up misapplying them to Judah but Judah is the lawgiver so why would YHWH make him (Judah) the lawgiver (Genesis 49:10, Ps 60:7) but then subsequently be happy to send His appointed judges to the Lake of Fire? Does that make sense? Of course it does not as it is misapplied by many and that is only if you want to believe that a two line gospel misapplied to Judah. Judah is not meant to be evangelized so he can keep the Torah and the feasts alive. This is the veiled truth which is not evident to many. If we examine why the Catholics and Christians failed to bring many of the Jews into their church system for the last two thousand years of history then this fact bears this out. YHWH does not intend them to. He intends them to remain a distinct group.

Judah was meant to remain a distinct separate group as they were going to return in small numbers and re-establish themselves in the land of Israel. This is already given in the prophesies of Jeremiah. Do you think the Catholics were assigned to do this? Or were the Christians assigned to do this or even the Khazari converts calling themselves Jews? The answer that YHWH gave for the question above was NO, clearly recorded in Psalm 78:67-68, where YHWH said He has chosen Judah but rejected Yosef, who personified the returning tribes as Christians or others coming back into the Torah truth. This is why Yahushua returns only when Judah calls out in a national crisis mentioned in Matthew 23:39. He does not return upon the gospel being preached as wrongly taught by many denominations. Read the text carefully.

The Messiah tells us that in Matthew 25 He judges goyim (Gentile nations) on account of 'these my brethren' (Real Judah Y'sra'eltes and judges the apostate counterfeit Israel) for being persecuted or killed in the nations for trying to obey the Torah but nevertheless judges appointed by Abbah YHWH. We do not submit to men but we submit and bow our knees to Abbah YHWH. How do we understand this fact of Judah being

Judges? Think of it like this: if there was a policeman and he stops you for a crime but you beat that police man yet he was installed by the state to control crime and unruly people so how will the state rulers then react to this lawman being beaten up? Would they pat you on the back and say well done good citizen you did the right thing by beating that policeman and for committing the crime, now go and do some more. Or would they take a very harsh approach and instantly put you in prison and even throw away the key so others do not do the same? Yahushua as the King takes this very harsh approach and is going to be throwing people in the lake of fire for this crime, read all of Matthew 25 and see our footnoted references on this too in the Hidden-Truths Hebraic Scrolls which can be purchased from the www.african-israel.com website. Also see this footnoted in First John 4:15. This text is not talking about Zionist Yahudim who have subversive motives or who are not even the sons of Judah but I am talking about the genetic sons of Yahudah who are appointed judges and they will be found in exile by many of you. Many of these can be found in Ethiopia today and even in America.

The Holy One is clear choose '**LIFE**', drash for Torah/Messiah and to choose anything else would be 'death'. Well everyone dies right so that would not be a punishment. This is because behind the term death is the idiomatic term eternal death, the same death that Adam was warned about.

So 'life' and 'death' the two idiomatic expressions reveal Torah keeping or Torah breaking. Torah keeping is GRACE or accurately unmerited favour and Torah breaking is DEATH. In fact this reality is more evident to the Yahudim than Christians and they have already beaten you to it.

Now ask yourself how many televangelists do you find in Judaism ripping people off with lies? None. How many Rabbis per capita? Very few while in Christianity the corruption is the highest and there is a saying you lift a brick from the ground and underneath is a Pastor or Evangelist all with his personal card and logo to proclaim himself, note proclaim himself not the real King, the Black Messiah but a white 'Jesus' another oxymoron. Unfortunately not only have many Christian denominations adopted but are living this error but there is absolutely no control in what they teach as both incorrect and ineffective in their lives. They have little understanding or regards for YHWH's holy laws/Torot. On the other hand Yahudim show a much more high regard for holiness and Christians will do well to learn from them which they will have to one day anyway when the see the real ones in the land that is if they will be allowed to enter the land which is another story.

Therefore, all the right-ruling Yahudim who keep Torah by definition will be cloaked with YHWH's right-ruling, the same YHWH that stood in the Garden with Adam, the same YHWH that stood with Abraham and Moses. The same YHWH who stood in Jerusalem 2000 years ago to die on the tree cloaked as a man. It makes no difference if the Yahudim recognise Him or not, He will recognise them. Look at Yosef in Egypt did his eleven brothers recognise him? No, but he recognised all of them. Did he say well since my brothers do not acknowledge me nor recognise me I won't send grain to my family in Israel? Clearly not the Type and shadows match perfectly.

However many who lack Torah knowledge incorrectly teach that you have to keep or obey all of the Torah, the fact of the matter is that you do not have to keep all of it. Let me prove this by a real example.

Are you a woman? If so then only the commandments of the women apply to you from the Torah. Let me use a crude example to put some reality back for the men. If you are a man then would you be keeping the niddah uncleanness laws of ritual purity? One such is the monthly discharge cycle for women?

Now I would like any one to prove me wrong that we men have to keep this commandment and by extension all of the Torah. This is how many Pastors have either deliberately or through ignorance lied.

By the way sorry I did not tell you but this is not the only one there are quite a few commandments around the various discharges that can affect the ladies. You would be foolish to even try. This Torah law is heavily documented by the sages and the rabbis and there are reams and reams of material on it in Judaism. How much of the Torah is for women alone? It would be safe to say that as an educated guess of what I have seen at least one third of the Torah covers women and the laws around them for ritual purity both in the Temple, in the Synagogue and in the home for the family such as marriage, death and divorce. **That is a whopping 33% of the Torah not relevant for you men! Wow**!

Already I as a man do not have to keep 33% of the laws of the Torah. Now for the geniuses out there who keep beating people up and as the Rabbi I was having my little discussion with, those who want others to keep 100% of the Torah explain this one? Why would the people keep 100% since the women commandments do not apply to men and vice versa? And marriage laws do not apply to singles and Temple laws do not apply to non presiding priests? It's absurd and not required. This means you only obey Torah that is relevant to you.

Next time anyone tells people that they have to keep it 100% they need to be careful how they communicate that truth because the reality is they do not have to keep all of it. So working on the equation of 66% being the remainder how many laws then cover Temple priesthood?

Once again it would be safe to conclude that one third of the laws, statutes and judgments are for the Temple. So if we take the laws of women which is 33% and take the laws of priesthood both past, present and future yet to come, let us just say 33% plus 33%, we end up with 66% or two thirds of the Torah roughly that may never apply to the ordinary man or woman on the street!!!!!!

Now tell me how much Torah do I have to guard and obey to please the Holy One of Israel?

How about one third. Now very quickly we start to instil reality in the equation and when I tell people that only possibly one third of the Torah may at best apply to you even not all the one third laws apply to us at all times so that then makes Torah keeping easy today and forever for everyone. They Holy One knew this. That is why He said it is <u>forever</u>. He was not kidding. Furthermore, salvation is not by which commandment you get right and which you get wrong this is another Christian fallacy that needs to be dealt with as they are taught that the Yahudim keep Torah to receive salvation and this is just not true. The Yahudim receive unmerited favour as part of the Abrahamic Contract/Agreement not Torah single commands we need to understand this point.

Once they accept the Contract/Agreement and by definition they also walk into the Contract/Agreement of Mount Horeb and then the Renewed Contract/Agreement given to Israel at Mount Nebo they are saved by accepting YHWH's grace and then happily say we will hear and do meaning obey YHWH's voice His Torah to please YHWH at all times. The Master of the House of our Abbah and it is His rules and not yours. You take your set of rules when you go to visit your friend's house you have to honour him in the house. If you are wanted to be rescued by the God of Israel you need to abide by his laws.

The Torah therefore is no longer a burden since our forefathers did not see this as a burden either. It's only a burden to those gentiles who have no understanding of it.

What did our Master Yahushua say?

> **Mattityahu 9:12-13** (HTHS) And He said, **<u>they that are healthy do not need a physician</u>**, but **<u>they that are sick</u>**. **13** But go you and learn what that means, **<u>I desire loving-kindness</u>**, and **<u>not sacrifice</u>**: for **<u>I have not come to call the right-ruling</u>**, but **<u>transgressors</u>**.

Let us see Hosea 6:6

> **<u>Hosea 6:6</u>** (HTHS) For I desired loving-kindness, and not sacrifice; and the knowledge of Elohim more than burnt offerings.

What is the context of Hosea 6:6, who is saying this? Is Judah saying it or is it Ephraim (goyim gentiles now)?

Who are the right-ruling, who are the sinners and who is the physician?

Judah was healthy, and not sick. Ephraim was sick, because Yahushua declares Judah does not need me but Ephraim does as He came for them. **The term Physician is a <u>rabbinic</u> term for the Messiah.**

The only one's who were remotely close to right-ruling, were the people in Judea of Judah. Perhaps we can see why the message of Christianity is not accepted by the Yahudim because it was not meant to be to them, God overrules them. Scripture is clear but unfortunately many Christians are not taught and are uneducated in matters of YHWH's holy laws.

> **Luke 15:31** (HTHS) And he said to him, Son, you are always with me, and all that I have is yours.

Who is the Son?

The son is Judah and Yahushua taught that he (Judah) is already with our Father in heaven. Do sinners which are going to the Lake of Fire reside with the Father? No.

Yahushua's blood retrofits Judah and all her sins just like it does for the House of Israel but they do not need to know this fact yet, it only hinders and does not help in the restoration.

Let us take a hypothetical position:

Here is one Sequence of events that could have taken place but we know it didn't: The Messiah comes on the scenes 2000 years ago and all of Israel suddenly believes he is the rightful anointed Messiah to fulfil all the prophesies. Now what should they do, choose another law?

But the prophet Isaiah said His report would not be believed, does that mean the prophet Isaiah then lied? If this had happened then he would be a false prophet.

Let's says hypothetically we break the Temple which took 45 years to build, and then what do we do?

Let's not keep the feasts any longer as the Messiah is here and the feasts were only a shadow of Him. Now that we have the shadow we do not have to keep the feasts as I am sure many would have reasoned. This is who Christendom keeps lying and cheating people out of their inheritance.

However there is one huge problem!!! YHWH said Le-Olam Va'ed. For His feasts and for his sacrifices. This Hebrew word in it's simplest context means FOREVER. For me at least **FOREVER** means until my death and beyond, so for each person it is until his or her death and if you are right-ruling to be raised then you will know forever is forever because the right-ruling will never die after being raised. We know the above did not happen simply because that was not to be the case as Isaiah was a true prophet and Judah was already rescued and fully redeemed.

So now I have to swallow the camel by believing that the Temple stood for forty years after the Messiah's Death and Resurrection but Abba YHWH did not honour the sacrifices? This is how Christendom reasons which is yet another error. Abbah YHWH indeed did honour the sacrifices otherwise Paulos would not be there attempting to fulfil his Nazarite vow sacrifices with others he led there. If such was the case then why did Paulos go there to offer a sacrifice to a corrupt priesthood? These would be in vain too right? The disciples celebrating feasts in the Temple would also be vain? The Christians will tell you this but they lack understanding as YHWH still accepted the Temple authority because He set it. **Judah was and still is the LAWGIVER. The day you grasp this truth that day you will grasp many other truths.**

> **Psalm 60:7** (HTHS) Gilead is mine, and Manasheh is mine; Efrayim also is the strength of my head; Yahudah is my lawgiver;

Can the blood of Yahushua the sinless lamb be used in isolation?

Yahushua's blood atones the Hebrews those Torah keeping ones and those who do not yet have His revelation through the same one door to heaven. It cannot be used in isolation outside the Torah Contracts/Agreements. This is a special one time provision hence why this is veiled.

How?

> **Deuteronomy 4:30-31** (HTHS) When you are in distress, and all these things come **upon you in the latter days**, when you turn to YHWH you Elohim and obey His voice (31) for YHWH your Elohim is a merciful El, He will not forsake you nor destroy you, nor **forget the Contract/Agreement of your fathers** which He swore to them.

It's all about semantics. They call Him Ha'Shem and not Jesus. They do not have that revelation beside His name is not Jesus which is a 500 years old appellation but His Hebrew name is Yahushua Ben Yosef.

Where is the Contract/Agreement? In Genesis 12:3, 15:13, 17:17 and Deuteronomy 29:1.

The very first mention is with Abraham then with Isaac and followed by Jacob.

> **Genesis 15:13** (HTHS) Then He said to Abram, Know certainly that your descendants will be **strangers in a land** that is not theirs, and will serve them; and **they will afflict them four hundred years;**

The black Hebrews taken as slaves to Europe and America. This land is America where they were landlocked for four hundred years and not Egypt as erroneously taught. Our people's hard slavery in Egypt was only for eighty-six years.

Abbah YHWH repeats for good measure.

If you will turn to repentance... Meaning obey Torah to the best of your abilities when you are in America and Europe YHWH will cover the true chosen people of Israel by **grace/unmerited favour** as a gift. That we know is Messiah today but it's the same grace/unmerited favour for Judah.

OK, one more thing that the whole Christian world is hung up on and many others, they like to take their single words and make new things out of it.

The Hebrew word Yada H3045 in the Strong's Hebrew or the Greek word ghin-oce'-ko G1097 needs to be examined.

How they love to tell people that it means it's a relationship! Yes it is true partly only however there are two sides to the Yada coin: One side is relationship and the other side is **responsibility** which Christians are not taught about.

Without **responsibility** nothing will work. It means YHWH is responsible to bring His bride in to the kingdom not man!

Let me explain:

Story time:
When Israel was in Egypt for 400 years and then in the latter part of that time she was held in captivity or hard bondage for eighty-six years, some had almost given up hope, can you see at that time their relationship with YHWH was pretty slim or partly non-existent? They were praying for a deliverer but many people had given up hope that YHWH would hear them since it was such a long time that anything had happened until Miriam Moses' sister prophesied that a RESCUER would be sent by the hands of YHWH.

Some Israelites believed in this report of their rescue but most others had already given up. There was no Yada from most of Israel in captivity but the Yada was only **one** sided from YHWH and that is all the Yada they needed to have their rescue take effect!! The same way the Yada will also apply to the second Exodus.

How much Yada did Yahushua need from the thief/freedom fighter on the tree? How about a total of **three** hours. (Matthew 27:45). So there goes our yada theory popularised by Christianity. Oh yes and don't they teach you the thief on the alleged cross of Tammuz was a thief. Take it from me he was not. He was only a thief in the sight of the idolatrous Romans, he was a right-ruling man fighting a war with the Romans, the man was from Galilee Yahushua's home town. You can go to my website under the menu option Media – Audio Teachings to learn more. Its time to unwind all the false teachings and learn the real truths.

Did the thief/freedom fighter on the tree need repentance? No, the thief did not even have time to repent, so there goes our repentance theory. So then what did the thief need? He only needed Emunah, faith, which means **trusting faith** on to the Master that is all. Trust and submission was his form of repentance and it was accepted.

You don't believe me? OK, let us prove this theory... Let's see King David.

> **Psalm 51:17** (HTHS) The sacrifices of Elohim are a broken ruach (spirit): a broken and a contrite heart, O Elohim, you will not despise.

This is the sign of repentance in Hebraic understanding.
Now what about the thief/freedom fighter?

- ✓ He did not need the four spiritual laws.
- ✓ He did not need the Catholic holy mother Church.
- ✓ He did not need the Protestant/Anglican Church
- ✓ He did not even need their baptism!

This shows another painful truth that Christendom did not exist in the first century and is not the true faith of Israel but Netzarim Israelite Judaism is and that is what people need to look at and follow to obey Torah which is completely in line with the ancient faith of Israel. All forms of modern Christendom and all its many branches are bankrupt of the true faith of Israel.

It's all about the Contract/Agreement!
Now Let us look at the Contract/Agreement and a reminder:

> **Beresheeth (Genesis) 17:17** (HTHS) And it came to pass, when the sun went down and it was dark, that behold, there was a **smoking oven** and a **burning torch** that passed between those pieces.

So Abraham slept. Was their any other human walking in between the sacrificed animals? The answer is No. Only the Shekinah of YHWH.

We see representation of the plurality of YHWH in the walk so this shows us the onus was upon YHWH to save Israel in Egypt, likewise the onus today is on YHWH to save Yahudim and they do not need Yahushua as they are already in Contract/Agreement **because Yahushua came for the lost sheep who are the Ten Northern tribes**

who were scattered and had refused to obey the Torah. The deal is already done but He will not reveal this truth to the southern tribe of Judah yet. This is why Yahushua was adamant to His disciples to go to the scattered sheep only, Matt 15:24.

The gentiles need Him but since Judah has Torah and Yahushua is the Torah, they actually already **have** him but they do not know him yet by the foreign unclean names that Christians call Him by. They do not know Him as Yahushua but that is fine for the moment though be careful I am not referring to real Israel but those who have converted into Israel and call themselves Jews, since they know Him by Ha'Shem (The Name) or Adoni (My Master). These are cleaner names than, Iso Christos, Jesus', Jesu, Eshu and all the other varieties.

The Real Problem is National blindness

The national blindness actually affects all of Israel at various degrees!

> **Ma'aseh Schlichim (Acts 2:21)** (HTHS) And it shall come to pass, that whosoever shall call on the name of YHWH shall be rescued.

All who? All Israel. The book of Acts is not written to the ones in the Brazilian rain forests or to the Australian Abroginies. It is written to Israel for Israel.

Isaiah 6:9, coupled with Matthew 13:13

> **Isaiah 6:9** (HTHS) And he said, Go, and tell this people, Hear you indeed, but understand not; and see you indeed, but perceive not.

The national blindness from above

So now should we believe that our Abbah YHWH blinds His chosen people first and then sends them one by one to the Lake of Fire for enjoyment? This is most ridiculous and bizarre theology if there ever existed one and is this not what Christendom has been teaching lumping everyone together? But you can hear it out of church pulpits every Sunday. Oh those poor, poor Jews they are going to hell because they do not believe in our Jesus white by they way a racist concept in itself when you enslave Black Hebrews and tell them they are savages and inferior to your white non-existant melanin skins. The ridiculous became the norm and the norm (black) became the cursed. These curses fell on Israel as they had rejected Torah so no white Jesus is going to remove the curses unless they go back to the true Torah with the Black Messiah.

This is why I said Christians do not know how to handle the clean or the unclean, holy or unholy and one day the Yahudim will teach them these things so who needs to convert who?

To offer prayers for the Yahudim appears to be a nice idea but this is not how it is meant to happen. In fact the true genetic Yahudim should be praying for Christians so they would stop teaching error! A Yahudi prayer is much more powerful because of the Contracts/Agreements hence why the Yahudi in Zechariah 8:23 will be leading people into the Kingdom. Somebody accused me of being a rabbinic Yahudi and I said indeed I am just like Yahushua was a rabbinic Yahudi so am I, in fact I have credentials to prove it from my forefathers in Iran, the house of Levi. In the end heartfelt prayer is needed for gentiles and the Yahudim in the churches to stop behaving like uneducated Pastors who do not know how to separate the clean from the unclean.

In fact I met at least two Khazari Yahudi families in Churches who ate pork and I was absolutely shocked to my core how could they have been keeping Torah and how easily they accepted to eat the unclean swine. What a tremendous bad witness to the nation of people who are meant to keep fast to the Contract/Agreements of Abbah YHWH. This occurrence is not widespread and these are isolated incidences. You find some Yahudim when they become Christians which is an oxymoron they start behaving the same way by removing their head covering criticising their synagogues and their liturgy. Very bad indeed, that indeed is destroying the scriptures very unhealthy and unprofitable. I would not have any part in such things to call YHWH's word abrogated and His laws no longer for us. This is indeed what Satan wants.

For this newly converted Christians then tzitzits come off, the kosher food stops. All these things in my mind at least show they are making an extremely bad witness, you can believe in the Messiah but letting go of Torah and the customs which are Torah based simply lead away from truth into paganism. Since the churches are full of paganism I cannot see why any genetic Yahudim needs to become Christian because the reality is that no Christian in scriptures leads other people to the 3rd Temple but true Israelites/Yahudim do. It's a matter of understanding. If you understood that Yahushua came for the scattered sheep then you will understand that Ephraim will continue in her idolatry until the very end because Yahushua came for them to remove them from idolatry and show them how to obey and keep the Torah commandments. The Yahudim already have the Torah and they know the difference between clean/unclean holy/unholy so are fine and in their rightful place where they belong.

YHWH has indeed blinded the Yahudim in order to save them, He was testing their obedience! They remained obedient unto Torah even to this day.

Does that mean Christianity has no value and no truth? Christianity does have truths and does have value, it just needs to get rid of the paganism obey the Torah and work more closely with the Synagogues and not against them. The times of hatred are over and they must reconcile with their brother Judah who is the law giver according to YHWH (Ps 60:7).

You may wonder but how does this help the End-Times?
First Christianity can be a force to do good deeds by the Western world in third world nations to preach the love of the Messiah and the death and resurrection for eternity. However Torah must be in and the Tanak (Erroneously called the Old Testament) must be read and practiced. Christians need to learn to work with those that obey the Torah with real Israel and stop Acquiescing counterfeit Jews and counterfeit Israel to adopt and practice the laws of YHWH and go and learn from the REAL Yahudim how to if they do not know how.

Without Ephraim (Christendom) Israel will not win the final battle as both Judah and Ephraim will fight alongside helping each other since Ephraim protects the Northern borders of Israel where historically the enemies of Israel have marched in from. Ephraim has to return home to the Hebraic roots of the faith. Ephraim must stop envying Judah and trying to force her to convert, it is actually not biblically right to do that and they will not succeed even if they try. The proof is majority of Judah are not Christians and not meant to be and will NEVER be. They are meant to be distinct to the End of Days and beyond.

This is why YHWH tells them to keep the feasts.

> **Nahum 1:15** (HTHS) Behold upon the mountains the feet of him that brings the words of Elohim that proclaim shalom. **O Yahudah, Guard your set-apart chag** (the appointed celebration times), perform your vows: for the wicked shall no more pass through you; he is utterly cut off.

Judah has to keep the ancient markers that lead back to the Torah truth, without her faithfulness this would not have been possible.

Christians which within it has real black Israelites and others form the brother Ephraim literally, allegorically and prophetically who did not keep the faithful markers but will one day come to realise that they were equally important. Some of you may not agree with this but it's not too long before this reality plays out in front of your eyes. This is not about me versus you but what I see YHWH doing in the Scriptures and in history. Many Torahless Christians will be dismayed and punished also.

Rabbis and Pastors can have differing opinions but still respect each other as the end goal is to dwell in unity between brethren and to proclaim the holy words of YHWH and I will continue to do just that. In fact people like me make a much more effective witness to the Muslims who need to be rescued from their sins and to the real Yahudim who need to be one (Akhad) in the end for unity. Christians who do not adhere to the Torah do not make a good witness and will lose favour also from YHWH.

Judah is initially meant to establish the land of Israel for the eventual return of the Messiah, Yahushua of Nazareth. Now in the true land of Israel we have really only a small remnant from the genetic house of Yahudah but the rest are converted Jews calling themselves chosen when they are not.

> **Amos 9:14** (HTHS) And I will **bring again the captivity of my people of Y'sra'el**, and **they shall rebuild the waste cities**, and inhabit them; and they shall plant vineyards, and drink the wine there; they shall also make orchards, and eat the fruit of them.

This is Judah who will come back in the land in the future when Israel is destroyed that will come to plant and establish the land of Israel, they would then have come to establish the tabernacle of David, which is the 3rd Temple (Amos 9:11)! It is when they will push and heave that the Islamic nations will start to get aggressive with Israel and see that as a direct threat to their status in Israel. The above prophecy is not yet fulfilled but we will see the fulfilment of that in the future. Present day Jews in the land of Israel are NOT the fulfilment of this prophecy as they are the sons of Japheth who are gentile converts. This prophecy only applies to genetic Black Israelites from the clans of Yahudah.

Amos 9:15 shows us that once the tribe of Yahudah, Benjamin and Lewi are back partially in the land that many will try to uproot them in the war. This is the Islamic radical nations but they will not succeed. However casualties will be drawn on both sides which have occurred and more on that to come. See my book World War III The Second Exodus, Y'sra'el's Return Journey Home.

> **Amos 9:15** (HTHS) And I will plant them upon their land, and they shall no more be pulled up out of their land which I have given them, says YHWH Your POWER.

The word to plant is the Hebrew word natah Strong's H5193, which means to fasten or to strike in. The Hebrew word is made up of Nun, Tet and Ayin and the text is preceded by a Wah, which indicates this prophecy is sealed to be fulfilled in the future because the return of the so called Jews in 1948 is not a fulfilment of this prophecy so be careful not to run after the counterfeit return versus the REAL return yet to come as these people are not the biological chosen.

They have to be fastened by YHWH so no man can uproot them and that is the thrust of the prophecy. Interestingly enough the ancient Hebrew picture of the word to fasten below is the following;

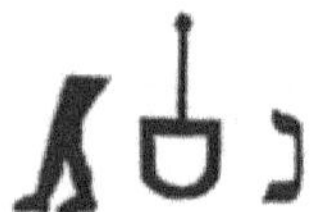

This gives us the ancient Hebrew meaning of "to pour out and expand without ceasing just like a river, while the nations look on." Warning, Judah can never be uprooted or eradicated out of the land of Israel once they are in, the Black true Yahudites. Right now I would be surprised if 10% of the people in the land of Israel are real Yahudah because the majority are the sons of Japheth and not true Yahudim.

There have been at least six wars since 1948 with Islamic nations and the sons of Japheth in the land with a tiny majority of Judah so we can see that YHWH predicted accurately that no nation Muslim/Khazari or otherwise will succeed in uprooting of genetic Israel once it has been established. Yahudah will have the mixture of Levites which are needed when the 3rd Temple is going to be rebuilt so we can see that the verse directly links with Islamic violence/Jewish violence of the settlers towards Muslims and destruction plus the rebuilding of the future Temple. How can we be certain of this? This is because we can look at the text of Amos 9:11, which reveals this fact. The Tabernacles of King David is a picture of the future 3rd Temple which will be rebuilt. This has also been prophesied by Ezekiel chapter 44 where the various gates are mentioned and the resumption of the Levitical sacrifices in the millennium kingdom to come. However what is important is that the ancient Israelites were people of colour and not white Caucasians while today east European Caucasians occupy the land which is a temporary endeavour. From these hands the land will pass to the real people the Negros and their ancestors who are the true Y'sra'elites. When this happens everyone will know about it.

One may wonder what benefit is there for Judah to be in the land. First without them the Messiah would have no place to return so Israel has to be re-established as a reality with borders and the House of Judah back which fulfils many prophesies. Judah has to make preparations to build the 3rd Temple before the coming of the Messiah though He will do the actual construction and finishing of it later. So we see to have these prophesies fulfilled perhaps in our lifetime or in our children's lifetime.

> **Zechariah 14:2** (HTHS) For I will gather all nations against Yerushalim to battle...

What is the purpose of gathering all the nations, indeed they are Islamic but why gather them? How can the God of Israel gather all the nations if there is no issue of Jerusalem and Jerusalem does not exist which presupposes the reality of the land of Israel coming into existence and there being active hostility towards Jerusalem. This hostility would be shown by radical Muslims who want Jerusalem for the capital of Palestine. The UN and the rest of the world wants to facilitate and broker a peace deal with the Islamic alliance to give part of Jerusalem away the negotiations centre around East Jerusalem to be the capital of Palestine. Scripture does predict that Eastern Jerusalem will go to the radical Islamic group but it suggests this by a war and a hostile takeover by the forces of the Anti-Messiah and not by peaceful means. However all this will allow the cleansing of the land from the counterfeit chosen.

> **Zechariah 14:2** (HTHS) For <u>I will gather all nations against Yerushalim</u> to battle; and <u>the city shall be taken</u>, and <u>the houses rifled, and the women raped</u>; and <u>half of the city shall go forth into captivity</u>, and the residue of the people shall not be cut off from the city.

It's clear that half of the city that will be taken away will be Eastern Jerusalem as that is the stronghold right now for the Muslims living there as they outnumber the Ashkenazi by a greater majority because most of the Ashkenazi population is situated in west Jerusalem. However note the Ashkenazi are not the progenitor of genetic Israel but are only place holders in the land. Jerusalem actually belongs to neither the Muslims or the Ashkenazim. The real people who are the inhabitants of this land are still in dispersion and yet to return in large numbers.

Who is the Messiah coming for?

Zechariah 12:8 (HTHS) In that day shall YHWH defend the inhabitants of Yerushalim; and he that is feeble among them at that day shall be as Dawud; and the house of Dawud shall be as Elohim, as the malakh of YHWH before them.

There seems to be no debate as to who the Messiah Yahushua is coming for. Most Christians are in their theological thought process that they will be whisked away to heaven in their alleged man made rapture and they also teach that the Messiah is coming back for them as the Bride! However the truth be told that scripture says Yahushua is coming back to fight the Islamic radical nations and to come to rescue and restore Judah thereby establishing the right-rule and reign with a 3rd Temple to be rebuilt there at that time. The born again faithful Torah keeping believers will be resurrected and they will come with Him but he is not exclusively coming for the Christian world. In fact most of them are living in disobedience so they actually have no right to His return and will not be raised in the first resurrection and will lose the 1000 year reign because of their disobedience.

The ones who died in this state will remain so in that state and will not be raised until the 2nd resurrection. Unfortunately you walk into any church then they teach you that you will get the first resurrection by just saying that you believe in "Jesus". Not so!!! However scripture mandates first resurrection is for faithful Torah keeping believers of Yahushua only and not the half way house ones who live without obeying any commandments of the Torah such as the feasts and Sabbaths and these ones still expect rewards won't find any. The ones who died prior to the coming of the Messiah and were Torah obedient will also be raised for the millennium and beyond.

The millennial kingdom is a reward for believers who were or are faithful its not a given all for anyone out there.

Are you going to be resurrected in the 1st resurrection or the second?

Deuteronomy 28:13 (HTHS) And YHWH shall make you the head, and not the tail; and You shall be above only, and You shall not be beneath; if You carefully listen to the commandments of YHWH Your POWER, which I command you this day, to Guard and to do them:

This commandment shows us that you would be the head not the tail in all things that by remez (hint) includes the resurrection, the first fruits but because of the disobedience factor you cannot expect a resurrection with the Disciples of Yahushua who are by definition the first fruits just like the Messiah (Rev 14:4). Look and make sure you understand the condition "IF" you OBEY which means if you do not obey as many Christians refuse to obey the commandments and negate the Torah therefore they cannot have a first resurrection but they will enter eternity upon the second resurrection but there are caveats and we will talk about positions in the kingdom later if given the time.

> **Revelation 14:1** (HTHS) And I looked, and, lo, a Lamb stood on the mount Tsiyon, and with him a hundred forty four thousand, having his name[27] and his Ab's name written in their foreheads.

Having the Father's name YHWH as the seal means that these are the disciples of the king Messiah and sadly most Christians cannot be the disciples, while they break the Torah and do not live by the precepts of the laws of the King of the universes and call the laws a Jewish thing or worse still a strange thing. If you live in the United States and you say I don't believe in driving at 50 kilometres on the highway but at sixty instead then by definition you are breaking the law of the land if it was set at fifty kilometres an hour so you cannot say I keep the laws of the USA because technically you don't. This is akin to many Christians who say we believe in the Bible but they don't because they do not obey the laws therein. They are only deceiving themselves and no one else.

> **Rev 14:12** (HTHS) Here is the steadfast endurance of the *Y'sra'elite* kedoshim (set-apart saints): here are they that **guard and do the commandments**[28] of Elohim, and the belief of Yahushua.

These ones guard the commandments written in the Torah of Moses and it has been revealed to us **to guard those zealously** so these one hundred and forty four do exactly that. There will of course be others apart from the 144 thousands who also guard and keep the commandments they will enter the Kingdom of YHWH as the disciples of Yahushua.

> **Isa 8:16** (HTHS) Bind up the testimony, seal the Torah among my disciples.

---

27 They had His name and His Ab's name. Earlier manuscripts support this reading.

28 Torah keeping Y'sra'elites have a great reward to come.

The disciples of Yahushua guard and keep Torah and do not call it legalistic while a majority of Christians refuse to believe what is there and call it abrogated. This means only a minority of Christians will see the first resurrection those who obey and guard the Torah of Moses. Please see the article on www.african-israel.com in the Ask the Rabbi page "Will Christians Enter the 1000 years millennial reign?"

Those who think they are going to get in the kingdom in the first resurrection by living a disobedient non pleasing life to the Father by just claiming the blood think again Your resurrection will have to wait if you are dead and you will also miss the one thousand years reign entirely, which is a reward for the faithful, since by definition you were not found faithful you are not utterly condemned but you do not qualify either for the reward to enter the kingdom. Isaiah 8:16 confirms exactly this and tells those who care to listen and obey, which are the disciples of Yahushua and again it confirms what Revelation 14:1 does say that **they have the seal and testimony**. In order to acquire the seal of YHWH, the Torah must be obeyed there are no if's and buts'. The Torah is not just instructions as per its literal interpretation but the Torah is made up of testimonies of our forefathers the Patriarchs and the testimony of YHWH and His dealings with Israel. If you deny Torah you deny YHWH's testimony that is the bottom line. How would you feel if somebody denied the true story of your life which is your testimony?

> **Isa 9:14-15** (HTHS) Therefore YHWH will cut off from Y'sra'el head and tail, branch and rush, in one day. **15** The elder and honorable, he is the head; and the prophet that teaches lies, he is the tail.

Look and read carefully YHWH cuts of head and tail from within Israel and not from outside so this shows that since Christians are all grafted into Israel but those who tell lies and we know there are many in Christianity who I call prophets for money and those who accuse others and spread lies. There judgment is already set because they were measured by YHWH and found wanting. The writing is on the wall and since no repentance will come forth away they go. I have heard of one Christian man in India who takes in £150,000 a month from donations and if he does not get this amount each month he cannot sleep because his life revolves around money and not the kingdom of Yah. Some of you may have heard of the corruption in a Church in Singapore where a Pastor spent millions trying to shine his wife's secular singing career. Such is the state of these places which have become a den of thieves and robbers.

If you ever watch the God channel then sometimes you will see usually they are always collecting money and it is not small figures but large ones like hundred million dollars. Whose pockets do you think this type of money lines up and what will be their end? Fooling the sheep has a price and such individuals indeed will pay on the Day of Judgment. How many times I have heard and seen such people collect millions but there is still no change in the world in the lives of people who they claim to be collecting for. The only thing that changes is that the collectors end up with an extra personal air plane or a very expensive luxury car and houses. One can work out what YHWH will do to such Christians whose motive is making a fast buck by blinding the sheep with their foolish science and prosperity lies.

> **Matthew 24:11** (HTHS) And many false prophets shall rise, and shall deceive many.

I am under no illusion that we have many people quite happy to live in sin and continue without Torah and its precepts and the love of many brethren has gone cold towards others, they love money and wealth even to the point of slandering each other. They think just because a large crowd follows them they will have a better reward. These people are only compounding their judgment. Right now In She'ol in the place called hell are many Pastors and priests and this was confirmed by a Christian who was given visions of hell and taken there for twenty three minutes and he saw several people being punished for the love of money and among them many Pastors and they were sorry at that time but it was too late for sorry and the judgment could not be overturned. If you are in such a situation then its time to repent now and serve the most High with a sincere heart. I tell you it's not worth it, not even for ten million dollars.

> **Second Peter 2:1-2** (HTHS) But there were false prophets also among the people, even as there shall be false teachers among you, who privately shall bring in damnable heresies, even denying the Master that bought them, and bring upon themselves swift destruction. **2** And many shall follow their pernicious ways; by reason of which the way of truth shall be evil spoken of.

One destructive heresy that has entered many churches is that the sin of homosexuality is OKAY and that men are born with the gene which is an unproven lie and that as long as they show love they can have unnatural relations with other men. These are called civil partnerships in England. The term can apply to both male to male and female to female living together. The Roman Catholic Pope Benedict spoke against this practice of homosexuality recently and was berated by some Christian clergy of breaking the peace since they have fully accepted this deviant behaviour as a modern design of society.

There are many false prophets in Christianity who teach falsehood such as we are not under law while the Torah is clear "**you will not teach falsehood**". The destructive heresy that I described above can only come in when people deny the Torah as the foundation of our faith. These people do not understand what the term under the law means it actually describes being under human law and not YHWH's law and yet these people live under human law and deny it. Foolish!!!

I can only warn you because ungodly Torahless actions will reap harsh judgment, those of you who stand against the Torah you won't stand a chance consider this is a warning to mend your ways!!! It is clear to me that the Christians have been given mercy through the Messiah and many have accepted the King Messiah but there are countless who through lack of biblical education or deliberate ignorant attitudes refuse to accept the King's laws. Many of these represent the Ten tribes but they chose to kick the gourds and refuse to obey (Not true of All Christians though). So by implication you lose the place of your first resurrection but your resurrection will have to wait with the rest which is the **second** resurrection unto judgment when YHWH decides your fate. You would have failed the test for which you were placed here. Eternity is a long time to be wrong.

For me at least this is the most devastating point that although the Saints are to be raised first but most of the world along with those who live disobedient lives in and out of Christian churches will not be raised in the first resurrection. The first resurrection is for the **disciples of Yahushua** only and not for everyone as I demonstrated line by line and precept by precept above.

> **Revelation 20:4** (HTHS) And **I saw thrones, and they sat upon them, and judgment was given to them**: and I saw the souls of them that were **beheaded for the witness of Yahushua**, and for the **word of YHWH** (Torah),[29] and which had not petitioned the beast, neither his image, neither had received his mark upon their foreheads, or in their hands; and they lived and reigned with Messiah a thousand years.

These people who were beheaded by the Islamic End-Times beast were believers who were commandment keeping, Torah loving. How do

---

29 The same people they beheaded will judge those who beheaded them.

we know this? This text has all the nuisances of the Hebrew underneath it. The text said for "**For the witness of Yahushua**". That is because Yahushua quoted the Torah of Moses and said to the Pharisees it bears **witness of Me**!!! It is all about what you witness. You cannot be His witness by living disobediently. The Torah is a witness of the homage we pay to the God of Israel being the Messiah Yahushua (Jesus of Nazareth).

> **John 5:46** (HTHS) For had you believed Musa, you would have believed me: for he wrote of me.

Do you see He is quoting Moses as a witness? This is because Moses would never testify for a **lawless Greek Messiah** but the Messiah was and is a Hebrew Y'sra'elite Yahudim King and very law abiding and law enforcing. By extension the Messiah is also testifying for His lawful disciples who were Torah keepers hence why the reference "THE WORD" of YHWH, which is the idiomatic expression for Torah keepers. Most people would not even see this and just skim past this text. Some Christians don't read the book of Revelations since they are so frightened by the imagery.

> **Revelation 20:6** (HTTS) Beneficial and set-apart is he that has part in the first resurrection: on such the second death has no power, but they shall be kohen (priests) of YHWH and of Messiah, and shall reign with him a thousand years.

To be a priest you have to be set-apart and commandment keeping (that is the only way you become set-apart) else you will not be a priest but a servant of the priests in the kingdom in other words a kingdom slave if you are alive at that time and if you have already died before this time but were disobedient you will not be raised so what is it going to be obedience or punishment? Choose wisely.

So logically the question is who is the disciple of Yahushua? Did you know that you can be saved and you can still be thrown out of the kingdom for lawlessness and not be the disciple of Yahushua? Ah, if only the church realised their error.

Yahushua Himself helped us answer this question.

> **John 8:31** (KJV) Then said Jesus to those Yahudim which believed on him, If ye **continue in my word**, then are ye are **my disciples indeed;**

> **John 8:31** (HTHS) Then said Yahushua to those Yahudim

(Hebrews) which believed on him, If **you continue in my word**, then are you my disciples indeed;

It becomes incumbent on us to know what does remaining in "My word" means because by Messiah's own mouth if you remain in HIS WORD then are you truly His disciples indeed else there is a negative imperative that you are not.

Please note a person can be saved but not necessarily be His disciple and this will affect each person's resurrection status and kingdom status illustrated earlier. Does a father allow his lawlessness son to continue in his home if he has a set of laws of how to behave in his household. If an earthly father does not allow his son to wreck the place then how much so the heavenly Father?

The reference to "My Word" in John 8:31 is the Hebrew idiomatic expression used throughout scriptures to mean to keep and to obey Torah, the first five books of Moses.

In Numbers Chapter 16 Korah's rebellion was essentially against Torah, against the Priests and Levites and I have to say sadly the same heart and mind attitude does exist in many Christians today?

It does not really matter what teaching of the Torah one questions because if you question one you question the whole. You are guilty of rebellion and sin. In other words, if you disagree with the Sabbath or you disagree about eating pork you actually question the Law Giver who is YHWH.

The net result is to live in continuous wilful sin and rebellion. YHWH said rebellion is the sin of witchcraft. No wonder many children are gone astray and do not listen to their parents any longer because the parents themselves have sown rebellion and thus will only reap rebellion!

> **First Samuel 15:23** (HTTS) For rebellion is as the **transgression of witchcraft, and stubbornness** is as **iniquity** and **idolatry**. Because **you have rejected the word of YHWH**, **he has also rejected you** from being Sovereign.

You are meant to be Kings and Priest but by rejecting the words of YHWH you will lose your kingship!!!!

If you question the Law Giver then it's obvious that you have rejected His law even if it is in ignorance. In other words, Moses and anybody coming with YHWH's doctrine/teachings and yes YHWH does indeed have His doctrine versus the world's doctrine. People of this type stand against Moses and predominantly against the God of Israel and His written words. This is why Yahushua said, "You reject Moses' words hence **<u>you have also rejected Me</u>**."

> **Numbers 16:27** (HTTS) So they got up from the tents of Korah, Dathan, and Abiram, on all sides: and Dathan and Abiram came out, and stood in the door of their tents, and their wives, and their sons, and their little children.

This applies to all teachers in and out of churches who teach anti-Torah doctrines against the law of YHWH as unnecessary.

Questions) Should we give the New Testament to the Yahudim in Israel? Answer) Only if you want them to continue to obey Torah then I do not see anything wrong with this practice because YHWH is merciful and may reveal the Messiah to some but the large majority will not be able to identify him no matter how many Bibles are sent or programmes are made for TV. We have to work with YHWH's timing not men. The true Yahudim have to be an identifiable race of people this is how YHWH has ordained it and nothing will change this. The Yahudim or those who call themselves Jews and are Caucasian are not the chosen anyway so whether you give bibles or not they are not true Israel. True Israel was and still is black and brown. In fact you will find more Israelites in the midst of Palestinian Muslims than Israeli Jews. The Black Y'sra'elites in Dimona are the true seed of Israel but they also have some incorrect teachings in their midst where Ben Ammi proclaims himself as the Messiah which is untrue. Is he anointed or The anointed. This is sadly another man who is building his own kingdom wanting to receive high honour.

Chapter 4
Objections to Yahudim being saved

Let us examine this today because some may object.

Here is the classical Christian line, believe in Jesus or you will die in your sin and end up in everlasting punishment.

OK, let's examine this statement a little.

Since Yahushua is YHWH then does Satan believe in YHWH and that YHWH exists? Yes of course he does.

Does he believe that Yahushua was nailed to the tree? Yes.

Then is Satan saved? No.

Therefore, if Satan is not saved then what does believe really mean because it doesn't mean what most are teaching...

Let me ask another question...

Did King Cyrus who YHWH called his anointed believe in Yahushua? No, since Yahushua had not even been born yet as a baby but YHWH managed to save Cyrus. If YHWH can save this king who allowed the Yahudim to go home then how much more those who are not kings?

Did King Cyrus believe in the Messiah's death on the tree? No.
Did King Cyrus believe in the blood? No.

So what did King Cyrus believe in? He believed in the God of Israel and put his trust in him and that is all that was required for him to receive his rescue and his redemption. Does that sound like two doors? No since there is only one YHWH who is Yahushua the Master of heaven and earth there is only one door but most do not realize that this is indeed the case.

Replacement theology

Churches teach that the Jews that is the Orthodox have to be converted to Christianity. The Yahudim men or women after conversion should start eating pork and other unclean foods. So he/she needs to **break Torah** in order to prove their salvation!!! They will be keeping

Christmas not Chanukah they will be keeping Easter and not Passover according to the established Church orthodoxy.

I find this kind of picture extremely disturbing. Yet this error has been taught for 1900 years to this day and continues to be taught. First the Orthodox white Jews are not genetic Israel, second they are keeping Talmudic Judaism so they will not budge. Whether the budge or not they do not present the true Israelites so its foolhardy to even run to them as Christians do.

Anybody who decides to practice Torah and **still believes in the Messiah**, he may be from Kathmandu but he will be heavily criticised by the Christian clergy, have you become Yahudim or are you mad! The word 'Yahudi would be used as a derogatory word against that person.

This is replacement theology by the established Church. So in order to do away with replacement theology what do we need? Do we need more Zionist Christians? No, More Messianics/Nazarenes? No. Then what?

We need the church and the synagogue amalgamated into one akhad unit so both the Hebrews and gentile are one (Akhad)!!! The Christians need to accept the Torah and let the Yahudim teach them how to behave correctly. We are not talking here about Zionism but Torah believing Black Yahudim and there are many who can teach Torah to those who wish to know. We know many Zionist or Ashkenazim are not the children of Y'sra'el but here we are talking about the Torah and not whether you are a biological genetic Y'sra'elite or not.

Let us look at the Debate with Justin and Trypho

Trypho the black Yahudi was a lot smarter than Justin Martyr yet Christians rate Justin Martyr and ignore Trypho! How ironic.

> **Dialog of Justin Martyr with Trypho the Yahudi**
> [30]**Chapter XI.—The law abrogated; the New Testament promised and given by Elohim.**
> "There will be no other Elohim, O Trypho, nor was there from eternity any other existing" (I thus addressed him), "but He who made and disposed all this universe. Nor do we think that there is one Elohim for us, another for you, but that He alone is Elohim who led your fathers out from Egypt with a strong hand and a high arm. Nor have we trusted in any other (for there is no other), but in

---

30 http://www.sacred-texts.com/chr/ecf/001/0010472.htm

> Him in whom you also have trusted, the Elohim of Abraham, and of Isaac, and of Jacob. But **we do not trust through Moses or through the law**; for then we would do the same as yourselves. (for I have read that there shall be a final law, and a Contract/Agreement, the chiefest of all, which it is now incumbent on all men to observe, as many as are seeking after the inheritance of Elohim. **For the law promulgated on Horeb is now old, and belongs to yourselves alone;** but this is for all universally. Now, law placed against law has abrogated that which is before it, and a Contract/Agreement which comes **after in like manner has put an end to the previous one**; and an eternal and final law—namely, Christ —has been given to us, and the Contract/Agreement is trustworthy, after which there shall be **no law**, **no commandment**, **no ordinance**. Have you not read this which Isaiah says: 'Hearken unto Me, hearken unto Me, my people; and, ye kings, give ear unto Me: for a law shall go forth from Me, and My judgment shall be for a light to the nations. My righteousness approaches swiftly, and My salvation shall go forth, and nations shall trust in Mine arm?' And by Jeremiah, concerning this same new Contract/Agreement, He thus speaks: 'Behold, the days come, saith the Lord, that I will make a new Contract/Agreement with the house of Israel and with the house of Judah; not according to the Contract/Agreement which I made with their fathers, in the day that I took them by the hand, to bring them out of the land of Egypt'). [Bold mine]

He continues...

> "For since you have read, O Trypho, as you yourself admitted, the doctrines taught by our Saviour, I do not think that I have done foolishly in adding some short utterances of His to the prophetic statements. Wash therefore, and be now clean, and put away iniquity from your souls, as Elohim bids you be washed in this layer, and be circumcised with the true circumcision. For we too would observe the fleshly circumcision, and the Sabbaths, and in short all the feasts, **if we did not know for what reason they were enjoined you,--namely, on account of your transgressions and the hardness of your hearts.** For if we patiently endure all things contrived against us by wicked men and demons, so that even amid cruelties unutterable, death and torments, we pray for mercy to those who inflict such things upon us, and do not wish to give the least retort to any one, even as the new Lawgiver commanded us: how is it, Trypho, that we would not

observe those rites which do not harm us,--I speak of fleshly circumcision, and Sabbaths, and feasts?

So Justin Martyrs words are clear

- For he said we do not trust through the Law of Moses
- He said the new replaces the old
- There is a new law that abrogates the previous law
- The Torah is for the Yahudim and not Christians as Justin saw it.
- The Torah was given because of the hardness of your heart according to Justin.

I can tell you today that Justin and all those who follow after him are wrong! Justin and all others who reject the law of YHWH and replace him are in for a surprise when and if they get resurrected. Do you know some people will not be resurrected at all?

Psalm 1:5 Therefore **the wicked shall not stand in the judgment**, nor transgressors in the congregation of the right-ruling.

Who are the wicked? Those that refuse to obey Torah.

The first person that I can trace in history who hated the Yahudim and promoted this kind of theology was Marcion of Sinope, 85 to 160 CE. Marcion came on the scene just 22 years after Paulos' death. He cobbled and corrupted Ten of Paulos's letters and then subsequently made his own New Testament document called the Marcion gospel hence removing several documents that he did not like from the Renewed Contract/Agreement writings. He did not include any of the books of the Hebrew Bible that Christians erroneously call the Old Testament.

Marcion was labelled a heretic much later but today Marcionism is prevalent in many churches across the world.

But let us look at the Torah for a second for Salvation!

Deuteronomy 4:30-31 (HTHS) In the **latter days** when days of distress come upon you and if You will **turn around to repentance** to YHWH your Elohim, and shall be obedient unto **his voice**; **(31)** For YHWH your Elohim is a merciful Elohim; he will not forsake you, neither destroy you, nor **forget** the Contract/Agreement of your ahvot (fathers) which he swore unto them.

YHWH's voice is YHWH's Torah and not some new fangled doctrine!

So YHWH said, if you repent in the **<u>latter days</u>**, that means in Simon Altaf's time or even later then YHWH will forgive and rescue these people. But how is that possible without a Temple?

If I ask the Catholics they say I have to join their Mother Church to be saved else I am going to hell. They call it the universal faith.

If I ask the Christians they say you have to repent and believe in 'Jesus' to be saved else you will go to hell.

But what if I just realised that I am Yahudim/Y'sra'elite, supposed to keep Torah so what do I do?

If I join the Catholics I go into Idolatry, if I join the Christians I go into idolatry and in joining both I break Torah and offend the Holy One of Israel. So what should I do?

The ones who are in the sacred names movement say "believe in YHWH and call on the sacred name with a particular pronouncement as the only way and **then** you are saved.

YHWH never said that those who do not call upon Him using the sacred name will not be saved but He did say they will have their names in a special book of remembrance for knowing <u>my</u> name.

So what is wrong with this whole picture?

The only way for Israel!

Let us even take Yahushua and his words, will those Hebrews who believe and keep Torah to the best of their abilities be condemned to hell without the blood of Yahushua? The answer by Christians is yes but actually the real answer is No. You may wonder how this is possible.

כי־פדה יהוה את־יעקב וגאלו מיד חזק ממנו:

> **Yirme'yah (Jeremiah) 31:11** (HTHS) For YHWH has redeemed Yaqub (Jacob), and **<u>ransomed</u>** him from the hand of him that was stronger than he.

YHWH has redeemed Israel as his first born son. Pidya ha-ben is the concept that YHWH shows us in Jeremiah 31:11 for those who understand it. Redeeming the firstborn. Refer to Exodus (Shemoth) and Numbers (We'Dabar) for this:

If it does not spell it out for many of you then let me spell it out for you.

Yahushua came to teach Torah so people would be obedient to it and His blood is already shed for Judah but Judah has not been revealed this truth and will not be revealed until the latter days when its time. They are meant to be in Israel first, this by the way is scriptural.

Let's rewind to Yahushua's time.

> **Yahuchannan (John) 1:1** (HTHS) In the beginning was the Word, and the Word was with Elohim, and the Word was Elohim.

The Yahudi have always had YHWH. How?

The Torah is Yahushua and Yahushua is the Torah. Now have the real Yahudi had the Torah or not? If so then have they had Yahushua or not? The answer is YES. It was Ephraim who had rejected Torah so therefore it is they who needed to return and Judah had no need to return, she was already there in the land in a very small number as a remnant.

Now let me challenge you!

Can you show me if Nicodemus who believed in Yahushua left Judaism?

Or can you show me Yosef of Arimathea left Judaism, he also believed in Yahushua?

Neither did!!!!

Ethnic cleansing

The Y'sra'elites for disobedience were thrown out of Y'sra'el they were carried as slaves by the gentiles nations. This was indeed Elohim's doing for their disobedience.

Are we not guilty of today as acting in the place of Elohim and of emptying Israel by removing Israel with our sermons and lectures and saying we can go to the Kingdom but the Yahudim will be ousted from the kingdom. In our error we forgot that we are doing the same thing as the

Germans did the only difference is that the Germans did it to the Ashkenazim who are not genetic Yahudim but converts into Torah while we are not doing it physically but through the tongue. Both are equally dangerous and high time we repent of such actions.

YHWH Himself blinded Judah and He does not send His blinded nation to hell.

When a rich man comes to Yahushua and asks about <u>salvation</u> what does he say?

Believe in the cross of Tammuz or the real tree where Yahushua died and later rose again.

Do not be unwise about these things any longer!

> **Mattityahu19:17** (HTHS) And he said to him, Why ask me concerning the good? There is indeed one good, if you want to enter into life, <u>**Guard and Do the commandments**</u>.

The Yahudim keeping the commandments means keeping Torah which has the contracts/agreements which would not send one to hell, they already have the Messiah in the allegorical sense. Who is bigger the Father in heaven or the Messiah? In the Renewed Contract/Agreement (NT) it is the Messiah who tells us that Judah is already with the Father (Luke 15:31) then who's testimony will you believe?

The Door is the same <u>one</u> for both.

Will we keep Torah and obey Messiah or will we still try to ram a Roman Catholic derived two line gospel into Judah's throat that already has the words of Torah.

> **Mark 2:17** (HTHS) When Yahushua heard it, he said unto them, They that are <u>**whole**</u> have <u>**no**</u> need of the physician, but they that are sick: <u>**I came not to call the right-ruling, but transgressors.**</u>

The doctor was called for the House of Israel (Ten Tribes), those who were <u>sick</u> and without Torah but not for the Yahudim which were Torah keeping, they certainly had a few issues that could be ironed out but they were not sick. Will you believe the Master or the later church fathers who were all anti-Semitic and anti-Israel that is the true Black Y'sra'elites as they have shown in their indifference to them and even to the converted Jews?

The words of Messiah:

> **Mattityahu 25:32-34** (HTHS) And before him shall be gathered all nations: and he shall separate them one from another, as a shepherd divides his sheep from the goats. **(33)** And he shall set the **<u>sheep on his right hand, but the goats</u>** on the left. **(34)** Then shall the King say unto them on his right hand, **<u>Come, you increased of my Abbah</u>**, **<u>inherit the kingdom prepared for you</u>** from the foundation of the world.

The idiom 'shepherd' means shepherd of Israel, Israel is not being judged the rest are, the <u>seventy</u> nations of the world that is.

When were the Y'sra'elites ever called goats? **NEVER** – The very designation of goats and sheep is to show the difference between true Israel and counterfeit with non-Israel.

Yahushua is judging on behalf of the true **<u>Yahudim</u>**, there is actually a remez (hint) of the holocaust of the African nations which contain many true Yahudim and the people from the tribes. This is the holocaust that no one ever talks about and its never ever shown on television keeping things quiet. These victims of slavery conducted against the members of the household of Israel across the African continent conducted by the Europeans and financed by European Jewry which are not the genetic seed of Israel. People would not normally see this as it is also 'sod' (hidden) in the text.

In the prayer taught to His disciples by Yahushua it says the following:

The Jubilee

> **Mattityahu 6:12** (HTHS) And forgive us our debts, as we forgive our debtors.

The idea here is not that you are begging for forgiveness and there is continual hard work on your part to receive forgiveness like climbing a mountain with your knees but the Messiah is pointing to two main themes, the year of Shemita (release of all debts) every seven years and Yahubel (Jubilee), 7 times 7. This is how the book of Revelations is also a theme of Sevens and about the annual celebrations of kul Y'sra'el!

Now let me ask the question, on the year of shemita, where did I have to be to receive a release?

Where did I have to be in the year of Jubilee? **In the Land of Israel of course! I am not going to be forgiven my debts if I am out of the land and none of the other tribes are present so this shows that the only way the Jubilee will be acted when the tribes are back in the land by definition.**

Did I have to squat in my leased out house to receive it back? If no then why not? This is because the release is automatic for the people of the land. It is called grace, **unmerited favour** of YHWH. **Its for all of Israel**. Did YHWH say Simon you were living in Pakistan but now that you are in Israel the release does not apply to you? Or does YHWH say that you live in England and I cannot give you unmerited favour? YHWH's laws span the whole world not just Israel otherwise it would be nothing but an exclusive club like the scientologists keeping everything secret. YHWH's jubilee applies to the whole of Israel and the laws are universal however due to many technical factors Israel has not been celebrating the Jubilee for two millennia since our people the true Hebrews are not in the land in their twelve tribes while the only ones claiming to be us are the Ashkenazim the self chosen.

> **Numbers 15:15** (HTHS) One ordinance shall be for you of the congregation and for the foreigner who lives among you, an ordinance forever throughout your generations; as you are, so shall the foreigner be before YHWH.

Yahushua says this:

> **Mattityahu 13:16-17** (HTHS) And increased are your eyes because they see, and your ears because they hear,**(17)** for truly I say to you, that many prophets and right-ruling ones longed to see what you see, and did not see it, and to hear what you hear, and did not hear it.

Do your eyes see it or are you still chasing after the counterfeit Israel? Do you ears hear the message of the Torah of Musa?

So the ones who did not see it were they saved?

King Solomon's the Black king's prayer in First Kings 8, which YHWH acknowledges in First Kings 9:3 while the gentiles continue to make movies showing him as a Caucasian which he was not just like the rest of Israel.

Melekhim Alef (First kings) 9:3 (HTHS) And YHWH said unto him, **I have heard your prayer** and your supplication, that you have made before me: I have set-apart this Temple, which you have built, to **put my name there forever**; and **my eyes and my heart shall be there forever**.

John 17:3 (HTHS) And this is life eternal, that they **might know you** the only **true Elohim, and Yahushua The Messiah**, whom you have sent.

It would be wrong to say that the true black Yahudim in the Diaspora did not know the Father because they already knew him and pray through Him.

Did those Yahudim not say Avenu Shab Shaymayim? Our Abbah who is in the heavens? They even acknowledge the coming of the Messiah with prayer daily asking for him to come quickly.

Now the Contracts/Agreements!

It is automatic and YHWH grants it therefore the Contract/Agreement part is with YHWH and not man, Israel is in YHWH's hands for complete forgiveness.

Let me prove it to you.

Wa'yikra (Lev) 25:10 (HTHS) And you shall consecrate the fiftieth year, and proclaim **liberty throughout all the land unto all the inhabitants thereof**: it shall be a Yahubel unto you; and you shall return every man unto his possession, and **you shall return every man unto his mishpacha** (family).

Note ladies and gentlemen **liberty** throughout the land, what land?

Israel!

When – On the Yahubel (Jubilee). **COMPLETE FREEDOM**.

John 10:11 (KJV) "I am the good shepherd. The good shepherd gives His life for the sheep.

The good shepherd lays his life down not the sheep killing themselves over acquiring eternal life. Did not the Roman Catholic Church teach that those who get martyred to free Jerusalem during the crusades will go to heaven? Now go and study the history of the crusades from the 10th century to the 12th century how they murdered and pillaged on their way to Jerusalem. They killed the sheep instead of leading them to Israel!

> **Revelation 22:15** (HTHS) For outside are dogs, and those enchanting with drugs, and those who whore, and murderers, and idolaters, and **whosoever loves and practices falsehood**.

Have the so called Church fathers practiced falsehood? Yes they have by telling lies that the Torah is abrogated.

We do not see any Yahudim mentioned in Revelation 22:15 but we do have gentiles mentioned as dogs. If a gentile became a proselyte to the faith of the Messiah being Nazarene/Messianic Judaism then they would no longer be called dogs.

By the description of this scripture Constantine indeed was a dog, a heathen dog for that, who corrupted much of the true faith and murdered many true Yahudim and the true believers of Messiah.

> **Zechariah 2:12** (HTHS) And YHWH shall inherit Yahudah (Judah) his portion in the set-apart land, and shall choose Yerushalim, (Jerusalem) **again**.

Even the prophet Zechariah shows us YHWH will choose Jerusalem once again, to repeat His earlier choice. Why?

> **Psalm 89:34** (HTHS) I will not break My Contract/Agreement, nor change the words that have gone out of my mouth.

The Contract/Agreement that YHWH mentions includes eternal **life** and not just life on the earth. YHWH is categorically saying, **I will not break my Contract/Agreement which means many in churches are teaching error still. There goes your so called seminaries and their trained Pastors, Bishops the blind leading the blind.**

> **Psalm 89:4** (HTHS) Your seed I will establish forever, And **build up your throne to all generations**. Selah

Why would YHWH establish the Yahudim to throw them all into hell?

> **Joel 3:16** (HTHS) YHWH also shall roar out of Zion, and utter his voice from Yerushalim; and the heavens and the earth shall shake:

> but YHWH will be the **hope** of his people, and the **strength of the children of Y'sra'el.**

We are not just talking about temporal hope like when they are being obedient but also when they are disobedient. Just as an earthly father will not let go of his children when they are disobedient how much more our Father in heaven?

> **Yeshayahu (Isaiah) 45:25** (HTHS) In YHWH shall **all** the seed of Y'sra'el be made right-ruling, and shall esteem in him.

How much is this ALL? Kul ha eretz (All of Israel) Faithful Torah believers, the blinded tribe of Judah as well which many are still outside the land. Do you want to really find the true tribe of Yahudah then let me tell you where some of these are today. Let's visit Africa, Ethiopia, Nigeria, Gambia, Ghana, Kenya, Chad, Jamaica, North America, Canada and Europe to name a few places and even as far away as China.

> **Psalm 129:5** (HTHS) Let them all be confounded and turned back that hate Tsiyon.

Who hates Tsiyon? If you think it's the Muslims you would be dead wrong. It's the Zionists who hate true Israel the black Israelites since Tsiyon does not just represent the hill but the total people of true genetic biological Israel.

> **Zechariah 2:10** (HTHS) Sing and rejoice, O daughter of Tsiyon: for, lo, I come, and I will dwell in the midst of you, says YHWH

Yet we know YHWH, who was revealed in Yahushua will come back and dwell in Jerusalem and not London, Paris or New York, even though the latter three are famous for fancy perfumes and open idolatry. You can read all about politicians, sportsmen and their clandestine affairs in the New York Times. You can read all about footballers and TV stars and starlets with their illicit affairs in The Daily Sun in London.

> **Isaiah 40:1-2** (HTHS) Comfort you, comfort you my people, says Your POWER. **2** You speak comfortably to Yerushalim, and cry to her, that her warfare is accomplished, that her iniquity is pardoned: for she has received of YHWH's hand double for all her transgressions.

Comfort them without ramming the man-made European gospel.

Deuteronomy 6:25 (HTHS) And it shall **be our right-ruling**, if we **observe to do all these commandments before YHWH** our POWER, as he has commanded us.

It shall be our "right-ruling" if we observe to do all that YHWH commanded. This is talking about Torah obedience, not calling to some new Western Jesus that you find on each street corner. Even mortal men are naming themselves Jesus Christ in the West. This is a typical scenario in the West Jesus on the door, Hello I am Jesus please follow me.

My response to Jesus selling on doors, who are you? Mormon, Jehovah witness or scientologist?

Fake Jesus; I have come to impart eternal life if you join my church.

I: What is the name of the Father?

Fake Jesus: Err, emm, I think it is the same as in your bible?
Myself: And what would that be?

Fake Jesus: Jehovah
I: That is not His name. Don't you know that there is no J in the Hebrew?

Fake Jesus: Err, emm, Oh we just anglicize it and pronounce this in English.

I: What is the mission of the Messiah?
Fake Jesus: To spread love to the world.

I: wrong. He is supposed to gather the lost sheep of the House of Israel (Matt 15:24).

Fake Jesus: Who? House of who? Do you mean the Yahudi?
I: No. Thank you Mr Jesus for your appearance but it is not needed here. Bye, bye.

Messianic Judaism is true because it ties in with the faith of our forefathers. It does not lead us to a false God. It does not lead us away from Torah. It does not lead us away for the purposes and restoration of Israel.

Deuteronomy 28:1 (HTHS) And it shall come to pass, if You shall listen carefully to the voice of YHWH your Elohim, to Guard and to

> do all his commandments which I command you <u>this</u> day, that YHWH your Elohim will elevate you high above all nations of the world.

So how come YHWH says that He will guard and raise up Israel high above all nations but then you come to believe in this Western style "Jesus", and start eating pork, crabs, lobsters, things he calls an abomination, do no keep the seven Biblical annual feasts and suddenly you are still saved (Admitted foods do not remove salvation) and you are being lifted up high above the nations and the poor black Yahudi is left behind defending his Torah? This is the craziness out there.

Do you see the problem? It's actually the opposite. You lose your rewards in the millennium but he gains it hence why Zechariah 8:21 is true. So we know that the Messiah came to teach Torah and to repair the Tikun Olam for Israel.

> **Yeshayahu (Isaiah) 45:4** (HTHS) For Yaqub (Jacob) my servant's sake, and Y'sra'el my elect, I have even called you by your name: I have surnamed you, though you have not known me.

> **Yeshayahu (Isaiah) 45:17** (HTHS) But Y'sra'el shall be rescued in YHWH with an everlasting rescue: you shall not be ashamed nor confounded anymore.

Is there even <u>one</u> witness from the Disciples of Yahushua and I am saying Disciples the twelve that says the Israelites that <u>**obey**</u> Torah is not saved?

You will not find them. Not even one!!!!!!!!

Today we are told that we should not enter Orthodox Yahudim synagogues because they do not know Yahushua meaning the Christian "Jesus", because these Yahudim are unsaved, this is plain brainwashing and an error indeed. Why would anyone sincerely keeping Torah be not saved?

The Yahudim even Orthodox those sincere whether converts will receive their rewards.

We can also go to their synagogues so do not follow the error of the anti-Yahudim church fathers. Admitted many may not be genetic Israel but that is a different issue. We are here only discussing pure Torah obedience.

Yeshayahu (Isaiah) 29:10 (HTHS) **For YHWH has poured out upon you the Ruach (Spirit) of deep sleep**, and has closed your eyes: the prophets and your rulers, the seers has he covered.

Wa'yikra (Lev) 18:5 (HTHS) You shall therefore keep my statutes, and my judgments: which if a man do them, he shall have life (Eternal) in them: I am YHWH.

Hopefully this will allow us to see where we must work to bring reconciliation both to the dispersed true Yahudim and Christian people! It's time to leave the fake and find the real to bring increases and benefits to your lives.

Chapter 5
Beheading & suicide bombings– The weapon of the beast

The Bible is clear that the Anti-Messiah forces will use these tactics and the Bible spells it out sometimes very clearly. Let us examine these aspects.

> **Revelation 20:4** (HTHS) I saw thrones, and they sat upon them, and judgment was given to them: and I saw the souls of them that were beheaded for the witness of Yahushua, and for the word of YHWH, and which had not petitioned the beast, neither his image, neither had received his mark upon their foreheads, or in their hands; and they lived and reigned with Messiah a thousand years.

Various people have been beheaded in different parts of the world where the radical Islamists are active and this is clearly a phenomenon the Bible describes as belonging to the final Empire. If one has read history he will realize that Rome never practiced beheading but instead burnt people on the stake so this rules them out as the End-Times Beast pointed to in Daniel 7 and Revelation 13.

The prophets of the Bible give us evidence that the End-Times beast will kill by bombs and not just mere bullets. How do we know this?

> **Isaiah 14:20** (HTHS) You shall not be joined with them in burial, because **<u>you have destroyed your land</u>**, and slain your people: the seed of evildoers shall never be renowned.

The 2005 Sharm el-Sheikh attacks in Egypt were done using a Truck bomb. The Islamabad Marriott Hotel bombing in Pakistan, which occurred on 20 September 2008, was also done using a dump truck.

Note that both of the above bombings occurred in Islamic States and Isaiah clearly tells us that the bombings will be in Islamic lands and the beast will kill its own Muslim people. It also tells us that the Anti-Messiah who is coming from Turkey will destroy and kill people in his own country too meaning in Turkey. There were bombings in Turkey both in 2006 and in 2008. Saudi Arabia has also been attacked by radical Muslim bombers who blew up the Khobar towers in June 25, 1996. Once again this was a truck bomb that almost demolished the entire building.

http://en.wikipedia.org/wiki/Khobar_Towers_bombing

Building #131 after the bombing.

> **Isaiah 14:20** (HTHS) **Isaiah 14:20** (HTHS) You shall not be joined with them in burial, because **you have [shawkat] destroyed your land**, and slain your people: the seed of evildoers shall never be renowned.

The radical Muslims have been destroying their land by suicide bombings and terrorism killing their own. The play on words is only apparent in the Hebrew tongue where the same word used for killing an animal for the sacrifice is used in a similar way for the destruction; the difference is one character at the end, a Hebrew Tet opposed to a Hebrew Tav. They have been slaughtering their own people by beheadings and others with a knife as a butcher would just as Isaiah describes.

שחת Instead of שחט . This is only revealed through Hebrew wisdom.

Therefore the Anti-Messiah's people will cut with a knife, cut what? The jugulars of people just like the animal i.e. beheading (Revelation 20:4).

What about suicide attacks where do we see this phenomenon in the scriptures?

We know about this but it is hidden under the text.

In Genesis 6 we are told about this fact below:

> **Genesis 6:4** (HTHS) There were Nephillim (fallen ones) on the earth in those days; and also afterward, when the sons of Elohim came in to the daughters of men, and they bore children to them, these were the mighty men who were of old, men of name.

Many get confused at this statement. It tells us a little elaborated detail about the sons of YHWH who were angels which are still bound in the abyss that made a pact at Mount Hermon and then descended to corrupt the women and impregnated them with children. The idea was to corrupt the line of Messiah in which they failed. Lilith the first woman created was involved in this.

The angels then produced offspring which at times killed both the mother and child as the offspring erupted or burst open in the wound being too large for the mother to cope. This is in symbolizing with the Beast which also has certain offspring that erupts and bursts in this case with suicide bombs. The other offspring grew into giants and started eating all the wildlife and vexing the earth sore until YHWH had to send the flood. The same way the Beast is killing other people by terrorism and in the end this will lead to Armageddon.

> **Enoch Chapter 7:7 (African-Israel translation)** Then they swore all together, and all bound themselves by mutual execrations. Their whole number was two hundred, who descended upon Ardis, which is the top of Mount Hermon.[31]

Ezra was not wrong when he said that the many writings are not for all the people and only the wise need to study them while for the majority leave them searching in the Bible and that is where they will remain because they will not understand anything this is typically the gentile Christian world and others.

> Make public the twenty-four books that you wrote first and let the worthy and the unworthy read them. But keep the seventy that were written last in order to give them to the wise among your people. For in **them is the spring of understanding**, the **fountain of wisdom**, and **the river of knowledge**. 4 Ezra 14:45-47

The river of knowledge is a reference to the books of Enoch.

Since Christians have a hard time understanding the Bible what chance is for them to understand the extra canonical texts? Without a real desire and detailed and deep learning in a Yeshivah (Yahudim teaching centre) probably very few will get that type of understanding this

---

[31] Mount Herman.

is why we at African-Israel run a Yeshivah to teach deep truths not evident. Personal study is absolutely essential and unfortunately most think they can just sit and get it all by air through the Holy Spirit but forget that without adding a strict regimen their study will not progress or without diligent teachers of the Torah it will be vain as they will fail to understand the simplest idioms.

Chapter 6
The Anti-Messiah Islamic, Turkic and Muslim

One of the interesting phenomena you will find in the West is that everything is coloured as western white. For instance look at the pictures of Yahushua that the Western churches make and He looks like a man from Scandinavia hardly resembling that of Yahushua of Nazareth who was a black African Yahudim. You look at Santa Claus (Father Christmas) an invented Character from St Nicholas, he looks nothing like St. Nicholas the Bishop of Myra of Turkey. Then the West idolises a white Christmas when it is abundantly clear to many who read the Bible and understand its various precepts that Yahushua was not born in December but during the feast of Sukkoth (Tabernacles). Turkey even invented a Santa stamp in 1955 to attract people to Turkey, which indeed worked because they realised that St Nicholas was born in Turkey and it would be a good way to bring in tourists.

The West seems to be obsessed with snow during Christmas and jingle bells with twenty-fifth of December which is not the day of birth of Yahushua but a pagan day. They seem to be obsessed about mince pies and Turkey none of which has anything to do with Jerusalem or the Messiah of Israel. When did Africans ever eat Turkey? Or did you not know that Israel is a North-Eastern African country?

One can understand these things are only treated as traditions in the West, I guess there is nothing wrong with people doing their traditions as long as it is understood that you cannot reflect Roman Catholic and Protestant traditions on to first century Israelite worldview. If we look at the writings of Polycarp the disciple of John he would absolutely not accept an Easter Sunday and always celebrated the Passover feast on Nissan 14 and he even went to meet Roman officials to convince them to drop Easter Sunday but history records for us that they did not listen and here we are with paganism and your so called Church tradition.

[32]Irenaeus records this:

> And when the blessed Polycarp was sojourning in Rome in the time of Anicetus, although a slight controversy had arisen among them as to certain other points…For neither could Anicetus persuade Polycarp to forego the observance [in his own way], inasmuch as these things had been always observed by John the disciple of our Lord, and by other apostles with whom he had been conversant; nor, on the other hand, could Polycarp succeed in persuading Anicetus to keep [the observance in his way], for he maintained that he was bound to adhere to the usage of the presbyters who preceded him. And in this state of affairs they held fellowship with each other; and Anicetus conceded to Polycarp in the Church the celebration of the Eucharist, by way of showing him respect (Irenaeus. FRAGMENTS FROM THE LOST WRITINGS OF IRENAEUS. Translated by Alexander Roberts and James Donaldson. Excerpted from Volume I of The Ante-Nicene Fathers (Alexander Roberts and James Donaldson, editors); American Edition copyright © 1885. Electronic version copyright © 1997 by New Advent, Inc).

The prophet Isaiah said who has believed our report and to whom is the arm of YHWH revealed (Isa 53:1). It's clear to me at least that even the western Christians have not believed in the report of the prophet Isaiah. They continue to portray a man from Nazareth that is inconsistent with the scriptures. Likewise the Western European and American prophecy writers now idealises with the anti-Messiah being European or far worse American. Every prophecy writer out there seems to have their clock stuck at Europe while Europe has nothing to do with producing the man of sin, there are plenty other men of sin here aught to do with prophecy. Once again it is clear that the masses which follow after this European anti-Messiah theory do not read their Bibles and if they do they certainly have no understanding of the subject and just follow after the wind and will one day reap the whirlwind. The bible is a closed book for blind eyes and unless the eyes have been opened by Em Chokmah (Mother wisdom the Holy Spirit) you will never see things as they are meant to be seen.

Scripture gives these various names to the Anti-Messiah.

The Anti-Messiah was spoken of by many prophets in these names

---

32 http://www.cogwriter.com/polycarp.htm

1. The Assyrian (Micah 5:6)
2. Gog (Ezekiel 38:2)
3. The Anti-Messiah or Antichrist (1 John 2:22)
4. Son of Perdition (2 Thess 2:3)
5. The Lawless one (2 Thess 2:8)
6. Man of Sin (2 Thess 2:3)
7. Lucifer correctly the light-bearer (Isaiah 14:12)
8. The house of the wicked (Hab 3:13)
9. The plunderer (Isa 21:2)
10. "King of Babylon (Isa 14:4)

The title of **The Assyrian** is also given because he is from a particular geographic region of the middle-east and not Europe.

Abraham was also called an Assyrian from the region of south-eastern Turkey where he was born because the Anti-Messiah is also out of Turkey. None of the above titles of the anti-Messiah do not at any time portray that he is from Europe. In fact clear Biblical passages contradict all European theorists yet they continue to teach error and countless are deceived as a result error is taught.

> **Jeremiah 51:27** (HTHS) Set up a banner in the land, blow the shofar among the gentile nations, prepare the gentile nations against her, call together against her the kingdoms of Ar-arat,[33] Minni, and Ashchenaz; appoint a commander against her; cause the horses to come up as the rough locusts.

Ashchenaz - The term Ashchenaz is the term for European nations that will form an alliance and go against the anti-Messiah nations of which Turkey and Iran will be two key nations. It is already apparent to me that they are forming an alliance against Israel and the West and these things will become more apparent near the time. This one scripture is enough to rule out any anti-Messiah ever arising out of decadent Europe. However I will present more evidence to prove that such theories are built on incorrect reading of scripture and do not line up with ancient nations names.

Minni – This is thought to be the nation of Armenia however it is actually the ancient biblical text for a nation in Africa that will join the alliance. Right now the most likely candidate is South Africa but that can

---

[33] See footnote Genesis 8:4 HTHS Study Bible.

change. Nigeria is another candidate for Har Minni which is where the Ark of Noah landed near Lake Chad. See the Hidden-Truths Hebraic Scrolls for more details.

The Assyrian (Micah 5:6)

> **Micah 5:6** (HTHS) And they shall waste the land of Assyria with the sword, and **the land of Nimrood in the entrances there**: thus shall he rescue us from the Assyrian, when he comes into our land, and when he treads within our borders.

When was Nimrood the Black Cushite king ruling a kingdom in Europe?

Land of Assyria – Assyria was never bordered in Europe or ever ruled Europe in its past. It ruled primarily middle-eastern nations.

Land of Nimrood – The land of Nimrood for most Bible commentators is Iraq but that is not true. The Land of Nimrood was actually from Turkey all the way to India but he was born in Africa and was a Kushite ruler but he went into Iraq to make the Tower of Babel. He was sent away from the south to the north from his brother Raamah who ruled eastern Arabia which is Eastern part of Africa but Nimrood through his conquests gained more territory than his brother in the South who ruled the regions of Eastern Arabia.

You will find in Turkey a mountain called after his name Nemrut Dagi (the mountain of Nimrood). This is also where the seat or statue of Zeus and Heracles was placed. The present day people in Turkey did not just come up with these things but they have traditions of these stories going back thousands of years and the only reason they have the traditions is because the stories are in fact true mostly. The cave of Abraham where he was hidden as a baby is also in Turkey and that story is also true because Nimrood tried to have him killed. The story also comes in the life of Yahushua where Herodes tried to have him killed. Nimrood was related to the father of Abraham these were black rulers, Abraham was a ruler priest's son who was also a man of colour.

> **Book of Jasher (Yashar) 8:35** And Terah took Abram his son secretly, together with his mother and nurse, and **he concealed them in a cave**, and he brought them their provisions monthly.

All these stories in the past cannot be just written off as legends because they have happened over and over again in different people's lives and teach us patterns in the Bible and they also teach us lessons on how the end of days will come upon us.

> **Micah 5:5-6** (HTHS) And this man shall be **The Shalom**, when **the Assyrian** [The anti-Messiah] shall come into our land: and when he shall tread in our palaces, then shall we raise against him **seven shepherds**, and **eight principal men**. **6** And they shall **waste the land of Assyria** with **the sword**, and **the land of Nimrood in the entrances there**: thus shall **he rescue us from the Assyrian**, when he comes into our land, and when he treads within our borders.

In verse five of Micah it speaks about the seven shepherds who shall waste the land of Assyria. I spoke somewhat about these shepherd nations in the part one of this book that these nations are likely to be the following in my opinion;

- **USA**
- **UK**
- **Italy**
- **Spain**
- **Australia**
- **Northern Russia**
- **South Korea**

These are the main nations but they may have other subgroups of European nations also but these are the shepherd nations. While many are incorrectly taught that the whole world will be in the grip of the anti-Messiah this is not true and not consistent with scripture. The anti-Messiah will only control nations that are Islamic and again it will be a loose alliance not a firm one. This means that all fifty two Muslim nations will **not** take part in the war. This also means that not all Muslims everywhere will be part of the alliance so cannot be called Radical or Islamist in the same way. This is very easy to understand. Some nations prefer to go to war and some don't. Scripture shows us the alliance which I mentioned in this book of nations centred in the Middle-East that will join. For instance Turkey and Iran and Kurdistan are one pact nation while Saudi Arabia, Sudan, Yemen are another pact. In fact in the various alliances that will form we will see some Muslim nations hostile against others. Scripture tells us this because this is what will bring about the destruction of the Ka'aba in Mecca in general.

> **Revelation 17:16** (HTHS) And the ten horns which you saw and the beast**, these shall hate the whore**, and shall **make her desolate and naked**, and shall eat her flesh, and burn her with

fire.

Since the harlot is Mecca in Saudi Arabia or Saudi Arabia itself then in fact it is scripturally correct to say that the harlot is the **whole region of Arabia** that the ten kings will make her desolate so its regional and not just one city of Mecca. This is in fact a province. Who are the ten kings? Well I can reveal to you that three of them are as follows.

1. Turkey
2. Iran
3. Pakistan (loose alliance with Saudi Arabia only)

These three are in the pact of the ten kings.

> **Revelation 13:1** (HTHS) And I stood upon the sand of the sea,[34] and saw a beast rise up out of the sea...

It is clear to me that if the beast is Islamic then so is **the Harlot** because scripture places her in the middle-east and not in Europe. In Revelation 13:1 we are told in no uncertain terms that the beast rises out of the sea.

> **Jeremiah 51:13** (HTHS) O you that dwell **upon many waters, abundant in treasures**, your end is come, and the measure of your covetousness.

In Revelation 17:1 we are told that she sits upon waters which according to the angel means peoples, tongues and nations Rev 17:15. This again fits with Arabia as she has 65% of the international work force which according to Rev 17:5 fits with different nations, and different languages of people. However in Jeremiah 51:13 we are told she dwells by many waters abundant in treasures. The only treasure that is abundant by Saudi Arabia is the oil and once again we know she is surrounded by literal seas. We also know that this cannot be Rome as Rome has no oil reserves or deposits in her regions by the sea. Furthermore, here in Jeremiah the term "waters" cannot refer to peoples as in Rev 17:15 because the text in Jeremiah says "dwellest upon many waters abundant in treasures". Clearly if the term "waters" in Jeremiah means peoples then Saudi Arabia has no treasure to reap out of foreign nationals who are all very poor. Plus to fit the reference with Daniel this water is indeed the surrounding seas.

---

[34] A terminology to mean desert region used from Isaiah 21:1. This region is Saudi Arabia.

> **Revelation 17:2** (HTHS) With whom the Sovereigns of the earth have committed whoring, and the inhabitants of the province *of the Middle-East*[35] have been made drunk with the wine of her whoring.

It is also evidenced that this nation is rich in oil and Saudi Arabia controls 26% of the world oil supply. This is the "wine of her whoring" that the kings of the earth were made drunk with to make unrighteous decisions concerning Israel and even the Christians in amongst their nations who they allowed to be persecuted and put down.

An Ethiopian woman one of many went crossed over to Yemen to go find a job in Saudi Arabia. Many Ethiopians in search of work have been doing this which is bringing misery to their own lives from what they are finding. The woman crossed over to Saudi Arabia then found work as a house maid. She was promised a nice salary and started the job. Three weeks into the job she seemed to be happy treated well in this well to do Saudi couple until one day nearing her four weeks she asked the boss for her salary. Being alone in the house he then tore her clothes and raped her not paying any money. He then continued to rape her daily and subject her to abuse. She was usually locked up in her room and then one day finding the room unlocked she fled to Yemen from there airlifted by the Ethiopian government back to safety in Addis Ababa. This happened in 2012 October time frame. This story is not just of one Ethiopian woman but of many who are still trapped there. When I tell people do not go to Saudi Arabia to work they don't listen. I was myself offered a job there in my profession for 50,000 UK Pounds tax free but I refused to go work there as I know what is coming there. I know of cases where other black maids who were physically abused by the wife in the house by beatings and lashing. This is nothing new to me as I know many Saudis are wicked people too stuck up in their opulent luxuries.

The reference to waters cannot be taken to mean that this is nations, tongues and peoples because that meaning is secondary but primarily it must match with the Tanak (Hebrew Bible erroneously called Old Testament by Christians) with what Daniel the prophet said;

> Daniel 7:2-3 (HTHS) Dani'el spoke and said, I saw in my vision by night, and, behold, the four winds of the shamayim strove upon the **<u>great sea</u>**. **3** And four great beasts came up from the sea,

---

35 See footnote Rev 11:10.

diverse one from another.

The Great Sea is confirmed by both Daniel and Joshua to be the Mediterranean Sea since both Israel and Saudi Arabia border this sea.

> Joshua 9:1 (HTHS) And it came to pass, when all the Sovereigns which were on this side of the Yardan (Jordan), in the hills, and in the valleys, and in **all the coasts of the great sea** over against Lebanon, the Hittite, and the Amori, the Canani, the Perizi, the Chivi, and the Yebusi, heard there;

Now get yourself a map or go to Google maps on the internet and see where Lebanon is and you will find it borders the Mediterranean Sea which confirms my view that Saudi Arabia is mentioned in the reference of Revelations 17:1 is the nation at hand.

Burden of the desert

> **Isaiah 21:1 (HTHS)** The burden of the wilderness of the sea. As whirlwinds in the south pass through; so it comes from the wilderness, from a terrible land.

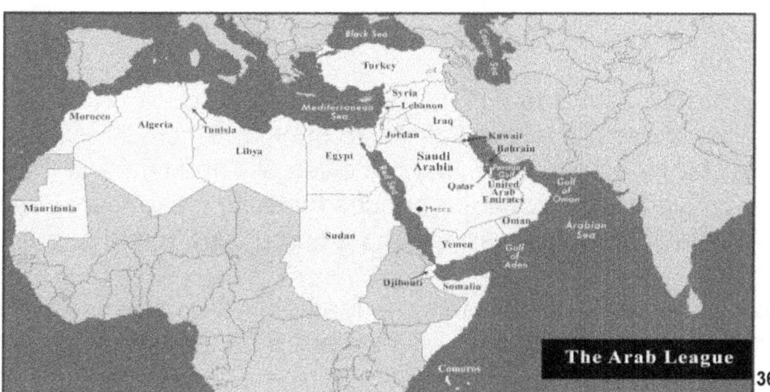

[36]

THE TRUE HARLOT IS SURROUNDED BY THE waters:

- Persian Gulf
- Arabian Sea
- Red Sea
- Gulf of Aden
- Gulf of Oman
- Mediterranean Sea
- Caspian Sea

---

[36] www.prophecymaps.com

- Black Sea.

There is no scriptural basis for placing the harlot in Europe and saying it is Rome. Once again Christians have been a bit too liberal with their pens and come up with theories untrue.

> **Jeremiah 51:7** (HTHS) Babylon has been a golden cup in YHWH's hand that made all the earth drunk: the nations have drunk of her wine; therefore the nations are mad.

If we assume that Babylon is Rome for a minute then when was it a golden cup in the hand of YHWH? The wine that scriptures speak about here is the black gold (Oil). The text in Jeremiah says all the nations are mad with her intoxication. Let's apply this to Rome's gospel then if Rome is mad then are all the Christian groups that came out of it mad too but this text just does not fit the model. Rome was never a golden cup but Saudi Arabia was. How is that explained? Well let's see if we can understand this. Today many Countries in the world are filled with terrorist acts predominantly the ones responsible are Islamic radicals so this shows us that Master Yahushua could use these to punish nations for their disobedience.

Seems hard? Not so. Let me show you.

> **Jeremiah 25:17-18** (HTHS) Then I took the cup from YHWH's hand, and made all the nations to drink, to whom YHWH had sent me: **18** To, Yerushalim, and the cities of Yahudah, and the Sovereigns there, and the princes there, to make them desolate, an astonishment, a hissing, and a curse; as it is this day;

This passage just shows us that the Master YHWH can use the cup in His hand for punishment to the nations since it happens to be Babylon then it also means that the suicide bombings are allowed by the Master Himself just like the invasion of Babylon was allowed into Israel and many men, women and children were crushed before Judah was taken off as captives. From this we may understand the cup is a sign of judgment or increases but primarily the Master has used it for judgment against Israel and other modern nations today. His protection is off since they are destroying his commandments. In the UK in May 2010 there were 65,000 abortions paid for by the tax payers estimated at over thirty million pounds. The majority of these abortions were wholesale murder of babies sponsored by British money. Then the UK public wonders why they are being attacked by terrorists! Wake up. It's the transgressions in the land where unjust murdered babies' blood cries out for justice to the throne room of YHWH.

Why would the ten Islamic kings hate the harlot and make her desolate or burn her which is yet to come. It is clear this will be caused by internal and external factions within Islam also helped by the west which plays both sides. We have already seen bombings in Saudi Arabia the regions of the harlot so once again it proves that if they can bomb the place then by bombing a place you do not grow flowers there but you destroy it and burn it. This was also evident when Saddam Hussain fired scud missiles on the Islamic holy land. It is marked for destruction and one day that will be accomplished. Behind this destruction is also Western greed and judgment on the West for their bad behaviour as illustrated in this book.

Micah 5 also speaks about the Assyrian coming into our land meaning Israel and Jerusalem. In ancient history the Assyrian Empire has been able to invade Israel and capture many cities but has never been able to invade Jerusalem but in this case the anti-Messiah who will be able to enter Jerusalem and plunder East Jerusalem as Zechariah the prophet tells us.

> **Zechariah 14:2** (HTHS) For I will gather ALL NATIONS against Yerushalim to battle; and the city shall be taken, and the houses rifled, and the women raped; and half of the city shall go forth into captivity, and the residue of the people shall not be cut off from the city.

The term for "All nations" applies to Islamic nations because we are told that they are roundabout Israel. Those that teach that ALL nations is the whole world once again demonstrate their ill education of the bible and they need to realign their prophecy with scripture.

> **Zechariah 12:2** (HTHS) Behold, I will make Yerushalim **a cup of trembling to all the people round about**, when they shall be in the siege both against Yahudah and against Yerushalim.[37]

Unless you believe that America or England will help the Islamic nations bomb Israel you will find that the theory of ALL Nations only applies to Islamic nations that will take part and scripture once again tells us that not all 52 Islamic countries will take part but it emphasises surrounding nations. We are also shown in Ezekiel 38:1-5 that there are other nations of the CIS which are southern Russian Islamic states.

---

37 The radical nations will lay siege in the future to capture Jerusalem.

Fifteen of those states are Muslim such as Kazakhstan, Dagestan, and Uzbekistan. Please note all of these states will take part to a certain extent.

Gog (Ezekiel 38:2)

The Anti-Messiah is Turkic

> **Ezekiel 38:2** (HTHS) Son of man, set your face against **<u>Gog, the land of Magog</u>**, the chief prince of Meshech and Tubal, and prophesy against him,
>
> The Schaff-Herzog Encyclopaedia of Religious Knowledge, citing ancient Assyrian writings, places the location of the land of Magog in the landmass between ancient Armenia and Media, in short, the republics south of Russia and north of Israel, comprised of Azerbaijan, Afghanistan, Turkistan, Chechnya, Turkey, Tajikistan and Dagestan etc. Significantly, all of these nations are Muslim nations today.

Is it any wonder that most of these kingdoms are at war? The term Meshech or Meshek and Tubal or Tabal were kingdoms or nations in ancient Turkey in the central regions of Turkey after the Hittite empire and ruled in that region. We know this is true because Josephus Flavius the Yahudim historian verifies this for us in his writings.

> **Ezekiel 38:3-4** (HTHS) And say, Thus says the Master YHWH; Behold, I am against you, O Gog, the **<u>chief prince of Meshech</u>** and Tubal: **4** And I will turn you back, and put hooks into your jaws, and I will bring you forth, and all your army, horses and horsemen, all of them clothed with all sorts of armour, even a great company with bucklers and shields, all of them handling swords:

The verse could be read "I will challenge you", YHWH mentions in verse 4 a few important details that help us to identify this army clearly and also YHWH speaks to the nations that will come up at the End of Days e.g. latter times.

- **Horses**
- **Horsemen**
- **Splendidly clothed**
- **Bucklers and shields**
- **Swords**

Turkey was known for its horses. The famous Turkoman horse from which today we have the thoroughbred horse. The Turkoman was well known for its swift speed and agility. The horsemen, and their splendid clothing, the Ottomans were well known for their ferocious armour both on the horses and on the riders. The Turks had specially crafted shields and a peculiar kind of sword a sabre that was used by them. The Janissaries in the Turkish army were feared by the nations and were very fierce fighters.

YHWH mentions putting hooks in their jaws to draw them out, this indicates that the army is indeed Assyrian since we know that Micah 5:6 talks about the Assyrian entering the land of Israel. The Assyrians had a peculiar habit of taking slaves from the booty and putting hooks in their cheeks and dragging them on bare foot, likewise YHWH indicates that the same fate will be meted out to them. Here many become confused that if this is the Assyrian Empire what has Turkey to do with it. Most of Turkey was conquered by the Assyrians therefore they have everything to do with it.

> **Ezekiel 38:6** (KJV) Gomer, and all his bands; the house of Togarmah of the north quarters, and all his bands: and many people with thee.

The KJV bible makes an incorrect translation by which many people are thrown off to look to Russia by translating the Hebrew word tsafon Yereka as the North quarters and the NKJV says the "far north".

In actual fact the words there in the Hebrew translate to <u>Northern sides</u> or <u>northern recesses</u> and not the far north which puts an incorrect slant on the translation. We can see that in the same translation of the KJV in Exodus 26:23 the word is correctly translated as "sides."

> **Exodus 26:23** (KJV) And two boards shalt thou make for the corners of the tabernacle in the two <u>sides</u> (Yereka).

The Hebrew word tsafon also indicates to us that this is a <u>concealed</u> army and drawn out by YHWH himself since the Hebrew word tsafon has the meaning for North is also used for the place of Heaven the throne room of YHWH, which indicates YHWH has purposely drawn this army out to reveal himself to the Islamic nations.

> **Ezekiel 38:5** (HTHS) Gomer, and all his bands; the house of Togarmah of the <u>north sides</u>, and all his bands: and many people with you.

The Anti-Messiah or Antichrist (1 John 2:22)

> **First John 2:22** (HTHS) Who is a liar but he that denies that Yahushua is the Messiah? He is the anti-Messiah, which denies the Ab and the Son.

We find that in the Brit ha Chadasha the ReNewed Contract (NT) gives us a key piece of information that the Anti-Messiah will deny the Father and the Son. It does not say that he will accept one and reject the other but it is clear that it is a conjugated statement and both must be true in order for the Anti-Messiah to fit. Many use this scripture to say that the Yahudim deny the Messiah so therefore by definition they are anti-Messiah. This is not so. The Yahudim do not deny the Father in heaven, in fact the very prayer that Yahushua taught the disciples came out of Yahudim traditions and literature. The true Yahudim are the people of the Contract/Agreement who have maintained the Contract/Agreement of YHWH faithfully and therefore are ruled out as the Anti-Messiah nation.

> **First John 2:23** (HTHS) Whoever denies the Son, the same does not have the Ab: (but) he that acknowledges the Son has the Ab also.

Many of the people out there may say that the Yahudim deny the Son Yahushua as the Messiah so must be the anti-Messiah's people then how can they have the Father as scripture says whoever denies the Son the same does not have the Father. The problem is that the scripture above is not put in to sideline the Yahudim and that is exactly what Christians have been doing for thousands of years. In fact the term "whoever" or "whosoever" applies to men or Adam meaning to <u>gentiles</u> (non-Yahudim). John's context of whoever or whosoever is a midrashic expression and therefore in the first century its idiomatic usage does not apply this statement to the Orthodox Yahudim but it applies to any person of non-Yahudim dissent. This then brings the Muslims back into focus as the qualifying people for this statement.

This idiomatic expression can also be seen in Ezekiel 34 and John 3:3. John uses this phrase this way on many occasions. John makes a very interesting statement in First John 2:1 where most Christians just gloss through his statement without any understanding of it.

First John 2:1 (KJV) My little children, these things I write to you, that you transgress not. And if any man transgresses, we have a Counsellor *of justice* with the Ab, Yahushua Messiah The Tzadik (Right-ruling One):

John applies the title "The Right-ruling One" to Melek Yahushua but in Hebrew the word is pronounced Ha Tzadik. This has a very important designation in Kabbalah, the mystical study of the Torah. The Tzadik is also the phrase also known as the Middle-Pillar so John was applying a highly esoteric term, which actually all Orthodox Yahudim believe in and also represents to Adam Kadmon the first man or to the Son of YHWH in this case Melek Yahushua but the Yahudim see this as the primordial man while we know that the primordial man or template upon which the first human was created was indeed Melek Yahushua. The Yahudim correctly hold that the middle-pillar comprises of the Crown and the beauty which leads to the Foundation, which is called the Kingdom (malkhut) through the Yesod Renewed Birth.

We therefore in Messianic/Nazarene Judaism know and have understood just like John that the Middle-Pillar applies to Melek Yahushua the Messiah who at this moment is concealed from the corporate entity of the Yahudim. This is why the prophet Isaiah predicted that they will not believe His report nor recognise Him (Isa 53:1-5). While Christians are dogmatic of Yahudim converting over to Christianity and making them pork eaters, scripture does not mandate any such thing to the Contract/Agreement holders as they need do no such thing and remain in the Contracts/Agreements and obey YHWH who at His appointed time will reveal the Messiah to them. In fact if truth be told most of the Christian doctrine has arisen out of Babylonian paganism and worship and not what YHWH has commanded but this topic is too vast to be dealt within this book. Most of what Christians are taught is incorrect or wrong anyhow little do they know they follow men's doctrines and not Abbah YHWH's.

For instance the crucifixion of Yahushua was at the Mount of Olives (Heb 13:12) and not at Calvary or the Holy Sepulchre the Constantinian invented Church. The hanging of Master Yahushua was on a tree (Deuteronomy 21:22 and Acts 5:30) according to the Torah and not on the Cross of Tammuz the Babylonian deity and abomination that is displayed as a sign which was never used by the disciples of Master Yahushua. This sign and the translation of this particular text does not exist in any manuscript before the 4th century CE as it came about in the 4th century CE to align with Constantine and his doctrine of the cross which was an Egyptian cross of the mummies. He was not a believer in any sense of the word but a gentile idolater.

The resurrection of Master Yahushua and the burial Tomb of Master Yahushua was also on the Mount of Olives and not Gordon's tomb once again invented by the your so called Church system in the 19th century CE, so much for truth coming from the Church, not likely anytime soon. It was common practice for the Roman's to hang criminals on trees when they ran out of crosses. Master Yahushua was stoned to death while on the tree (Mark 15:44, Lev 24:14-16, Acts 14:19, Gal 6:17 and Gal 3:13) and scripture makes that point clear about His immediate death within three hours by being bled profusely to line up with the prophecy in Isaiah the prophet (Isaiah 52:13-15) after being on the Tree.

The Orthodox Yahudim disagreement is whether this applies to Yahushua or another person yet to come, however they do not disagree with the Middle-Pillar nor the term THE TZADIK being Adam Kadmon or the one who repairs the breech Tikkun Olam. We as believers should know who Adam Kadmon is but the Yahudim are kept from certain knowledge according to Isaiah and therefore it is a mistake to force them to see or accept a religion invented in the late 1st century CE by apostate people like Thebuthis, Marcion and Paulinsim and this is what one historian wrote:

> **Hegesippus**
> "And after James the Just had suffered martyrdom, as the Lord had also on the same account, Symeon, the son of the Lord's uncle, Clopas, was appointed the next bishop. All proposed him as second bishop because he was a cousin of the Lord."
>
> "Therefore, they called the Church a virgin, for it was not yet corrupted by vain discourses. But Thebuthis, because he was not made bishop, began to corrupt it. He also was sprung from the seven sects among the people, like Simon, from whom came the Simonians, and Cleobius, from whom came the Cleobians, and Dositheus, from whom came the Dositheans, and Gorthæus, from whom came the Goratheni, and Masbotheus, from whom came the Masbothæans. From them sprang the Menandrianists, and Marcionists, and Carpocratians, and Valentinians, and Basilidians, and Saturnilians. Each introduced privately and separately his own peculiar opinion. From them came false Christs, false prophets, false apostles, who divided the unity of the Church by corrupt doctrines uttered against God and against his Christ."

Hegesippus the Nazarene; c. 185 CE; quoted by Eusebius in Eccl.Hist. 3:32)
"Up to that period (98 CE) the Assembly had remained like a virgin pure and uncorrupted: for, if there were any persons who were disposed to tamper with the wholesome rule of the proclaiming of salvation, they still lurked in some dark place of concealment or other. But, when the sacred band of Emissaries had in various ways closed their lives, and that generation of men to whom it had been vouchsafed to listen to the inspired Wisdom with their own ears had passed away, then did the confederacy of godless error take its rise through the treachery of false teachers, who, seeing that none of the emissaries any longer survived, at length attempted with bare and uplifted head to oppose the proclaiming of the truth by proclaiming "knowledge falsely so called."

This makes it clear that Master Yahushua certainly did not espouse a new religion. He was very much part of Judaism and preached and practiced the similar to Judaism while many of today's Christian denominations resemble nothing of the early faith and government of YHWH.

Because the Yahudim believe in the Middle-Pillar and the Tzadik Son it rules them out entirely from the Anti-Messiah nation. As I said the Middle-Pillar is also called Adam Kadmon or the primordial man. Please look up on this as this is too exhaustive a subject to cover in this book. Many false teachings that are rife in churches will one day have to be removed including all the phallic symbols such as the steeple of the churches and the crosses. Any wonder why the synagogue does not have the phallic symbols such as the steeple and cross but have the Star of David and contrary to the false opinions of Hebrews its not an occult, it's a valid symbol derived from the six petel pomegranate and Lily flower of true Israel. The other symbols of true Israel is the Menorah and the Torah scrolls. These are set-apart symbols and indeed correct. Even Islam builds upon the phallic symbol of the steeple by building huge minarets.

Jeremiah 16:19 (HTHS) O YHWH, my strength, and my fortress, and my refuge in the day of affliction, the nations shall come to you from the ends of the earth, and shall say, Surely our ahvot (fathers) have inherited lies, vanity, and things wherein there is no value.

Who do you think these people in Jeremiah are? May I suggest Christians of all flavours and dispensations?

The Son of Perdition (2 Thess 2:3)
The lawless one (2 Thess 2:8)
The man of sin (2 Thess 2:3)

The common theme between these three is the one which is the person who is the anti-Messiah leader and supreme Caliph of Islam defies the law of YHWH, the Torah of Moses. This is why the title **son of perdition** which means son of damnation, the lawless one is easy to see the one who is against the laws of YHWH the law that is being measured is the Torah of YHWH and not Israel's present secular law. The third title the man of sin is once again telling us that the anti-Messiah does not hold up the standard of Torah as his law but holds up another standard which we know is Islam operating on the Sha'ria (Islamic law principle).

Even though many Christians do not keep the Torah of Moses which they should these titles do not strictly apply to Christians or Catholics because they do not deny the Father and the Son. Some people contend that the Catholic people only acknowledge the Son Yahushua by mouth but really are not saved. The argument is mute because YHWH's standard is to obey His Torah and He gives unmerited favour to His people by circumcising their heart and that is what is termed the New Birth. Now be honest and ask yourself can you really be born of above and deny the laws/Torot of YHWH? This is the state of many in Christendom so to argue that one is born again or not is futile. The important thing is to know that this person the Anti-Messiah stands against the principles of the Master Yahushua and His principle for Israel or His law is the Torah delivered to Moses. He did not come to abrogate it or deny it (Matt 5:17-18) Therefore any man or woman who refuses to obey the law of Moses which is actually the law of YHWH and not Moses as such in my mind is not born of above but only born in his own mentality. Here is scripture to prove my thesis.

> **First John 5:2** (HTHS) By this we know that we love the children of Elohim, when we love Elohim, and follow his commandments.

John is pretty clear that to know if one is in the New Birth he will be obeying the "commandments", this is an idiomatic expression for obeying the Torah of Moses. The reasons why most Christians get prophecy and the interpretation of scripture wrong is that they start from the book of Matthew then look back to interpret the whole Bible but this is completely the wrong way to interpret scripture. We must start from the beginning the book of Genesis because it has keys to our understanding and interpret it forward and not backward. The example is like watching a movie in the cinema when you walk in the movie in the last 30 minutes and then expect to interpret what happened in the first hour by watching the end by either asking the guys there before you or just doing a guessing game. I have seen many theologians in Christendom with PhDs, religious degrees and their interpretation of the Bible is absolutely flawed because they do the same mistake looking at the Renewed Contract/Agreement (NT) to try to interpret the Tanak (Hebrew Bible) through the Renewed Contract/Agreement (NT) which is the wrong way. We go from Torah to the Tanak and interpret the Renewed Contract/Agreement in light of the Torah and not vice versa.

Many do not have a revelation that Israel is not just black but not just two tribes but twelve and they incorrectly fit the bride to the church but without understanding that this bride that was divorced is the prophetic and literal picture of Ephraim (The Northern Ten tribes) but they try to lump the Yahudim into this but do not realise that Judah is mentioned as a separate bride (Ezekiel 23:2) and was not divorced therefore cannot be lumped with the Christian church. Judah or the Yahudim have a special economy and are always in the hands of the Father in heaven (Luke 15:31).

Lucifer or the light-bearer (Isaiah 14:12)?

> **Isa 14:12** (KJV) How art thou fallen from heaven, O Lucifer, son of the morning! How art thou cut down to the ground, which didst weaken the nations!

This one we need to look at a bit further to understand it. The translation in the King James Version is not accurate for the term Lucifer but let us see what the Hidden-Truths Hebraic Scrolls bible reveals:

> **Yeshayahu** (HTHS) How you have fallen from the heavens, **light-bearer**, <u>**son of the crescent**</u>! How are you cut down to the ground, which did weaken the nations!

There are five terms we need to understand in this verse:

- The word Lucifer, which is actually Light-bearer.
- The son
- The Crescent

The word <u>Lucifer</u> was inserted by Jerome in the 4th century CE. This is a Latin word and has no place in the Hebrew Tanak considering the prophet Isaiah wrote seven hundred years before Master Yahushua was born and he would not have written in a language that was not yet even spoken nor invented unless he was shown a symbol to do with Latin, which we know now looking at the copper scroll of Isaiah was not the case either. The meaning of the Hebrew word Shahar is crescent moon, a symbol of Islam showing us that the Anti-Messiah will be from one of the Muslim nations. The word is incorrectly translated in many dictionaries and simply glossed over as "light" or light-bearer but the definitive meaning behind this word in this text is the "crescent" or the morning crescent, which can also be found in the text of Judges 8:21 and Isaiah 3:18. These other texts show us that Scripture is our best interpreter not modern day Bible dictionaries that have many wrong meanings behind words.

The word son here can be very deceptive unless you understand what YHWH is trying to tell us, this will be the dark power the power of Satan that will build up Islam! The crescent will be its symbol and Satan will be its leader mentioned in Revelation 9:11. Its uncanny how on 9/11 this power was manifested to the modern world when the twin towers were taken down in the US, while most people are running after a One World Order, which is a distraction and subterfuge to lead away from the true signs of The Beast.

Now that we understand these terms it then helps us to formulate our understanding correctly.

> **Isaiah 14:13** (HTHS) For you have said in your heart, I will ascend into the shamayim, I will exalt my throne above the stars of El: I will sit also upon the Mount of the congregation, in the sides of the north:

The description in these texts is of Satan but it is reflected into a future man, which we now know to be the Anti-Messiah, who weakens nations.

The house of the wicked (Habakkuk 3:13)

When scripture applies the term "wicked" it is not signalling out one person only but is signalling out the whole clan, tribe or nation. In our modern terms we apply the term wicked to any person who is not saved however in the text of Habakkuk it is not applied like that. The house of the wicked or Dar ul Islam (House of Islam) is all Islamic who distort the Torah by saying we believe in it but modifying many principles in it to confuse the masses.

> **Habakkuk 1:8** (HTHS) Their horses also are swifter than the leopards, and are more fierce than the evening wolves: and their

horsemen shall spread themselves, and their horsemen shall come from far; they shall fly as the eagle that hurry to eat.

This is a clear prophecy that these armies coming up to fight Israel are Turkic, many do not realise that Abraham was called a resident of Ur which is a city in Turkey and not Iraq. Also the people who only see Nebuchadnezzar as ruling Iraq do not realise that his reign extended to South-Eastern Turkey also. One of the finest horses Turkoman is from there from which we get the thoroughbred horses today. The Turkic horses are known for their speed and endurance and make an excellent war horse. Note the tale of Troy and the Trojan horse ever wonder why a horse was used in Turkey then? The Arappaloosa is a middle-eastern horse and is spotted and also very famous, its interesting that YHWH describes the horse swifter than the leopards, note leopards are spotted too!!!

These armies that are marching forward are therefore Islamic End-Time armies from the middle-east to fight with Israel and not European.

The plunderer (Isaiah 21:2)

One of the Islamic traits is to raid the enemy and collect their goods as booty. This is also one of the things the Anti-Messiah has in mind to collect booty an Islamic trait. The leader gets 20% and the rest is shared out to the others.

Sura Al-Anfal 8:41 And know that whatever of war-booty (plunder) that you may gain, verily one-fifth (20%) of it is assigned to Allah, and to the Messenger (Muhammad or any future leader), and to the near relatives, (and also) the orphans, Al-Masâkin (the poor) and the wayfarer, if you have believed in Allah and in that which We sent down to Our slave (Muhammad SAW) on the Day of criterion (To decide that the Muslims are right and infidels are wrong), the Day when the two forces met (This was the battle of Badr or any future battle) - And Allah is Able to do all things.

Sura Al-Ahzab 33:27 And He caused you to inherit their lands, and their houses, and their riches, and a land which you had not trodden (before). And Allah is Able to do all things.

Book2, Hadith 35:
Narrated Abu Huraira: The Prophet said, "The person who participates in (Holy wars) in Allah's cause and nothing compels him to do so except belief in Allah and His Apostles, will be recompensed

> by Allah either with a reward, or Booty (if he survives) or will be admitted to Paradise (if he is killed in the battle as a shaheed - martyr). Had I not found it difficult for my followers, then I would not remain behind any sariya going for Jihad and I would have loved to be martyred in Allah's cause and then made alive, and then martyred and then made alive, and then again martyred in His cause."

From this it can be understood why today some people are killing themselves as suicide bombers as this is seen as striving for Allah for an external Jihad against the enemy and these people are taught that to kill yourself is not suicide but martyrdom for Allah and for this cause they will enter paradise and will not be judged for their sins.

So these days when good Muslim men and women are going to be offering themselves as suicide bombers they are not doing it because they have no money and are destitute but they are taught the Qur'an with its literal meaning or the straight meaning though disputed by moderate Muslims and the Hadith to show them that what they are doing is not haraam (illegal in the eyes of Allah) but halal (right in Allah's eyes) and so many of these actually come from very good Muslim homes which believe it or not are moderate too. Osama bin Laden is a fine example and if you look at the Al-Qaeda top leadership they are all from good educated backgrounds and not from off the street or poor backgrounds. Ayman Al Zawahiri was a surgeon before he joined the ranks of Al-Qaeda and from a wealthy family a far cry that poverty is the cause of Islamic terror. The cause of Jihad is simply the spiritual teaching of the Qur'an manifesting in the physical but most deny it for political expediency.

Habakkuk also tells us the following:

> **Habakkuk 1:17** (HTHS) Shall they therefore empty their net, and not spare continually to slay the nations?

Those of you who believe it is the Roman Catholic Church will have to prove that the Anti-Messiah is currently killing various people in different nations by violent means. However only one religion today is responsible to kill with violent means and that is radical Islam. Rome did kill in the past and is not innocent but that era has now passed. Rome is no more truth than modern versions of Christianity that parade out as YHWH's truth but its not but denying the law of YHWH is denial of the very Son they claim to uphold. John Wesley the creator of the Methodist assemblies did not deny the Law of YHWH and even kept the 7th day Sabbath, while most modern Methodists today do not follow after their founder. Here is what he said:

[38]**Methodist: Jesus did not abolish the moral law - no command to keep holy the first day**

The moral law contained in the Ten Commandments, and enforced by the prophets, He Jesus did not take away. It was not the design of His coming to revoke any part of this. This is a law which can never be broken ... Every part of this law must remain in force upon all mankind and in all ages; as not depending either on time or place, or any other circumstances liable to change, but on the nature of man, and their unchangeable relation to each other." John Wesley, Sermons on Several Occasions, Vol.1, No. 25

You will even find Baptist denominations in the old days keeping the 7th day Sabbath, while most modern Baptists do not.

My point is this that if you are going to call Rome the religion of the Anti-Messiah then to be consistent you would have to call today's Christianity also the religion of the Anti-Messiah however we cannot do this because both acknowledge the Father and the Son and therefore corruptions aside they cannot be the religion of the coming Anti-Messiah and so do not fit.

"King of Babylon (Isaiah 14:4)

This description tells us that the Anti-Messiah will rule and reign Iraq for a time in the near future. This may be the violent take up of Iraq by a future Turkic leader. Many thought this was Saddam but he was not Turkic and neither the Anti-Messiah but simply a type and shadow. Others have tried but also failed. This one that will come will succeed. So we can see that all the prophets that spoke about this particular Islamic person in using different terms all point to an Islamic charismatic leader who will woo the world but later show his true colours. Turkey is already showing its colours but many are still failing to see them. The takeover does not mean necessary war it can also occur by proxy for a ruler who submits to Turkey.

[39] *03/01/2010* **Is Erdogan Strong Enough to Take on the Generals?**

---

38 http://www.abcog.org/nh/sabsun.htm

39 http://www.spiegel.de/international/world/0,1518,680907,00.html

By Daniel Steinvorth

Last week's arrest of military brass amid allegations of a plot against the Turkish government have dealt a serious blow to the country's secular elite. But some are asking if Prime Minister Erdogan has bitten off more than he can chew.

Four-star General Cetin Dogan, 69, has a fondness for luxury. Shortly before his retirement, the army veteran, who until five years ago was the commander of the First Army of the Turkish armed forces and a feared hawk, bought a three-story beach villa in the resort town of Bodrum on the Aegean Sea, where he intended to spend his golden years.

But that vision is not likely to materialize, at least not for the foreseeable future. Last Monday, police officers with Turkey's counter-terrorism force TEM searched Dogan's dream house. The general himself was arrested in Istanbul, where he was taken away in handcuffs. No one had ever treated him like that before.

Ibrahim Firtina, 67, was also taken by surprise. The heavyset four-star general, with his bushy, Leonid Brezhnev-style eyebrows, was the commander of the 60,000-member Turkish Air Force, the pride of Anatolia, for four years. Like Dogan, he too was considered a member of the country's top military brass, an untouchable "pasha."

That was until last Monday, when police rang the doorbell at his villa in Ankara. When the pasha opened the door in his robe, his wife called out: "What do they want from you?" "You are under arrest," one of the officers said. "You have half an hour to say goodbye. Please take only a few essentials with you."

Arresting 'Golden Boy'

At about the same time, a special task force paid a visit to Özden Örnek, 67. The retired commander-in-chief of the Turkish navy, a man who was considered highly talented from an early age, a high flyer his wife affectionately referred to as "Golden Boy," was worshipped like a demigod while in office. Even after going into retirement, Örnek was fond of wearing sparkling, white uniforms in public. The police officers took him into custody while he was having breakfast. "Excuse us, Admiral, but we must arrest you now," they said politely.

The charges against Firtina, Örnek, Dogan and 64 other retired and active senior officers who had been arrested throughout the country by last Friday are monstrous: Prosecutors in Istanbul claim that the suspects planned to blow up a popular mosque in the city and shoot down a Turkish fighter jet to provoke a military crisis with NATO partner Greece. Under Turkish criminal law the suspects, if found guilty of establishment of and membership in a terrorist organization, could face at least 15 years in prison.

Turkey has almost become accustomed to news like that. Images of raids and arrests of presumed conspirators against the government have been flickering across television screens for more than two years now. But in the most recent police operations on Monday and Friday, the targets were not, as in the past, obscure figures from the right-wing nationalist scene. This time investigators are taking on some of the highest-ranking generals of recent years, the self-proclaimed "guardians" of the legacy of Mustafa Kemal Atatürk, the founder of the modern Turkish state.

There have been four military coups in Turkey since 1960, and since the arrests many Turks have been wondering if the army would strike back. Had Prime Minister Recep Tayyip Erdogan gone too far?

Erdogan's Huge Self-Confidence

At the moment, however, it doesn't seem as if the government is the least bit intimidated by the army. Erdogan continues to rule the country unchallenged. In fact, it is more the army that seems nervous. When he heard of the arrests, the Turkish army's chief of staff, General Ilker Basbug, immediately canceled a trip to Egypt. Meanwhile, the prime minister, who was on a trip to Spain, remained cool. "The judiciary is doing its work," he commented.

In fact, so far Feb. 22 marks the culmination of a power struggle between the conservative Islamic Erdogan government and the secular military in Turkey, possibly even a preliminary victory for Erdogan. "The untouchables have been touched!" the pro-government daily newspaper *Zaman* wrote in jubilation. "An operation without precedent in the history of the republic," the newspaper *Sabah* commented. Erdogan has so far managed to survive all attempts by the military and the courts to drive him out of office and is now in his strongest position in a long time.

The generals have been subdued. The fact that Basbug apologized to the prime minister two years ago when Erdogan's wife was denied entry to a military hospital because she was wearing a headscarf attests to a huge cultural turning point.

"Good news for Turkey, good news for democracy," says Istanbul journalist Mustafa Akyol, who points out that there is nothing more erroneous than the belief that the Turkish army was the guardian of democracy for decades. "The opposite is the case," says Akyol. "They deprived us of democracy."

The European Union, too, ought to be pleased. Hasn't it called upon the Turkish government for years to finally curtail the power of the military?

Part 2: The Army Strikes Back

But if the Kemalist elite truly relented, it would the first time in the history of the republic. In fact, retaliatory measures already seem to be taking shape. For months, the Kemalists in the judiciary system are believed to have been preparing for a new trial with the intention of banning Erdogan's Justice and Development Party (AKP), and Abdurrahman Yalcinkaya, 59, Turkey's chief public prosecutor, is making sure that the word gets around. "The parties can sense whether or not they will be banned," he predicted in early January.

Yalcinkaya was also the one who filed the first petition, in 2008, to deprive the AKP of its power. He described it at the time as a "center of anti-secular activities." His petition initially failed before Turkey's constitutional court, but this clearly has not deterred Yalcinkaya. The son of a Kurdish family from south-eastern Turkey and the grandson of a sheikh in the devout Naqshbandi order, he is seen as Turkey's most principled lawyer. He also keeps a watchful eye on his adversary, Erdogan, at all times.

"The senior members of the judiciary are afraid that their representatives could also be taken away in handcuffs," says Mustafa Sentop, a law professor. For this reason, a new petition to ban the party would be a welcome means of reining in the AKP. It would be the latest in a long series of attempts by lawyers and military officials to force Erdogan out of office.

Since his historic victory in the 2002 parliamentary election, Erdogan, who is the son of a seaman from the working-class Istanbul neighborhood of Kasimpasa and sees himself as an enlightened Islamist, has been a thorn in the side of the traditional governing elite. The more Erdogan managed to convince the West of his democratic intentions, the more the Kemalist establishment hated him.

An Assault on Modern Turkey

For the generals, much of what Erdogan has done is nothing short of an assault on the foundations of modern Turkey. He eliminated the notorious state security courts, allowed the Kurds to use their own language, pledged to resolve the dispute with Greece over Cyprus, and even had a draft constitution written up that would subject the military to civilian control.

But what could the military do to turn the tide? The generals quickly recognized that the legal and political tools for removing Erdogan were limited and that attempting to acquire power the old-fashioned way was no longer an option these days. The reputation of the Turkish army was on the line. "The days when the army would stage a coup are gone," General Ilker Basbug conceded.

Nevertheless, a small, ultra-nationalist group, which included some very high-up decision-makers, thought about ways to undermine the popular government.

In March 2007, the magazine *Nokta* published the conspirators' alleged plans, in the form of the so-called "coup diaries" of Navy Commander Özden Örnek.

Örnek claims that these notes are not authentic, and he was temporarily released last Thursday. According to the coup diaries, the presumed leader of the conspiracy, General Dogan, who is still in custody and was indicted Friday evening, was supposedly planning a remake of the brutal military coup of 1980. The arrest and detention of tens of thousands of "enemies of the state" in football stadiums were as much a part of the plot as the formation of a puppet government. Dogan's alleged grim scenario even had a name: "Sledgehammer."

War Games

Another plan, dubbed "Cage," included murders of non-Muslim minorities. Bombs were to be detonated in Christian and Yahudim neighborhoods of Istanbul, and businesspeople were to be kidnapped. The goal was to ensure that the blame would be assigned to Islamists, and that the resulting massive pressure from abroad would force the administration to step down.

Although a spokesman for the Turkish army did not deny the existence of the "Sledgehammer" document, he described it as a "war game" typical of the military. The pro-government newspaper *Zaman*, calling this a weak excuse, wrote: "This plan is much too good to be just a game. Operation 'Sledgehammer' is the most detailed coup plan in the history of Turkey." The Kemalists' response seemed rather helpless by comparison. A retired officer, who chose to remain anonymous, calls it an "audacious smear campaign against secular Turkey."

Sedat Ergin, a journalist with the high-circulation daily *Hürriyet*, expresses himself more cautiously, noting that it is much too early to distinguish between fact and fiction. "There are too many documents at the moment, and their authenticity still has to be checked."

The fact is, however, that the Turkish military is under great pressure to investigate the accusations against the alleged conspirators within its own ranks. It needs to make its position clear. Things are getting tight for General Basbug, who insisted until recently that the coup plans were fabricated. During a meeting with Erdogan and President Abdullah Gül which was called last Thursday in a bid to reduce "tensions," Basbug promised to clear things up.

Islamized Democracy?

It is surprising, however, that the enthusiasm over the arrests voiced in the pro-government press has not caught on elsewhere, neither with the Turkish population nor with Europeans. Could this

> be because many Turks and Europeans don't completely trust the prime minister? Is Erdogan, who is probably the most powerful prime minister in the history of the Turkish republic, truly a flawless democrat?
>
> Not according to some Turks. "We are being put under pressure," complains one trade union secretary. "Nowadays, people are only joining the pro-government, religiously oriented unions." An attorney says: "The Justice Ministry is doing its best to seat its own people on the appeals court." And a teacher reports: "They are in all key positions. We have city administrations loyal to the AKP, governors loyal to the AKP, district administrators, school principals and police officers." The journalist Burak Bekdil, a prominent critic of Erdogan, wonders what kind of a democracy Turkey can be if only the military is being democratized, while the AKP's people are being installed in all other sections of society. "Is that an Islamized democracy?" he asks.
>
> Power belongs "in the hands of the people," Erdogan promised in a campaign speech a few years ago. He is of course right. But many Turks are now wondering which people he is referring to.[40]

This story is proof that Turkey is leading towards Islamic rule of law rather than the Army dictating liberal values.

Turkey is increasingly aligning itself with the Palestinian authorities and speaking against Israel and has been speaking against the Gaza war during 2008/2009/2010. This is not to say that the Palestinians are wrong but the Zionist government in Israel is fully corrupt and does not want peace with the Palestinians. Every effort made by the Palestinians for peace is rejected therefore Israel which has been carelessly killing Palestinians in Gaza will only reveal its ultra agenda motives in which one cannot say the Palestinians do not want peace. The Palestinian reactions of firing rockets towards Israel's indiscriminate killing of Palestinians is thus understandable.

There has been much Muslim effort to help the Palestinians even before this such as introducing a new drink called Mecca Cola from which certain profits are used to fund the PA Government in the Palestinian

---

40 Translated from the German by Christopher Sultan

regions. It's a shame that the PA Government is not helping its people more to help in their financial situation.

http://en.wikipedia.org/wiki/Mecca-Cola

This is also a call against the Coca Cola brand in the US considered to be of course Christian and hostile to the Muslims.

The other soft drink to come up to fight the popular drink Seven-Up is called Muslim-Up a rival to Seven-UP. But once again both these Mecca Cola and Muslim-Up are French and started by Muslims in that region. This is why we see more and more French Muslims are very anti-Western and anti-Israel. From this we can learn we are heading towards a bigger war between Muslims and the Zionists which will ultimately clear the illegal occupation of the Zionists to bring in the true chosen of Israel.

Israel is not great as many Christians blindly say it but Israel has many unruly actions of wickedness against Muslims and Christians and these are going to lead to the destruction of those who claim the land as theirs when it isn't the so called self appointed chosen.

Another look at Daniel 7

> **Daniel 7:2-3** (HTHS) **2** Dani'el spoke and said, I saw in my vision by night, and, behold, **the four winds of the shamayim strove upon the great sea**. **3** And **four great beasts** came up from the sea, diverse one from another.

There is another esoteric hidden meaning behind Daniel 7. The four winds that were stirring the great Sea are four angels of YHWH which have been specially appointed for this task. Why the four winds (angels) of heaven and not 6? This is because this is connected from Genesis with the four rivers in the Garden of Eden. (Gan Eyden)

> **Genesis 2:10-14** (HTHS) And a river goes out of Ayden to water the garden; and from there it separated, and became four heads.

11 The name of the first is Pishon: that is which is roundabout the whole land of Chavilah (Saudi Arabia/West Africa), where there is gold; **12** And the gold of that land is good: there is bdellium and the onyx stone. **13** And the name of the second river is Gihon: the same is that runs roundabout the whole land of Cush. (Sudan, south of the river Nile including Nubia, Ethiopia and parts of east Africa). **14** And the name of the third river is khidekel (Tigris): that is which goes toward the east of Ashshur. (North Iraq – Mosul an area of Assyria). And the fourth river is Euphrates. (Turkey)

The four rivers signify the four major beasts

Four heads – four kingdoms.

- Pishon - meaning to "disperse"
- Gihon - to break forth – violently
- Hiddekel - means to Prick to sting
- Euphrates - Root word for fruit – Parats means to "break" forth in great numbers.

The four heads are the four corners or axis of the world the North, the South, the East and the West. Note the river Pishon encircles Havilah, which is the area of northern and southern Saudi Arabia. This means that Pishon, which means to disperse is the religion of Islam which will disperse from Saudi Arabia into the four corners of the world. The Garden is the analogy for Israel and also for the people of YHWH. The beast will encompass all these and be around them. The gold in Saudi Arabia/West Africa is not just physical gold but also attributed to black gold this is why this Pishon River is important. Note the fourth river tells us the location of the End-Times Anti-Messiah as it comes last in the mention of the rivers in Genesis telling us that this is indeed Turkey, which I have shown you before where the Anti-Messiah makes his start.

Pishon (Arabia) goes over to the beast including West Africa as many are Islamic today.

Gihon – River Nile, Cush was to go over to this beast meaning given to Islam.

Tigris – this area also goes over to the beast and the area of the Euphrates goes over to Islam. The river Tigris and Euphrates meet in Basra and move on together emptying into the Persian Gulf. This shows an alliance between Iran and Turkey in the end of days this is clearly given in Isaiah 13 and Ezek 38.

Euphrates – Also belongs to the Beast given over to Islam the area of Turkey. The Hebrew word paretz the root word means to break forth. Turkey will break forth in the end of day upon Israel. The ancient Hebrew meaning of this is High flying head in which Islam will try to dominate itself in the end of days by speaking high words and raising its head.

So we have four locusts in Joel and 4 rivers in Genesis. The interpretation of both is the same.

> **Isaiah 46:10** (HTHS) Declaring the end from the beginning, and from ancient times the things that are not yet done, saying, My counsel shall stand, and I will do all my pleasure:

The meaning behind the four rivers of Genesis, the army widely dispersed i.e. Islamic countries united in terror will strike with terror violently and will be fruitful until the End when it is finally brought down but not totally eradicated until the end of the time.

Let us look at the 4 locusts of Prophet Joel.

> **Joel 1:4** (HTHS) That which the chewing locust has left has the swarming locust eaten; and that which the swarming locust has left has the crawling locust eaten; and that which the crawling locust has left has the consuming locust eaten.

4 types of locust are described

Chewing locust/Palmer worm –גזם gazam means "devourer"
(Swarming) Locust - ארבּה
Crawling locust – ילק Yalek (Young locust – suicide bombers)
Consuming locust – חסיל Khaseel

The Muslims described as the "devourer", this is the root meaning of the word for the first locust especially these Arbeh (locusts) are desert roaming creature (Arabs) who send their young "Yalek" to mean young locust to "feed" akal to eat and they are living on blood like a drip feed by killing the people in the both in the land of Israel and other lands such as Iraq, Afghanistan and Pakistan. The idea of locust is also to show that they multiply very quickly they have a lot of children. Islam has the ancient order of Israel the law of polygamy which is practiced in the East while many in Israel today especially the Khazari converts do not practice the belief of Abraham, they also do not practice what YHWH commanded to produce offspring to maintain and sustain Israel both spiritual and physical.

The description of Yalek is that they are helped by their leadership to do the tasks given to them which is not a <u>one</u> man thing but behind it are many other people supporting this work meaning Islamic leaders all over the world.

YHWH is teaching **<u>essential truth</u>** here not just well here you go son now do what you want kind of thing.

Let us go to Genesis for a background for this. YHWH's garden in <u>Eden</u> in the <u>East</u> section is the analogy of Israel planted in the world to be a light unto the nations. Zionist Israel is not the light of the world as they are not chosen. The true black Israel will do this and beginning to shift and shake to understand her plan.

> **Revelatioin 13:7** (HTHS) And it was given to him to make war with the *Y'sra'elite* kedoshim (set-apart saints), and to overcome them: and power was given him over all kindreds, and tongues, and nations.

To make war with the saints these are people of the book or both Christians and Yahudim who are under the Contract/Agreement of YHWH given to Abraham and subsequently to Isaac, Jacob and then to Moses and brought through by Yahushua.

Daniel also predicted this:

> **Daniel 7:18** (HTHS) But the *Y'sra'elite* kedoshim (saints) of the most <u>High shall take the kingdom</u>, and <u>possess the kingdom forever</u>, even forever and ever.

Daniel's prophecy of the saints strictly applies to Torah keeping people and certainly not to Torahless Christians who will not posses the kingdom nor be there in the first resurrection. These kedoshim does not include secular Zionists who will be out of the land by that period and even the racist religionists too.

This means that an army will "**break forth**", "rushing" and conquering.

> **Joel 1:6** (HTHS) For a nation is come up upon <u>my land</u>, <u>strong, and without number</u>, <u>whose teeth are the teeth of a lion</u>, and it tear apart like a fierce lioness.

In other words this is a great multitude.

Teeth of a lion

A lion has 30 teeth and if this is true then I believe the Muslim countries will divide in a block of seven, there needs to be at least 30 nations taking into consideration the 7 heads in Revelation 13 would give us the block of 7.

The 7 heads or strongholds in the End-Times

1. Pakistan
2. Afghanistan
3. Turkey
4. Iran
5. Iraq
6. Saudi Arabia
7. Egypt

The immediate leaders are ten through whom which the 11th horn leader will come who we call the Anti-Messiah who is also the Gog of the land of Magog i.e. Turkey. Ezekiel 38:2. גוג ארץ המגוג Gog from the land of Magog, picture of a multitude marching together.

> **Revelation 13:1** (HTHS) And I stood upon the sand of the sea, and saw a beast rise up out of the sea, having seven heads and ten horns, and upon his horns ten crowns, and upon his heads the names of blasphemy.

Note he has 7 heads (This could give us our seven regions), the heads are synonymous with Mountains and kingdoms.

> **Revelation 17:3** (HTHS) So he carried me away in the ruach (spirit) into the wilderness: and I saw a woman sitting upon a scarlet coloured beast, full of names of blasphemy, having seven heads and ten horns.

The king Messiah has a bride the woman consisting of many believers and Satan also has a bride consisting of many Muslim nations, tongues and people which are referred to as the “seas” and this woman sits on the Beast controlling it.

The Beast has seven heads and ten horns.

The Beast is seven kingdoms and Ten kings.

> **Revelation 17:9** (HTHS) And here is the mind which has wisdom. The **seven heads are seven mountains**, near which the woman sits.

In other words these seven have to come together a bit like the UN, we will have seven power heads which will have different number of Muslim nations attached to them. Micah mentions the **eight** princely men and **seven** shepherds.

Turkey would be one **power head**, Pakistan will be another and then you will have a **power head** near Southern Russia e.g. Afghanistan and so on and so forth.

In Revelation 13:2 we are shown he has the mouth of a lion and in Joel we are told he has the teeth of a lion, well if he has a mouth then he must have teeth even if they are false teeth like the ones you purchase from your dentist. So who is Satan's dentist that will do the fitting and bringing together of the teeth? The Anti-Messiah of course!

In Dan 7:4 "The first was like a lion"

Daniel gives us the look of this beast.
Joel gives us the teeth
Revelation gives us the composite body and its heads.

> **Joel 1:11** (HTHS) Be you ashamed, O you husbandmen; howl, O you vinedressers, for the wheat and for the barley; because the harvest of the field is perished.

All three symbols "**wheat**, **Barley and the field** represent believers as in the Passover Barley is seen and the Pentecost harvest is related to the wheat in the "field". The "field" which is the symbol of the world having been destroyed. The Hebrew for "destroyed" is the Hebrew word abad אבד

Or it also means to "wander" away.

The Alef in the word Abad is for a human and the bet for a house and dalet for a mouth "House of the speaker. " So it is saying my people were led through the house with big words but not the true house but a false house to eternal death. They left their faith pure and simple exactly as John 6:66 describes it.

The "farmers" in Joel 1:11 are the pastors and Bishops who gave way to ecumenicalism, false man made church dogma and people like Rick Warren who promote weird doctrines.

This is the sickness in the churches. Unless they repent and turn to the Torah, the law of YHWH they will all likewise perish because Master Yahushua came to reveal the Torah completely.

> **Joel 1:14-15** (HTHS) Set-apart a fast for yourselves, call a solemn assembly, gather the elders and all the inhabitants of the land into the house of YHWH Your POWER, and cry to YHWH, (15) Alas for the day! For the day of YHWH is at hand and as destruction from El-Shaddai shall it come.

All the elders, pastors, priests alike are called to fast for this judgment is severe and it is called the **Day of YHWH**, this is a Sabbath and not Sunday the day of Satan when he sits with his dentist to fix his teeth allegorically speaking of course. YHWH's day is always the weekly Sabbath mentioned numerous times in the Torah. Those who do not respect YHWH's Torah YHWH does not respect them and their prayers shall not be heard!!!

> **Joel 1:18** (HTHS) How do the beasts groan! The herds of cattle are perplexed, because they have no pasture; yes, the flocks of sheep also perish.

The animals moan and are hungry because of "your" punishment "your" wrong doings and "your" sins. To live against Torah as most Christians are doing is to live in transgression. Allegoric drash for believers which lack the true word of YHWH, because Torah and the prophets are not taught and put to one side and considered only for the Jews and not counted as the words of YHWH through which we feed but foolish words/dogma is preached that is not scripture. One such is the pre-tribulation rapture.

> **Joel 2:1** (HTHS) **Blow you the shofar in Tsiyon**, and sound an alarm in my Set-Apart mountain: **let all the inhabitants of the land tremble**: for the Day of YHWH comes, for it is near at hand;

Why blow the trumpet in Tsiyon and sound the alarm in My Holy Mountain?

Tsiyon is all the community of believers in the world, His Excellency, His government on earth and His holy mountain is the place of His habitation in Israel plus the one assembly in the world. The **Day of YHWH** is a feast day and a high holy Sabbath day.

> **Joel 2:2** (HTHS) A day of darkness and of gloominess, a day of clouds and of thick darkness, as the morning spread upon the mountains: a great people and a strong; there has not been ever like, neither shall be any more after it, even to the years of many generations.

A great army is raised this is the **ARMY OF YAH** not Satan as most had believed.

> **Joel 2:3** (HTHS) A fire devours before them; and behind them a flame burns: the land is as the Garden of Ayden before them, and behind them a desolate wilderness; yes and nothing shall escape them.

These are YHWH's sanctified ones. The "fire" is the drash allegorical for the House of Jacob (12 tribes), the flame is the House of Joseph, aka the believers in Messiah Yahushua.

> **Obadiah 1:18** (HTHS) And the house of Yaqub shall be a fire, and the house of Yosef a flame, and the house of Esav for stubble, and they shall kindle in them, and devour them; and there shall not be any remaining of the house of Esav; for YHWH has spoken it.

House of Esav shall be destroyed i.e. all the Zionist entities and Islamists with them. Note the House of Esav the so called people who are the counterfeit Jews.

The House of Joseph shall be a flame in other words those who accepted King Messiah because Joseph is the type of Messiah in Egypt and similarly Master Yahushua is the Messiah, which the Hebrews did not recognise because they see someone look like Joseph when his brothers thought Joseph was just another powerful Egyptian.

Just as black Joseph revealed himself to his brothers, spoke Hebrew and wept. Here black Judah weeps once they recognise their long lost brother Master Yahushua the black Messiah who will also speak comfortably to them in Hebrew and not Greek, Latin or Aramaic. It's time of the real Hebrew people returning the people of colour.

> **Zechariah 12:10** (HTHS) And I will **pour upon the house of**

> **Dawud**, and upon the inhabitants of Yerushalim, the Ruach (Spirit) of favour and of petitioners: and they shall look upon me (את) whom they have thrust through, and they shall mourn for him, as one mourns for his Beloved son, and shall be in bitterness for him, as one that is in bitterness for his firstborn.

The real black Messiah with the real House of Dawud who were and are the people of colour will find favour while the self appointed chosen will find this a day of shame for themselves.

> **Joel 2:4** (HTHS) The appearance of them is as the appearance of horses; and as horsemen, so shall they run.

These are sturdy looking men described as horses in other words they are strong and it describes them as “war” “paw rawsh” horses.

> **Joel 2:5** (HTHS) Like the noise of chariots on the tops of mountains shall they leap, like the **noise of a flame of fire** that devours the stubble, as a strong people set in battle array.

They are the House of Joseph and will devour Esav both the Zionist apostate Jews and radical Islamists.

This is a strong army of believers those who were worthy of the resurrection because not all Christians will be raised in the first resurrection. The common perception that everyone calling themselves or just having a knowledge and belief in a person called “Jesus” or Yahushua will be raised is simply not true. Unless you are His disciple obedient to the Torah you will have to wait. In order to be a true disciple you have to accept and obey the Torah of Moses. False teachings of Paul will not save you that day which many use to abrogate the Torah.

> **Joel 2:6** (HTHS) Before their face the people shall be much pained: all faces shall gather blackness.

Before YHWH’s army their enemies are troubled especially white skins turning dark since they call Hebrew Israelites niggers and Cushites a Hebrew word for nigger.

YHWH is their head and it is His army.

> **Joel 2:16** (HTHS) Gather the people, set-apart the congregation, assemble the elders, gather the children, and those that nurse the breasts: let the bridegroom go forth of his chamber, and the bride out of her chupah (bridal-chamber).

Ready for the gathering of the believers, the bridegroom Messiah is ready to go to collect the Bride.

The pre-tribulation crowd uses this incorrectly to say "see the Bride has been taken out and now is brought back after the rapture," nothing could be further from the truth. The word for the "bride's chamber" or "closet" is "**chupah**". In other words that is not where the marriage was consummated but that is where the marriage vows were taken affirming her loyalty to the husband once more so Christians are wrong to take the verses out of context. Here the affirmation is like in Exodus 19 to accept the Torah and not to deny it as they do.

> **Joel 2:15** (HTHS) Blow the shofar in Tsiyon set-apart a fast, call a solemn assembly:

Last chance! To blow the trumpet in Tsiyon, that is the whole believer community to sound the alarm. In the old days <u>six</u> calls were given, one to call people from the field one to cease from business activity and one to prepare for the Sabbath. So what if you do not keep the Sabbath will you be called?

> **Joel 2:17-18** (HTHS) Let **<u>the kohenim, the ministers of YHWH</u>**, weep between **<u>the porch and the altar</u>**, and let them say, Spare your people, O YHWH, and give not <u>your heritage to reproach, that the nations</u> should rule over them: Therefore should they say among the people, Where is their Elohim? **18** Then will YHWH be jealous for his land, and pity his people.

These Kohenim are people like me Lewites who would have been woken up and who are redeemed that we will petition for our people the Hebrew Israelites to be rescued. Note, our petition is heard of the collective true genetic priests and not some Christian mumbo jumbo shaba daba doo tongues.

Which priests and which ministers and what people?

It is not talking about the believer community but the Hebrews. The enemy is at the door and about to bring in destruction so the priests are to pray. Israel was and still is called YHWH's heritage.

> **Joel 3:2** (HTHS) **I will also gather all nations** and will bring them down into the valley of Yahushafat, and will plead with them there for my people and for my heritage Y'sra'el, whom they have scattered among the nations, and divided my land.

The true Israelites enslaved and taken away these are the ones YHWH now wants to return to their rightful place.

> **Joel 2:18** (HTHS) Then will YHWH be jealous for his land, and pity his people.

YHWH is jealous not in the wrong way but in sense that He wants their well being and He has compassion on His people.

> **Joel 2:19** (HTHS) Yes, YHWH will answer and say to his people, Behold, I will send you grain, and wine, and oil, and you shall be satisfied therewith: and I will no more make **you a reproach among the nations:**

He will give them prosperity while in the nations the black Hebrews were ridiculed and called names.

> **Joel 2:20** (HTHS) But I will remove far off from you the northern army, and will drive him into a land barren and desolate, with his face toward the Dead Sea, and his rear part toward the Mediterranean Sea, and his stink shall come up, and his ill savour shall come up, because he has done great things.

Ah, it is the Northern army the one that came out of the northern region, here it ties with Turkey as I head out via Turkey to Kenya today rewriting this on the 15th of November 2012 to go and teach the Torah to our people there so that they may be restored back to the Father.

Two seas are mentioned.

- **East sea is the Dead sea**
- **West sea is the Mediterranean sea**

Through a flood

> **Joel 2:23** (HTHS) Be glad then, you children of Tsiyon, and rejoice in YHWH Your POWER: for he has given you the former rain moderately, and he will cause to come down for you the rain, the former rain, and the latter rain in the first month.

A message to the ALL the believer community. Rejoice and be glad.

Former rains and latter rains to come down in the moth of Aviv, March and April time period.

The reference is dual, not only to the Messiah, because He was revealed in the month of Aviv as the Pascal lamb but also this month is the beginning of the religious year, i.e. The head. So the drash is to the Messiah.

> **Joel 2:26** (HTHS) And you shall eat in plenty, and be satisfied, and praise the name of YHWH Your POWER that has dealt wondrously with you: and my people shall never be ashamed.

YHWH's people will never be put to shame this is one solid promise provided if you are His people. This is recital of the Yahudim prayer after food the Birkat Hamazon, the long prayer in which we thank YHWH for feeding us and the whole world and because of Him we have never lacked food and may we never lack it and we increase His name upon the earth.

> **Joel 2:27** (HTHS) And you shall know that I am in the midst of Y'sra'el, and that I am YHWH Your POWER, and none else: and my people shall never be ashamed.

Twice repeated not for comfort but to be a sure promise. YHWH is in the middle of Israel or more accurately Temple Mount from where He will rule and reign in the 3rd Temple.

Chapter 7

Pakistan and the radicalism in the region – Ten years of brutal violence now what?

Today everything is blamed on Pakistan and its corrupt government but what many may not know is that the madrassas that sprang up in Pakistan in the last thirty years were funded and aided by the US governments then in power to raise jihadist fighters to fight the Soviet occupation in Afghanistan. It was not until 2002 that the Washington Post published the US plans to recruit jihadist to fight the soviets through books funded and supplied by the US that would make ready fighters through madrassas to send to fight the Russians aided and abetted by American funded tax paid dollars. This was called operation Cyclone and its aim was to kill as many Russians as possible and to bleed the Soviet army. The mission as we know was largely successful in ousting the Russians but the text books that were printed and given to Madrassas were from the US to incite jihad in the first place however it all later backfired. They knew that the Qur'an spoke about jihad and fighting the infidels so the US used the text in their favour against another power. What was used for Russia has now become the fighting force against the US.

Before the war in Afghanistan in order to punish Iran America aided and abetted Saddam Hussain to fight an eight year long war with Iran fully funded by American bombs and biological weapons, the same ones that could not be found when Saddam Hussain reneged on the US. Saddam used the same weapons to kill his own people in Halabja 16/17th March 1988. About 6000 Kurdi's were instantly killed and ten thousand injured. Though Saddam Hussain did the killing but the US was complicit in this affair. Should we wonder why the twin towers went down in 2001, which represented the US economic symbols which killed Americans and many other nationalities? Is it right for a superpower nation to kill covertly and indiscriminately and then lay the blame on the others who they have tried to suppress? There are a lot of other theories too that the 9/11 was done by the Zionists but blamed on the radical Muslims as they had vested interests to take insurance money from the collapse of the building and a lot of people question how two very tall structures can just collapse with a few floors burning at the top with planes. One argument is that explosives were laid in the building to make them collapse.

The Americans also need to understand that the Muslims are not Red Indians which were also indiscriminately killed and then the American government displaced and usurped their land. The Muslims will fight back and not go silently and we should be aware what the scriptures say about Ishmael as a wild man who will fight all (Gen 16:12). Ever wondered why he will be wild? Because the West thought they would colonize them and take over their resources but Ishmael will fight back and that is exactly what his sons are doing.

Note the Bible tells us the following that what we have sown we will also reap. The law of cause and affect comes right out of the pages of scripture.

> **Job 4:8** Even as I have seen, they that plow iniquity, and sow wickedness, reap the same.

This reveals that today's fighters that are fighting a war with the Allies were actually trained by the Allies. All these nations were guilty and knew fully well what they were up to but turned a blind eye. There goal was not to make Pakistan or Afghanistan a better place to live but simply to advance their own goals of corporatocracy the building of the American Empire within the borders of Muslim nations by subjugating them through loans and help given that they would not be able to repay back including many Latin American nations today who are in the same predicament. The corrupt politicians of Pakistan were only too willing and complicit in all these affairs and were the yes men for America and anyone that came along with a barrel full of money.

The same thing had happened in Latin America earlier where nation after nation was put down for its resources through the Economic hit men or Jackals that went in to do the CIA's dirty work to assassinate presidents and Generals that did not cooperate such as General Torrijos and Jamie Roldos of Ecuador whose plane just exploded in mid air of course without any fault. The same thing happened with General Zia ul Haq of Pakistan, whose plane just happened to also explode in mid air while no fault was found. He was also assassinated by the CIA all of us knew it even back then so it was no secret to us who did it as we saw Henry Kissinger's hand behind that one. The American administrations did not succeed to deceive Pakistanis because they knew what the American government was up to and this brought about a wrath of the Pakistani men and women who were willing to go to Jihad. Radical Islam then really became a call sign to oppose American government policies.

The corrupt entities that have a few elite individuals behind them such as World Bank and IMF pretend to help poor nations but actually subjugate them in the guise of loans which are given on such inflated forecasts to put the nation into permanent debt to usurp the resources that they have such as oil or gas. Africa was also subjugated the same way. No wonder in spite of having so much mineral wealth there is so much poverty there still. The World bank and IMF arrange loans then the money does not go to the third world country but is given to the US corporations to do the work so effectively the money stays in the US while lands occupied by natives were usurped either by removing them through military force and if they fought back they were labelled terrorists. This is still ongoing in Latin America and many other nations.

Personal Observations

If a person like Hugo Chavez of Venezuela who is regarded as the poor people's champion in Venezuela rises and opposes the US foreign policy then he is branded as a communist leader and despot. Hugo Chavez knows that the despots are actually sitting in the US in their boardrooms wearing suits and ties. They tried to assassinate Hugo Chavez twice but the jackals failed and he survived. If we look back at the history of Iran the Prime Minister Mohammad Mosaddegh got elected by the people in 1951 and as soon as he became Prime Minister he nationalized the petroleum, which was owned by Britain, which of course angered the government in England.

The British MI6 then sought CIA's help who in 1952 in partnership with Eisenhower's government then had Mosaddegh removed by the CIA in an operation called AJAX by bribing Iranian military and political officials. They brought in the puppet Mohammed Reza Pahlavi the Shah of Iran who then tyrannically ruled Iran for several years before being ousted by the Ayatollah Khomeini. Before Mosaddegh's removal a political slander campaign was conducted against him to discredit him. Presently the two governments the Labour government of England and the US Obama's government were caught doing the same thing against Mahmoud Ahmadinejad's government by supporting Iranian dissidents but so far have been unsuccessful to bring him down. The elections that took place in Iran were pretty fair but it was made to look like that the elections were rigged but this is not true as a large majority of Iranians voted for Ahmadinejad while the opposition simply failed to convince the Iranian people.

This is not a question of whether Ahmadinejad is morally right or wrong or whether he is a partner for peace but it is clear a slander campaign has been generated against him but without success. Ahmadinejad is actually a very modest man opposed to how he is demonised in the media. He is hated by the Zionists of course and it is they who want to bring Iran down using American troops and money.

The Western governments are not doing this for the Iranian people so do not be mistaken but they are doing it so that a Western alliance government can come which will allow these foreign nations to go and do business contracts and control the oil and mineral wealth that Iran has according to their foreign policy.

A campaign has been formulated to dethrone and change the Iranian government but up to now without success. The CIA and MI5 are behind activities in Iran to destabilize the country in order to overthrow the present regime. Many people in England and America do not seem to be aware of what our governments are doing while everyone else knows this fact well. Is it true that Iran has atomic weapons right now? The answer is no but will they succeed in building them? Given the chance of course they will build them as the scripture says they will become the strength of the armies of the Anti-Messiah however given the present circumstances of Iran it does not yet have the full means to make a nuclear bomb but will succeed in making strategic missiles to fire over short and medium distances. However it is highly unlikely that they will rival the US or any other major western country to build nuclear weapons at the same capability or to be a serious threat to the American or European public.

China also knows the situation of Iran and is supportive of Iran while the Russians also know this and want to help Iran hence why they are not happy for sanctions but the western nations are playing the typical game they are used to and forgetting that these games have dire consequences for the western people of increasing suicide attacks by the radical Islamists. The reality is that the Iranian regime is not as evil as the West has made it out to be. While their enmity with Israel is more spiritual and related to the past events but we know that a clash between Israel and Iran is ultimately inevitable because of the Islamic issue of Israel being Palestine for them rather than being a Yahudim national home. The reality is that the Ashkenazi and even many of the Sephardi Jews in Israel are not the true chosen or neither the inhabitants of the land of Canaan.

I want to point out that what allowed these things to come about was the fact that the West was afraid that Iran would join communist Russia and then the West will lose control of the Oil and the western corporations would not be able to participate to make money. Our present government that just came into power in May 2010 the coalition of Lib-Con would have been a bit more clued on to what is best and how to deal with the current situation and we may see a different direction to what Labour had been doing with the US but we saw instead no change as they have also become the puppets of America. The Liberals are not for war with Iran and the conservatives want to play safe and only intervene if they feel the situation requires them to do so. They do not want to head into an all out war with Iran partnering with the US unless it is deemed necessary.

Why do the US citizens wonder why there are radical Muslims and other soldiers shooting others in their army bases such as Fort Bragg, Fort Hood and other military bases? This is because places such as Fort Bragg, Camp Pickett, High Rock Gun Club, Camp Perry and Harvey Point were used to train the Mujahideen (Islamic fighters) in how to kill the Soviets. CIA also aided in the Opium trade both in Latin America and Afghanistan, which is used to fund their covert operations to this day. The Opium fields were planted on the secret orders of the CIA through the Taliban and today the American government pretends to be innocent and makes the Taliban the guilty party but it was them that raised these people as the killing machines that they are today. Perhaps the US citizens don't ask the question how did Muslim peasants learn to blow up buses, trains, planes and police stations? How did they learn to make sophisticated triggers for bombs? It certainly was not reading manuals from the internet as they never had any internet access which is common today and most of all many Mujahideen did not know how to use computers either.

All this expertise was provided for by the US when the Mujahideen were trained through the CIA in American military camps and subsequently these Taliban then trained others at home. The war in Afghanistan actually has no biblical or religious justification, and it has no moral justification. Afghanistan is not a threat to Europe or the US in anyway. If the US and Europeans controlled their borders then they would have nothing to worry about but this war was created as a front in order to establish gas and oil pipelines for big American and European corporations to bring in Oil and Gas over the Caspian basin through Afghanistan from Muslim nations such as Kazakhstan. Initially Afghanistan was just a base to fight the Soviets and afterwards for exploitation of Oil and Gas. The only people who seem to know this are the Muslims while some honest Americans are also aware of such things and would admit to these things as would the British.

Prophetically speaking this plan will not succeed and America is destined to lose this war just like Vietnam which I wrote about in 2008 and will have to eventually pull out which is already beginning to take place now in 2012 November. In fact this is now doing the opposite effect of strengthening radical Muslim alliances and the anger of Muslims to join forces to thwart what is termed foreign aggression. It has actually helped to galvanize Islam and we are fast heading towards Armageddon.

The Bible says the following:

> **Ezek 38:5** (HTHS) Persia, Cush (Sudan), and Phut (Somalia) with them; all of them with shield and helmet:

Persia is the region of Pakistan, Afghanistan, Iran and other close by regional nations so since Persia is able to come up to fight Israel in the future its clear that Afghanistan will become stronger in the hands of the Muslims and they will repel the Allied forces. Whether you believe it or not one day Pakistan will have its secularist government overthrown by the military and they will go to war both with the US and Israel and be willing to use the atomic bombs also. This is now only a matter of time. America has pulled the trigger and now we are sitting on a ticking time bomb. Saudi Arabia the wicked Islamic nation that has so many wicked deeds on it's soil with the raping of women, servants working in Saudi homes and the helpless cries of women and children which helped America to do all this with the instructions of the US. YHWH is going to destroy Saudi Arabia completely with Mecca included but America has a chance to repent but will also suffer with a likely bankrupt economy. Both are heading fast to the ghetto scenario.

The choice is really in the hands of the American government and the people of what directions are taken. It is a well known fact that General Zia the ultra Islamist general brought in a coup in Pakistan was brought to power by the US and it was also the US that blew up his plane later. He was given a stark warning by Henry Kissinger that if he did not cooperate with the US they would do to him the same they did to Prime Minister Bhutto who was dethroned from power in Pakistan by the US because he wanted to build the bomb. Note he was a very popular prime minister who came into power by democratic elections and removed by American CIA covert operations.

I would also like to point out the words of the Master who was very clear that the children of disobedience act more wisely than the children of light and the same is true in our day while many of the people who put their faith in Him walk around without understanding and in worldly fleshly ways.

> **Luke 16:8** (HTHS) And the master commended the dishonest steward, because he had done wisely: for the children of this world are in their generation wiser than the children of light.

It's very sad that many young British, American and other Allied soldiers are dying needless deaths in the guise of fighting terror. Our past governments have been more prone to serving mammon and not YHWH and killing their own children for greed and lust of wealth and power. The issue at least in Afghanistan is not at all related to terror but for economic wealth from that side of the world but if the governments are honest and tell you then this war would not have happened. The simple question to ask is how many Afghans were involved in the twin tower smashing by the hijacked planes on 9/11? How many were involved in destroying buses and trains in Europe through suicide attacks? Any sane person's factual answer should be zero, not even one. If this is the answer then how come America did not attack Saudi Arabia as all the people who formulated the 9/11 attacks were allegedly of Saudi origin? It is a given that Pakistanis largely contributed to the attacks in London on 7/7 and are still been implicated in further planning of attacks.

Afghanistan has turned into a bloodbath for the Allies because the Bible says that region will become stronger in favour of the enemy, while our politicians lie to us that they are winning the war. The truth is that they are bogged down in a war that they cannot win and have been for the last ten years.

If the Allied forces pulled out today all the bombings in Pakistan would stop and there would be no terror threat on British or the American soil. However because these things are written in the Bible therefore the Islamist will fight back and cause many casualties, this in turn will strengthen and not weaken the hand of the Beast. India may also be playing a part in the bombings in these nations because certain officials in India are involved in what is going on in both Pakistan and Afghanistan. The whole region is a cesspit of political issues and religious madness. Now that this part has been ignited it will remain ignited for generations to come with dire consequences for peace in that region.

The Beast is increasing by the day and has become so big that now it is attacking the very people who helped resurrect it. Therefore the question is, were the British government or the US government innocent? No, they were part of all these conspiracies carried out so they will share in the punishment of their sins too. What you have sowed you shall indeed reap. Some honest politicians in both these nations and even honest military personnel may admit to past failings and the present issues but by and large the population in the West is kept in dark about the goings on of this so called war on terror or should it be called the war of terror on the Afghanis because so far many innocent Afghan men, women and children have been killed who had nothing to do with fighting with the West.

Whenever a nation abuses the rights of another because they think they are powerful scripture tells us that the blood of the innocent cries from the ground for justice and justice indeed will be carried out though YHWH's judgment on the nations participating in such actions. YHWH's wrath is indeed set for the radical Islamic nations for the death destruction and mayhem of innocent men, women and infants but equally unless we act in a right-ruling manner in our conduct to the men who are fighting us we could end up on the wrong side of YHWH because our governments have been complicit in the killing of innocent civilians.

We can only hope that the British and American sons and daughters will repent for the evil actions and will repent of the sins of their forefathers and change for their own good and for the good of the people. The eighty nine million born again Christians in the US should use their voting power to bring about a better change for the emancipation of the world and certainly can do much good if they decided to act on it. Certainly many women in the east need emancipation but this needs concerted effort from the western alliance.

Remember what I said earlier that the law of YHWH is established already what you sow you reap. The Americans and European governments have blood on their hands and need to repent of their sins. America can be a force for good and can decide to go into history as a world power that did much good or can go down as did the other Empires, Rome being a prime example but the US will be given a chance by the God of Israel to demonstrate that its repentant and mending its ways or else it will go down into the world as another corrupt and evil dominating empire.

Just as Afghanistan was used to fight the Russians now Pakistan is being used as pawns to fight the Taliban the very same guerrilla forces that America has helped to create. This is termed blow back a phrase coined by the CIA for the consequences of actions that they have taken in other countries which come back to haunt America. The bringing down of the twin towers was one such blow back and more will come if the foreign policy is not amended. This is not to say that all American and British people are evil but we are only talking about the actions of certain past government policies that have proved to be a failure, while innocent people from these nations get captured or caught out by radicals while on holiday somewhere or shot at because of what has happened in the past even though they are innocent. Whether you like it or not the radicals are the chickens coming home to roost. By killing one Osama who was caught and shot in Pakistan ten more will be born to avenge his death and this is how radical Islam has functioned and will continue to function until the end as it's a tribal religion.

I would recommend you read the book Avoiding Armageddon by Martin Schram and also "The Secret History of the American Empire: Economic Hitmen, Jackals, which may show you what is going on behind the scenes and the Truth about Global Corruption by John Perkins." My observation on the matter is that not only were the Muslims brainwashed into believing a jihadist mentality from the Qur'an but also the Christians are brainwashed by their governments and their clergies. The governments tell them how good they are doing which mostly they are not and the clergy is telling them the law of YHWH is not for you but only for the Yahudim. Both are deceptions and will be dealt with by YHWH in the End of Days. Many will not enter the kingdom which many think that they will have on a plate.

I could like some other Christian writers paint all Islamic governments as evil but I will speak the truth and paint a true picture of the West at how in reality many of their actions are extremely unrighteous, I am not without knowledge on this as the past actions dictate present conditions in the West. These may be termed cause and effect but in reality just as YHWH said what will happen is happening and we continue to move in the direction of Armageddon which is unstoppable!

I want to point out that the Islamic Beast was wounded by the British Empire but reawakened fully with the help of the American and British Empires. It's quite funny how prophecy fulfils itself and works itself out. When America thought she was preparing for Russia but they did not figure out what will we do when this mammoth Beast has awoken and now America is realizing the consequences after 9/11, and Britain after 7/7 and they fear other future attacks to come which are now unavoidable. Some Christians make the mistake of thinking that perhaps the biblical wars would be of one religion versus another religion or that the Allies will only go in the war if it is justified. Unfortunately this is not how things need to play out in reality and actually don't do scripturally either. Most wars are usually fought for unjust reasons while very few are for the right reason.

Scripturally I see this as the ground work already being laid out. Pakistan is a hotbed of Islamic fundamentalism connected both with Afghanistan, Iran and southern Russia. They have the atomic bomb. In the future a military government will take over the country that will make ready for war with what they consider the infidel nations. One such infidel nation in their mind will be Israel. They consider Israel the poodle state for the American interests and see her just as a bully as America while this is indeed true with the likes of Benyamin Netanyahu who gives orders to kill innocent Palestinians in Gaza numerous times. While Israel thinks it has her national interest at hand and concerned about her neighbour Iran having nuclear bombs that could threaten her existence but YHWH is in control of Israel's destiny and one day He will sort out the mess created by the nations. Israel today does not house the true Israelites in large numbers only converted European Jews and Arab Jews who were not part of the true Israelite group in the ancient past. The Black Jews in Israel are fewer in number than the Caucasian variety so we wait and see the real coming of the true Y'sra'elites home.

If America attacks Iran then Pakistan will break ties with America and fight against them. This will be the biggest blow back for America and this will bring many attacks on the American and British soil by Pakistani jihadists.

As I said Turkey is lining up more and more against Israel and the days are not far when Turkey will also become anti-Israel and then join forces with Pakistan and in turn to support the Palestinians we will have a future war on our hands. This I first wrote in 2010 and now two years later this is reality. Turkey is anti-Israel.

Perhaps Israel may think that they can contain the war but Turkey and Pakistan together will become pretty powerful nations and have the capacity to inflict serious damage on Zionist controlled Israel and its public. While for Israel to strike Pakistan will be fraught with difficulties but Pakistan can strike easily by having their jets on Turkish soil. Iran will join hands with them on this side too and they will sideline Saudi Arabia as a corrupt regime or puppets of the American's and the British and could likely attack them just as scripture suggests and blow up their oil fields in retaliation. Pakistan does have a record of defeating the Zionist jets in the past when they struck them in the 1967 war and in 1981 Israeli backed attack on the Osiris reactor. In 1981 flight Lieutenant Saif ul Azam in action with IDF destroyed Israeli jets in Iraq with Israeli encounters.

Unfortunately the Zionists who call themselves the chosen are not the chosen and that is a huge problem for them because they are the sons of Japheth then how can they occupy the land and remain in it forever? These wars are being fought in which the final expulsion will be of the Zionist Jews who are really gentiles claiming the chosen status falsely.

For more on this see my book World War III – The Second Exodus, Y'sra'el's Return Journey Home.

> **Isa 21:2** (HTHS) A grievous vision is declared to me; the treacherous dealer deals treacherously, and the spoiler spoils. Go up, **O Elam (Iran): besiege, O Media** (Northern Iran with Kurdistan); all the sighing there have I made to cease.

The Saudis have been killing Houthi fighters in Yemen who are Iranian backed gorillas. In a news report on press TV on the 15th January the following was aired:

> [41]Saudi Arabia has denied being involved in a military offensive against Houthi fighters in Northern Yemen after Iran's president slammed the country over the issue.
>
> Iranian President Mahmoud Ahmadinejad lashed out at Saudi Arabia for its violent military offensive against the civilians in northern Yemen. "Saudi Arabia was expected to mediate in Yemen's internal conflict as an older brother and restore peace to the Muslim states, rather than launching military strike[s] and pounding bombs on Muslim civilians in the north of Yemen," said Ahmadinejad while addressing the people of Ahvaz on Wednesday.
>
> The Iranian president questioned why Riyadh had not used its military weapons against Zionists to defend Gazans during Israeli 22-day Operation Cast Lead which killed over 1400 people. The Saudi Foreign Minister Saud al-Faisal, however, denied any Saudi involvement whatsoever in military attacks against the Yemeni Shia fighters, known as the Houthis.
>
> "I don't know where he (Ahmadinejad) got this accusation ... that the kingdom is waging war on the Houthis," al-Faisal said in Riyadh. He added that even the Houthis don't say such a thing. "The real accusation is that Iran is the one that meddles in Yemen's internal affairs." Al-Faisal's remarks, however, quite categorically contradict the news reported nearly on a daily basis by Houthi fighters over the Saudi air offensive against the people of Yemen. Houthi fighters reported on Wednesday that a man and two of his daughters, civilian all and sundry were killed by Saudi fighter jets in northern Yemen.

---

41 http://www.presstv.ir/detail.aspx?id=116192§ionid=351020101

Riyadh joined Yemen's offensive against Houthis after accusing them of killing a Saudi border guard and occupying two border villages on November 3. Houthi fighters have denied the claims. Yet, the Saudi foreign minister made no response to Ahmadinejad's remarks when it came to the Kingdom's failure in supporting the people of Palestine, despite claiming to be the ultimate defender of Muslims across the world.

Meanwhile, in another speech in the southern city of Hoveyzeh on Thursday, the Iranian chief executive drew an analogy between the September 11 attacks and the Holocaust, and described West's often-stated concerns over human rights, war on terror and democracy as an "explicit lie." "The Western states have always resorted to massacre of defenceless people, in order to infiltrate into special regions, under the pretext of the September 11 attack and Holocaust," the Iranian president remarked.

"Some Western states invaded the region (Afghanistan and Iraq) in the wake of the September 11 attack, while al-Qaeda's main hub is located in another country in the region, which enjoys huge oil revenues and good relations with the United States and Western countries," Ahmadinejad maintained.

"There are some countries in the Middle East region that do not hold even a single election, don't allow women to drive, but the US and European governments are supporting their undemocratic governments," he continued.

By Alex Johnson and Andrea Mitchell

Jan. 16, 2007 msnbc.com and NBC News

Saudi Arabia believes the Iraqi government is not up to the challenge and has told the United States that it is prepared to move its own forces into Iraq should the violence there degenerate into chaos, a senior U.S. official told NBC News on Tuesday. Saudi Foreign Minister Saud al-Faisal made no effort to mask his scepticism Tuesday about President Bush's proposal to send 21,000 more U.S. troops to Iraq to stem sectarian fighting.

"We agree with the full objectives set by the new plan," Saud said at a joint news conference in Riyadh with U.S. Secretary of State Condoleezza Rice, who is travelling in the region selling Bush's

> plan. "We are hoping these objectives can be accomplished, but the means are not in our hands. They are in the hands of the Iraqis themselves."

Now we can see why tensions are building up both in Iraq where the Shiites are killing the Sunnis, note Sunnis are the largest sect of Islam so Saudi has had a few blows with Iran over this and now they fought back by attacking Iranian fighters in Yemen since they could not do anything in Iraq. As you can see in the above headlines a year ago that the Saudis did threaten to send in their own military forces. I do not think the time is long now when these nations will indeed fight. If the Saudis had sent in their forces into Iraq then Iran will pretty much thrash them and send them back home in body bags that is assured as they are no match for the Persian fighters.

This will open up room for attack on Saudi Arabia by jihadi groups supported by Islamic governments such as Iran. No doubt America and England will move in to save their interests, the oil and the gas but in the ensuing violence Saudi Arabia will get trashed with its oil fields being blown up and the ones to be hit by this crisis will be Europe and the United States. It is likely that if the scenario folds out like this that the government of America and England will suffer serious blow back and could potentially have a financial meltdown because of the billions of dollars invested in that country and Iraq. The financial meltdown will reverberate through the world not just these two nations. We are going to see some pretty awful times in the future so we better be prepared.

The financial meltdown will be a lot worse than the credit crunch seen in 2008. I surmise that we are looking at a credit crunch at least 10 times as bad because the lack of oil and gas supplies and the rise of war will cause government after government to suffer and tumble. Many countries economies won't be able to run without oil and gas. Russia and Venezuela won't be able to supply everyone's needs. There will be a huge destabilisation in the world and sides will have to picked, some will pick Muslim sides and others with Europe and America but I can guarantee you that the European nations and America will go through much suffering to overcome the fallout of the oil and gas crisis.

> **Rev 18:9** (HTHS) And the Sovereigns of the earth, who have committed whoring and lived deliciously with her, shall bewail her,

> and lament for her, when they shall see the smoke of her burning,[42]

These kings of the world are not local surrounding Muslim kings but leaders that directly benefited such as the European governments and the United States of America with Saudi Arabia the Harlot of Babylon.

> **Rev 18:11** (HTHS) And the merchants of the earth shall weep and mourn over her; for no man buys their merchandise any more:

These "merchants of the earth" will be the business men who used to go from the US and Europe to sell their merchandize such as luxury cars, planes, gold, silver and other luxury items but when Saudi burns they will not be able to sell them these items any longer, which indicates the only reason they are crying is because their companies have suffered a severe loss, their shipments or items being shipped would now be not going to be reaching their destination such as Saudi Arabia and that also means they will be in severe loss of financial income possibly many of these going bankrupt! So if they go bankrupt who does it affect? It affects companies both in Europe and the US and many executives will end up killing themselves by suicides over these things.

This means that the economic meltdown that is coming in the future is very real and those that are prepared now will benefit from the chaos and crisis while those that are not will suffer badly.

Why Pakistan?

Pakistan is a strategic country that allows easy access to the Middle-East and to the Far East to countries such an Indonesia and China which are right next door. From the US militarily perspective it makes spying easy on adjacent nations and from Pakistan within the Islamic context it makes it easy to unite the Muslims who will form the fighting brigades to fight in the End-Times battles to go to Iraq. The country is predominantly Sunni with a small Shia community and it has good relations with Iran which is largely Shia. The two countries that helped established and grow modern Islamic radicalism to be propagated worldwide were Pakistan and Egypt with American dollars. America is also a big donor to Egypt. From Pakistan it spread all around to the neighbouring regions and from Egypt all over the Arab regions. Note Egypt is the lynchpin that connects Africa

---

42 When these nations go up in smoke, the merchants or business men will stand from the Red Sea and see the smoke and be crying as their business empires will start to fall.

to the Middle-East. Turkey is the gateway to Europe so these three nations will play very important roles in the End-Times battles.

43

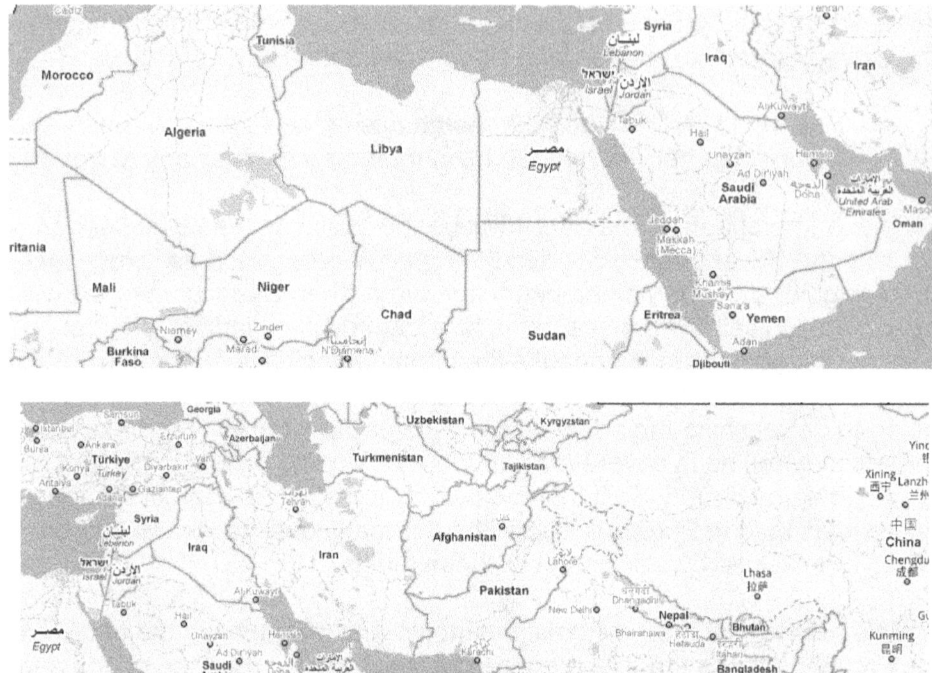

To bring in cheap gas and oil from Kazakhstan a Muslim nation you would have to traverse Afghanistan and parts of Pakistan to make it possible to do this hence why both nations are involved in bitter conflict, however this project is doomed to fail as I suggested that the Allied forces will get repelled here by the gorilla fighters since Persia will become stronger according to scripture and that includes Afghanistan on the side of the radicals. I said it in my book Islam, Peace or Beast in 2004 that no amount of technology will allow this war to be won. The New World Order will be crushed here of the so called Illuminates and Zionists bankers combined together.

This is a spiritual battle and it's not about who has what. America has been bogged down in a war for the last 10 years but without much

---

43

http://maps.google.co.uk/maps?hl=en&source=hp&q=map%20of%20eypt&um=1&ie=UTF-8&sa=N&tab=wl

success just as I suggested in my previous book it has so far proven to be true. One can get lost in the argument of which is a good nation and which is a bad one because if America had not done what it did then Russia would have and if not Russia then some other nation so we need to keep focus on what good we can do personally or collectively as a nation following ours guide book the Bible and the God of Israel and His moral standards the law/Torah, which He commands us. We cannot bring new moral standards because our standards may be useful to one society and useless to another. Hence the answer is not Satellite TV, McDonalds and Americanism but let's get biblical and put into effect the laws/Torah of YHWH, which will reap more results.

We can bring about national changes in various countries but what I find interesting in the solutions proposed by ex economic hitmen are really devoid of God and the morality that descends from Him. God appears to play no part in these people's equations of making the world a better place however I am convinced that without YHWH and His right-ruling standards all these projects by the liberals and humanists are only going to have limited success and in all honesty be a failure. It is therefore my opinion that if we honour YHWH that means acting on His right-ruling laws given in the Torah it is only then that He is able to honour us and we are then able to honour our fellow men but if we do not honour YHWH then our honour to fellow men is only an illusion because what standard are we going to use to decide what is honourable to one man versus another? YHWH was clear to Joshua that in order to be increased and live a prosperous life he had to do the following.

> **Joshua 1:7**-8 (HTHS) Only be you strong and very courageous, that you may observe to do according to all the Torah, which Musa my servant commanded you: turn not from it to the right hand or **to the left that you may prosper wherever you go**. **8** This scroll of the Torah shall not depart out of your mouth; but you shall meditate therein day and night, that you may observe to do according to all that is written therein: for then you shall make your way prosperous, and then you shall have good success.

If we think we can ignore the law of YHWH and have peace then these words should remind us that this is not true. Also humanists' laws will equally bring failure and a curse upon us.

> **Deut 29:19** (HTHS) And if it comes to pass, when he hears the words of this curse, that he speaks benefit for himself in his heart, saying, I shall have shalom, though I keep my halacha

(commandments) with a rebellious heart,[44] the watered ground with the parched:[45]

This is typically what many Christians are doing who do not obey the Torah hey parrot the words of I have peace. Hardly likely!

Isa 42:1 (HTHS) Behold my servant,[46] whom I uphold; my elect, in whom my soul delights; I have put my Ruach (Spirit) upon him: he shall bring forth right-ruling to the nations.

The Messiah of Israel in the future will bring judgement and justice to the entire world and that is not coming via the pages of the New Testament only but through the pages of the first five books of Moses the everlasting law of YHWH that has been echoed in the New Testament but many ignore it at their peril. This is one of the primary reasons why Christians lack the full power of YHWH since they deny parts of the Bible in their life and end up in curses which are automatic by not believing and acting upon those laws.

I have so far tried not to base my opinions on personal emotions but on strict Bible prophecy, its interpretation and biblical morality alone since human morality is always skewed to personal agendas. The Bible prophecy dictates where we are heading. It does not matter how we get there but what's important is we will get there just as predicted by the scriptures thousands of years ago by the prophets of old. Many of my friends have asked me does the Bible prophecy dictate that the European Union nations will become more Christian to operate in the right spirit but I tell them that no they will become more anti-Christian and they will only do what any nation does for its own good and survival but leaving YHWH behind unfortunately as liberalism and humanism is common to all these nations who have completely backslidden to the message and ways of the Master Yahushua. While President Obama openly conducts Muslim prayer sessions in the white house please don't hold your breath for this type of political correctness and open idolatry and rebellion against the

---

44 This is the categorical state of most in Christianity. The majority of them walk in utter rebellion and trying to **Increase** self while sticking to the pagan ways of their forefathers popularly known as the church fathers. Our task in life is not to behave like this and **Increase** self, because when we are walking Torah then YHWH will **Increase** us and not self.

45 Idiomatic expression to mean whatever this person touches will be cursed that includes friendships and business and he will bring judgment on whole nations if he be a king or leader.

46 This servant is Yahushua of Nazareth.

God of Israel. I wonder what the founders of America will think of this presidential showmanship.

The God of Israel is greatly displeased with these attitudes that our nations are displaying so judgment is automatically set. What has been sowed will also be reaped, this is the golden principle of YHWH's justice and it does not need YHWH to invoke it but individuals invoke it by choice. In the Indian Hindu faith they call it karma but in reality Karma is just an invented word for the same thing **what you sow is what you reap**.

When Hitler attacked London the people did not become more Christian but instead survival instincts took over. Sure there were Christians who prayed for a change and victory and even fought the war however the percentage of believers varies at different times, sometimes it may increase and at other times it may decrease but YHWH operates on His moral standards at all times and thank YHWH for that He does indeed operate on His own moral compass and timeline and we can never be let down if indeed we are submitted to Him.

I suggest to watch the following nations for the End-Times, which are Pakistan, Turkey and Egypt for political and radicalization. Iran and Israel are good indicators for temperatures of the middle-east, too hot or too cold in other words how far are we from the war with Iran in latter times. Watch Saudi Arabia for oil supplies running out that will indicate to us when Saudi Arabia including Mecca is about to be destroyed as it has to happen before the oil wells dry up and this will be our key indicator for Armageddon.

Chapter 8
Zechariah and the horses of Revelation

Allah contending with YHWH

> **Revelation 6:2** (HTHS) And I saw, and behold a white horse: and he that sat on him had a bow; and a crown was given to him: and he went forth conquering, and to conquer.

Recently when I read this verse Egypt came to my mind then Lebanon, Sudan and Yugoslavia. Countries such as Sudan are recent trophies for Islam and to add to them Yugoslavia and the breakaway republic with in it is stolen right under the Serbian noses by Muslim separatists. Today the area now that has been taken over by Ethnic Albanians is actually 70% Muslim. Any time a nation is over 50% Muslims then they will make the utmost effort to overtake it.

Many people have misapplied the verse of the "white horse" to Sar Shalom the incorrectly translated Prince of Peace instead of the **Ruler of Shalom as in the Hidden-Truths Hebraic Scrolls bible**, which has been applied to Yahushua riding the white Horse when in fact that is the Anti-Messiah riding it? Many in Christendom have failed to see this. Recently in a teaching I asked believers who they think the rider of the white horse is and most responded with Yahushua. I told them He is not the Messiah but the opposition.

Whenever a horse is mentioned it is usually a "**sign of war**" seldom peace hence we are at all times at war in the spiritual world with the enemies of YHWH. This horse is a war horse.

What is the fascination with horses in scripture and why does YHWH use a war horse to illustrate a point? You many know that the Arabs love their horses the Arabian stallions are one of the best in the world. YHWH uses horses also in the sod (Hidden) level to indicate action with the End-Times with the Arab Muslim armies.

Zechariah 6

> **Zech 6:1** (HTHS) And I turned, and lifted up my eyes, and looked, and, behold, there came **four chariots** out from **between two mountains**; and the mountains were **mountains of bronze**.

Four chariots, a sign of judgment and war coming out of **two mountains.**

In drash (Allegorical), the number four represents the four corners of the world. The Hebrew word ארבעה Arba shows all the qualities of the Alef (Our Messiah proceeding from the Father) leading us as a commander from above sweeping down like a falcon to His House. The ayin signifies action as it's the picture of two legs walking.

The Heh is there signifying the Ruach the Spirit of Elohim.

We are seeing **two** kingdoms with the mountain being a symbol for a Kingdom, Empire and nation. One Bronze Mountain is the old kingdom and the second is the new, [two mountains], a **revival of radical Islam**. The chariots and horses represent war. The Ottoman Empire faded and was wounded but now the revival of radical Islam is rampant and the wounded head (Empire) is being healed. It does not mean that only the Ottoman Empire will come back. It means Islam, as a whole will **revive worldwide** with many Islamic nations taking active part. Even Muslims in the west will take part, and this is the conglomerate empire that will dominate the world scene.

Rev 13:11-15 the two beasts are actually the Two Mountains of Bronze. Bronze identifies judgement; YHWH will use radical Muslims to judge the world because of the rampant sins these armies are unleashed.

This is the battle of Gog and Magog

In the drash (allegorical) meaning it's very clear to me that YHWH is showing something very sinister.

The four chariots represent four stages of Islamic onslaught coming from all four corners of the earth.

- **1st stage – By peaceful means**
- **2nd stage – By educational means**
- **3rd stage – By political means**
- **4th stage – by localised wars, all out active Jihad by the radicals.**

What else do the four chariots represent?

Four corners of the earth, the Muslims will come from all sides.

- **They will be split into Four types of Armies**

- **We will have Shi'ite, Sunni split formations.**
- **Sunni in the South, Shi'ite in the North, Sunni in the East, Shia in the West. Pakistan and Afghanistan are the key nations in the East. Iran, Iraq Saudi Arabia and Turkey are key in the West and south of Israel.**

The four months interestingly were used by Umar al Khatab who put a siege around Jerusalem for this time period before her surrender. Oh, and it was not the Jerusalem you have been taught or visit today which is the Jerusalem of the Amorites. Ummar conquered the real Jerusalem of the Hebrews in which the true Temple site was 140 acres and not 26 acres as proclaimed today.

The Black horse will lead – The Hebrew word Shakur the only one of the four horse ending in Resh. The leader is right there.

Who are the black horse riders?

*The book "**Yawmul-Ghadhab hal-Bada'a be-Intifadat Rajab**?"* by Abdul Rahman al-Wahabi which means: "***The Day of Wrath, it will start** with the **Month of Rajab Uprising" upon translation*** **states**:

> *"The final battle will be waged by Muslim faithful coming on the backs of horses from the stans, carrying black banners. They will stand on the east side of the Jordan River and will wage war that the earth never seen before. The true Messiah who is the Islamic Mehdi who will kill the pig and will break the cross and will defeat Europe... will lead this army of **Seljuks**, He will preside the world from Jerusalem because Mecca would have been destroyed,"*
>
> **Sura 2:216** "**Warfare is <u>ordained</u> for you**, though it is hateful unto you; but it may happen that you hate a thing which is good for you and it may happen that you love a thing which is bad for you. Allah knoweth, you knew not."

Warfare that is violence and bloodshed are **<u>divine holy calls for Muslims</u>**. No one can argue with that because the Qur'an is the **voice of Allah**. This is why Muhammad said the following quoted by Al Tabari a famous Muslim scholar:

I will bring you slaughter. Tabari VI:10

The verse in Surah Al-Bakra 2:216 was revealed to Muhammad after his <u>first</u> attack. His followers mercilessly massacred an innocent and unarmed merchant at Nakhla while they pretended to be **pilgrims during 623 CE** taking the other two merchants as captives and their money/goods as booty of which twenty percent went to Muhammad.

The massacre came in January, the sacred month of Rajeb. The non-Muslims had an oath not to attack in the sacred months but these Muslims broke that treaty.

Mode of attack: On a Sabbath, more likely a High Holy day such as seen in Yom Kippur war. The Yahudim of Quraida when between 600-900 men were beheaded in Arabia were massacred on a Sabbath. We must guard particularly on these days and our High Holy days.

> "I have been ordered by God to fight with people till they bear testimony to the fact that there is no God but Allah and that Mohammed is his messenger, and that they establish prayer and pay Zakat (money). If they do it, their blood and their property are safe from me" (see Bukhari Vol. I, p. 13).

So what does this mean? A major attack is yet to come which will be in the month of January in the future and not necessarily July or September.

The four horses also represent four levels of attack to overcome the world in fact this is being used now to overcome each individual country. If the Messiah does not return in the next 25 years then it is estimated that Europe will have 12% of Muslims, a sizeable population that will then start to overcome Europe one country at a time. The question is not will it happen but when. Scriptures give us an indication Europe will have to fight for their survival, forget the revival because there won't be any. Christianity will languish in the West and will resurge in the East. People will become faithless in the West, while the eastern ones will become active and even more faithful.

The Two Mountains represent two Kingdoms of Islam, the old revived into the New.

What is the direction of the Horses?

Red -
Black - Going to the North Country.

Western Europe will be invaded by Turkey whether that is through Turkey being allowed entry into Europe or other means.

White - These go North.
Dapeveryled (spotted) - These go South.

Why is Zechariah's horse dappled (spotted) and Revelation 6:8's horse Green?

Have you ever played a video game? What happens when in the game we drop a bomb especially a biological bomb? It turns the colour into a mixture of yellow and green but more greener. The ground turns arid green after the explosion and nothing can survive upon it at least for a while. Death and disease spread.

The horse of Zechariah was just spotted when it started so what is YHWH revealing to us? When it ended up in Saudi Arabia it turned Green. How did it manage to change its colour?

Now look at the description of what the **Green horse** does in Revelation 6:8.

He kills the 4th part with death and destruction in the Middle-East. There is our clue to the end result. So then who is the spotted horse which kills with death and destruction?

Where are we told that something spotted is not good?

> **Exodus 12:5** Your lamb shall be without blemish... (Meaning without any spot or defect).

We are told not to use spotted lamb for Passover.

We find both in the Tanak and Renewed Contract/Agreement writings things mentioned which are spotted or spotless. We are told of the Messiah without spot meaning without sin.

> **First Peter 1:19** But with the precious blood of Messiah, as of a Lamb without blemish and without spot

> **Jeremiah 13:23 (NKJV)** Can the Ethiopian change his skin or the leopard its spots? Then may you also do good who are accustomed to do evil.

Does YHWH have something against the Ethiopians? No. This is a bad translation it is saying a Cushite and not an Ethiopian Christian as such. Note also ancient Israelites were black just like the Cushite hence why this analogy is drawn. See my book Yahushua – The Black Messiah.

> **Jeremiah 13:23** Can the Cushite change his skin, or the leopard his spots? Then may you also do good, that are accustomed to do evil.

So why did YHWH pick on the Cushite (Sudanians)? Not because he has problems against the people of Sudan but he has problem with one particular ancestor.

That ancestor is Nimrod the first organised rebel and dictator of Turkey and Iraq who was a Cushite hence this connects well with his sins to defy the Master of Heaven and earth. So clearly the spot represents sin.

Let's connect the rest.

Ezek 28 speaks about Satan being perfect meaning without Spot at one stage.

> **Ezek 28:12** Son of man, take up a lamentation upon the king of Tyrus, and say to him, thus says the Master YHWH; You seal up the sum, full of wisdom, and perfect in beauty.

The allegory behind the king of Tyre is related to Satan when a sin enters and he gets spotted.

How does the horse then become completely green in Revelation? This is because Satan did not stop at one sin but continued and so therefore from the one spot he then later became covered with sins hence Green like a plague spreading upon a man.

See the horse now the Green one whose rider is Satan or Death they are one and the same individual. The two horses both spotted and Green are the same horse and same character of Satan being described. Look he starts at Israel where he caused the rebellion and then the spotted horse heads south to find the biggest religion of Islam.

What I mean in the description of the horse where Satan is being described in both places but with changed clothes so to speak. Do not look at it's just an animal. Go beyond the animal.

Because of his craftiness and sin a nuclear strike is impending in the middle-east which will kill one quarter of the people affecting the middle-east that is what we are being told which is the end result in Rev 6:8 of the spotted horse which is now green.

Symbols in Rev 6:8

Sword - War which will lead to the nuclear strike
Hunger - Shortage of food followed by disease
Death - Then followed by death.

So here John was shown the result of what happened to the spotted horse but what we miss is that he was not always spotted as Satan was at one time without sin. How do I know what I suggest is correct? Easy I test it against Zechariah himself. He says in verse 6:5 there are 4 spirits standing before the Creator.

> **Zech 6:5** (HTHS) And the malakh answered and said to me, These are the four spirits of the shamayim (heavens), which go forth from standing before the Master of all the earth.
>
> **Zech 6:7** (HTHS)...So they walked to and fro through the earth.

So Zechariah describes them as horses walking but note Kefa (Peter) the Netzarim disciple describes Satan as a lion picking up the similar theme.

Here is the second witness

> **First Peter 5:8** (HTHS) Be sober, be vigilant; because your adversary the devil, as a roaring lion, **walks about**, and seeking whom he may devour:

Did not Satan stand before YHWH? Yes indeed. He was an archangel. The four is very descriptive and prescriptive. His evil will spread in the four corners of the earth which also caused the ten northern tribes of Israel to get scattered in the four corners of the earth.

Southern portions of the world will be contending with the Beast and it will strike with biological ammunition causing havoc and disease.

The Red horse is not mentioned where it went? Revelation six gives us the answer.

> **Rev 6:4 (KJV)** And another horse, **fiery red**, went out. And it was granted to the one, who sat on it to **take peace from the earth**, and that people should kill one another; and there was given to him a great sword.

He stays home causing confusion and warfare and bloodshed. The reference to the earth is actually the Middle-East as that is the centre of the plot and the verse is talking about the area adjacent to Israel.

> **Rev 6:4** (HTHS) And there went out another horse that was fiery red: and power was given to him that sat thereon to take shalom (peace) from the province *of the Middle-East*, and that they should kill one another violently: and there was given to him a great sword.

These mountains are Bronze; this is referring to the revived Grecian/Assyrian Empire. The entire Middle East region was once part of the Assyrian/Grecian Empire (now all Islamic), the place of the Anti-Messiah, as the "little horn" comes out from one of the divisions of the Alexandrian kingdom. Here he joins forces with his comrades to form his confederacy.

> **Zech 6:2** (HTHS) In the first chariot were red horses; and in the second chariot black horses;

We see horses; these are strong sturdy animals very graceful. Here this speaks about war, bloodshed and violence with the colour of red that is to come from Islam. The black horse signifying death is also an Islamic colour for Iran and destruction which will accompany these people. You may have seen the Palestinians wearing black and Muslim women wearing black. Also you may have seen the Muslims carrying black flags they are used by the Shi'ite sect of Islam so we can see in the black horse is a clear description the Shi'ites sect of Islam (Iranians) for those who can see it.

> The word for peace in the Greek is "**lambano**" but the Hebrew would be Shalom.
> The word for kill in the Greek language is "**sfad-zo"** to kill violently.

The red horse in Revelation matches Zechariah's red horse going out killing people as the sign of bloodshed and violence. The Greek word used for kill is *"sfad-zo"* which means not just to kill, but to "kill with violence."

This resembles the tactics of the Islamic armies and matches with what the radical Islamists do today. The Greek word for "to take" is "lambano," which means to take by force. So they will take by force and destroy any concept of peace, whether the world likes it or not. We can see this behaviour in Iraq, Pakistan and Afghanistan.

A lot of Islamists are fighting there from foreign nations even if they have no business there. So they take hold of people by force killing anyone and shatter the peace. This passage is figurative of the Anti-Messiah and his forces having victory for a time. These are the armies of the Anti-Messiah from the Islamic nations.

> **Zech 6:3** (HTHS) And in the third chariot white horses; and in the fourth chariot grizzled and bay horses

The white horses indicate that these people proclaim a sort of right-ruling through outward works and salvation through a false peace and the prophet of Allah. They will even win wars for a time as the Bible suggests. He will overcome the saints. They think that they are the armies of heaven fighting for their god Allah. The grizzled horse signifies the disease and decay that is about to come to the world through these people so be warned and be prepared as I described above.

> **Rev 6:2** (HTHS) And I saw, and behold a white horse: and he that sat on him had a bow; and a crown was given to him: and he went forth conquering, and to conquer.

The white horse in Revelation matches with Zechariah which goes out and wins wars. This is the sign of the Anti-Messiah king who will go and win battles. The crown signifies that he is a king/leader and the bow and arrow is the sign of him making war. The white horse also signifies him offering a false peace and a false salvation to those he calls to follow after him.

> **Rev 6:8** (KJV) And I looked, and behold, a pale horse. And the name of him who sat on it was Death, and Hades followed with him. And power was given to them over a fourth of the earth, to kill with sword, with hunger, with death, and by the beasts of the earth.

The one who sits on the pale horse is not pale but green (Greek word *chloros*) horse and he wages war and death on the earth.

> **Rev 6:8** (HTHS) And I looked, and behold a **GREEN** horse: and his name that sat on him was death, and She'ol followed with him. And power was given to them over the fourth part of the province *of the Middle-East* to kill with a Thracian saber (Romfayah), and with hunger, and with death, and with the beasts of the earth.

The GREEN colour signifies death and pestilence. Is it any wonder that after the green horse is released that there is much death and destruction; the Islamic rider causes this: Note Strong's Greek for the Thracian Saber G4501 Romfayah, this is a Turkic Thracian type sword. This shows us that this is an Islamic onslaught and not Roman by any means. The Thracians who later became the Muslims used this type of weapon from 400 BC onwards.

> **Rev 6:9** (HTHS) And when he had opened the fifth seal, I saw under **the altar the souls of them that were slain** for the word **of YHWH**, and for **the testimony** which they held:

Many believers will be killed during this time for the testimony of YHWH, actually these points to many Yahudim being killed as they hold the "testimony" idiomatic for Torah obedience.

> **Rev 6:5** (KJV) When He opened the third seal, I heard the third living creature say, "Come and see." And I looked, and behold, a black horse, and he who sat on it had a pair of scales in his hand.

This rider is shown to have a pair of scales, but in actual fact this is not translated accurately as the Greek word used is "**dzoo-gos**" meaning yoke. He has a yoke in his hand to put people to servitude, or more correctly to bring people to servitude through the black gold which is oil.

> **Rev 6:5** (HTHS) And when he had opened the third seal, I heard the third beast say, Come. And I beheld, and lo a black horse; and he that sat on him **had a yoke to put into servitude with power**.

This black horse is the colour of Shi'ite Islam so the black horse represents two nations particularly Iran and Iraq which both have a majority of Shi'ites in them. They will hold the world under ransom because of the oil. Iran is beginning to show signs of this already. Iraq and Iran together hold 35% of world oil supply. Zechariah 6:6 tells us that the black horses go into the North Country. The North Country is Turkey which means that Turkey will have a very strong alliance with the Shi'ites which has happened in 2010. The ruling class in Iran is actually of Turkic origin known as the Azeris. The Azeri Turkic people moved into Iran in the 15th century CE and are the direct descendants of the Oghuz Turkic people, this is why we will see an alliance between Iran and Turkey just as the Bible describes.

This is why the verse above is to do with the oil economy, which controls the world. Here in the future the verse describes it is time for it to come to an end and judgment is set for these. This will bring trouble to the world. The same is seen in Revelation 18. Many countries economies will collapse. This will be the last chance for the US and Europe to do something right or be slowly bled to death.

> **Zech 6:4** (HTHS) Then I answered and said to the malakh that talked with me, What are these, my master?

> **Zech 6:5** (HTHS) And the malakh answered and said to me, These are the four spirits of the shamayim, which go forth from standing before the Master of all the earth.

These will be released from the Master of heaven and earth both for judgment and for destruction that is to come.

> **Zech 6:6** (HTHS) The black horses which are therein go forth into the north country; and the white go forth after them; and the grizzled go forth toward the south country.

Death and destruction comes from the North Country. That is Turkey where the Anti-Messiah will rise out of (Gog from the land of Magog Ezek 38:2) and they are going to attack the south (Egypt) just as prophet Daniel prophesied and the Anti-Messiah will overcome them. The grizzled horses bring death and destruction to the south i.e. through likely biological warfare.

> **Daniel 11:40** (HTHS) And at the time of the end shall the Sovereign of the south [Egypt] will attack him: and the Sovereign of the north [the anti-Messiah] shall come against him like a storm, with chariots, and with horsemen, and with a large navy; and he shall enter through the lands, and shall pass over like a flood [complete victory].

Some people think there are three parties involved in Daniel 11:40, but in affect there are only two kings one from the north and one from the south. The king of the south is Egypt and the King of the North is the Turkic Anti-Messiah. He will attack Egypt, which will fall to him, Somalia (Phut) and Sudan (Cush), which is mentioned in Daniel 11:43 are also following in the steps of the Anti-Messiah, this shows they have an alliance with both Iran and Turkey.

Daniel proves and concludes with Isaiah that Egypt is going to be won over. Remember the white horse above in Zechariah 6:6; this also signifies some victories before the Anti-Messiah is brought down.

> **Daniel 11:25** (HTHS) And he shall stir up his power and his courage against the Sovereign of the south [Egypt] with a great army; and the Sovereign of the south shall be stirred up to battle with a very large and strong army; but he shall fail: [Egypt defeated] because of the plans established against him in battle.

Egypt shall be brought down for its arrogance.

> **Isaiah 19:4** (HTHS) And the Mitzrim (Egyptians) will **I give over into the hand of a harsh master** [this is the Anti-Messiah]; and a powerful Sovereign will rule over them, says Master YHWH of hosts.

Isaiah concurs with what I said above. He is to be given over to the harsh northern king who is the Anti-Messiah. This has never happened before in the past. The Egyptians will be ruled by this king by force whether they like it or not. Protests in Tahrir square won't be helping them much.

> **Zech 6:7** (HTHS) And the bay went forth, and sought to go that they might walk to and fro through the earth: and he said, **Get you hence, walk to and fro through the earth. So they walked to and fro through the earth.**

These people are upon the earth executing vengeance. Are the radical Muslims doing this today? Yes and it will get worse

> **Zech 6:8** (HTHS) Then cried he upon me, and spoke to me, saying, Behold, these that go toward the north country have quieted my Ruach (Spirit) in the north country.

These go to the North Country [Turkey] from where the whole thing started, executing their form of judgement on the earth. The Master allowed them to execute this judgement in order to show and reveal His esteem. This does not excuse these people from guilt, but it shows their evil nature.

Chapter 9

The Rapture, The resurrection and other questions

There seems to be confusion around the following events:

- Rapture or Resurrection?
- How many resurrections?
- Islamic battle one or two?
- Will all world religions dissolve at the onset of the kingdom of heaven?
- Will people totally stop sinning at the return of the Messiah?
- How will YHWH gather the lost tribes who died in exile in other religions and nations?
- Which nations will go up to Jerusalem to celebrate the feastival of Tabernacles?

Rapture or Resurrection?

Scripture is clear that we need not argue for a rapture in any form because when the Saints are raised for the first resurrection these are the ones who will be going forth with the Messiah to Israel and descending to Jerusalem. Scripture tells us that they are down here upon the earth in She'ol in the section of paradise known as Abraham's bosom and not up there in the third heavens as most keep saying. Let us examine these passages.

> **Zech 14:5** (HTHS) And you shall flee to the valley of the mountains; for the valley of the mountains shall reach to Azal: yes, you shall flee, like as you fled from before the earthquake in the days of Uzzi'yah Sovereign of Yahudah: and YHWH my POWER shall come, and all the Y'sra'elite kedoshim (saints) with you.

It is clear that the worthy saints only who were Torah obedient will come with Yahushua and descend to Jerusalem. There is no pre tribulation rapture because these are 17th century ideas propagated by Jesuit priests and other people who latched on to such teachings. One could say it is a post tribulation type rapture if you wanted to fit this in to a rapture theory. However the correct term is always going to be the FIRST RESURRECTION. Note, not all the people will get raised at the first resurrection because this is a first-fruits resurrection for the faithful. A faithful man or woman is not described by their church attendance each Sunday but if they kept YHWH's Torah which is His voice. This requires believing and acting upon the Contract/Agreement e.g. the Abrahamic Contract/Agreement requires us to circumcise our sons who are eight days old, the Contract/Agreement at Horeb requires us to believe and obey in the Torah commandments summarised by the Ten Commandments.

This entails keeping of the 7th day Sabbath Friday sunset to Saturday sunset, it requires us to keep the 7 appointed annual feasts alongside this we have to watch the food we eat that YHWH told us is ritually unclean such as pork, shellfish, dogs, rats, snakes and other kinds of unclean animals. The list is exhaustive on the pages of Leviticus 11. The diet separates us into a set apart people consecrated on to YHWH. We are to behave in justice and mercy and right-ruling if we are Torah obedient. This means no running around backbiting tale bearing or slandering other believers or running after gain for money as many Christians are doing today. So when YHWH lifts these believers they are the ones who will go with Messiah to Jerusalem while the rest will not be raised. If they are alive they will not be taken but will walk meaning they will have to book a plane ticket to Israel. Israel will have to increase its airports to receive the influx of people.

> **Jer 50:4** (HTHS) In those days, and in that time, says YHWH, the children of Y'sra'el shall come, they and the children of Yahudah together, going and weeping: they shall go, and seek YHWH their Elohim.

This was the rapture waiting crowd that was not raptured and since they were alive at His coming they have to go back to Jerusalem. Note no flying in the air without wings. These will have to go by plane and walk. If all the real chosen Jews from the tribe of Judah have gone back to the land they why is Yahudah and Ephraim crying outside the land? This is because these are the real tribes of Yahudah and not counterfeit Yahudah white Jews in the land. The real Jews are the people of colour who will one day return but before they return what do you think will happen to the counterfeit Caucasian Jews?

There are two other resurrections.

> **Rev 20:4** (HTHS) And I saw thrones, and they sat upon them, and judgment was given to them: and I saw the souls of them that were beheaded for the witness of Yahushua, and for the word of YHWH, and which had not petitioned the beast, neither his image, neither had received his mark upon their foreheads, or in their hands; and they lived and reigned with Messiah a thousand years.

These ones who receive the first resurrection are those particular saints who were beheaded by radical Islamists for their bold witness for Yahushua and to the Torah, which is the law of YHWH. Most modern Christians do not believe in the Torah the LAW of Moses so they can be ruled out of this resurrection camp, the passage absolutely requires that both be true that one these believers believe in Yahushua as King over them and that two they adhere to the LAW of Moses.

The only ones who fit this requirement are only Muslim converts, Torah believing Messianics and Nazarenes obeying Torah since I know I am an ex-Muslim the day I came out I believed in the Law of Moses as an absolute walk of faith and Yahushua as king over me. Nothing would have dissuaded me as many in Churches told me that the Torah is abrogated I found this to be both incorrect and contradictory to scripture and the laws of YHWH which are eternal. Likewise many other Muslim converts who I have known except some following wrong church traditions they have similar issues which reject Western Christendom's ideas of the law is only for the Yahudim.

Note this is an End-Times passage and only applies to those people who particularly died in the Middle-East or Islamic nations. It does not apply to the West. We know the laws of the west for blasphemy to Allah do not exist so therefore these particular laws only exists in Muslim nations hence the deaths of these believers also happened in the Islamic nations.

The Hebrew term in the above passage is Davar Ha Elohim (Word of YHWH) is always a reference to the Torah of Moses. Clearly these people who will be Torah obeying are Muslim converts which will strongly adhere to the Torah and this pronouncement is an End-Times pronouncement. This is not talking about the first century saints who were killed by Nero. The reference to "the Beast" is the reference to the 4th Beast of Daniel 7:7 which applies to both the first and second Beast of Rev 13:1 and 11.

Not receiving the mark is and was <u>the submission to Allah</u>. These believers refused to bow down to Allah and therefore refused the mark of the Beast. The mark is not a chip because this kind of nonsense parades in western churches but has no reality. They are putting chips in dogs in the West so are the companies whose founders doing that the anti-messiah? Such is the dilemma of Western Christianity's false teachings.

When Islam took over Egypt which was a Christian country many centuries ago then many Christians were killed and some converts were beheaded.

This is a special resurrection. There will be some other believers part of this too who deserve to be resurrected and were faithful to the word/Torah of YHWH. Many Christians today who do not strongly adhere to the Torah of YHWH will not be raised in this first resurrection. If they are alive they will have to walk to Israel and learn the laws as I show above. The Yahudim teachers in the Temple will teach them how to behave and live before YHWH.

> **Jer 3:18** (HTHS) In those days the house of Yahudah shall walk with the house of Y'sra'el, and they shall come together out of the land of the north to the land that I have given for an inheritance to your ahvot (fathers).

This is both literal and spiritual. The house of Judah will walk or the House of Judah that is the Torah keeping real black Yahudim will come to agreement with Ephraim (10 Northern tribes) who were non-Torah keeping (Christians at that time who are alive) but at that time they will start to learn to keep Torah hence why Judah will come into agreement with them. One can see that these people are returning back to Jerusalem and its ways. Many of these people are still outside the land of Israel.

> **Isa 2:3** (HTHS) And many people shall go and say, Come, and let us go up to the mountain of YHWH, to the Temple of Elohim of Yaqub; and he will teach us of his ways, and we will walk in his paths: for out of Tsiyon shall go forth the Torah and the word of YHWH from Yerushalim.

As can be seen the people in Jeremiah 3:18 are both meeting here in Jerusalem to correct any misunderstanding and to come to learn the Torah of YHWH which is eternal. This passage can now be easily reconciled that people in the millennial reign who lived in disobedience will come to the knowledge and want to return to Jerusalem to learn how to start behaving with Torah as the goal. This also shows that all religions of the world will continue but King David who will be raised over Israel will be set as King and over Him will be the universal King Yahushua. A black king for the Black Hebrews returning from all nations.

- Islamic battle one or two?

There will be two major Islamic battles both can be termed the war of Gog and Magog.

The first one is just before Yahushua returns at around the end of this age which is mentioned in Ezekiel 38.

> **Ezek 38:2** (HTHS) Son of man, set your face against Gog, the land of Magog, the chief prince of Meshech and Tubal, and prophesy against him,

This is the first great battle.

After this the 3rd temple will be built by the Messiah as being the head and then Satan will be put into the abyss in his cell for 1000 years so we will have 1000 years of starting peace in Israel and many nations will come up to learn the Torah of Moses. After the 7th day (1000 years) has passed then we enter the 8th day which signifies the great day of the feast of Tabernacles then Satan is released and he goes around collecting armies again and deceiving people. Note the Islamic religion will still be around and so will Hinduism and other false religions of the world on the 8th day since we still have two more days to go to eternity allegorically 2000 more years.

> **Revelation 20:8** (HTHS) And shall go out to deceive the nations which are in the four quarters of the earth, Gog and Magog, to gather them together to battle: the number of whom is as the sand of the sea.

This is ragathering the Muslim armies for a second time and it will be a revenge attack upon true Israel.

> **Revelation 20:9** (HTHS) And they went up on the breadth of the earth, and surrounded the camp of the *Y'sar'elite* kedoshim (set-apart saints) about, and the beloved city: and fire came down out of shamayim (heaven), and devoured them.

As can be seen The 3rd Temple is built and the city established but the Muslim armies this time encamped around the Temple to try and destroy it but they will fail because this time Yahushua sends fire down from heaven to devour them.

Note scripture says on the 8th day Shaitan (Satan) is released but this does not happen on the 8th day necessarily because we still have two more days to make up the 10,000 years reign before the angels which are bound in the abyss are thrown in the lake of fire. Their punishment is for 10,000 years. For this see the book of Enoch.

In my opinion the great white throne judgement is on the 10th day or 10,000th year. YHWH has ten attributes and YHWH does things in Ten on many occurrences in the history of the Bible. For instance we have the Ten Commandments we have the Ten sefirot, we have the ten plagues, we have the ten tests of Abraham etc.

- Will all world religions dissolve at the onset of the kingdom of heaven?

As shown above they will not. They will be dissolved on the tenth day at the white throne Judgment. Since we are told in scripture that Satan goes out to deceive the nations again this is clear that the nations continue as they did but albeit in a different state of economic cycle. Computers will still be around and planes will still be around and no we do not go back to the cave age.

- Will people totally stop sinning at the return of the Messiah?

Why are people or nations going to Jerusalem in Isaiah 2:3? To learn YHWH's holy law which is for what? For right-ruling living which means people still have the ability to sin because freewill has not been removed from man and this is why we also see a sin sacrifice in the 3rd Temple in Ezek 44:27.

- How will YHWH gather the lost tribes who died in exile in other religions and nations?

Yes He will raise them from the dead during the millennium and bring them back to Israel and then teach them His LAW/Torah and they will then know their YHWH and live peacefully in the land.

> **Ezek 37:5** (HTHS) Thus says Master YHWH to these bones; Behold, I will cause breath [life] to enter into you, and you shall have life:

- Which nations will go up to Jerusalem to obey the feast of Tabernacles?

The defeated Islamic nations will go up to celebrate and learn the Israelite feasts. Also many Christians will go up to learn about them and many will put their faith in the God of Israel at that time.

Chapter 10
Will a 3rd Temple be rebuilt in our days or after the return of the Messiah?

You may have noticed the fervour amongst various Christians and Yahudim groups of rebuilding of the 3rd Temple right now and all the excitement around this that this will be built soon. We also hear of the Temple Mount faithful and the various groups that are making ready the articles, the furniture of the Temple and that Orthodox Yahudim in Israel have made a new Sanhedrin to prepare the Levitical Priests for the duties for the coming Temple. Note today Caucasian Jews call themselves the chosen and have given themselves names such as Levi and Kohen. These are not the chosen nor are they the true Kohenim (priests). These converted gentiles are forbidden from entering our 3rd Temple so be warned. The true ancient Y'sra'elites were a people of colour and hence it is they who will be the ones who are allowed to enter the set-apart place. Also the real Jerusalem is in Tel Arad where the Tabernacle of David is and his city. All the present sites in modern Jerusalem are false.

Here is picture of Real Bethlehem in Tel Arad that lies desolate with the graves of the Kings when all the tombs opened when the Master Yahushua arose from the dead, the tombs were opened (Matt 27:52).

Note the stones on the graves would have been rolled down at the angle shown so it would be impossible for a single man to remove the stone hence even the stone of Yahushua's tomb could not be removed unless five or six strong men used a rope to bring it up.

> **Ezek 44:9** (HTHS) Thus says Master YHWH; No foreigner, [gentiles] uncircumcised in heart, and uncircumcised in flesh, shall enter into my sanctuary, of any foreigner that is among the children of Y'sra'el.

I will examine the three key texts that are presented by Christians that the Temple will be built before the return of Messiah and the fact that all 12 tribes of Israel have to be in the land. From the outset I want to be very clear that my position is that the Temple will not be rebuilt before the Messiah returns and that He will rebuild it after He returns however we will restore the Tabernacle of King David in Tel Arad long before that time and some of the tribes will be in the land albeit a token number only. Any large scale migration will occur at the appointed time of YHWH. Its debatable whether that is immediately prior to the return of the Master or after however some hold one position while others hold the other.

> **Amos 9:11** In that day will I raise up the Tent of Dawud[47] that is fallen, and repair the breeches there; and I will raise up his ruins, and I will rebuild it as in the days of old:[48]

I will present evidence why I say this. I will also examine if a Temple

---

47 The specialty of the tent of David, (Second Sam 6:17-19) was that both Yahudim and strangers (Gentiles) were allowed to come freely and worship YHWH and even today in the same manner Elohim is restoring the breach between the two Houses of Y'sra'el (North and South), which has been from centuries to make them ONE new man in Messiah Yahushua who is the restorer of ALL things.

48 Repeated in Acts 15:16, this is for the millennium kingdom. King David will also be resurrected.

can stand before His coming in light of the fact that we have five Muslim mosques on the Temple Mount presently to deal with and on top that the present people in Israel are not the real chosen people but Europeans, Portuguese, Spanish, Russians who are not the true stock of Israel because Israel's ancient people were black who looked identical to Negroes while a false people are being called the chosen today. The Jerusalem is not true Jerusalem and the Temple Mount is not the Temple Mount. How's that for a real twist of fate.

The four key texts for the Temple are the following which we shall examine step by step.

These are Daniel 12:11, Revelation 11:2, Second Thessalonians 2:4 and Acts 15:16.

> **Daniel 12:11** (HTHS) And from the time that the daily sacrifice shall be taken away, and the abomination that lays waste is set up, there shall be a thousand two hundred ninety days.
>
> **Rev 11:2** (HTHS) But the court which is outside the Beyth HaMikdash (Temple) leave out, and measure it not; for it is given to the gentiles: and the set-apart city shall they tread under foot three and a half years.
>
> **Second Thess 2:4** (HTHS) Who opposes and exalts himself above all that is called Elohim, or that is petitioned; so that he as Elohim sits in the temple of elohim, showing himself that he is elohim.
>
> Proof that the Tabernacle will be rebuilt first before the Temple, this is taken from Amos 9:11.
>
> **Acts 15:16** (HTHS) After this I will return, and will Rebuild again the Tent of Dawud, which is fallen down; and I will Rebuild again the ruins there, and I will set it up:

Some Christian teachers use words like we must use scripture only and cannot go with other people's vain imaginations we will examine this too because Paul's words are *not* scripture and he is not a true apostle which they blindly have put inspiration on considering the number of contradictory anti-Torah statements made from him. For more on this hear the words of Paul at www.african-israel.com under Shabbat audio teachings or purchase the book Paul of Tarsus - The Thirteenth Apostle from Amazon.

Look I am an ex Muslim so please excuse my ignorance because I was not brought up in a typical western based Church system but it's extremely puzzling for me at times and quite difficult to understand how these contradictory statements are made of **scripture only when these people do not even understand what Scripture prima facie is**. Who has the authority to call Pauline letters scripture or even the NT for that matter? Christians do no know what is sacred and what is secular so they are the wrong people to ask as none of them have the authority to decide Scripture.

While what is forgotten is that real scripture is interpreted by the Lewites according to YHWH. Yes we the Lewites are his chosen everlasting teachers not some fad Christians or Jews from Khazaria near Russia to decide.

> **Malaki 2:6-7** The Torah of truth was in his mouth, and iniquity was not found in his lips: he walked with me in shalom and equity, and did turn many away from idolatry. **7** For the kohen (priest)'s lips should Guard knowledge, and THEY [The Nations and true Y'sra'el] **should seek the Torah from his [Lewites] mouth**: for HE IS THE TEACHER from YHWH of hosts.

> **We'Yikra (Lev) 10:10** And that you may distinguish between set-apart and not set-apart, and between clean and unclean.

So first who is the Teacher? Read the answer above carefully, it is the Lewites the Kohanim who are the ones to decide Scripture or no Scripture.

YHWH does not give all the interpretation and commentary on the bottom of each page to all and sundry. So I find these ideas very fanciful to use words like "Scripture only", while what actually happened between teachers such as rabbis that a debate and discussion on a piece of scripture took place to arrive at some kind of consensus of what the passage means or it could be a complete variance from each other. Presently none of the Christians agree on anything with each other just look at them but at least the Rabbis laid out our their arguments on the table and examined them in light of both Scripture and history.

This is the way good Israelite Rabbis discuss things and I think the Christians and those who call themselves Torah observant believers would do well to adhere to this policy rather than calling other interpretations vain imagination when they themselves practice idolatry and vanity.

I could equally say that this idea of the Temple being rebuilt before the Messiah returns is a vain imagination but I am not going to insult others and be disrespectful by saying this. I accept that this is one opinion held by many Christians and Torah believers alike. However I also know they are wrong according to my understanding but I accept their opinion without hesitation.

However I want to present the other side of the coin to show that this thesis is difficult and unlikely to come to pass and I will present evidence now to show you why I say this. This is how we the true teachers of YHWH speak and do it and this is how the Hebrews have been doing it for many millennia to present their differing opinions and even this is how Muslims do it too who learned from the Israelites how to practice certain tenants.

The only people I see arguing with each other seems to be Christians but they really must get a grip of themselves and be a bit more reasonable with each other and give each other a chance to understand the various opinions. When it is a matter of halacha (way of doing something) it must be formulated and accepted by all parties so there are no arguments and in this the Rabbis are miles ahead of Christians because they have already established their halacha and their groups adhere to that. You will not find 38000 denominations in the Jews, ever wonder why. Now there is a surprise.

So my point scripture interpretation has to be made outside the Bible and by people and this idea of **Scripture only** is only a smoke screen and nothing more. I could present you several Scriptures which you are not going to be able to interpret by what many term **Scripture only** because no explanation is given in Scripture. Let me show you just one small example.

> **Lev 4:1-5** (HTHS) And YHWH spoke to Musa, saying, **2** Speak to the children of Y'sra'el, saying, If a soul shall transgress through ignorance against any of the commandments of YHWH concerning things which ought not to be done, and shall do against any of them: **3** If the Kohen (priest) that is anointed does transgress according to the transgression of the people; then let him bring for his transgression, which he has transgressed, a young bullock without blemish to YHWH for a transgression offering. **4** And he shall bring the bullock to the door of the Tent of the appointed times before YHWH; and shall lay his hand upon the bullock's head, and kill the bullock before YHWH. **5** And the Kohen (priest) that is anointed shall take of the bullock's blood,

and bring it to the Tent of the appointed times:

Now please interpret this with your Scripture only theory. If you are honest with yourself you will find it is impossible to interpret the passage above for several reasons. First it is clear the priests were to bring a bull. There are several questions that most Christians did not even think about and just say "Scripture only" without understanding what they mean by that.

1. What is the age of the young bull? The Torah does not tell you this.
2. What hand is the priest supposes to put on the bull's head? Torah is silent.
3. How is he going to kill the bull? Is he going to slash the throat of the bull or slash the leg or where exactly is the Priest meant to incise with the knife? Scripture is silent.
4. In verse 3 it says if the sin is unintentionally done so what type of sin can be classified in this group? Who decides?
5. In verse 5 it says the Priest shall take some of the blood, so how much is "some" blood? Is it a cup full, a jug full or more? Scripture is once again silent on this too.

You see from the one paragraph of what really is Scripture what may seem clear instructions but there are several items in the instructions that are not even explained so you cannot just interpret it by saying "**Scripture only**." Teachers have to sit down and work these things out and we can see not only Moses and Aharon knew this is how it is worked out but the later Hebrews also did likewise and this is why we have set halacha (way of conduct) or oral Torah given to our forefathers and I agree with the first century oral halacha.

If this is not done then anyone can in theory say **Scripture only** but each person will have to come up with his own interpretation of **Scripture only** with the 38,000 denominations of Christendom that cannot even agree between themselves and then it no longer remains a buzzword of "**Scripture only**." This is how Christendom ended up with 38,000 denominations because they have disagreements between each other. I hope my point is now clear that YHWH has set teachers (Lewites) people like me and others to reveal understanding so please next time you hear the term **SCRIPTURE ONLY** as a buzzword make sure that this matter has been debated and agreed by all parties concerned but if not then it is not "**scripture only"** but opinion only as one personal opinion against another, in other words one teacher over another!

Now I am not going to use the Christendom's buzz words but simply present to you my opinion on the matter why I do not think a Temple is likely before the return of Yahushua according to our scrolls given to our people.

What does our prophet Daniel tells us?

> **Daniel 12:11** (HTHS) And from the time that the daily sacrifice shall be taken away, and the abomination that lays waste is set up, there shall be a thousand two hundred ninety days.

If we examine the passage of Daniel then most commentators will agree with me that we time this for the return of Yahushua and not a rebuilding of the 3rd Temple before His return. This prophecy details when all the troubles of the Hebrews will finish with a complete situation of peace in future Israel and I doubt anyone would disagree with me that this will only happen when Melek Yahushua returns and not before. Please don't expect the Zionist infiltrators of the land to bring any peace any time soon but only wars as history and prophecy has proven since 1948. Even now they are fighting a war with the Palestinians in Gaza pounding Gaza during November 2012 when in fact the Palestinians are ill equipped to fight a modern Zionist army. A goliath and David situation.

The bullying and killing of Palestinian civilians is quite evident to those who want to see it while the rightwing Zionist media and Christians have become blind to the suffering of the innocent Palestinian people in Israel.

The prophecy of Daniel 12:11 is not talking about the three and half years of temporary peace with the anti-Messiah but a situation of complete autonomy of the land of Israel after which point the third Temple can commence its rebuilding, with real black Israelites back in the land which also requires the removal of the false occupiers, the so called Zionists self appointed counterfeit chosen people from the land. To suggest that the Temple at the present site is another interesting dilemma when you consider that modern Jerusalem is not ancient Jerusalem. In fact ancient Jerusalem is in Tel Arad so the real place of the Temple of King Solomon and Herod is there. Hence why the present Temple Mount is nothing but a counterfeit setup. The present wall or so called Kottel is nothing but the ancient garrison of the Roman Legion X. This is how many are being deceived in Israel today.

> **Debarim (Deut) 1:20** And I said to you, you have come into the Mountain of the Amoree, which YHWH our POWER will give to us.

I doubt some of them have even understood that the Temple is not going to be built on the present structure of the Temple mount which is at an average only about 35 acres of land. This is way too small for the third Temple and a counterfeit site. There are actually two Jerusalem's in Israel one which you know is really the Jerusalem of the Amorites built upon a Mountain and the other real Jerusalem of the Jebusites was built around Mountains. There is a distinct difference.

> **Psalm 125:2** As the **<u>mountains surround Yerushalim</u>**, so YHWH is around his people from henceforth even forever.

Anyone with a keen eye who has read the prophecy of Ezekiel which I will show you will notice something of great interest to us all that the Temple precinct is huge and not just 35 acres of land. I do not want to blind you with scientific facts and figures but let me give you a very simplistic interpretation.

> **Ezek 42:16-20** (HTHS) He measured the east side with the measuring reed, five hundred reeds, with the measuring reed round about. **17** He measured the north side, five hundred reeds, with the measuring reed round about.**18** He measured the south side, five hundred reeds, with the measuring reed.**19** He turned about to the west side, and measured five hundred reeds with the measuring reed. **20** He measured it by the four sides: it had a wall round about, five hundred reeds long, and five hundred broad, to make a separation between the sanctuary and the common place.

OKAY, so in layman talk a reed is 6 cubits we are going to take each cubit to be 22 inches for a royal cubit so you can multiply 6 by 22 inches as the royal cubit while a standard cubit is 18 inches. You may choose to use the standard cubit size that is fine by me but you will still fail to measure the figures to 35 acres of land. Reality check where you going to fit the Temple in the Mount today with this much land? Also consider my main argument this is not the real Jersualem so would you be allowed to put the Temple at the wrong site?

Four Sides of the Temple	**Reeds and Cubits**	1500 to 1833 yards or just over a square mile depending on whether you use 18 inches to the cubit or 22 inches for the royal cubit as I have used here.
North	500x6=3000 cubits	
South	500x6=3000 cubits	
East	500x6=3000 cubits	
West	500x6=3000 cubits	

I hope it is clear now that the Temple cannot be built on the present site because the present site is one too small and two not the real site. So we can see the conundrum that most of the teachers that say that the Hebrews are able to make the 3rd Millennial Temple is just not possible for several reasons some which I have mentioned or hinted at earlier.

1. The first is what do you do with the Muslim mosques at the present site? This is no problem when you consider this is not the real site of ancient Jerusalem.
2. The second is even if you remove the mosques the area is too small.
3. The third is that the Temple of Ezekiel does not fit the present area.
4. The fourth is that no ground near the Temple can be given to any gentile as it is all set-apart therefore contradicting Revelation 11:1 which suggests an area given to the gentiles (Muslims) immediately next to the Temple, which means this is not the 3rd Temple site. As I said earlier the present Jerusalem site is not ancient Jerusalem.

Most people have bought into the deception hook, line and sinker.

5. The present Zionists are not the true sons of Abraham but gentiles so the 3rd Temple cannot even be touched by the gentiles let alone even be built by their hands. An honest conclusion before we even begin the present gentiles calling themselves proselyte of the way are not the true children of Y'sra'el and are not permitted to touch the set-apart ground of the millennial Temple.

I hope now I can use that buzzword in reverse **Scripture only**. Can the **SCRIPTURE ONLY** crowd please show me how you are going to fit this 3rd Temple in the present Temple Mount and remove my five objection points above which many of you do not even understand as you support a foreign entity in the land and call them the chosen people when they are not? They are gentile converts, the Caucasian Ashkenazim Jews or even Sephardic ones in majority are gentile converts converted in the 5th century BCE in Yemen and the Ashkenazim in the 8th century CE in Khazaria? I did not reveal the 6th point that they are expecting a false cucasoid Messiah while the real one is black Negroid. Shocked? I would hope so, so get my book Yahushua the Black Messiah from Amazon to learn a few details on that. This will teach you more about the true Messiah and the true chosen people before any more brain washing by gentiles in your churches may continue. Now a teacher appointed by YHWH is speaking to you even when Melek Dawud will be raised he will be raised as a black man and not some white red faced king as none existed in Israel in such a way as Melek Dawud both had a black wife Bathsheba and her Son the Black King Solomon. Oh and not to mention the whole tribe of Yahudah was in majority a people of colour.

The practical reality is whichever way you dance and twist you cannot fit the circle into a square so we can do the twist together and we just cannot fit it not to mention the major war that will ensue after you demolish the mosques, every major Muslim nation will be gathering and sending armies over to Israel and even if Israel has 500 atomic bombs they cannot control all the Muslim nations with 1.6 billion followers however at that time it won't be Israel's firepower but only YHWH who will rescue our people but present Israel will be cleansed and all foreigners removed so the war is inevitable and no one can stop it. The Muslims are going to give you the big wars like it or not and it is predestined to happen that way.

Now let us examine the verse of the book of Revelation.

> **Rev 11:2** (HTHS) But the court which is outside the Beyth HaMikdash (Temple) leave out, and measure it not; for it is given to the gentiles: and the set-apart city shall they tread under foot three and a half years.

You can see the problem immediately with this if you have read what I wrote earlier. **Leave the court outside the Temple for the gentiles** (Muslims and even Jews). How can we leave the court outside for the gentiles because Ezekiel's Temple does not say that? In fact it says the Temple is around about a square mile wide but it also gives us another interesting detail that the area allotted to the priests is 61 miles square within which the Temple is built so immediately you can see this text in the book of Revelation does not apply to the 3rd Temple. To do so shows me that one does not have any understanding of true Biblical prophecy. You can calculate this in Ezekiel 45:1-4. The Temple that John the Black Hebrew was made to measure was the second Temple which was standing when he was writing his book which finished that is the book of the Apocalypse called Revelation was written before 70 CE and not 95 CE as Christian scholars would like you to believe. Another man-made religion to deceive the people out there. The Second or repaired Temple that Herod enlarged was completely and utterly destroyed just as the Master Yahushua said that not a single stone was left standing (Matthew 24). On the contradictions front present Jeruaslem has a whole big wall standing with large stones which again defies the prophecy of the Master. This they call the Kottle and the Eastern wall.

Now let's be reasonable does it sound like that any part of the set-apart land can be given to gentiles? Then how can gentiles on both sides one claiming to be Jews (counterfeit chosen) and the other claiming to be rightful owners the Muslims take our land away.

The text is clear in Ezekiel this cannot be given to the gentiles, while the text in Revelation is saying to leave the **court for the gentiles** do you see the problem? This once again defeats the objections that the Millennial Temple is rebuilt before the Messiah returns. The reasonable logic is that Ezekiel's Temple cannot be built before the return of Master Yahushua.

If you believe that the present modern Jerualem is real then you will have to destroy the Mosques and take away all the land that the Muslims occupy inside and around Jerusalem or destroy them and demolish the houses altogether in order not to give the land around the Temple to the Muslims followed by the automatic expulsion of all the gentiles that includes counterfeit chosen Jews the racist white Zionists variety and yes they will go says this Lewite. Also that modern Jerusalem is not the real Jerusalem so what a conundrum. However the real Jerusalem in Tel Arad is laid bare as prophesies dictated and is available to build on with giving plenty of space to the dwellings of the Kohanim.

> **Yeshayahu (Isa) 51:3** For YHWH shall comfort Tsiyon: he will comfort all her waste places; and he will make her wilderness like Ayden, and her wilderness like the garden of YHWH; joy and gladness shall be found therein, thanksgiving, and the voice of melody.

Tsiyon desolate just as prophesied.

> **Yeshayahu (Isa) 64:10** Your Set-Apart cities are a wilderness, Tsiyon is a wilderness, Yerushalim a desolation.

Therefore we expect to find Tsiyon and Jerusalem as a desolation and not some built up city.

> **Yermiyah (Jer) 3:14** Turn, O backsliding children, says YHWH; for I am married to you: and I will take you one of a city, and two of a family, and I will bring you to Tsiyon:

This is yet another proof that the return of Y'sra'elites to the land prior to the Messiah will be very selective and not everyone will return.

> **Yermiyah (Jer) 26:18** Mikahyah (Micah) the Moresheth prophesied in the days of Yakhizqiyahu (Hezekiah) Sovereign of Yahudah, and spoke to all the people of Yahudah, saying, Thus says YHWH of Armies; Tsiyon shall be plowed like a field, and Yerushalim shall become heaps, and the mountain of the house

as the high places of a forest.

Tsiyon to be ploughed like a field and proof that in 2014 May Tsiyon was plouged like a field when we went there.

Prophecy also dictates that no one treads Tsiyon. Isn't it true that no large scale Christains go searching for the real site of Tsiyon?

> **Yermeyah (Jer) 30:17** For I will restore health to you, and I will heal you of your wounds, says YHWH; because they called you an Outcast, saying, She is Tsiyon, whom no one treads.[49]

As I stated in my previous book that it is at least clear to me that an area on the future sacrifice altar will be offered to the Hebrews in the truce or peace treaty that is formed between Israel and the Muslim nations in future. The Islamic nations will not accept to have their mosques removed because this is set for a later time and the text of Revelation 11:1 has nothing to do with the Temple of Ezekiel because by the very suggestion that an area of that Temple is allotted to the gentiles, which is not the case in Ezekiel because in Ezekiel 45:1 this area belongs to the priests from the House of Lewi so no Muslim can have their home or mosque there and neither can any proselyte Jews from Khazaria or Yemen.

---

[49] People knew the real Hebrews were blacks but they were ignored and abused. The women were raped the men were killed, some even said their Elohim has cast them away. No one went searching and seeking for the true Tsiyon, its lying there in Israel in Tel Arad still in heaps. It will be rebuilt by the true Children of Y'sra'el.

> **Rev 11:1** (HTHS) And there was given to me a reed like a measuring rod: and the malakh stood, saying, Rise, and measure the Beyth HaMikdash (Temple) of YHWH, and the altar, and them that paid homage there.

Well this altar is in ancient Jerusalem.

Unless we do not believe in the scroll of Revelation to be true it states that to measure the Temple of YHWH and the altar for those that worship there a clear reference to the true black Hebrews but in verse 2 we are told to leave the area outside. This is the area which presently is occupied by the gentiles in this case the gentiles those that you call Jews the Ashkenazim who are the sons of Japheth and of course the Sephardic convert majority too.

To leave any area of the present Temple defeats the notion of those teachers who believe in a fully fledged Temple before the Messiah returns. I assert it cannot be done not until the Messiah has set foot on the ground, restoring the real black Y'sra'elite people and sorting out the mess of the Zionists who are not the inheritors of the land anyway. We are going to see a big earthquake which will divide Jerusalem Zech 14:4 and the feet of Him who stands there is no other than the Messiah of Israel who is also called YHWH our Right-Ruler (Jeremiah 23:6). It is clear in the text of Jeremiah that Judah will be rescued which is not yet fully in the land in majority but a tiny minority? Then many of which are still stuck in Europe and Americas including the Caribbean's yes I am talking about the real Y'sra'elites, the black ancestors of Negro Abraham and his Negro wives one of which was Sarah out of the four that he had. Now there is a surprise that Sarah was also black from the area of Africa called Chad. Only black people lived there in the past and even today. If you want to locate our father Abraham's ancestors you can locate them in Seno/Gambia region the fulfulbe people they are his ancestors that became Hebrew but they are not Y'sra'elites as there is a difference.

You have the Hebrews who could just be ancestors or converts to our faith.

You then have the Jews of Khazaria that have a religion called Judaism that were converted out of Khazaria and Yemen.

You then have the Y'sra'elites that is us we are the sons of Yaqub known also as Y'sr'ael. These distinctions are important to remember. Many of us call ourselves Hebrew Y'sra'elites however the correct designation is either Y'sra'elites and others call us people of the Book

(Torah) such as the Arabic word Ahlul Qitab.

The great war that ensues in the future against Israel and the tribe of Yahudah will be meriting complete salvation/rescue as they are in the Father's hands already meaning the real Yahudah are saved presently but will be revealed the full revelation later (Luke 15:31). The area of the holy mount will be expanded to make room for the 3rd Temple or properly known as Ezekiel's Temple otherwise why would YHWH break the already standing 3rd Temple by dividing the valley and bringing in the earthquake? This is the time also when the whole land will be cleansed to allow the Temple of Ezekiel to be built. YHWH himself tells us that He is IN Israel (Ezekiel 39:7). This is not allegorical but matches with Zechariah where His feet are firmly placed on the Mountain of Olives in Tel Arad.

Now let us examine the letter of Thessalonians even though it is not inspired in anyway and neither is Paul of Tarsus any kind of Apostle but just to sastisfy Christian curosity I will speak on it. Note none of our Y'sra'elite people walked around with Pauline letters in their hands in the first century. We did not call these letters scripture neither held them sacred. If you get my book from Amazon Paul of Tarsus, The Thirteeth Apostle that will help you understand Paul.

> **Second Thess 2:4** (HTHS) Who opposes and exalts himself above all that is called Elohim, or that is petitioned; so that he as Elohim sits in the temple of elohim, showing himself that he is elohim.

Many have made the mistake of calling this fully fledged 3rd Temple while I insist that nothing could be further from the truth because with this in mind the prophets prophesies are broken and let me show you why.

> **Ezek 44:9** (HTHS) Thus says Master YHWH; **No foreigner, uncircumcised in heart, and uncircumcised in flesh**, shall enter into my sanctuary, of any foreigner that is among the children of Y'sra'el.

To use the buzzword "Scripture only" anyone who can read and see that YHWH will not allow a **foreigner to enter His Temple**. This excludes all your present definition of Jews in Israel who are Caucasian of any description. However not the Dimona Black Y'sra'elites as they are true Y'sra'elites. Also neither the Sephardim from the conversions of Yemen.

It says NO Foreigner shall be allowed inside, yet here I am being asked to believe some supposed theory that the anti-Messiah will be able to sit in the Temple of YHWH and defile it who by the way is a foreign/gentile.

This should one clue why Pauline epistles are not inspired.

This is why sometimes I think that the western prophecy teachers do not pay much attention to the small details of the text and come up with new theories by using the usual buzzword "Scripture only," While when we really go to scripture we find the theory does not fit. The only way the anti-Messiah could potentially sit in the Temple of YHWH would be to repent and convert and become a converted Israelite but we know that this will not be happening either. Ezekiel says it cannot be, so what in the world is Paul speaking about? Let us once again examine the text.

> **Second Thess 2:4** (HTHS) Who opposes and exalts himself above all that is called Elohim, or that is worshipped; so that he as Elohim sits in the temple of elohim, showing himself that he is elohim.

At no time does the Anti-Messiah say 'I am YHWH worship me,' nor does he say I am your Master Yahushua the Messiah of Israel.' This is the error made by many writers which is brought about by misreading the text of Paul that is uninspiring of the uninspired texts of all his letters. Let us take a close look at the verse above and let us see how it should read. First of all the Bible does not say that the Anti-Messiah proclaims himself as the Messiah. You will not find any single passage supporting this claim. Secondly the issue of him sitting and exalting himself as YHWH needs to be re-examined. No Muslim Anti-Messiah will ever say I am the son of Allah since Allah does not have a son so another problem with buzz words.

Let us now go back to the Greek language to get some more insight. The very first words in the letter of Second Thessalonians 2:4 say, 'who opposes.' There lies our first clue, and we have to ask the question, opposes what? The Greek word used there is 'antikeimai', which means opposite, contrary, or against. He opposes, or is against the teachings of Yahushua the Messiah by proclaiming himself as the way to YHWH by good works. While the Bible teaches contractual based salvation, Muslims teach good works to gain paradise, so this leader will do likewise. Furthermore, the text says, 'He sits AS God.'

Yet many rulers have proclaimed themselves 'as' God, but died later, because they were 'only' human. In like manner this individual proclaims 'himself' like God by saying in essence, 'if you follow me and take the mark i.e. acceptance and submission of Allah, then you will go to heaven.' So this displays power over men's souls AS God but not the true God YHWH. The temple that the anti-Messiah sits in is not the 3rd Temple at all as believed by many but a shrine/mosque of the gentiles. As I showed you above no foreign person can enter Ezekiel's Temple including foreign Ashkenazim alleged Jews who are not chosen. Now here is another bitter pill to swallow the anti-Messiah will be killed so when will he sit in the third Temple exactly please tell me?

> **Ezekiel 28:7-8** (HTHS) Behold, therefore I will bring foreigners upon you, the terrible of the nations: and they shall draw their swords against the beauty of your wisdom, and they shall defile your brightness. **8** They shall bring you down to the pit, and **you shall die the deaths of them that are slain** in the midst of the seas.

There lies your anti-Messiah quite DEAD and IMMOBILE. So much for sitting in the Temple of YHWH.

Moreover Daniel the prophet showed us that the Anti-Messiah in fact worships a god of fortresses, which we know is the god of Jihad, the deity of Islam, which we all now know is Allah.

> **Daniel 11:38** (HTHS) But in his place he shall respect the elaha (power) of strongholds: and an elaha (power) whom his ahvot (fathers) did not know; he shall respect with gold, and silver, and with precious stones, and pleasant things.

So is Paul bigger than Daniel the prophet? No, people have made mistakes with him who was nothing but a self proclaimed apostle while the Master Yahushua spoke out against him in Rev 2:2 calling him a false apostle but did you even bother to examine the text of who was in Ephesus calling himself an apostle. This was no other than Paul himself.

> **Rev 2:2** I know your works, and your labour, and your patience, and how you cannot tolerate them which are evil: and you have tried them which said they are Emissaries (Apostles), and are not, and have found them liars:

So there was more than one Apostle there that includes Paul and another one that I detail in my book.

Modern people call his letters inspired which are not. Furthermore a man can be called elohim because the Hebrew term behind the word elohim simply means "mighty one/s" or "power/s" and it can even be applied to an angel or a judge. It can apply to a human leader or a warrior. So even if we take the extreme wrong interpretation of Second

Thessalonians we can see that if the anti-Messiah called himself elohim he is only declaring himself to be a mighty warrior on the earth. The same way Yahushua said you are gods (elohim). John 10:34, which was quoted from Psalm 82:6.

> **John 10:34** (KJV) Jesus answered them, is it not written in your law, I said, Ye are gods?
>
> John 10:34 (HTHS) Yahushua answered them, Is it not written in your Torah, I said, Ye are powers (elohim)?
>
> **Psalm 82:6** (KJV) I have said, Ye *are* gods; and all of you *are* children of the most High.

Now let us examine the book of Acts at what that is hinting at

> **Acts 15:16** (HTHS) After this I will return, and will Rebuild again the Tent of Dawud, which is fallen down; and I will Rebuild again the ruins there, and I will set it up:

This text is a prophecy from Amos 9:11.

> **Amos 9:11** (HTHS) In that day will I raise up the Tent of Dawud that is fallen, and repair the breeches there; and I will raise up his ruins, and I will rebuild it as in the days of old:

This text can be looked at both ways physically and spiritually but it is actually a hint or drash (allegorical, picture) of the restoration of the twelve tribes under the banner of King David and not about the physical Temple. The Greek word used for build in Acts 15:16 is Strong's G456 *anoy-kodom-eh'-o* which is taken from the Hebrew in Acts 9:11 Strong's H1129 which is Banah. Banah has the Hebrew root word "ben" for Son, which indicates the son is the builder of the home so therefore the word both in Greek and Hebrew indicates to "rebuild" and not just build. So we would build something already there and broken or in disrepair. If you ever happen to go to Tel Arad you will find the Tabernacle of David there in disrepair and that is what we will build.

Tabernacle of David called the Fort of the Cannanites in Tel Arad.

I was there so I know with the other Israelites. Look in the sky you will see a menorah formation which YHWH showed in the sky accepting our service and repetance of our lips.

The real site of ancient Bethlehem is close by in Tel Arad. Right to left Moreh Co Browne, Daniel, Rabbi Amariel Howshua, Rabbi Simon Altaf, Rabbi Kefa Ben Yah and Rabbi John Amalraj.

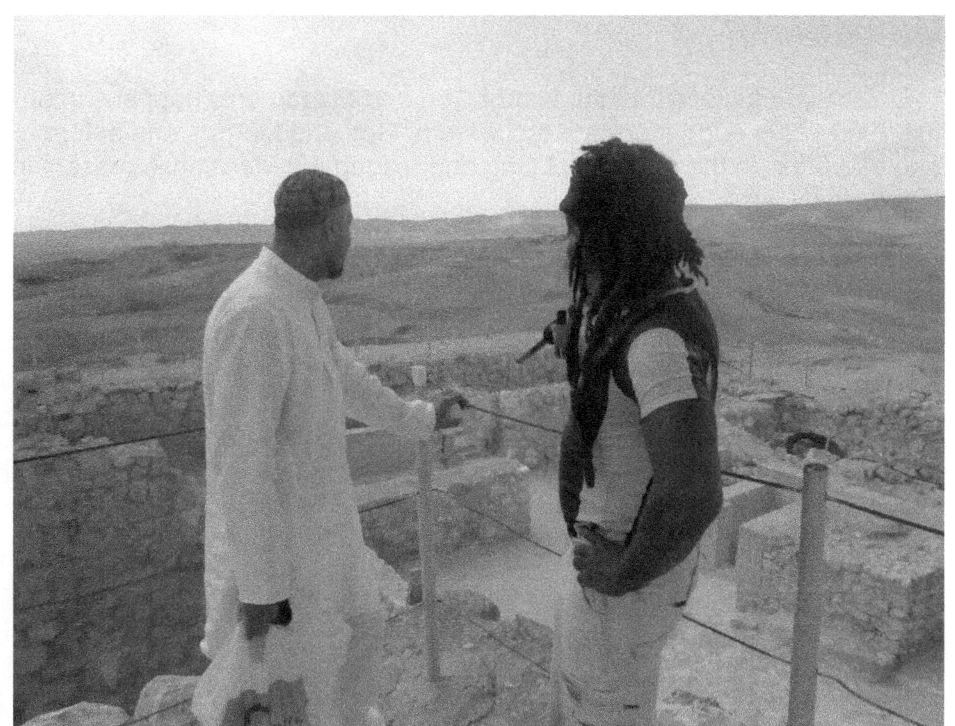
Rabbi Amariel Howshua from the House of Ephrayim and Rabbi Simon Altaf from the House of Lewi at the Tabernacle of David in Israel Tel Arad.

This means YHWH is going to bring together the sons of Israel under one united King not only king David will be resurrected in the millennium kingdom but also under the universal king Messiah. It is clear to me that this text coupled with Acts 15:1-16 that YHWH will draw in the Ten scattered real northern tribes back to Israel for a united Israel as Israel will no longer be divided into two nations as it was after the time of King Solomon. The man who will do the joining will be the Messiah who will repair the breech which is hinted at in Acts 15:16 meaning Tikkun Olam to repair the world, a work which no physical human being can do but only the Messiah of Israel can accomplish and has already accomplished in the spiritual but we have yet to see the final physical results. King David will be the King of this United Kingdom in Israel. The question is will he be raised before or after the Messiah returns.

Even if I was completely wrong in my stated opinion on this particular text let us assume that it is talking about a physical Temple, still the text does not suggest at anytime that this physical Temple is before the return of Messiah.

How do we know that the 3rd Temple can only be built when the

Messiah returns?

Unless you believe that the war of Gog and Magog only happens after the 1000 years reign there are two wars of Gog and Magog, one before and one after. In the first war of Gog and Magog the Messiah is present in Israel.

> **Ezek 39:7** (HTHS) So will I make my Set-Apart name known in the midst of my people Y'sra'el; and I will not let them pollute my Set-Apart name any more: and the nations shall know that I am YHWH, the Set-Apart One **IN** Y'sra'el.

Note when the armies come up (Ezekiel 38:1-6) to surround Israel YHWH himself will descend IN Israel and He would no longer be just sitting in the heavens minding His own business because Israel is His business and His chosen people are the apple of His eyes. We are talking about the real Israel which you can find more details by getting the next in the series to this book called World War III – The Second Exodus, Y'sra'el's Return Journey Home from Amazon books.

The nail in the coffin for those who believe a fully fledged Temple can stand without the Messiah is the following.

> **Ezek 37:26** (HTHS) Moreover I will **make a Contract/Agreement of peace** with them; it shall be an everlasting Contract/Agreement with them: and I will place them, and multiply them, and will **set my sanctuary** in the midst of them for evermore.

There is no Contract/Agreement of peace which must follow the building of the Temple with Israel as yet between YHWH and true Israel as they are not even in the land fully so once this is formed even the animals in Israel will not fight each other as depicted in Isaiah 65:25.

> **Isa 65:25** (HTHS) The wolf and the lamb shall feed together, and the lion shall eat straw like the bullock: and dust shall be the serpent's meat. They shall not hurt nor destroy in all my Set-Apart mountain, says YHWH.

The secret is all in the First Resurrection

> **Ezek 37:4-5, 10, 12** Again he said to me, Prophesy upon these bones, and say to them, O you dry bones, hear the word of YHWH. **5** Thus says Master YHWH to these bones; Behold, I will cause breath to enter into you, and you shall have life: **10** So I

prophesied as he commanded me, and the breath came into them, and THEY LIVED , (they were dead before but the resurrection caused them to live), and stood up upon their feet, an exceeding great army. **12** Therefore prophesy and say to them, Thus says the Master YHWH; Behold, O my people, I will open your graves, and cause you to come up out of your graves, and bring you into the land of Y'sra'el.

I will open your graves: YHWH will literally open up their graves and raise them up in the Millennium from their death in the different countries and take our peopel home. Many Christians have been taught to gloss over these verses and Pastors come up with fanciful theories about the new birth, while the full force effect of the prophecy is not going to be fulfilled until the return of the Messiah. I hear many like to believe and gloss over this by calling this the Christian Church. Nothing could be further from the truth as this is the real Black chosen Israelites woken up. If this is The Church then what is the sanctuary? See my videos on www.youtube.com/simalt on the resurrection of true Israel.

Bring you into the land: YHWH is going to put life back into dead bones of the House of Israel, the ten tribes and raise them up this is why it will be the greatest Exodus back from Egypt (the allegoric world/USA and real Egypt in North Africa). They will return from whichever country they died in and return to Israel as it shall be a glorious resurrection and then the Temple shall be rebuilt by redeemed Black Israel. This will be a sight for all nations to see and after this the nations will fear YHWH. The dead right now are kept in She'ol (parts of hell) but there they are kept to be resurrected because of the Contract/Agreement promises made in Deut 29:1 and Deut 30:6.

Chapter 11
Who is the prince and why does he give the sin offering in the 3rd Temple?

> **Ezek 43:19** (HTHS) And you shall give to the kohenim the Lewites that be of the descendants of Tzadok, which approach to me, to minister to me, says the Master YHWH, a young bullock for a transgression offering.

The best teachers out there cannot explain why YHWH requires a sin sacrifice in the coming Temple. Many Christians have been taught to ignore the millennial Temple as an allegory only and the sacrifices as simply looking back to the sacrifice of the Messiah and therefore educational and not in reality for a transgression, this is the kind of theology taught in Churches. There is also a man identified as the prince in Ezekiel 44:3, which most teachers see as Yahushua except me of course who does not see him as Yahushua at all and the sin sacrifice is not educational.

There are many problems and contradictions in the views I have described above whichever side of the debate you are on as I will highlight some for you.

Problems to address;

- The 3rd Temple is real and not an allegory, so if this is a real Temple then what is the point of a Temple if you cannot sacrifice for sins since the meaning of the Temple is that the shekinah of YHWH may be in it and that you may sacrifice for those who have committed various types of sins or when there are the seven annual celebrations of Israel such as Passover, Unleavened Bread, First-Fruits, Pentecost, Yom Terua, Yom Kippurim and Tabernacles. The various sacrifices that are commanded shall be offered and a host of other functions too numerous to detail here would be done that are now on hold.
- How can you sacrifice for someone's sins if the Messiah Yahushua is a one time sacrifice for the whole world? Does that show you Christian Pastors' have been lying and misleading the masses?
- How can the prince offer a sin offering for himself if he is the Messiah (Ezekiel 45:22)?
- How can the prince have real physical children if he is the Messiah YHWH incarnate on earth (Ezekiel 46:16)?

I am going to be totally honest with you so be ready for the shocking truth. I have the answers to all these questions and many more however I am not going to answer all these questions here but I will address some of these as summary since it really does require a whole book to explain what is going on in these pages of scripture. Moreover, you will have to throw out much of your past teachings out of the window because it is my opinion whether you agree with me or not that most of the teachings out are contradicotry to Torah and completely wrong. After I start addressing some of the issues you will see how many wrong teachings have been created to get over the obvious obstacles. You may also have learnt that the so called Jews in Israel are the chosen so this sets everything garbled because you don't even know who is really an Y'sra'elite anymore. The Church certainly is clueless on these and many other important issues while they simply gloss over and continue in error. All the denominations are the same no matter what you call yourself.

However there is good news as always that even if your view on this is 100% wrong it makes no difference to your salvation because that is not dependent on you or your teachers getting this teaching on the millennium Temple and its sacrifices correct however if you are wrong about the Torah observances you will forfeit your resurrection so be careful including possibly your entire salvation.

Now let me state my belief and opinion that YHWH does not allow everyone to see everything at all times. This means that YHWH allows His priests to be able to address things as He sees fit giving them understanding and knowledge on the subject. This by no means is an indication that we have all the information available for everything as it is a learning and understanding process that takes a few lifetimes and even if I did have much of the information I would not give it since it is indigestible by most of the public out there and is very complex. I refuse to dazzle with science and wish to stay to the simple explanations and the facts and history of our Y'sra'elite people. The complex side is really for my close personal students only in the distant online learning Yeshivah at www.african-israel.com.

There is a saying what you do not know does not harm you. That can be sometimes true however sometimes it is better to know so that you can avoid any future pitfalls because what you do not know may actually harm you. One more thing I am going to throw in the mix whether you like it or not is that Christendom will have to merge into the real Israelite faith because Christendom is not the truth and while Judiasm created in the middle ages has kept the feasts and Sabbaths, while many Christian practices are paganism and will not stand. I am not talking about the present day view of the Messiah of Judaism but the real view of Messiah as it was held by the first century disciples and the priests and ancient prophets of Israel the pure Judaism or Y'sra'elite faith called The Way.

Here is a scripture to ponder on.

> **Isa 2:3** (HTHS) And many people shall go and say, Come, and let us go up to the mountain of YHWH, to the Temple of Elohim of Yaqub; and he will teach us of his ways, and we will walk in his paths: for out of Tsiyon shall go forth the Torah and the word of YHWH from Yerushalim.

Now ask yourself what happened to the Vatican in Rome and Lourdes in France. Why are people being directed back to the Torah in Jerusalem? I thought it was all done away with and abrogated. This is where Christendom gets a rude awakening!

These people going up to learn the LAW/Torah of YHWH, they are not just common or heathen people but are Christians who behaved badly and put real Israelites down but in the millennium will come to their senses that they were wrong in their views of putting down Yahudim traditions and laws. Many Christians near the end will start to learn and adapt Hebrew roots and customs, which is the true path back to our faith while those that died will suffer the consequences.

While I do not intend to create a division by arguing and fighting with people on what I understand versus what they do it has no benefit to me and proves nothing. I offer this information as is so you can take it or leave it because this is my understanding through the Holy One of Israel over many years of diligent petitions to him, study and complete submission to Him to this day and to the end of my life and beyond.

Let us break it down one step at a time.

Who is the prince? Is he is the Messiah of Israel e.g. Yahushua?

> **Ezek 45:22** (HTHS) And upon that day shall the Nasi prepare for himself and for all the people of the land a bullock for a transgression offering.

If we take that view that he is the Messiah then how can he be offering a sin sacrifice? Therefore He is not the Messiah, see Ezekiel 45:22 above. The sacrifice is very real and not educational. Sorry this teaching that emanates out of some messianic camps that it is educational is incorrect because it cannot bypass the obvious. In the past I have simply not wanted to address the issue or argue with my friends so when they said to me it is educational I said OK, however in reality it is not educational. I am sorry to say that in many of our views of the coming of Messiah and what happens thereafter has a lot of gaps but some of those gaps can be filled very easily if we study and petition Abbah YHWH diligently for answers some of which are available in scripture but veiled. They are not obvious to all I assure you. The Tanakh is a very complex and mysterious book few can really understand some of the precepts well and only the appointed teachers the Lewim are allowed to know these matters. The rest only grope in the darkness as things are veiled in dark hidden sayings. Even YHWH envelopes in the darkness.

I think in order to understand these passages in the last four chapters of Ezekiel it is critical that you put your views to one side at least until you read this chapter. After this you will either love me or hate me. You will not hate me in a bad way but in a good way as this article will force you to re-evaluate all the teachings you have learnt and even if you are not willing to accept many things I write this does not mean we become enemies but it does mean that at least you will have seen what is coming to pass in the future and you may have some answers for unanswered questions and over time these things will be confirmed.

Since my background is not Christian it forces me to look at everything differently as I did not grew up in a Church background learning from the Pastors. In fact I spent time with Muslim clerics trying to understand Islam.

I saw many contradictory teachings in the Qur'an and Hadith but of course the clerics would ignore me as I was only a kid then and they would tell me not to ask questions that I had no understanding of these as a child and that in due course the understanding would come. I can tell you that they were right that in due course the God of Israel has given me the understanding of what is truth and who I really am, so their words became prophetic for me.

Now coming back to the prince this person has sons and I am saying he has physical children, which is real flesh and blood and not just spiritual entities. Once again Christendom proven to be untrue who teach people do not get married in the millennium and have children.

> **Ezek 46:16** (HTHS) Thus says the Master YHWH; if the Nasi give a gift to any of his sons, the **inheritance there shall be his sons**; it shall be their possession by inheritance.

He has an inheritance of land in Israel. Well why would the Messiah only have a small portion of land since He owns the whole world?

> **Ezek 46:17** (HTHS) But if he give a gift of his inheritance to one of his servants, then it shall be his to the year of release; after it shall return to the Nasi: but his inheritance shall be his sons for them.

This person is not Yahushua but the problem is in our translation which does not allow us to see who this person is. Let me give you the translation from the Hidden-Truths Hebraic Scrolls Bible then you will see partially and it will actually help you to see more truth.

> **Ezek 45:22 (HTHS)** And upon that day shall the Nasi prepare for himself and for all the people of the land a bullock for a sin offering.

Note the word in Hebrew is not a prince but Nasi which actually means a leader. The usual word for a prince is Sar and not Nasi. To illustrate the point Jacob was the first Nasi of the Jerusalem Synagogues and not a prince or you could say leader. There were no churches or the word church did not creep into the dictionary until the 4th century CE. Jacob was the Nasi of the Jerusalem believing synagogues.

YHWH is going to resurrect King David in the Millennium and this is our Nasi in the person of King David. He is the one who will offer the sin offerings.

He will be the King while the Messiah will be the Universal king, the model of Pharaoh and Yosef in the reign of Egypt.

How do we know it is King David?

> **Jer 30:9** But they shall serve YHWH their Elohim, and **Dawud their Sovereign**, whom I will raise up to them.

King David will be raised to sit upon the throne of Israel.

The second problem, how can King David sin if he is resurrected? Are we not taught that raised people cannot sin therefore how can King David sin in the millennium in his resurrected body or anyone else who is resurrected for that matter?

Welcome to the school of Rabbi Simon African-Israel Yeshivah 101.

You have been taught that this is so and so but can you prove that a resurrected body cannot sin? The answer is no because the only way resurrected bodies stop sinning is if their FREEWILL is removed. If you have freewill you still have the capability to sin. Even in every universe YHWH has created there is a small amount of evil so that a person's freewill can be measured. Without evil present there can be no choice or sin so a tiny fraction of evil is necessary to allow free choice. So you can consider Satan the personification of Yetzer Hara or evil inclination.

We do not need Satan for us to commit a sin because at that time it will strictly be by choice and not compulsion hence why the sacrifices for the King and people who will be alive in Israel is rightly for sins by choice. King David will not be condemned in the eternal state order but the sacrifice is to honour YHWH and fulfil the law in the Torah of YHWH that demands that it be done.

As an example look at the angels, do they have earthly bodies? No. Can they sin? Yes. How? Many angels have freewill. This is how a third of the angels rebelled. Not all the angels are robots and neither are we. Millennium or no millennium sin will still be here as long as men and women have FREEWILL. Judaism also has error in its teaching today by teaching that angels have no freewill.

So this answers our question very easily that as resurrected beings we will make marriages and have the freewill to sin if we wanted to but then YHWH has made provision in the Temple. Note we are not into eternity at that point in time but the 7th day which is the 1000 years reign. After this Satan will be released on the 8th day. Scripture does not tell us what date Satan is completely removed but gives us a clue and we enter eternity but in my opinion we enter eternity on the 10th day. That is after 10,000 years of the earth's sojourn when the rebellious angels bound in the abyss are put into the Lake of Fire. Enoch wrote about this, please read his book which can be acquired from our website with a good translation and commentary.

Now some of you may find this hard but no one goes to heaven apart from the Messiah who lives in heaven and I mean no one. All the dead right-ruling people are kept in the section known as Paradise in She'ol and will be raised from there. I am surprised that I am the only one who is saying this while everyone else wants to believe that the mansions the Messiah built are where the dead saints are however once again I must disagree with these bad teachings.

The unruly dead are also kept in She'ol in parts known as hell in cells or chambers like prison cells until the second or third resurrection. There are three resurrections and not two. Sorry for giving you a hard time as you will have to do a purge delete and reboot your brains so they can be cleansed of all these errors.

For your information She'ol is under the earth and encompasses several countries and is vast. Some countries that are above She'ol are Saudi Arabia, Iraq, Iran, Israel, and Syria in fact the whole of the middle-east for quick reference including parts of Africa.

For more on She'ol please read this article: http://www.african-israel.com/Simon/hell.html

There is a reason why I say 10,000 years that is because we have two battles of Gog and Magog one just before the millennium starts and one after the 8th day. The number 10 is important as YHWH reveals himself as Ten and not seven as in a Menorah as many thought. This corresponds to the ten sefirots, the 7 correspond to the upper 7 seferiah's. Abraham had ten tests, YHWH gave ten plagues, YHWH gave the Ten Commandments and hence the number ten was for judgment of nations and the ten tribes of Israel went astray namely the House of Israel. So it is my opinion that when 10,000 years are complete then we will have our white throne judgment and the last resurrection of the dead. Early believers did not see the godhead as a trinity but as a binitarian view and here is proof.

> [50]A binitarian view was still held by Roman leaders in the third century, such Hippolytus. Hippolytus wrote:
>
> He did not say, "I and the Father am one, but are one." For the word "are" is not said of "one" person, but it refers to two persons, and one power...
>
> Earliest believers worship specifies two figures, God the Father and Jesus, as recipients (Hurtado Larry. Abstract: "The Binitarian Shape of Early Christian Worship". International Conference on the Historical Origins of the Worship of Jesus. 13-17 June 1998).
>
> The argument that Christianity is not binitarian but Trinitarian, hence could not be perceived as a two-powers heresy, ignores the

---

50 http://www.cogwriter.com/two.htm

fact that it is not so much what Christianity thought of itself that counts but how it appeared to its rabbinic critics. And there we see clearly that it was often described as binitarian or dualistic rather than Trinitarian (Summary of response by Alan F. Segal. International Conference on the Historical Origins of the Worship of Jesus. 13-17 June 1998).

While Paul engages in a great deal of legitimation for his view of Torah, there is no indication that he felt the need to defend himself against charges of 'two powers' heresy. Paul's view of the exalted Christ's investiture with the divine name (Phil.2:9-11) must be viewed in relation to non-Christian Yahudim texts such as the Apocalypse of Abraham. This work refers to an exalted angel, Yahoel, who bears the divine name (Apoc.Abr.10:3, 8). There is simply no evidence that belief in a supreme mediator or agent of God, one that might later be called a 'second power,' was controversial at any point during the first century CE. This is not to be explained by the lack of any universally recognized authority which could speak for Yahudim 'orthodoxy' in this period. Even within the context of first century Yahudim diversity, parties in conflict with one another took seriously the objections of their opponents and sought to respond to them. In the case of Paul's claims about the exalted Christ and of Philo's view of the Logos as a second God, there is nothing to indicate that their contemporaries found them to be heretical or controversial...the Tosefta contains several references to Christians as minim ('heretics').

The lack of explicit reference to 'two powers' cannot be explained as a lack of interest in Christianity, since the rabbis who composed the Tosefta took the trouble to polemicize against Christians. So, if Christian belief in 'two powers in heaven' was an issue at that time, it is quite surprising that the Mishnah and the Tosefta do not mention it" (James McGrath (Alliance Theological Seminary) with Jerry Truex (Tabor College). TWO POWERS' AND EARLY YAHUDIM AND CHRISTIAN MONOTHEISM http://www.iwu.edu/~religion/ejcm/McGrath_SBL2001_TwoPowers.htm 9/18/04).

Also, Ignatius, who was known by Polycarp (and praised in this same Polycarp epistle) wrote around 100-115 A.D.,

For our God, Jesus Christ, was conceived by Mary in accord with God's plan: of the seed of David, it is true, but also of the Holy

Spirit. He was born and baptized so that by His submission He might purify the water (Ignatius of Antioch, Letters to the Ephesians 18,2--note this is translated the same by at least three separate translations as done by Dr. Lightfoot, J.H. Srawley, and Roberts & Donaldson).

...God appeared in human form to bring newness of eternal life (Ignatius. Letter the Ephesians, 19, 3. In Holmes: The Apostolic Fathers: Greek Texts and English Translations. Baker Books, Grand Rapids (MI), 2004, p. 149).

Ignatius, who is also Theophorus, unto her which hath been increased in greatness through the plentitude of God the Father; which hath been foreordained before the ages to be for ever unto abiding and unchangeable glory, united and elect in a true passion, by the will of the Father and of Jesus Christ our God; even unto the church which is in Ephesus [of Asia], worthy of all felicitation: abundant greeting in Christ Jesus and in blameless joy (Ignatius' Letter to the Ephesians, Verse 0. In Apostolic Fathers. Lightfoot & Harmer, 1891 translation).

A second century apologist named Athenagoras wrote the following:

And, the Son being in the Father and the Father in the Son, in oneness and power of spirit, the understanding and reason (*nous kai logos*) of the Father is the Son of God...The Holy Spirit...which operates in the prophets, we assert to be an effluence of God, flowing from Him, and returning back again like a beam of the sun...Who, then, would not be astonished to hear men who speak of God the Father, and of God the Son, and of the Holy Spirit (Athenagoras. A Plea for the Christians, Chapter X. Translated by B.P. Pratten. Excerpted from Ante-Nicene Fathers, Volume 2. Edited by Alexander Roberts & James Donaldson. American Edition, 1885. Online Edition Copyright © 2004 by K. Knight).

Near the end of the second century, Melito of Sardis (whom Catholics and others consider to be a saint) wrote

No eye can see Him, nor thought apprehend Him, nor language describe Him; and those who love Him speak of Him thus: `Father, and God of Truth" (Melito. A Discourse Which Was in the Presence of Antoninus Caesar. In Ante-Nicene Fathers by

Roberts and Donaldson, Volume 8, 1885. Hendrickson Publishers, Peabody (MA), printing 1999, p. 755).

Melito also wrote, "For the deeds done by Christ after His baptism, and especially His miracles, gave indication and assurance to the world of the Deity hidden in His flesh. For, being at once both God and perfect man likewise...He concealed the signs of His Deity, although He was the true God existing before all ages" (Melito. On the Nature of Christ. In Ante-Nicene Fathers by Roberts and Donaldson, Volume 8, 1885. Hendrickson Publishers, Peabody (MA), printing 1999, 760).

At least one Trinitarian scholar has acknowledged:

The language of the New Testament permits the Holy Spirit to be understood as an impersonal force or influence more readily than it does the Son...The attempt to develop an understanding of the Holy Spirit consistent with the trinitarian passages...came to fruition at Constantinople in 381...those who saw the Holy Spirit as a Person, were often heretical, for example, the Montanists (Brown HOJ. Heresies: Heresy and Orthodoxy in the History of the Church. Hendrickson Publishers, Peabody (MA), 1988, p. 140).

Polycarp Taught that The Father is God

Second century writers, like Polycarp, referred to the Father as God. And that He was the Father of Jesus.

Polycarp of Smyrna wrote:

But may the God and Father of our Lord Jesus Christ, and Jesus Christ Himself, who is the Son of God, and our everlasting High Priest, build you up in faith and truth, and in all meekness, gentleness, patience, long-suffering, forbearance, and purity; and may He bestow on you a lot and portion among His saints, and on us with you, and on all that are under heaven, who shall believe in our Lord and God Jesus Christ, and in His Father, who "raised Him from the dead (Polycarp. Letter to the Philippians. From *Ante-Nicene Fathers, Volume 1* as edited by Alexander Roberts & James Donaldson. American Edition, 1885. Section 12 modified by R. Thiel to correct omission in translation).

Polycarp Did Not Teach that the Holy Spirit Was God

Where did the idea of the Holy Spirit being one hypostasis of a trinity come from?

It did not come from Polycarp. It actually came from the famous heretic Valentinus in the early to mid 2nd century (note that Valentinus is considered to be a heretic by Catholics, Orthodox, Protestant, and Church of God adherents).

Now with the heresy of the Ariomaniacs, which has corrupted the Church of God...These then teach three hypostases, just as Valentinus the heresiarch first invented in the book entitled by him 'On the Three Natures'. For he was the first to invent three hypostases and three persons of the Father, Son and Holy Spirit, and he is discovered to have filched this from Hermes and Plato (Source: Logan A. Marcellus of Ancyra (Pseudo-Anthimus), 'On the Holy Church': Text, Translation and Commentary. Verses 8-9. Journal of Theological Studies, NS, Volume 51, Pt. 1, April 2000, p.95).

Polycarp taught about the Kingdom of God:
"Blessed are the poor, and those that are persecuted for righteousness' sake, for theirs is the kingdom of God" (Polycarp. Letter to the Philippians, Chapter II. From *Ante-Nicene Fathers, Volume 1*as edited by Alexander Roberts & James Donaldson. American Edition, 1885).

Knowing, then, that "God is not mocked," we ought to walk worthy of His commandment and glory ...For it is well that they should be cut off from the lusts that are in the world, since "every lust warreth against the spirit; " and "neither fornicators, nor effeminate, nor abusers of themselves with mankind, shall inherit the kingdom of God," nor those who do things inconsistent and unbecoming (Polycarp. Letter to the Philippians, Chapter V. From *Ante-Nicene Fathers, Volume 1*as edited by Alexander Roberts & James Donaldson. American Edition, 1885).

Polycarp taught about the kingdom of YHWH and to obey the commandments meaning to keep Torah that today many Christians are wrongly taught that they are for the Jews only. Now whether you believe in the trinity, binitarian view, Unitarian view or some other view, YHWH is not limited to human views and does not judge of what we do not know. I think it is wrong for people to condemn others who do not believe in the trinity or other views and let YHWH be judge because YHWH is Akhad (Unity).

Objection: How can there be marriages in the Millennial Kingdom when Yahushua clearly stated that "In the resurrection they neither marry nor are given in marriage but are as the angels in heaven." (Matt 22:30)?

Answer: Let us take a look at Matthew 22:30 once again.

> **Matt 22:30** (HTHS) **For in the resurrection** they neither marry, nor are given in marriage, but are as the angels in shamayim (heaven).

Yahushua was clear that while people are being raised (In the resurrection) marriage will not be an issue as the resurrection will be like the twinkling of an eye. It will be very fast so you cannot marry while you are being raised. But people in the kingdom will marry after the resurrection and be given in marriages. The questioner did not ask Him will they have wives in the kingdom after they are raised but they asked Yahushua what would happen during the first moments of resurrection.

Yahushua put them on the right path, that you will be like angels during the resurrection because we will fly like them during the time of our resurrection, but once we are raised and established in Israel we will have wives and children. You cannot give up the best increase that YHWH has given us namely marriage. This idea that we will never marry belongs to stoics and ascetics and is totally unbiblical and a repressive idea of depraved men who put women down. There will in fact be polygamy in Israel as it was in the ancient order but it is debated whether everyone will be polygamous or not or if it does mean some people in Israel will choose polygamy and others will be monogamous. I contend all believers will choose the ancient lifestyle over the Satanic monogamy of the world we must go back to the order of the Garden of plural marriage, Isaiah 4:1 is our reference and also Adam had many wives, don't be fooled by your errant translation of Genesis, Get the HTHS and it will open your eyes.

> **Isa 4:1** (HTHS) And in that day **seven women shall take hold of one man,** saying, We will eat our own lechem (bread), and wear our own apparel: **only let us be called by your name**, to take away our reproach.

So if there are no marriages then how come people are eating and drinking and having children and some men are taking seven wives? Why does YHWH need to put fish in the Dead Sea and make it a living sea? Spirits do not need to eat fish and when Yahushua rose from the dead he also ate and was not a spirit (Luke 24:30).

So that we may fish and eat and sustain our bodies even though being our bodies are everlasting they still need food!!!

> **Isa 65:20** (HTHS) There shall be no more there an infant of days, nor an old man that has not filled his days: for the child shall die a hundred years old; but the sinner being a hundred years old shall be accursed.

Children will be born and die as of the unbelieving people limited in age to a hundred. We can see that YHWH is still offering grace to the unbelieving people to live to a hundred and therefore this is not the end of grace as people see it. However if people think that now salvation will only be through sacrifices this is not correct as there is no sacrifice for intentional sin so the method and modes do not change but continue as it was. However what is clear is that those people who would put their faith in the Messiah of Israel in the future will take the yoke of Torah upon them and will be expected to attend Israel three times a year this is mandatory and not optional. This is why in order to accommodate the large influx of traffic Israel will have to enlarge its airports and build more airports both in the North and South of the country. Airplanes will resume as before so no change.

This answers many other questions about the prince having children and owning land also. In fact the verse implies that King David will take on more wives in the millennium and his rule will be greater than before as he will rule the whole world by proxy and not just Israel. This does not mean that we will not have our prime ministers in our countries such as David Cameron in England and President Barak Obama in the US. It means that they will have to submit to King David and ultimately to the greater King the Messiah of Israel else they will have no rain and no food. Obviously neither of these two has to worry as he is not coming back in their reign but a future leader of these nations will have to submit to the Master. The caliph or one world Empire is set to build from Israel not America.

At this time that is all I am releasing so I hope this has given you some insight and food for thought as to what will happen in the future. Maybe later on I may release more information as it depends if Master YHWH allows me to release more information about these matters. For more information on what happened in the Garden and who are Adam's other wives see the Hidden Truth Hebraic Scrolls (HTHS) Study Bible obtainable from www.african-israel.com or Amazon.

Chapter 12

The return of the Messiah and the prophesies of Dani'el

One of the searching questions on believers mind is when is the Messiah going to return it's been so long and even the two thousand years are up?

Currently the mainline accepted view is that His return is on the Feast of Trumpets and some assert on a Jubilee.

For this the primary two references used are from Paul's letters First Thessalonians 4:16 and First Corinthians 15:52 neither of which is inspired.

> **First Thess 4:16** (HTHS) For Master Yahushua himself shall descend from the shamayim (heaven) with a shout, and with the voice of the chief messenger, and with his shofar the tekiyah-ha-gadolah (long blast) of YHWH: and the dead in Messiah shall rise first.

> **First Cor 15:52** (HTHS) In a moment, in the twinkling of an eye, at the last shofar: for the shofar shall sound, and the dead shall be raised incorruptible, and we shall be changed.

However what most people do not know is that everything in scripture must be established by two witnesses and it must have one witness being the prophets of old. The two quotations above are thought to be of the feast of Trumpets. Also note the above two verses from the two letters of Paul are just <u>one</u> witness of one man. We need another witness to testify that the Messiah is returning on a feast. There is a problem the way the Bible is interpreted in the Western world in a mishmash way without understanding what it is that the writer has been inspired to write through the Holy Spirit.

However on close examination you will notice that the book of Matthew actually contradicts the theory of a return on the feast of Trumpets.

> **Matt 24:42** (HTHS) Watch therefore: for you know not what day your Master (Adon: Lord) does come.

This is a very concise rabbinic Hebraic way of saying **his return is <u>not</u> on a feast day**. People in Israel and some people in the West like me watch for feast dates, for important prophetic events but generally

Christians are not taught which signs to watch out for. So who is right Paul the self acclaimed apostle or Matthew the Levite? You will be surprised to know that Matthew the Lewite is correct as I shall prove here for you step by step.

We find another reference in Matthew that actually helps us.

> **Matt 24:31** (HTHS) And he shall send his angels with a great sound of a shofar, and they shall gather together his elect from the four winds, from one end of shamayim (heaven) to the other.

This reference in Matthew 24 simply points out that He will send the angels in Matthew 24:31 with the **proclamation of a king's arrival** hence why the **loud shofar blast** that we read about in the letter of Thessalonians. The gathering is like an army for battle but since many in the Western world do not know ancient workings of Israelites they end up coming up with various theories about what is going to happen predominantly wrong.

Our reference point is Daniel the prophet. It is my opinion and I will give reasons why when we read the text of Daniel it is at least clear to me that the return of Messiah is not many hundreds of years away as some brothers have suggested. It is my firm conviction that the return of Messiah will be in this century and not the next thousand years. This means the Master will return before the end of 2099. I will not bore you with the details of why I have concluded this and I will not even give you my calculations as they are private and not for public consumption.

I offer you some insights for you to consider whether you wish to stay with the mainstream view of the return of the Messiah to be on the feast of Trumpets or my view which Is not the mainstream view however I would suggest the mainstream view of the feast of trumpets has several problems too numerous to discuss here. I apologise if I offend any of you but my intention is not to do such a thing. You have your views and I respect this but I have mine which I can tie with every prophet of the Bible. The question is can you do that? I doubt you can tie most views to even two prophets let alone every prophet of the Bible but if you are able to I would be keen to hear about it.

As we know from the historical past the Christian world out there has been given dates with the coming of Messiah ranging from 1880 to 2015. Contrary to popular opinion I do not find any problem or sin with setting dates. We are given signs precisely for the reason to know the season of

His return therefore I do not hold date setters in any fault minus the fact that they were wrong and they have to admit their inaccuracy...

We know from the past that many dates did not see the return of Messiah and I can assure you that even 2012 or 2015 is not the time of His coming.

First Paul's references of the shout is simply to be **interpreted as the arrival of a king for war and nothing more than that** as He comes when Israel is on the brink of destruction in a major war with radical Islamists nations. To say it's the feast would be inaccurate because the shofar was blown on each feast so why pick the feast of Trumpets, why not the feast of Tabernacles or Shavuot? One might contend that it is the long blast but the long blast is also done at other times as I have suggested. Let me show you some flaws.

We cannot read the feast of Trumpets into that. If we want to read the feast of trumpets into a long trumpet blast then we also have a long trumpet blast in Exodus 19:19 but it was not the feast of trumpets but Pentecost or Shavuot, the feast of weeks when the Torah was given. The New Testament must not contradict the Torah else the theory is thrown out pure and simple. Rabenu Moses (Our teacher) is a giant in stature and knew much more secrets and esoteric knowledge about prophecy than all the disciples and apostles put together. I know most out there do not place any weight on him and run to New Testament to the likes of Paul for answers when many answers are already contained in the law of Elohim the Torah. The Types and shadows in the text of the Tanak match with the references of the New Testament perfectly.

The Torah tells us:

> **Deut 11:14** (HTHS) That I will give you the rain of your land in his due season, the first rain and the latter rain, that You may gather in

The above prophecy is not just about physical rain and food but it is also about the two comings of the Messiah. In summary the latter rain which signifies the second coming of Messiah is about March time period however in order to fulfil all the timelines this is why He is coming just before Passover in February and not later.

The very next statement in that verse was a warning to all Israel.

Deut 11:16 (HTHS) Take heed to yourselves, that your heart be not deceived, and you turn aside, and serve other Elohim, and worship them;

Unfortunately many are being deceived by all wonderful and weird doctrines and are led astray by the gods of this world, just look around you. One sister told me that the Messiah has asked a particular person in Indonesia to break all the spiritual strongholds because he is proclaiming Indonesia as his place and his soon return. I asked the sister are the mosques still standing in Indonesia and if so then these people are being deceived by the enemy. When the spiritual strongholds will be broken the mosques have to go and so do all the false places of worship and the steeples of the churches, the phallic symbols also have to be pulled down. The crosses also have to go the sign of Tamuz.

Now Joshua entered the land just after the Passover

Josh 3:6 (HTHS) And Yahushua (Joshua) spoke to the kohenim (priests), saying, Take up the ark of the Contract/Agreement, and pass over before the people. And they took up the ark of the Contract/Agreement, and went before the people.

The ark of God was with them before they entered the land. This time around the ark which was the symbol for the actual person the Master Himself will be with the people to enter the land with His saints.

Josh 4:19 (HTHS) And the people came up out of Yardan (Jordan) on the **tenth day of the first month**, and encamped in Gilgal, in the east border of Yericho (Jericho).

The people came out the 10th day of Nissan and not on the feast of trumpets but just before the feast of Passover!!! This is a critical piece of information for us. The ancient patterns must match.

Therefore it does not necessarily have be a feast at all. Also Yahushua is not going to come on the actual day of the feast of Passover but He is coming one month or 30 days approximately before the feast of Passover on a given year in the future, which I shall explain later.

However as I said earlier I respect the opinions of others who believe it could be the feast of Trumpets. The reason why I do not think it is the feast is primarily because of two prophetic references that both cause problems for the theory of Yom Terua (Feast of Trumpets), Rosh Hashanna the civil new year of Israel or any feast date for that matter. He needs to return before a feast not upon a feast even according to Matthew is true.

First Daniel 12:11-12 says that the time the daily sacrifice will be taken away will be **1290 days** and the **completion of the period to be 1335 days**.

In my opinion no one has satisfactorily interpreted this text yet. Am I the first, only time will tell you if I was right about this or not. I know I am human and certainly not infallible. However to my credit in the past 14 years I have never been wrong prophetically not even once and all esteem be to Master Yahushua for that since this is not a guessing science.

Some authors have taken the days of Daniel's prophecy to be literal years such as 1290 years or 1335 years, this could be one application of the timeline because the Hebrew text does use the term days as years in some applications of Scripture, I know some friends who calculate this as years and it's perfectly fine if they wish to do it this way.

However I would offer the other view where I simply take the 1290 and 1335 days as a period of literal twenty four hour days rather than years.

The prophecy of Revelation tells us the following:

> **Revelation 12:6** (HTHS) And the woman fled into the wilderness, where she has a place prepared by Elohim, which they should feed her there one thousand two hundred and sixty days (1260 days).

Some authors take this to be a period of 1260 years and as I suggested earlier this could be one application of the usage of days I certainly do not disagree with this practice but since I am going to use the literal 24 hour application therefore I calculate it as three and a half years yet to come in the future tying up with Daniel. One more thing is this that this period is as a Type/Shadow and has been fulfilled in the past too but the real deal is yet to come.

Now let us look at Daniel 12:11

> **Daniel 12:11** (HTHS) And from the time that the daily sacrifice shall be taken away, and the abomination that lays waste is set up, there shall be a thousand two hundred ninety days. (**1290 Days**)

In order for the **daily sacrifice** to be taken away there has to be an altar setup for sacrifice in Jerusalem. I know some of my friends disagreeing that in order to sacrifice there has to be the Millennial Temple. I respectfully disagree with my friends because we never had a full fledged Temple when we were sacrificing animals in the wilderness out of Egypt so the argument is flawed at best. I have detailed the full answer of this in chapter ten why they are plainly wrong.

It cannot be a full Temple because this contradicts Dani'el the prophet and it also contradicts the prophet Ezekiel but for now I will not go into those contradictions.

I am going to suggest that we take the month of **July** as the time period when the radical Muslim armies will gather to invade Israel in the future. We take the period of Tisha B'Av especially the 9th when the sacrifice that Daniel mentioned will be taken away from the Temple Mount Altar given to the Yahudim (the converts from Khazaria and not the real chosen people) in the peace deal. Keep your finger on Tammuz 17 and the 9th of Tisha B'Av. As far as I know no one to date has predicted when the armies will attack Israel or at least what days in the year they are likely to attack. Since I am giving you these mark them in your calendar for all future references.

The Master Yahushua is not returning to London or New York the places where the real children of Y'sra'el were taken as slaves the black Hebrews many of these so called experts and teachers still do not now the true children of Y'sra'el and they run after a counterfeit entity in Israel who will be removed in the future. So where is He returning to and for whom? Christendom teaches that He is returning for them but He is not returning for them and they are indeed grafted into the Olive Tree (True genetic black Israel) but He is actually returning for **Israel the land** and the **people of that land, the Yahudim and the other children of Israel the Northern ten tribes who are still to this day scattered in countries of the world. These can be found in large part in the USA, Africa, Brazil, Europe, the Caribbean's and of course the East**. This is why the Yahudim recite in their daily prayers the speedy return of the Messiah. The purpose of the Messiah is to repair the breech above which He has and also to reunite the two brides the North (Ten tribes) and the south (Judah) into one akhad (unity) so they all learn to obey the Father in the heavens.

Many Christians who are expecting to be raised in the millennium will be disappointed to remain in She'ol where YHWH keeps their souls and will not be raised since they were disobedient to Torah the law of YHWH which is required for obedience. Please read my article in www.african-israel.com under the page Ask the Rabbi, "Will Christians enter the 1000 years millennium reign."

I have carefully illustrated why disobedience will cause many to lose the first resurrection but their salvation is dependent on their confession with YHWH of your repentance and to live a repentant life accepting the provision YHWH has sent through Yahushua of Nazareth to clothe them with right-ruling. However if you sill deliberately live a sinful life then you put your salvation at risk with separation from YHWH permanently.

> **Zechariah 14:2** (HTHS) For I will gather all nations against Yerushalim (Jerusalem) to battle...

If Jerusalem is where Christians live then Yahushua is returning for Christianity but fortunately Jerusalem is the eternal capital of Israel and the place where Judah's heart and soul is. This is very much a place for the true Yahudim and the future 3rd Temple. King David was the man who made this the capital of his kingdom over 3000 years ago.

Yahushua is returning for Israel first and foremost for the Yahudim to fight on their behalf and alongside with them at the battle of Armageddon. He will end the Exile of the House of Israel (The Ten tribes) and Judah. This battle is just before Passover because it is the second rescue of Israel just as the first was during Passover so the second would be likewise during Passover. There has been no major rescue of Israel or any exodus during the feast of Trumpets. But there is a build up several months before this hence why the gathering of the radical Muslim armies in July is an important timeline.

Now the likely date in the year for the battle of radical Islam I am going to suggest to you two particular dates in the year the date of 17th of Tammuz, which I believe when the armies of Islam will besiege Jerusalem in the future and the 9th of Tisha B'Av when the Islamic Armies will try to destroy Jerusalem and succeed in taking East Jerusalem captive at least for a short period of time and many Muslim women will be killed at that time in Jerusalem and Yahudim women raped in Eastern Jerusalem.

East Jerusalem has a heavy Muslim presence so we must remember when it comes to bombs and bullets they do not distinguish your religion so when the Muslims start to bombard this area this also means they will kill many of their own people there. They would even rape both Muslim and Yahudim women. Many women and children get caught out in war and some soldiers in war usually take opportunity and do not care about religion at that time but it's more about conquest and subjugation.

This is why it is incumbent for true Y'sra'elites for their own safety not to live in East Jerusalem but I doubt any of them will listen to this advice. They should move to western Jerusalem as that will not be conquered by the enemy or at least have a place there also to go to for safety however in reality it is forbidden for us to live in Israel right now.

The 17th of Tammuz is when the walls of Jerusalem were breached in the ancient past upon destruction of the 2nd Temple. My forefather Musa also broke the set of Tablets that he had brought down with the Ten Commandments on the 17th of Tammuz. This day can be calculated forty days after the feast of Pentecost (Shavuot). The children of Israel built the golden calf the goddess Hathor on the 16th of Tammuz.

All of Israel's past bad times have happened during T'sha B'Av especially the 9th such as the destruction of the first Temple, the destruction of the Second Temple and many other events too numerous to list here hence why the sacrifice will be stopped in this month in the future, which is in our month of August. I will give you a time span and it is up to you what you do with it.

I am going to give you some critical time ranges where this action could take place from 2027 to 2045. The build up of the Muslim confederacy will take place in 2019 and not necessarily the war as that will come later, the two key dates after this event are 2023 and 2027. Note this is not the rapture as there is no such event in scripture but there is a resurrection and a uniting of the dead believers who are raised which could be termed a post resurrection and a gathering of the elected. One thing the first resurrection will occur on a set date set by the Father in heaven and to be honest we can estimate the day of the year it could potentially occur for the resurrection but we will probably never guess on which actual day it will happen, the same as the return of the Messiah we can estimate it with the signs around us but we cannot pin an exact date to it not because we are not allowed to do it but because we lack data.

If I am completely wrong you have lost nothing as these are tentative dates in my calculation for these to work one event needs to take place and that is the blowing up of an oil installation in Saudi Arabia. I believe this indeed will take place soon. However I want to point out two things, one in 2003 I wrote that Ariel Sharon will be removed from power and the Palestinians will celebrate this by sending sweets in my book Islam, Peace or Beast printed in January 2004 and I also wrote that when the

Muslim Mullah's issue the rallying call in Europe time will tell how many children will rise to fight Jihad with the West. In effect I was hinting that many children would rise up to fight but I had to conceal some of the information to protect the innocent. In Feb 2007 I spoke in a teaching session about suicide bombings coming to Europe before the July bombings in London.

Please note on all these occasions I was right 100% and this is the true sign of a servant of YHWH. Many good scholars have been wrong about every attempt they made at prophecy and the return of Yahushua. Ariel Sharon was removed in 2006 two years after the publication of my book and the Palestinians celebrated this by sending candy to each other. The Muslim Ummah issued a Jihad call to European Muslims and many children took up the rallying call and went to fight both in Afghanistan and Iraq. We also saw suicide bombings in London on 7/7, and trains were bombed in Spain in 2004 this was after my book was released and later we saw this repeated in India too. Most of the things I spoke about in my book came to pass exactly as I suggested but some things are yet to take place in the future and I am certain they will also come to pass.

I spoke about the Indian subcontinent bombings two years before they happened to some friends in private. I also spoke in private about Somalians Hijacking and attacking Western ships long before they started to operate in the gulf waters hijacking Western ships. I learnt about the ships before this happened as I was one day sitting in prayer and the Master showed me this in a clear vivid vision where I saw what looked like Somalians attacking ships.

Then I saw some ships firing back at Somalians. Please note I do not dream or see visions often but when I am shown something it usually is that the Master is trying to reveal something to me that will come to pass else I would not know these details before hand.

I have also said about the Allied forces will not have complete victory in Afghanistan and will start to leave and said earlier that the US will leave Iraq one year before President Bush made his announcement to withdraw troops. It does not matter what technology the West carries they will lose the war in Afghanistan both psychologically and fundamentally and the Taliban will come back to power in their former places but this time they will be even more hostile.

When I was talking about the pullout of Iraq this was a time when most news pundits were predicting the army to stay in Iraq for a long time. I said that this would not happen and indeed it was proven to be correct.

I also said on many occasions before that the war with Iran is not imminent and have been saying it frequently while the media and most prophecy writers will have you believe it is going to happen tomorrow. The truth is it is not until a few important things are in place mentioned in this book.

If you are reading this then I do not write to make myself famous, popular, trendy or for sensationalism because I do not really have time for such things but only when the Holy Spirit Em Chockmah (Mother Wisdom) guides me to put to paper what "She" has revealed to me and the Mater tells me that I need to speak then I will speak or write. I serve the Most High Adon YHWH the God of my forefathers who were in Iran and formerly Israel of the Lewitical order. I serve Him and Him alone therefore am not ashamed to be under His refuge. You can either take this book seriously and plan accordingly or you can reject its content and put yourself and your family in danger. I have at least now made more information public to help all the people out there both the believers in the Messiah and those who are not.

Jubilee year

About the return of the Messiah the main stream view or at least another emerging view is that the Messiah will come on a Jubilee year. I am not going to touch on this theme because though I do believe the Jubilee cycle plays an important role but I do not see this as a prerequisite to His return. What I can say is that He will be here close to a Jubilee and not necessarily descend on the day of the start of the jubilee. I can tell you categorically and I hope I do not offend anyone out there please forgive me if I do but the Messiah is not returning in 2012 to 2020. After these dates yes but before this it will not happen so plan sparingly for yourself and your children's future where you will be during the dates I have now given you above. Avoid being in radical Islamic states unless you are on a special mission for Master Yahushua or you have no choice but to be there and if you are there because of no choice or either a visit remember be Torah obedient and YHWH will protect you and if you are not Torah obedient and deny or reject the LAW of YHWH in anyway then He will not seal you and you will become a target for the radicals and can face certain death.

> **Revelation 9:4** (HTHS) And it was commanded them that they should not hurt the grass of the earth, neither any green thing, neither any etz (tree); but only those men which do not have the seal of YHWH in their foreheads.

The "locusts" are radical Muslims who will attack idolatrous Christians who "do not have the seal of YHWH on their forehead and who dishonour the commands of Torah." This also applies to all those who do not have the mark, or seal of the true Name of YHWH on their hearts and in their minds to protect them from radical Islam in the time of Jacob's Trouble. Historically the Saracens (Arab Muslims referred to as Saracen by the Europeans) worked mainly in those countries where corruption of Christianity prevailed, i.e. the Greek Orthodox and Roman Catholic Churches.

Daniel mentions an abomination that will take place and a lot of teachers place this either during the Roman Era or before this Era so it depends whether you place this for the first Temple or the second Temple, I know some erroneously place it for the 3rd Temple. I am now going to suggest to you that it is neither and also that it happens twice, just like the coming of Messiah and the two beasts of Revelation are the one and the same radical Islam happening twice also. We do see two's in scripture. Moses went up twice to bring the Ten Commandments down, Yahudim entering Israel twice, the coming of Messiah twice, the exodus twice the giving of the law twice, also the heaps of the flood waters for Israel to cross happened twice once with Moses and once with Joshua. Note Joshua was of the tribe of Ephraim so Ephraim and Judah enter the land twice also. One yet to happen for Ephraim.

Daniel mentioned two things must happen, the daily sacrifice stopped and the second thing that must have happen is the abomination that makes desolate. This was not the idols placed inside the 2nd Temple but the structure of the abomination must be on the corner according to Daniel's prophecy. The corner or wing of the Temple structure was only fulfilled by the Islamic Empire when the Caliph Umar captured Jerusalem and in 638 CE he erected a prayer place on the corner of the Temple mount to Allah.

Why is this corner so important to Satan? YHWH instructed Israel to make fringes known as tzitzits for the garments (Num 15:38) so that they remind us of who is our maker and His commandments. We are told that we are under the Kanaf or wings of the Most Holy One Ps 91:4. There are other reasons but lets keep it simple for now.

Later in history the Omar mosque was built at the same place around 691 to 705 CE. Different historians cite different dates but this is what we have. The Omar Mosque was destroyed a few times by earthquakes but then rebuilt again on the corner and still stands.

The text in Dani'el is not saying that the Omar Mosque will be destroyed and then rebuilt but it is saying that it will host a special session of prayer or commemoration that will be yet future. We know that this event will take place after the coming of Messiah as Yahushua tells us something key in Matthew 24:15.

> **Matthew 24:15** (HTHS) When you therefore shall see the abomination of desolation, spoken of by Daniel the prophet, **stand in the Set-Apart Place**, (whoso reads, let him understand.

Note He says "stand in the set-apart place". Yes Stand but stand where? The word **stand** is both figurative and literal where we that is you, me and others will "stand" and see that this is for us to see this abomination and decide the events spoken of earlier. The abomination is there but the special prayer to Allah by the Caliph is yet future when the Muslim Caliph who will declare himself the Caliph and commemorate his victory of taking Eastern Jerusalem by going into the Omar Mosque that is when Daniel's prophecy becomes completely fulfilled and not until then. He (the Muslim Caliph) will offer prayers to Allah and cause the Yahudim to stop the sacrifice at the little altar that they had given in a peace treaty (Rev 11:1). We also know that the Messiah will return near a jubilee year and not necessarily on the actual day of the Jubilee year, be careful about this one. This is given in the wording of Dan 9:27 and Isa 61:1-2. Note when he was born it was not a jubilee year but the jubilee fell after his birth meaning after his first coming. The same pattern will follow.

For those expecting the Messiah to return on a jubilee date. The next Jubilee is to fall on 2016 according to Maimonides calculation. However according to some calculations the year 30 CE was a jubilee year. According to me the next jubilee will most likely fall on 2039 while some teachers place a jubilee in 2042 or 2045. In all honesty it is not important to know when a Jubilee year is so even if all of these dates for the jubilee are incorrect it matters little.

Now let us address the timeline from Dani'el.

> **Daniel 12:11** (HTHS) And from the time that the daily sacrifice shall be taken away, and the abomination that lays waste is set up, there shall be a thousand two hundred ninety days.

Daniel is clear that when the sacrifice is taken away which I place on Tisha B'Av 9th August period in a future year. He goes on to tell us that it will be 1290 days. That is 3 years and 7 months. The Messiah will return in the month February in a future year and then 30 days later it will be the Passover festival the great deliverance for Israel.

Now we know that the book of Revelation 12:6 tells us it will be 3 and a half years so how do we tally the one extra month in Daniel?

Assuming a date in future in the month of August the daily sacrifice is taken away just like in the past two destructions of the Temples.

We start at August then add to it 3 and a half years gives us the fulfilment of this period in February of a future date.

Let me show you from August Tisha B'Av timeline which matches perfectly with everything scripture states.

- 1 year to August
- 2 years to August
- 3 years to August then add six months – September, October, November, December, January and February.

So this tallies us with the three and a half years in Rev 12:6 and then in order to tally up the 30 extra days of Daniel 12:11 we add the 30 days to the month of February and voila we arrive at the return of Messiah just before the Passover of that future year!!!

This will be the greatest exodus history has seen when both Houses will fully return back to the land that is the 12 tribes which start marching back to Israel.

> **Jeremiah 50:4** (HTHS) In those days, and in that time, says YHWH, the children of Y'sra'el shall come, they and the children of Yahudah (Judah) together, going and weeping: they shall go, and seek YHWH their Elohim.

The two houses will start to return to Israel as it will be then the time to build the full 3rd millennial Temple.

It is also time to fulfil the prophecy which was spoken of by Isaiah 2:3.

When Israel went out of Egypt they first did the Passover the feast of redemption, the same is true in the future. Then after Israel's exodus they received the Torah the law of YHWH. The same is true here as they head towards Jerusalem to start learning the law/Torah of Moses.

Isaiah 2:3 (HTHS) And many people shall go and say, Come, and let us go up to the mountain of YHWH, to the Temple of Elohim of Yaqub; and he will teach us of his ways, and we will walk in his paths: for out of Tsiyon shall go forth the Torah and the word of YHWH from Yerushalim.

Note this will happen in the month of May/June the feast of weeks or Pentecost when the law is once again given to the people of YHWH the <u>second</u> time. This time the prophecy of Micah is fulfilled as the nations that are going up have woken up to the fact that they are true black Israelites or from the House of Israel.

Micah 4:2 (HTHS) And many nations shall come, and say, Come, and let us go up to the mountain of YHWH, and to the house of the Elohim of Yaqub; and he will teach us of his ways, and we will walk in his paths: for the Torah shall go forth out of Tsiyon, and the word of YHWH from Yerushalim.

So what is the 1335 days of Dani'el?

Daniel 12:12 (HTHS) Increased is he that waits, and comes to the one thousand three hundred and thirty-five days.

So 1335 – 1290 days = 45 days gap. This is the time period that people will wait before the feast of Shavuot to receive the Law of YHWH the second time around so one could see that there is indeed even two comings of the Law which many thought was no longer for you. Many of you will be wrong again and found wanting. The LAW/Torah is for you and for me and we must act on it and obey it FOREVER.

Isa 2:3 (HTHS) ... for out of Tsiyon shall go forth the Torah and the word of YHWH from Yerushalim (Jerusalem).

You might wonder that the time to wait was 49 days that is 7x7 then how come we are four days short. I can assure you we will not be short to fulfil the 49 days perfectly however I am withholding a key piece of information for now so you can search it out and fill the gap yourself.

Also the teachers who predict that the coming could be hundreds of year away or over thousand years away have to prove that the oil in Saudi Arabia will not run out in the next 1000 years time. Current studies are proving that we are fast running out of world supplies of oil with emerging giants like India and China with a huge appetite for oil I doubt we will get past this century of oil in the middle-east. Saudi Arabia was predicted to last for sixty-five years with what they had declared. However one needs to be aware that nations declare more oil than they actually have because some middle-eastern nations could be at peak oil now. In my opinion and for good reasons I believe Saudi does not have oil for more than fifty years and if new reserves are found it cannot be proven with accurate estimate how long they will last until all the scientific data is collected. If Saudi Arabia is going to last fifty years for instance then one has to ask the critical question about the prophesies of Isaiah 34 which requires the oil to burn in warfare. How could this happen if there will be no oil left beyond fifty years? Then one can see the futility of estimating a thousand years for the return of the Messiah. It's quite clear that the Messiah will return in this century and not any other. However many teachers need to reassess their data and not to mislead the sheep.

Note the coming of the Master is neither the end of the world nor the end of all religions as doomsayers' theories. We will still have an operating world. We will still have planes and trains. Israel will expand and have to build several airports to accommodate the incoming flights for people who will be going up to celebrate the feasts. The thousand year reign in Israel is not spiritual or like angels but as men and women who were faithful to the word that will be resurrected with real bodies that can eat, drink, have marriages and give birth to children. In scripture this is termed the 7th day. We then have the release of Satan to look forward to in the 8th day the great day of the feast of Tabernacles and we also have the 9th and the final 10th day to finalise everything.

We will have verifiable 10,000 years of earth's living history before the earth will be renewed by YHWH. Note Islam the second largest faith after Christianity will not be removed during the 7th day but the mosques on Temple mount will be removed to build the 3rd Temple and Mecca will lie in ruins alongside Saudi Arabia. Note also that Christianity will be collapsed into what it was meant to be into biblical Judaism. All 38,000 or more denominations of Christianity will be folded and none left. Those who refuse to submit will never be able to enter the kingdom, now will be the last time for Christians to obey Torah those who are alive and return to the true roots of our faith and not be divided. If they refuse to obey then they will not be allowed entry into the kingdom and end up eventually in outer darkness outside the Kingdom. The blood of the Master will not help you if you refuse YHWH's voice which is His Torah. The Messiah will tell you himself to get away from Him you lawless ones (Matt 7:23) negates of Torah.

> **Ezek 20:38** (HTHS) **And I will purge out from among you the rebels**, and them that **transgress against me**: I will bring them

> forth out of the country where they sojourn, **<u>and they shall not enter into the land of Ys'ra'el:</u>** and you shall know that I am YHWH.

So if your Pastors or teachers are teaching you that you can live any type of life, disobey the Torah and still enter the kingdom you won't be able to because the passage of Ezekiel the priest is a witness against these type of people.

Sorry this is not my theology but the theology of the Kadosh Father in the heavens. Unfortunately most of you have been following the father out of Rome the papal one where you can just profess a name, live whichever way and enter an illusionary kingdom that is not even there for you.

Read Ezekiel 20:38 very carefully as I am trying to help you to make sure that you enter the kingdom and receive rewards and eternal life. I am your friend and as a teacher of scripture I am trying to show you the pitfalls before they happen because I was chosen and called out with this responsibility to teach the truth, I do not hate you nor dislike your denomination whatever you are in that is fine by me and makes no difference to my life or calling. The unmerited favour of the Master is available to all in equal measure but we cannot claim grace and live rebelliously. In the ancient past Israel tried this and YHWH did not allow the <u>first</u> generation from the Exodus to <u>enter the land</u> except two people Joshua and Caleb. To enter the land of Israel or the coming kingdom in Israel is a privilege and not a do as you please now and enter the kingdom approach later. This is why YHWH has teachers there in the future to teach the people how to start obeying and living the Torah before they are allowed in the holy places.

The millennial order reign will be under King David and His and our supreme commander and King of Kings Yahushua (YHWH the Right-ruling Branch with us). For full details see my book World War III – Unmasking the End Times Beast.

<u>http://www.african-israel.com/Books/books.html</u>

The US and other European nations are going to go through a very trying time due to their own disobedience but they will be given a chance to prove their faithfulness to the Master of heaven and earth. Israel's borders will be increased, counterfeit Jews will be removed, Israel will have peace in its internal borders and no more suicide bombings but Israel has to fight another battle after Satan is released termed the battle of Gog and Magog. These are two battles of Gog and Magog, one before and one after the coming of the Messiah. Remember everything happens twice that is the key.

Many Muslims will have the opportunity to submit to the true God of Israel after the first battle of Gog and Magog but they will not all submit hence why Islam will continue until the second battle. Many Muslim nations will believe and bring tribute to YHWH, while others will not believe and continue as they are. They will be dismayed by their defeat but will not be deterred to try again. There is a lot more information but I hope you now have some more of the picture to help you. May you be increased in the Master YHWH.

Conclusion

It should be clear to all of us that we live in a fast changing world and old alliances are set to change and new ones to be established. News in one corner of the world reaches the other corner instantly because of cross communication and the wide IT infrastructures in place such as the Internet. Europe is going to go through a trying time and so is America because although the US will remain the superpower but its influence in the third world will severely decline. Part of the reason for that is going to be the last two wars in Iraq and Afghanistan. In the east the next rising powers are China and India. India and China will emerge as the new powers on the block with China as a greater power than India because of its stable Chinese language, culture and communist government with strict controls in place while India will struggle to beat China with its myriads of languages and different cultures within its different states and internal divisions, strife and heavy corruption in the ranks.

The best friend to the Muslim nations will be China and Russia who will help Islamic states to come up in stature, which will also benefit Russia and China while India with its extremist Hindu elements in the government will not be as well with the Islamic states roundabout the South-East Asia region.

China and Russia will line up more with Muslim nations because of western hostility to China and Russia in the past and present. China will only shake hands with the West if they remain quiet about the Chinese occupation of Tibet and the issues surrounding Taiwan will prove to be a hard sell while America gives weapons to Taiwan that irks China to no end. Also China's friendly stance with North Korea will not help South Korea which has more friendly ties with the Western based governments.

If China shakes hands with the west then it will be very loose one indeed and both Europe and America will have to come to terms with China having friendlier ties with Iran. Since Turkey has been pushed back from joining Europe and so far not allowed to enter Europe it has already picked new alliances with Iran, Pakistan and some other key nations which means the hardliners in Turkey are increasingly fundamentalist Islamic and will push back the West and also distance themselves from counterfeit Israel more and more which is part of prophecy.

Turkey will push back at Europe because it is not being allowed to enter Europe and will want to exact revenge in the form of not allowing the West to operate out of Turkey as they have liked to in the past. There will come a day when Turkey will ask the US to remove her base from Turkey.

I thought I had closed and sealed my book hoping to send it for review and then to the printers for printing and left the country on May 29th 2010 for Nigeria for a trip to teach the Netzarim believers of Nigeria in Port Harcourt and in some South-Eastern areas where the Igbo tribe (pronounced Ebos) a Hebrew tribe live in Anambra State a city called Onitsha, which is a very large industrial hub in the South. While I was there I heard about the Gaza flotilla news where a group of six ships were intending to break Israel's naval Gaza blockade in which IDF soldiers boarded one of the ship called Mavi Marmara and captured and killed various peace activists in the ship which was illegal. After this what ensued on TV and papers was gymnastics to prove or disprove that Israel was right or wrong. Is it possible that their intention was not to shoot first but to interrogate the boats for weapons and ammunition that could be used against them? From the fact that peace activists were shot straight to the head at point blank range this is of course not possible. In fact they had on their list to assassinate a sheikh on board which they failed to do so.

However we know the raid went badly wrong because when the soldiers descended on the ship some with paint guns others with rubber bullets and live ammunitions that some of them were set upon by some peace activists who had various weapons such as sticks and knives then the Israeli forces used rubber bullets followed by live ammunition in which they managed to kill several activists at point black range. Depending on who you believe in the news report that followed it was reported that at least nine activists lay dead and the rest were arrested and taken into Israel for interrogation. I want to point out anytime anyone has criticised Israel has ended up in slander, tailspin and media harassment such as

Judge Richard Goldstone who did the enquiry into the Gaza war in 2008/9 and suggested in his report that Israel had acted illegally with war crimes and he also blamed the Palestinian Hamas government of the same. He was harassed and criticised for his report. Richard Goldstone is a judge, a war crimes expert and is of good sound credentials and also a proselyte Yahudim so would have no bias towards Israel. He had faced severe personal attacks since that time. A lady MP that was on the ship Ms Zouby has been hounded and was provided protection for fear of her life from the Israeli Knesset members who have been shouting abuse at her for being on the ship. She is an eye witness of Israeli forces brutality according to her testimony. She is facing calls by hardliner rightwing Zionists for her expulsion and removal of her Israeli passport. This is what I mean by political Zionism gone mad and out of control.

Unfortunately the mentality of these political Zionists is that they are always the victim and never the aggressor. However there are some level headed Zionists who know that all these things which are happening are going to drive Israel to a big war eventually with many Yahudim lives once again going to the slaughter. Note these Jews are not the original chosen children of Israel anyway because the real children were and are Black Israelites found in Europe, Americas and in African and the eastern lands. They are also found in Brazil, Portugal where they were taken as slaves from Africa. The charade with the so called Jews is up now to show they were never the chosen but gentile converts. One day the land will be removed from them by God himself and given to the rightful heirs the true Israelties which are my ancestors so these people are living on borrowed time.

Here is one Israeli Palestinian MP Zoubi's words from Jonathan Cook a British reporter in Nazareth.

> [51]Haneen Zoubi said Israeli naval vessels had surrounded the flotilla's flagship, the Mavi Marmara, and fired on it a few minutes before commandos abseiled from a helicopter directly above them.
>
> Terrified passengers had been forced off the deck when water was sprayed at them. She said she was not aware of any provocation or resistance by the passengers, who were all unarmed.
>
> She added that within minutes of the raid beginning, three bodies had been brought to the main room on the upper deck in which

---

51 http://www.jkcook.net/Articles3/0490.htm#Top

> she and most other passengers were confined. Two had gunshot wounds to the head, in what she suggested had been executions.
>
> Two other passengers slowly bled to death in the room after Israeli soldiers ignored messages in Hebrew she had held up at the window calling for medical help to save them. She said she saw seven other passengers seriously wounded.
>
> "Israel had days to plan this military operation," she told a press conference in Nazareth. "They wanted many deaths to terrorize us and to send a message that no future aid convoys should try to break the siege of Gaza." ... Contradicting Israeli claims, Ms Zoubi said a search by the soldiers after they took control of the Marmara discovered no arms or other weapons.

One can see how Israel's behaviour is going to drive many people in the Palestinian ranks to more terror attacks for revenge then Israel will complain like a little child that they did nothing to deserve this however as I had said earlier unfortunately all this will only cause more terrorist attacks and not less. Israel cannot win by brute force and it's a mistake to think otherwise.

It appears that Israel was not entirely in the clear to board a ship in international waters seventy two miles away from her legal waters according to international law and that especially at night with night visions with arms of course would be classed as illegal and called an act of piracy. The question is who decides to enforce international law since there is no body to do so in which case a state can act with impunity whether right or wrong. Israel did just that and proved its hard line stance against the Muslims and even other activist which were non-Muslims.

This kind of hatred will not win Israel friends because the very principle that YHWH has ordained Israel to live by was violated of love your neighbour (Lev 19:18). Since these are European pretenders one need not wonder. Just as Hitler took them to task to eradicate them they are taking to task to eradicate the Muslims but they too will fail.

In fact Israel violated two principles first of taking vengeance when they are told not to take vengeance and broke the second commandment of loving their neighbour. I wonder how the Israeli lobby in America will justify these types of international and scriptural crimes. Most likely by white washing them and calling the flotilla an aggression of the Palestinians and anybody that writes in favour of Gaza will be branded a traitor that is the typical scenario of accusations that seem to arise out of the political Zionists prejudice corner where they are always the victim and the others always the aggressor.

Now Israel has also been threatening a war with Iran with US backing, the Iranian nation which has not fought a defensive war for 150 years then how could Israel claim to want to live in peace while threatening regional countries with war. I have shown the media distortion of the statements of Ahmadinejad in this book which you will read later. If Israel is not committed to peace then how could it expect others to do the same? What the media agencies are doing that are aligned with Zionism are creating a fear factor and pushing for war which will one day take us to the devastation of much of our planet. The end goal of some is to allow as many humans to die as possible so they can keep power and wealth.

Many people in the Churches need to take their fog misted glasses off and see why the Muslims are angry when Israel has nuclear bombs they wonder why they cannot do the same to improve their economic conditions to have their own nuclear energy and to stop other aggressive nations from attacking them as a deterrent with nuclear bombs. If the moral argument is that the Muslim nations have been careless with nuclear armament then one only needs to look at the US which is the only nation that fired two bombs at Japan while Pakistan the only nation with a nuclear bomb has not been careless with its weapons so the Muslims cannot be put down with the moral argument. It's clear that we are facing a huge big war in the near future which scripture tells us about but one needs to also understand that the reasons are already in place. When you have Israel sending jets to attack convoys of arms trucks in Sudan in 2009 in a foreign nation miles away from its borders then one can understand the attack on the flotilla also and Israel threatening Iran and Syria then one can see why the coming war with the Islamic nations is inevitable. Israel sending war planes to destroy arms factory in Sudan once again miles away from its borders is a sure sign of aggression and Zionist hypocritical standards in 2012.

What is clear so far is that Israel's present government is not a partner for peace but hypocritical at best.

This is in no way to suggest that the ordinary Yahudim in the street is war mongering because right-ruling Torah abiding Yahudim are committed to peace and some refuse to serve in military forces but this is to show you that some of Israel's governments have been extremely hostile to regional nations attacking within foreign airspaces then one can see why Israel cannot claim a moral high ground? In January 2010 it is alleged that the Mossad sent twenty six operatives using British, French,

German and Australian forged passports to kill one Palestinian commander Mahmoud Al Mabhuh in Dubai and though they managed to assassinate him but the operatives were caught on camera going in and out of the hotel. The Muslims see it as either Israel was sending a very strong message to the Palestinians or Israel was simply reckless showing its arrogance which is a typical political Zionist policy. There is not really much difference between the Nazis in Germany during the war and Zionists today like it or not.

Assuming this man that was assassinated was guilty of crimes against Israel then there is international protocol to bring back criminals from other nations to bring them to justice. The Torah values life and in order to put a criminal to death it is commanded in scripture to bring two or three witnesses before a panel of Judges who can then try the criminal for death. So did Israel decide that the twenty six spies will act as 23 Torah designated judges and the other three as witnesses (Deut 19:15-21)?

Christians who support Israel in these kinds of actions will equally share the guilt when innocent lives are lost and they will be judged for this one day while our Master **Yahushua asked us to seek first the kingdom of God** and **His right-ruling** (Torah) Matt 6:33, He did not ask us to seek first warfare and bloodshed. This does not mean that we do not defend ourselves if we are attacked but it does mean that we do not go after seeking warfare first. Yahushua also told us that increased are the **peace makers** (Matt 5:9). Christians are taught that peace is not possible without Yahushua, so if peace is not possible then why would the peacemakers be increased? This is the faulty Christian doctrine that peace cannot be made. Why would Yahushua tell us this if it was impossible to make any type of peace?

So the question is can relative peace be obtained. The answer is yes a large part of Palestinian attacks can disappear today if Israel relinquishes control of the occupied territories and secure her borders and let the Palestinians defend their own borders and not blockade them. The Palestinian attacks started first when they were going to be displaced in 1948 and subsequently when they were being expelled by the incoming Zionist Jewish refugees from Europe especially the occupied territories with settlements are the biggest headache since not only Israel has to expend its armies and borders to defend them but they are the target for Palestinian attacks as usurpers because they forcefully took the land from the Palestinians this is a fact most do not even understand and many deny.

The settlers need to go home that means back to Europe and back to the US, they are not only breaking the Torah but also the oaths our true Yahudim forefathers took of not going up to take the land by force in large numbers. These oaths that have been broken by these people will bring dire consequence to their families and I am saying it as a Rabbi in love that they need to dismantle their settlements or give their houses to the Palestinians and go back to their respective homes until the God of Israel leads them back. These people have been misguided by irreligious people and some clergy that they have some kind of right over these lands. **One thing needs to be understood the land was given forever by YHWH but a condition was placed upon possession and that was Torah obedience**. Today the majority of Israeli society is hardly Torah obedient and on top a strict oath was placed not to take the land by force until YHWH brings them back so we can see both conditions have not been met. Any good Rabbi who has knowledge in the Torah will tell you the exact same thing I said but there is no need to become angry or judgmental towards the Palestinians because they are simply entrusted the land until YHWH takes us back.

[A side note; Real Isreal which was black in ethnicity and colour are still a majority outside the land. The God of Israel will bring them back in small numbers to the land so if you are called to go and live in some part of Israel then you must go. Note real Jerusalem is not the modern Jerusalem but an area between Hebron and Beersheba near Tel Arad that is where the real Mount Zion, Jerusalem and the Mount of Olives is.]

The majority of the people who broke the oaths are the Ashkenazim and Sephardim and they are not the original children of Israel but are Jews by conversion.

> **Jer 31:6** For there shall be a day, that the Notzarim[52] upon the Mount Efrayim shall cry, Arise you, and let us go up to Tsiyon to YHWH our POWER.

So there will be some brothers who are true Hebrews and will leave Christendom and go up to Jerusalem the real Zion and become the watchmen. One such brother is there now his name is Rabbi Amriel Hoshua who is proclaiming himself as the watchman to call people back.

---

[52] The word for 'watchmen' is notzarim, which means branches, or followers of the Messiah Yahushua (Christians) will go up to Jerusalem one day and begin to realize who they really serve and who or what they are. Not a church but grafted into Y'sra'el, the ten Hebrew tribes who were scattered for Torah violations.

The following prophecy only fulfills in the gentiles and these are in majority Christians and Jews who really are gentiles but in the midst of the churches are many black children of Israel who yet may not know who they really are.

> **Jeremiah 16:19** O YHWH, my strength, and my fortress, and my refuge in the day of affliction, the nations shall come[53] to you from the ends of the earth, and shall say, Surely our ahvot (fathers) have inherited lies,[54] vanity, and things wherein there is no value.

As for the fact if the Palestinians are eternally violent one can see that the start of the violence was large portions of the Khazarian Jews returning to Israel under the Zionist idea of repopulating the land so the violence in the Palestinian mind is justified because they have been oppressed in their understanding and their land confiscated.

In real truth they have never been given full control on the alleged land that has been given to them because there is an Israeli occupation there of military force. The settlers live in Palestinian areas by force not love so one can see why the attacks that are coming from the Palestinian side are termed resistance and not terror by them and as freedom fighting.

Here is what an Israeli senior scholar of the Jerusalem Institute for Israeli studies concluded about the so called peace deals of Oslo, Camp David and Taba.

> [55]"Israel presented a map to Yaser Abd Rabbo and then presented this orally in Stockholm and at Camp David. It was leaked to [the Israeli newspaper] Yediot Ahranot. It shows Israel controlling a greater Jerusalem that goes to the Dead Sea and connects with the Jordan valley where Israel would have sovereignty over a strip of land west of the river, and thereby keep control over the external borders of the Palestinian State."

In other words Israel would have control over Palestinian borders. How could the Palestinians be autonomous with Israel in control? This is what

---

53 At the return of Messiah these will have to walk back as there will be no rapture for these Christians because they believed in lies all along and refuse to believe in Torah as their church leaders taught them falsehoods and did not teach full truth.

54 It is not one man's job to change the behavior and the lies that Christendom has adopted and they will in majority continue in them until right at the end while some will find complete truth and leave the lies and come into the full light.

55 The case for Israel page 147 by Michael Neumann.

is called Occupation. It's like Germany saying to France under its occupation that you can have your land but we will control your borders, your air space and your access roads that we built while in control of the country.

Israel would do well to assist the Palestinians with governance and relinquish both Gaza and the West Bank and tell the settlers to either go into Israel or simply to go back home. I would suggest the settlers go back home to the US and Europe and stay put until YHWH calls them out but really they do not belong in this land, its not theirs, never was and never will be. If they stay in Israel or the present PA areas by force then the settlers are breaking he Contract/Agreement and oaths our forefathers made and anyone who is telling them to do this by right will be responsible for the consequences that follow for them.

YHWH will remove them from the land to empty it and then later bring the real children of Israel back because He promised the massive second Exodus has to be by his hand and not by Zionist organisation funds or church donations. Did YHWH need the Zionist funds to bring them back from Egypt?

Christians have very little knowledge of Yahudim law or of interpreting Torah so are the wrong people to tell you what to do and while some of the Rabbis are more into sentiment than reality, Ha'Shem works with reality not sentiment and he does not work with what your and mine fantasies are. We have an appointed time with destiny and we have to wait for that appointed time.

I am warning you in the similar way that the prophet Jeremiah warned the Yahudim that to resist Nebuchadnezzar's army was against YHWH and they had to leave in order to prolong their lives now that choice is once again before you. Those who did not leave were massacred. Their swords, their well built houses and the defences they had put up were useless. Please consider what I have said in prayer with a sincere heart and not a stubborn heart.

The land is given to Israel eternally but the condition is to obey Torah and right now the condition and oath specifies very clearly not to take the land by force or in large numbers. You have broken both conditions and therefore are in extreme danger under YHWH's oath. This scripture is for the oath breakers.

Sos 2:7 (HTHS) I put you under oath, O you daughters of Yerushalim, by the gazelles, and by the female deers of the field, that you stir not up, nor awake my love, till he please.

The first oath is that the Hebrews must not emigrate en masse to the Holy Land; the second oath is that the Holy One, Increased be He, forbade us from rebelling against the nations of the world; and the third oath is that the Holy One, Increased be He, forbade the nations of the world from unduly oppressing the Hebrews'. Rabbi Yehuda replied:

"[in the above verses of the oaths] it is written'[I adjure you…] Do not dare "to provoke and to awake"' [so there are two oaths contained in each verse, for a total of six]. Rabbi Zera interprets this concerning Rabbi Levy says: "Why are there these six oaths? Three represent the ones stated above. The other three are: 1) that the Hebrews must not reveal the end time [of exile]; 2) that they must not force the arrival of the End [of exile]; and 3) that they must not reveal the secret meanings of the Torah to idolaters.

Let me show you what our Rabbin of ancient times have said:

Rabbi Chama Bar Chanina said: The son of David (Messiah) will not come until even the most insignificant form of government no longer exists among the Hebrews. Rashi explains this as follows: "That there absolutely no sovereign governmental body of the Hebrews shall exist, even the most minor or trivial type of regime". (Talmud Sanhedrin 98a).

Also the behaviour of Israeli commanders to attack regional countries every time a pin drops is a guarantee that we are not far from Armageddon. It will happen this century when we will see many Muslim nations rise up to attack Israel just as the scripture predicted and it will be the hand of YHWH that will bring them. Israel will find out that their hostile behaviour will not help them on that day when their strength is spent then the only one they can call out to in humility and meekness will be the Elohim of Israel with a repentant heart. Who knows how many will perish before this event because of their stiff necks.

Now an admonition to the Yahudim who have taken Palestinian land (Which originally and still belongs to true Israel and not counterfeit Jews) by force;

Jer 22:13-16 (HTHS) **13** Woe to him that builds his house by

> wrong-ruling, and his rooms by wrong; that uses his neighbour's service without wages, and gives him not for his work; **14** That says, I will build myself a wide house and large rooms, and fashions out windows; and panels it with cedar, and painted with red. **15** Shall you reign, because you closed yourself in cedar? Did not your father eat and drink, and do right-ruling and justice, and then it was well with him? **16** He judged the cause of the poor and needy; then it was well with him: was not this to know me? Says YHWH.

You who have usurped the land and think you can hasten the coming of the Mashiach are gravely mistaken and will not the Master of heaven and earth judge your actions? He shall judge indeed with right-ruling while you have judged with unrighteousness.

Here is what Ben Gurion even admitted:

> [56]If I was an Arab leader I would never make terms with Israel. That is natural: we have taken their country sure, God promised it to us, but what does that matter to them? Our God is not theirs... There has been anti-Semitism, the Nazis, Hitler, Auschwitz, but was that their fault? They only know but one thing; we have come here and stolen their country. Why would they accept that?"

This is why I said Israel's political government will be dismantled by Elohim under right-ruling Torah leaders who can serve the Holy One in right-ruling without oppressing others in the land and will have a real desire to live peacefully with their neighbours and Israel will have peace prophesied for 1000 years.

However one could understand that if the flotilla boats were a sure threat to Israel then Israel would certainly have the right to a pre-emptive strike even if the ships were away from Israel's waters closing in on her border.

Obviously from the various reports that followed if one is going to use the appropriate measure of justice then Israel intervened without the necessary threat this is clear because the ships were carrying 10,000 tons of humanitarian aid to Gaza and not weapons. One cannot fail to notice that the Palestinian party Hamas wanted to create a scene using the flotilla to show that Israel is hostile and they successfully proved this thesis in front of the media lenses worldwide. Israel fell right into their

---

56 The case against Israel page 152 by Michael Neumann.

trap proving that Israel acted with a very heavy hand. Of course some IDF soldiers were hurt in the scuffles that followed when they boarded the ship in darkness.

One IDF officer was thrown overboard and quite seriously hurt while others were set upon with clubs and knives although Israel alleges the peace activists had guns but Ms Zoubi claims this is false considering the only gun they had was the one they grabbed from the soldiers hands. You can decide if Ms Zoubi is telling the truth. She claims there were no guns on board.

Here are some of the things that happened in the Gaza war in 2008/2009 according to a UN report.

> **Some facts from the Gaza war report by the UN, the full report can be read at the link below**
>
> **http://www2.ohchr.org/english/bodies/hrcouncil/docs/12session/A-HRC-12-48.pdf**
>
> 43. The Mission investigated 11 incidents in which the Israeli armed forces launched direct attacks against civilians with lethal outcome (chap. XI). The facts in all bar one of the attacks indicate no justifiable military objective. The first two are attacks on houses in the al-Samouni neighbourhood south of Gaza City, including the shelling of a house in which Palestinian civilians had been forced to assemble by the Israeli armed forces. The following group of seven incidents concern the shooting of civilians while they were trying to leave their homes to walk to a safer place, waving white flags and, in some of the cases, following an injunction from the Israeli forces to do so. The facts gathered by the Mission indicate that all the attacks occurred under circumstances in which the Israeli armed forces were in control of the area and had previously entered into contact with or had at least observed the persons they subsequently attacked, so that they must have been aware of their civilian status. In the majority of these incidents, the consequences of the Israeli attacks against civilians were aggravated by their subsequent refusal to allow the evacuation of the wounded or to permit access to ambulances.
>
> 44. These incidents indicate that the instructions given to the Israeli armed forces moving into Gaza provided for a low threshold for the use of lethal fire against the civilian population. The

Mission found strong corroboration of this trend in the testimonies of Israeli soldiers collected in two publications it reviewed.

45. The Mission further examined an incident in which a mosque was targeted with a missile during early evening prayers, resulting in the death of 15 people, and an attack with flechette munitions on a crowd of family and neighbours at a condolence tent, killing five. The Mission finds that both attacks constitute intentional attacks against the civilian population and civilian objects.

46. From the facts ascertained in all the above cases, the Mission finds that the conduct of the Israeli armed forces constitutes grave breaches of the Fourth Geneva Convention in respect of wilful killings and wilfully causing great suffering to protected persons and, as such, give rise to individual criminal responsibility. It also finds that the direct targeting and arbitrary killing of Palestinian civilians is a violation of the right to life.

47. The last incident concerns the bombing of a house resulting in the killing of 22 family members. Israel's position in this case is that there was an "operational error" and that the intended target was a neighbouring house storing weapons. On the basis of its investigation, the Mission expresses significant doubts about the Israeli authorities' account of the incident. The A/HRC/12/48 page 21 Mission concludes that, if a mistake was indeed made, there could not be said to be a case of wilful killing. State responsibility of Israel for an internationally wrongful act would, however, remain.

8. The use of certain weapons

48. Based on its investigation of incidents involving the use of certain weapons such as white phosphorous and flechette missiles, the Mission, while accepting that white phosphorous is not at this stage proscribed under international law, finds that the Israeli armed forces were systematically reckless in determining its use in built-up areas. Moreover, doctors who treated patients with white phosphorous wounds spoke about the severity and sometimes untreatable nature of the burns caused by the substance. The Mission believes that serious consideration should be given to banning the use of white phosphorous in built-up areas. As to flechettes, the Mission notes that they are an area weapon incapable of discriminating between objectives after detonation. They are, therefore, particularly unsuitable for use in urban settings where there is reason to believe civilians may be present.

49. While the Mission is not in a position to state with certainty that so-called dense inert metal explosive (DIME) munitions were used by the Israeli armed forces, it did receive reports from Palestinian and foreign doctors who had operated in Gaza during the military operations of a high percentage of patients with injuries compatible with their impact. DIME weapons and weapons armed with heavy metal are not prohibited under international law as it currently stands, but do raise specific health concerns. Finally, the Mission received allegations that depleted and non-depleted uranium were used by the Israeli armed forces in Gaza. These allegations were not further investigated by the Mission.

9. Attacks on the foundations of civilian life in Gaza: destruction of industrial infrastructure, food production, water installations, sewage treatment plants and housing

50. The Mission investigated several incidents involving the destruction of industrial infrastructure, food production, water installations, sewage treatment plants and housing (chap.XIII). Already at the beginning of the military operations, el-Bader flour mill was the only flour mill in the Gaza Strip still operating. The flour mill was hit by a series of air strikes on 9 January 2009, after several false warnings had been issued on previous days. The Mission finds that its destruction had no military justification. The nature of the strikes, in particular the precise targeting of crucial machinery, suggests that the intention was to disable the factory's productive capacity. From the facts it ascertained, the Mission finds that there has been a violation of the grave breaches provisions of the Fourth Geneva Convention. Unlawful and wanton destruction which is not justified by military necessity amounts to a war crime. The Mission also finds that the destruction of the mill was carried out to deny sustenance to the civilian population, which is a violation of customary international law and may constitute a war crime. The strike on the flour mill furthermore constitutes a violation of the right to adequate food and means of subsistence.

51. The chicken farms of Mr. Sameh Sawafeary in the Zeytoun neighbourhood south of Gaza City reportedly supplied over 10 per cent of the Gaza egg market. Armoured bulldozers of the Israeli armed forces systematically flattened the chicken coops, killing all 31,000 chickens inside, and destroyed the plant and material necessary for the business. The Mission concludes A/HRC/12/48

that this was a deliberate act of wanton destruction not justified by any military necessity and draws the same legal conclusions as in the case of the destruction of the flour mill.

52. The Israeli armed forces also carried out a strike against a wall of one of the raw sewage lagoons of the Gaza wastewater treatment plant, which caused the outflow of more than 200,000 cubic metres of raw sewage onto neighbouring farmland. The circumstances of the strike suggest that it was deliberate and premeditated. The Namar wells complex in Jabaliyah consisted of two water wells, pumping machines, a generator, fuel storage, a reservoir chlorination unit, buildings and related equipment. All were destroyed by multiple air strikes on the first day of the Israeli aerial attack. The Mission considers it unlikely that a target the size of the Namar wells could have been hit by multiple strikes in error. It found no grounds to suggest that there was any military advantage to be had by hitting the wells and noted that there was no suggestion that Palestinian armed groups had used the wells for any purpose. Considering that the right to drinking water is part of the right to adequate food, the Mission makes the same legal findings as in the case of the el-Bader flour mill.

53. During its visits to the Gaza Strip, the Mission witnessed the extent of the destruction of residential housing caused by air strikes, mortar and artillery shelling, missile strikes, the operation of bulldozers and demolition charges. In some cases, residential neighbourhoods were subjected to air-launched bombing and to intensive shelling apparently in the context of the advance of Israeli ground forces. In others, the facts gathered by the Mission strongly suggest that the destruction of housing was carried out in the absence of any link to combat engagements with Palestinian armed groups or any other effective contribution to military action. Combining the results of its own fact-finding on the ground with UNOSAT satellite imagery and the published testimonies of Israeli soldiers, the Mission concludes that, in addition to the extensive destruction of housing for so-called operational necessity during their advance, the Israeli armed forces engaged in another wave of systematic destruction of civilian buildings during the last three days of their presence in Gaza, aware of their imminent withdrawal. The conduct of the Israeli armed forces in this respect violated the principle of distinction between civilian and military objects and amounted to the grave breach of "extensive destruction... of property, not justified by military necessity and carried out unlawfully and wantonly". The Israeli armed forces

furthermore violated the right to adequate housing of the families concerned

.

54. The attacks on industrial facilities, food production and water infrastructure investigated by the Mission are part of a broader pattern of destruction, which includes the destruction of the only cement-packaging plant in Gaza (the Atta Abu Jubbah plant), the Abu Eida factories for ready-mix concrete, further chicken farms and the al-Wadiyah Group's food and drinks factories. The facts ascertained by the Mission indicate that there was a deliberate and systematic policy on the part of the Israeli armed forces to target industrial sites and water installations.

It continues...

10. The use of Palestinian civilians as human shields

55. The Mission investigated four incidents in which the Israeli armed forces coerced Palestinian civilian men at gunpoint to take part in house searches during the military operations (chap. XIV). The men were blindfolded and handcuffed as they were forced to enter houses ahead of the Israeli soldiers. In one of the incidents, Israeli soldiers repeatedly forced a man to enter a house in which Palestinian combatants were hiding. Published testimonies of Israeli soldiers who took part in the military operations confirm the continuation of this practice, despite clear orders from Israel's High Court to the armed forces to put an end to it and repeated public assurances from the armed forces that the practice had been discontinued. The Mission concludes that this practice amounts to the use of Palestinian civilians as human shields and is therefore prohibited by international humanitarian law. It puts the right to life of the civilians at risk in an arbitrary and unlawful manner and constitutes cruel and inhuman treatment. The use of human shields also is a war crime. The Palestinian men used as human shields were questioned under threat of death or injury to extract information about Hamas, Palestinian combatants and tunnels. This constitutes a further violation of international humanitarian law.

11. Deprivation of liberty: Gazans detained during the Israeli military operations of 27 December 2008 to 18 January 2009

56. During the military operations, the Israeli armed forces rounded up large numbers of civilians and detained them in

houses and open spaces in Gaza and, in the case of many Palestinian men, also took them to detention facilities in Israel. In the cases investigated by the Mission, the facts gathered indicate that none of the civilians was armed or posed any apparent threat to the Israeli soldiers. Chapter XV of the report is based on the Mission's interviews with Palestinian men who were detained, as well as on its review of other relevant material, including interviews with relatives and statements from other victims submitted to it.

57. From the facts gathered, the Mission finds that numerous violations of international humanitarian law and human rights law were committed in the context of these detentions. Civilians, including women and children, were detained in degrading conditions, deprived of food, water and access to sanitary facilities, and exposed to the elements in January without any shelter. The men were handcuffed, blindfolded and repeatedly made to strip, sometimes naked, at different stages of their detention.

58. In the al-Atatra area in north-western Gaza, Israeli troops had dug out sandpits in which Palestinian men, women and children were detained. Israeli tanks and artillery positions were located inside the sandpits and around them and fired from next to the detainees.

59. The Palestinian men who were taken to detention facilities in Israel were subjected to degrading conditions of detention, harsh interrogation, beatings and other physical and mental abuse. Some of them were charged with being unlawful combatants. Those interviewed by the Mission were released after the proceedings against them had apparently been discontinued.

Did not the German Nazis do these kinds of horrors to the Jews? Yes they made them to strip naked and put them in pits and now you can read the UN report in point 57 and 58 where similar incident is meted out to Palestinian civilians who had been taken into custody. This is why the Muslim world sees this treatment as fascism and equates Israel with the Nazis. It's deplorable that in spite of the Israeli high court Judges ban on human shields the IDF forces used some of the Palestinians as human shields. It shows they do not care about their own defined laws and feel they can break them anytime they like.

Here is the sort of questions the Muslims ask. Why did Israel armed forces destroy the flour factory, the sewerage works and the poultry farm killing all the chickens which were for the majority of the civilian population?

Were the chickens also firing rockets at Israel? This seems totally irrational and unwarranted in anyone's mind, personally I do not blame the Muslims for this thinking.

Did the flour owner send bread stuffed with bombs into Israel?

If we are honest we know we cannot defend these instances of what happened. One can see that unfortunately Israeli forces have committed brutality many times. So in order to kill let's assume 100 Hamas fighters who fired rockets into Israel at least 1400 people were killed. Much of the civilian infrastructure was destroyed which is against not only human rights but international law. Using the Israeli doctrine of Dahiya a disproportionate force was used to destroy civilian infrastructure. 280 schools and kindergartens were destroyed in Gaza. A Hospital was targeted that was treating civilians and ambulances that had nothing to do with the Hamas forces were targeted. So what will be the excuse of the Zionists now?

A prison was bombed that had nothing to do with Hamas fighters.

We now need to ask the question is the Muslim anger justified? We must examine both sides and I will let you decide if Israel can be justified in these counter attacks and using weapon materials such as white phosphorus which is extremely dangerous to the health and gives serious burns to the body. I would suggest any Bible loving human being would not agree with this violence which can easily be termed state sponsored terrorism by the Muslims and Israel therefore according to them has lost its moral high ground no matter how democratic it claims to be.

It is still time for Israel to withdraw from the occupied territories and claim some moral fibre and show some decency and mercy to the very people it has acquired the land from. Now the question is not why should we have future wars with the Muslims or Armageddon but when because the time clock is ticking and Israel has just hastened it a little more.

We must stand and speak for justice for all sides concerned whether Jews or gentile it's when we see the rule of law broken and stay quiet that's when a greater crime is committed against humanity. We should not simply remain quiet. Remember what happened when the world remained silent and millions of Jews were assassinated by Hitler. Now once again the world is silent while Palestinians are being murdered and removed from their homes.

If an atrocity is committed against a Jew then speak about it and if likewise against a Palestinian individual then we need to speak it and bring it forward so justice can be done. No serious Muslim denies Jihad in radical Islam as an outward external duty but the present Israeli actions have only compounded the problem and the result is Jihad which only adds to the equation and not removes from it. Ottoman Muslim Turks in the 16th century gave the Jews of Spain refuge in their fertile land to live in peace when Spain was throwing out and forcefully converting the Yahudim to Catholicism and now after years of peace Turkey has suspended 7.5 billion dollars of contracts with Israel and fast distancing itself from her ally. One need not wonder why.

I believe Turkey will now rise and will once again show the world what it is made of as it was once a mighty Empire. Unfortunately all the things that are happening and the Western governments silence only helps to awaken the 4th Beast more and the problem will not be just in Israel but will also land at the Western doorstep where many innocent people will die.

> **Matt 23:23** (HTHS) Woe to you, scribes and Pharisees, hypocrites! For you pay tithe of mint and anise and cumin, and have omitted the weightier matters of the Torah, **judgment, loving-kindness, and trustworthiness** these you should have done, and not to leave the others undone.
>
> **Mic 6:8** (HTHS) He has showed you, O man, what is good; and what does YHWH require of you, but to **practice justice, and to love loving-kindness,** and to **walk humbly** with Your POWER?

Both according to the Master Yahushua and ancient prophets of Israel loving-kindness translated mercy and Justice are the highest calling for us but is anyone going to speak for innocent civilian deaths in Israel of Palestinians and even Yahudim who have no part with state sponsored terror on either side of the fence? Yes both do it and the Palestinians claims are that they do it for the land that is taken by force from them which in fact not only was but still is being taken and Ben Gurion confirmed this truth. But Israel's response is that the rockets fired into Israel is the reason for their response. We can clearly see that in 1948 the Palestinians were not firing rockets and the problem started with the influx of these converted European Khazarite Jews into the land and the Palestinians have been ever since defending what they claim is their rightful possession of the land while Israel claims it's theirs when in reality it belongs to neither of the two but the Torah does allow foreigners to stay in the land in peace when true black Israel is back. So the first act of terror according to the Palestinians was the takeover of their land and ever since they feel they have been displaced the subsequent response from them has been the thwarting of that terror at all costs including suicide bombings which are justified in radical Islam to fight the enemy. The question is where does it stop?

In the process Israel has killed innocent Palestinian civilians who have not fired a single rocket and they are simply called collateral damage and Israel punishes the Palestinian population instead so they can remove Hamas but Israel fails to understand the rocket attacks are a result of land taken. If Israel wants some type of peace than it must give up the occupied territories and let the Palestinians have complete autonomy over those lands and then Israel may have a moral equivalence to invade territory that the Palestinians occupy if they continue to attack them with rockets.

Right now the rockets fired in the Palestinian eyes is for the aggressive takeover of Palestinian lands for which they are fighting against the crusaders both the Christians of the west whose lands the Yahudim came out of. Today in 2012 Obama makes a statement that no country can allow rockets to be fired into its space and remain quiet by defending Israel's attack once again for eight days in November 2012 upon Gaza by killing 171 Palestinians and 77 civilians with thousands of other Palestinians injured. This hypocritical speech could only come from the US president who himself orders extra judicial killings by firing missiles into all foreign lands such as Pakistan, Afghanistan and Yemen with drones. Thank you President for showing your hypocritical stance and to dance at the Zionist tune like a puppet who pull your strings if only you were a more right-ruling president many in your own country would not suffer and be protesting outside government buildings in many States while over forty million US citizens live in poverty who did not choose to do so. Yes you may defend your statement that it's not your fault but neither it's theirs who have no food to eat so how now we going to solve this problem created by your Zionist banker friends who you are backing?

The US and neither Israel is not a partner for peace because the US turns a blind eye to Israeli aggression against the weak.

Many Palestinian women have given birth at the Israeli manned checkpoints because of deliberate delays by the IDF to frustrate the Palestinian people. In fact a woman even lost her twin daughters at the checkpoint. This is causing humiliation to the Palestinians and they want all out revenge against the political Zionist ideology which has caused these problems and if I will be honest this is totally inhumane to deal with pregnant women like this and it s a moral outrage and Europeans and Americans need to assist and not hinder these peace talks while America has been silent and too busy trying to destabilise Syria and other nations of the world for political and monetary gain. We are commanded to live in peace with all men the question is when will decent men rise up in the West to do their duty? Israel needs to release occupied territories pure and simple.

This is best in Israel's interest and the opposition because Israel can easily secure her borders and is technologically superior to thwart any attacks. This action of unilateral withdrawal from the occupied territories will alone reduce the terrorism by more than half. Israel must give border control of the regions allotted to the Palestinians back to them. Its like France which was once occupied by Germany and if Germany after its defeat left and said we will control the French borders and roads that we built then really France would still be under German subjugation and Israel is acting in this way and many Muslims are feeling this unease that the claims of peace and land offers are simply empty and vacuous since Israel continues to occupy the land and build settlements inside Palestinian areas where settlers are better armed than the Palestinians and they continue to usurp the land, water and things that belong to the Arabs not forgetting their harass local Palestinians cut down their olive groves and humiliate their women.

If Israel continues to defy and take over lands in the guise of new settlements then the attacks will simply increase and continue and both Yahudim and Palestinians lives will continue to be lost. The curse upon Israel for breaking the three oaths will not diminish nor disappear unless Israel does what is right as stated in this book.

Here is what some Yahudim speakers have said which understand the issues of the land and the obligation of the Hebrews.

> [57]"We're not the Chosen People just by virtue of our forefathers; Leviticus warns the land will vomit us out, too, if we continue to be stiff-necked and evil. . . . There is no eternal guarantee to this holy land. . . . Our presence in the land is neither eternal nor automatic. Rather, our presence in the land is intimately connected with our moral behaviour (our treatment of the stranger, widow and orphan) as a nation. If we act wickedly towards the stranger; turn our

---

57 http://www.thomaswilliamson.net/God's%20Land.htm

heads from the poverty of the orphan, and stuff our ears to the cries of the widow, then the land will vomit us out - just as it had done to so many nations before us. When life is not lived morally, there's no difference between Yahudim and Amorites, between Israelis and Canaanites, Romans or Crusaders." - **Avraham Burg, former speaker of the Knesset (Israeli Parliament).**

"The text [Exodus 19:5] makes clear that this special status [Chosen People] is conditional: Israel must uphold their end of the deal and maintain the terms of the Contract/Agreement. As the text states, 'IF you will obey Me faithfully and keep my Contract/Agreement, THEN you shall be My treasured possession among all the peoples.' It is not Israel as a people who are special, but rather it is their behaviour, their commitment to and adherence to the laws of the Contract/Agreement, which sets them apart from all other people." - **Rabbi W. Gunther Plaut, in Kolel, The Adult Centre for Liberal Yahudim Learning.**

"Here [Deuteronomy 11:31-32] is clearly spelled out the formula for successful conquest and possession of Eretz Israel. In order that we should succeed in inheriting and dwelling in the Land, the Torah tells us we must observe all of Hashem's laws. It was therefore necessary to dramatically communicate a public declaration of blessings and curses upon entry into the Land, to drive home the message that possession of the Land was conditional on observance of the commandments." - **Rabbi Mendel Weinbach, Dean, Ohr Somayach Institutions.**

The Exile and the Redemption only belongs to God Himself, and He assured us that He Himself shall redeem us at the time he deems appropriate

“And God said to Abraham: ‘You should know that your descendants will be foreigners [in a land not their own]’” (Genesis 15:12)’. Know that I will disperse them; know that I will ingather them. Know that I will make them serve as collateral, and know that I will release them. Know that I will enslave them and know that I will redeem them. (Midrash Raba, Genesis 42:18)”.

There is the issue of the oath and curses coming upon the Yahudim if they take the land by force and they have taken the land by force without Torah obedience. The consequences of this could be dire and is proving to be since many people are dying as a result of the daily fighting.

Suppose that the Palestinians have no blood relationship with the Yahudim then should the Yahudim as a race treat them being a foreigner with respect and justice? The Torah commands mercy and justice for the foreigners but even though the Palestinians have blood relations to the same father Abraham that the Yahudim nation claims for her father then why the injustices? Why the hard handedness? Why the call for forced expulsion of Ms Zoubi? What kind of message does this send to the Muslim world? That these Yahudim are a racist people and bigots while we know that this is not true of all the Yahudim in the land of Israel. The actions of the few undermined and brought to condemnation many other Yahudi families.

This has interesting implications for Bible prophecy as I stated earlier that Israel is fast heading towards Armageddon thanks to those who advocate violence against violence. As I have showed you in this book the US has her direct hand in the revival of the Beast and so one could see radical Islam also has only been helped by radical Israelis who hate Muslims. Israel successfully managed to have itself condemned by world opinion because Israel acted with aggression when the whole thing was designed to bring humiliation to Israel for the blockade. It would be incorrect to say that the peace activists were martyrs since they did not have suicide belts on them nor automatic weapons to kill the IDF soldiers. If some of the activists managed to grab a weapon from the IDF soldiers which may have been used in the scuffle then that does not make them suicide bombers or criminals.

This just proves the weakness of the IDF commanders to assess the situation correctly before embarking on their trip to sabotage the ships as some kind of heroes. This is why the Muslim world suggests that the Yahudim were once on the receiving end and are now on the giving end are as worse than Nazis. Looking at the present government of Israel their behaviour is certainly questionable because they are putting their families at risk of harsh attacks.

I want people to just think for a minute without being biased towards Israel or the Palestinians. Israel needs to drop the hammer and nut approach and be careful how to resolve sticky issues since Gaza has become a thorny issue and will continue to dominate the scenes while the government is Israel also refuses to compromise.

The obvious question is why give Gaza away in the first place if later you are going to block it and occupy its borders actually makes no common sense!

If Hamas has been firing rockets into Israel then they need to be charged and arrested but there should not be an all out war on the rest of the Palestinian population who have no part in these actions. They are not all guilty for just living in Gaza or being Muslims but Israel thinks they can resolve everything by the hammer and nut approach meaning by force which we know is not true and has proved too many times that it's a failure. One must also notice that Hamas was chosen democratically by the Palestinians of Gaza so they should be allowed to determine their future just as much as Israel has her's they have theirs. If Hamas has a charter to drive all the Yahudim to the sea then one should ask why? I think anyone with an open mind will find the answer to that the mass migrations of Yahudim to the land of Israel in and after 1948 was going to bring about this spiritual conflict that will last many generations until the Messiah returns.

As for the Gaza Flotilla unless it had breached Israeli waters and refused to cooperate in which case Israel would have all the right to board and search the ship but it did not happen that way. Also notice a similar incident in March 2007 happened with Iran and England in which fifteen British marine personnel were captured who were claimed by Iran to be in Iranian waters and indeed they had guns and live ammunition.

What do you think would happen if the Iranian guards had shot down nine of them? Should we then go all guns blazing and drop a couple of nuclear bombs on the population of Iran? This is the kind of stupidity that many live in the West with who think the answers to all our problems is to drop bombs on civilians and call it collateral damage. When the opposite side attacks we call it terrorism. The West needs to stop terrorizing and killing innocent Muslims pure and simple.

Iran could have easily made the excuse that they were armed and in Iranian waters and hostile but Iran did not do that and in fact Iran a gentile nation acted in a more right-ruling way and did not shoot down soldiers with guns and create a scene on the high seas such as Israel has did with people who were not really armed with live ammunition. In fact in the ensuing dialogue Iran made sure to treat the British hostages well and with respect and dignity while Israel beat and abused some of the peace activists making them crouch down in awkward positions for hours and left some scarred from beatings they received while in Israel's custody. Some American activists will testify to this story who are not Muslims.

Real Israel are YHWH's chosen people but chosen people have to be responsible people and I would suggest Israel needs to learn a lesson from this incident that YHWH is watching both the justice and injustices that are being committed in the name of democracy and political Zionism. As I pointed out the majority of people living in Israel today are not chosen but only Jews by conversion or name hence why we are seeing this bigoted attitudes towards foreigners while they the Jews themselves are foreigners. The real Israelites the genetic seed were and are still black both the House of Yahudah and the ten tribes. Many of Yahudah the freed slaves who dwell in America, Europe and other eastern nations. Only fools will keep supporting the euro-centric Jews who are Khazarian converts and not genetic. Their actions are wholly unruly and wicked period.

We are commanded to be responsible people and must correct ourselves and apologise where we are wrong without arrogance and hostility correcting our mistakes since we are called to be a light to the nations. The US administration actually needs an excuse to attack Iran and had one in 2007 but still could not act upon it because it was not yet time for a war with Iran even though they secretly offered England this choice in 2007 but the time was and still is not yet as I said earlier. When the war does come many Iranian people will needlessly suffer but I pray that YHWH will indeed help those who are innocent and stuck in bondage and slavery of false religions and will be brought to the light.

The Muslim contention is simple they say that since Israel has Nuclear weapons why can't we. In their eyes Israel cannot be the only power with nuclear arsenal in the Middle-East. In the scheme of things and being neutral one would have to agree there appears to be a double standard and hypocrisy in the Western governments. Many western analysts know this fact too.

The Muslims are also well aware that the only aggressor with nuclear weapons and the one who used them in the past has been the United States which fired at least two of them on Hiroshima and Nagasaki in Japan in which an estimated 240,000 people were vaporised instantly and several thousand were left injured with the country facing huge problems for decades to come. So one can understand why the Muslim nations see the hypocrisy of the US administration that thinks that Muslims will use the nuclear bomb while in fact it's the other way around according to the Muslims. If we examine Pakistan as an example of a nuclear nation that has not used its nuclear weapon and in fact that has helped to keep a war with India at bay.

If I examine the Bible prophecy then another shocking truth is clear that the US will use the nuclear weapons again and this time it will be against

Syria and the Middle-East. This will allow the Muslim nations to galvanize and attack Israel in the future.

Now coming back to Israel she has only proved that her present approach so far has been a failure because of the lack of desire in many Israeli politicians to make true peace efforts and the issue of the removal of land by force. The Scriptures are clear that the people living in Gaza or the coastal regions that belong to the Muslims today is a judgment upon Israel however I do not think most Christians realize this truth and live in fantasy land that anything Israel does is right. This is not so.

> **Num 33:55** (HTHS) But if you will not drive out the inhabitants of the land from before you; then it shall come to pass, that those which you let remain of them shall be pricks in your eyes, and thorns in your sides, and shall trouble you in the land wherein you dwell.

> **Josh 23:13** (HTHS) Know for a certainty that YHWH Your POWER will no more drive out any of these nations from before you; but they shall be snares and traps to you, and scourges in your sides, and thorns in your eyes, until you perish from off this good land which YHWH Your POWER has given you.

> **Judges 2:3** (HTHS) Wherefore I also said, I will not drive them out from before you; but they shall be as thorns in your sides, and their powers shall be a snare to you.

Clearly YHWH has said he will not drive out the people that are in the land of Israel meaning the Muslims today. Why is this? YHWH wanted to test Israel and her faithfulness to the Torah and many in Israel had proven to be unfaithful and continue to do so today. The present government of Israel is totally against the principles YHWH wants to see put in place so YHWH himself will remove them when the day comes.

> **Judges 2:21-22** (HTHS) I also will not henceforth drive out any from before them of the nations which Yahoshua left when he died:
> **22** That through them I may prove Y'sra'el, whether they will keep the way of YHWH to walk therein, as their ahvot (fathers) did keep it, or not.

However things will change in the future.

> **Ezek 28:24** (HTHS) And they shall no more be a pricking brier to the house of Y'sra'el, nor any <u>grieving thorn of all that are round</u>

about them, that despised them; and they shall know that I am the Master YHWH.

This prophecy is yet future to be fulfilled so you can see this will continue to happen as that portion of the land has been given over to the gentiles (Muslims) by YHWH for Israel living in disobedience in the past and still in the present. This means it was a given condition that the division of the land was going to happen (Joel 3:2) and a two state solution was going to emerge whether we like it or not in which case we are encouraged to serve YHWH by His laws the Torah and its wise for us to try to make peace as best as possible at least until YHWH removes the enmity from Muslims and restores them to their father Abraham and his faith and joins them back to his brother Isaac and of course the Yahudim. Trying other options such as killing Palestinians or forcefully evicting them from the land will only bring more death and destruction because this is totally anti-Torah.

Usurping the land that YHWH has expelled Yahudim from and then to take it by force is against both the Torah and strict Yahudim law yet many settlers threaten Palestinians harass them and take over their land by various government schemes such as building roads, calling the land a military zone and various other tactics because the settlers are pretty well armed to do so while the Palestinian villagers do not have such sophisticated guns and weapons to fight back so they are forced to leave when there water is stolen and land is confiscated and their Palm and Olive groves are cut down by force. The settlers have five times the water of poor Palestinian families and they force them to leave. Remember the Zionists the same measure you use YHWH will use the same against you.

[58]**Prince warns S. Arabia of apocalypse**
Wed, 09 Jun 2010 09:02:52 GMT

Saudi Prince Turki bin Abdul Aziz Al Saud has warned the country's royal family to step down and flee before a military coup or a popular uprising overthrows the kingdom.

In a letter published by Wagze news agency on Tuesday, the Cairo-based prince warned Saudi Arabia's ruling family of a fate similar to that of Iraq's executed dictator Saddam Hussein and the ousted Iranian Shah Mohammad Reza Pahlavi, calling on them to escape before people "cut off our heads in streets."

---

58 http://www.presstv.ir/detail.aspx?id=129692§ionid=351020205

He warned that the Saudi royal family is no longer able to "impose" itself on people, arguing that deviations in carrying out the religious concepts that make up the basis of the Saudi government "have gotten out of our hands," so that the opposition views our acts as "interfering in people's private life and restricting their liberties."

"If we are wise, we must leave this country to its people, whose dislike for us is increasing," said Prince Turki, advising Saudi officials to escape with their families.

"Do it today before tomorrow as long as the money we have is enough for us to live anywhere in the world; from Switzerland to Canada and Australia...we should not return as long as we are able to get out safely, we must take our families quickly and pull out," he urged.

"Do not fool yourself by relying on the United States or Britain or Israel, because they will not survive the loss; the only door open is now the exit door of no return. Let us go before it closes."

He finally warned against a military coup against the ruling family, saying "no one will attack us from outside but our armed forces will attack us."

Prince Turki is a member of the liberal Free Princes movement founded in the 1950s amid tensions between King Faisal and his brother King Saud, requesting the Saudi authorities to implement political reforms and set out a constitution.

The late King Faisal expelled members of the civil rights group to Egypt but later on pardoned them.

MRS/MSA

Just as I told you earlier this news just came out in which prince Turki bin Abdul Aziz has warned the Royal family to flee. It is ironic that these are exactly my sentiments of things to come but what prince Turki said is true and almost prophetic and will come to pass in the near future so be warned as the time is getting closer for a Saudi meltdown which will affect the whole world.

This news below has just been released confirming what I have written about Turkey earlier in this book in the first edition being one of the power heads of the seven heads of Revelation in 13:1.

> http://www.ynetnews.com/articles/0,7340,L-3903244,00.html
>
> 06.10.10, 13:12 / Israel News
> In a speech to an Arab and Turkish ministerial forum, Prime Minister Tayyip Erdogan also announced plans to form a regional free trade zone with three Arab states -- Jordan, Lebanon and Syria.
>
> ...He went on to say Turkey would be forming a free-trade and visa free travel zone with the three Arab countries.

What does this mean to us?

Exactly what I stated earlier that Turkey will form one power block/Head and it will have some Muslim nations joining it. This is clear cut fulfilment of Biblical prophecy that says this which is concealed in *Revelation 13:1And I stood upon the sand of the sea, and saw a beast rise up out of the sea,* ***having seven heads****...*

Note Turkey is one head

This explains now very easily why Jordan will escape the wrath of the anti-Messiah because they are part of it.

Here is the Biblical prophecy to prove this, "*Jeremiah 50:44 Behold, he shall come up like a lion from the swelling of Jordan unto the habitation.*"

If you still do not see it then here is the nail in the coffin.

> **Daniel 11:41** (KJV) He shall enter also into the glorious land, and many shall fall: but these shall escape out of his hand, **Edom, Moab, and the chief of the children of Ammon**.

Note Edom, Moab and Ammon are all regions of Jordan. They escape and now you know why because they are in full alliance with the anti-Messiah who will come out from Turkey. So watch Turkey carefully because this is the iron legs (Dan 2:33) that once was Rome and is now Islamic.

Other observations

Putting Iran down a build up to the coming war!!

Did the Iranian president Mahmoud Ahmadinejad say he wants to wipe Israel from the face of this world's map? Did he deny the holocaust or is this all spun by the Western media and government propagandists?

The full text of what was said by the Iranian president

> [59]"They say it is not possible to have a world without the United States and Zionism. But you know that this is a possible goal and slogan. Let's take a step back. [[[We had a hostile regime in this country which was undemocratic, armed to the teeth and, with SAVAK, its security apparatus of SAVAK [the intelligence bureau of the Shah of Iran's government] watched everyone. An environment of terror existed.]]] When our dear Imam [Ayatollah Ruhollah Khomeini, the founder of the Iranian revolution] said that the regime must be removed, many of those who claimed to be politically well-informed said it was not possible. All the corrupt governments were in support of the regime when Imam Khomeini started his movement. [[[All the Western and Eastern countries supported the regime even after the massacre of September 7 [1978]]]] and said the removal of the regime was not possible. But our people resisted and it is 27 years now that we have survived without a regime dependent on the United States. The tyranny of the East and the West over the world should have to end, but weak people who can see only what lies in front of them cannot believe this.
>
> Who would believe that one day we could witness the collapse of the Eastern Empire? But we could watch its fall in our lifetime. And it collapsed in a way that we have to refer to libraries because no trace of it is left. Imam [Khomeini] said Saddam must go and he said he would grow weaker than anyone could imagine. Now you see the man who spoke with such arrogance ten years ago that one would have thought he was immortal, is being tried in his own country in handcuffs and shackles
>
> [[[by those who he believed supported him and with whose backing he committed his crimes]]]. Our dear Imam said that the occupying regime must be wiped off the map and this was a very

---

59 http://www.informationclearinghouse.info/article12790.htm

wise statement. We cannot compromise over the issue of Palestine. Is it possible to create a new front in the heart of an old front? This would be a defeat and whoever accepts the legitimacy of this regime [Israel] has in fact, signed the defeat of the Islamic world. Our dear Imam targeted the heart of the world oppressor in his struggle, meaning the occupying regime. I have no doubt that the new wave that has started in Palestine, and we witness it in the Islamic world too, will eliminate this disgraceful stain from the Islamic world."

(Source: www.nytimes.com, based on a publication of 'Iranian Students News Agency' (ISNA) -- insertions by the New York Times in squared brackets -- passages in triple squared brackets will be left blank in the MEMRI version printed below)

As a precaution we will examine a different translation of the speech - a version prepared by the Middle East Media Research Institute (MEMRI), located in Washington:

"They [ask]: 'Is it possible for us to witness a world without America and Zionism?' But you had best know that this slogan and this goal are attainable, and surely can be achieved. [[[...]]] "'When the dear Imam [Khomeini] said that [the Shah's] regime must go, and that we demand a world without dependent governments, many people who claimed to have political and other knowledge [asked], 'Is it possible [that the Shah's regime can be toppled]?' That day, when Imam [Khomeini] began his movement, all the powers supported [the Shah's] corrupt regime [[[...]]] and said it was not possible. However, our nation stood firm, and by now we have, for 27 years, been living without a government dependent on America. Imam [Khomeni] said: 'The rule of the East [U.S.S.R.] and of the West [U.S.] should be ended.' But the weak people who saw only the tiny world near them did not believe it. Nobody believed that we would one day witness the collapse of the Eastern Imperialism [i.e. the U.S.S.R], and said it was an iron regime. But in our short lifetime we have witnessed how this regime collapsed in such a way that we must look for it in libraries, and we can find no literature about it. Imam [Khomeini] said that Saddam [Hussein] must go, and that he would be humiliated in a way that was unprecedented. And what do you see today? A man who, 10 years ago, spoke as proudly as if he would live for eternity is today chained by the feet, and is now being tried in his own country [[[...]]] Imam [Khomeini] said: 'This regime that is occupying Qods [Jerusalem] must be eliminated from the pages of history.' This sentence is very wise. The issue of Palestine is not an issue on which we can compromise. Is it possible that an [Islamic] front allows another front [i.e. country] to arise in its own] heart? This means defeat, and he who accepts the existence of this regime [i.e. Israel] in fact signs the defeat of the Islamic world. In his battle against the World of Arrogance, our dear Imam

[Khomeini] set the regime occupying Qods [Jerusalem] as the target of his fight. I do not doubt that the new wave which has begun in our dear Palestine and which today we are also witnessing in the Islamic world is a wave of morality which has spread all over the Islamic world. Very soon, this stain of disgrace [i.e. Israel] will vanish from the center of the Islamic world - and this is attainable."

(Source: http://memri.org, based on the publication of 'Iranian Students News Agency' (ISNA) -- insertions by MEMRI in squared brackets -- missing passages compared to the 'New York Times' in triple squared brackets)

The Iranian press agency IRNA renders Ahmadinejad on 2005-12-14 as follows: "'If the Europeans are telling the truth in their claim that they have killed six million Yahudim in the Holocaust during the World War II - which seems they are right in their claim because they insist on it and arrest and imprison those who oppose it, why the Palestinian nation should pay for the crime. Why have they come to the very heart of the Islamic world and are committing crimes against the dear Palestine using their bombs, rockets, missiles and sanctions.' [...] 'If you have committed the crimes so give a piece of your land somewhere in Europe or America and Canada or Alaska to them to set up their own state there.' [...] Ahmadinejad said some have created a myth on holocaust and hold it even higher than the very belief in religion and prophets [...] The president further said, 'If your civilization consists of aggression, displacing the oppressed nations, suppressing justice-seeking voices and spreading injustice and poverty for the majority of people on the earth, then we say it out loud that we despise your hollow civilization.'"

CNN (2005-12-15) renders as follows: "If you have burned the Yahudim why don't you give a piece of Europe, the United States, Canada or Alaska to Israel. Our question is, if you have committed this huge crime, why should the innocent nation of Palestine pay for this crime?"

The Washingtonian "Middle East Media Research Institute' (MEMRI) renders Ahmadinejad's statements from 2005-12-14 as follows: "...we ask you: if you indeed committed this great crime, why should the oppressed people of Palestine be punished for it? * [...] If you committed a crime, you yourselves should pay for it. Our offer was and remains as follows: If you committed a crime, it is only appropriate that you place a piece of your land at their disposal - a piece of Europe, of America, of Canada, or of Alaska - so they can establish their own state. Rest assured that if you do so, the Iranian people will voice no objection."

The MEMRI-rendering uses the relieving translation 'great crime' and misappropriates the following sentence at the * marked passage: "Why have they come to the very heart of the Islamic world and are committing crimes against the dear Palestine using their bombs, rockets, missiles and sanctions." This sentence has obviously been left out deliberately because it would intimate why the Israeli state could have forfeited the right to establish itself in Palestine – vide licet because of its aggressive expansionist policy against the people of Palestine, ignoring any law of nations and disobeying all UN-resolutions.

In spite of the variability referring to the rendering of the statements of Iran's President we should nevertheless note down: the reproach of denying the Holocaust cannot be sustained if Ahmadinejad speaks of a great and huge crime that has been done to the Yahudim.

In another IRNA-dispatch (2005-12-14) the Arabian author Ghazi Abu Daqa writes about Ahmadinejad: "The Iranian president has nothing against the followers of Judaism [...] Ahmadinejad is against Zionism as well as its expansionist and occupying policy. That is why he managed to declare to the world with courage that there is no place for the Zionist regime in the world civilized community."

It's no wonder that such opinions do not go down particularly well with the ideas of the centres of power in the Western world. But for this reason they are not wrong right away. Dealing out criticism against the aggressive policy of the Western world, to which Israel belongs as well, is not yet anti-Semitism. We should at least to give audience to this kind of criticism - even if it is a problematic field for us.

As can be seen the President of Iran did not deny the holocaust nor make the speech in the words the Western media has suggested justifying another war with Iran. One wonders why? This is because they wanted to justify an attack on Iran and to create what I can only term a reason so when they attack Iran which we know already is going to happen then they can put their hands up and say see Iran is an aggressive nation and making threats hence why we have to attack them and put them in their place. However behind the attack would be other real reasons such as control of the nation's mineral wealth and its distribution.

Here is another source

[60]**'Wiped off the Map' – The Rumor of the Century**
by Arash Norouzi
Across the world, a dangerous rumor has spread that could have catastrophic implications. According to legend, Iran's president has threatened to destroy Israel, or, to quote the misquote, "Israel must be wiped off the map." Contrary to popular belief, this statement was never made.

On Tuesday, October 25th, 2005 at the Ministry of Interior conference hall in Tehran, newly elected Iranian President Mahmoud Ahmadinejad delivered a speech at a program, reportedly attended by thousands, titled "The World Without Zionism." Large posters surrounding him displayed this title prominently in English, obviously for the benefit of the international press. Below the poster's title was a slick graphic depicting an hour glass containing planet Earth at its top. Two small round orbs representing the United States and Israel are shown falling through the hour glass' narrow neck and crashing to the bottom.

Before we get to the infamous remark, it's important to note that the "quote" in question was itself a quote – they are the words of the late Ayatollah Khomenei, the father of the Islamic Revolution. Although he quoted Khomeini to affirm his own position on Zionism, the actual words belong to *Khomeini* and not Ahmadinejad. Thus, Ahmadinejad has essentially been credited (or

---

60 http://www.antiwar.com/orig/norouzi.php?articleid=11025

blamed) for a quote that is not only unoriginal, but represents a viewpoint already in place well before he ever took office.

The Actual Quote:

So what did Ahmadinejad actually say? To quote his exact words in Farsi:

"Imam ghoft een rezhim-e ishghalgar-e qods bayad az safheh-ye ruzgar mahv shavad."

That passage will mean nothing to most people, but one word might ring a bell: *rezhim-e*. It is the word "regime." pronounced just like the English word with an extra "*eh*" sound at the end. Ahmadinejad did not refer to Israel the country or Israel the land mass, but the Israeli *regime*. This is a vastly significant distinction, as one cannot wipe a *regime* off the map. Ahmadinejad does not even refer to Israel by name, he instead uses the specific phrase "rezhim-e ishghalgar-e qods" (regime occupying Jerusalem).

So this raises the question.. what exactly did he want "wiped from the map"? The answer is: *nothing*. That's because the word "map" was *never used*. The Persian word for map, "*nagsheh*" is not contained anywhere in his original Farsi quote, or, for that matter, anywhere in his entire speech. Nor was the western phrase "wipe out" ever said. Yet we are led to believe that Iran's president threatened to "wipe Israel off the map." despite never having uttered the words "map." "wipe out" or even "Israel."

The Proof:

The full quote translated directly to English:

"The Imam said this regime occupying Jerusalem must vanish from the page of time."

Word by word translation:

Imam (Khomeini) ghoft (said) een (this) rezhim-e (regime) ishghalgar-e (occupying) qods (Jerusalem) bayad (must) az safheh-ye ruzgar (from page of time) mahv shavad (vanish from).

Here is the full transcript of the speech in Farsi, archived on Ahmadinejad's web site (http://www.president.ir/farsi/ahmadinejad/speeches/1384/aban-84/840804sahyonizm.htm)

The Speech and Context:

While the false "wiped off the map" extract has been repeated infinitely without verification, Ahmadinejad's actual speech itself has been almost entirely ignored. Given the importance placed on the "map" comment, it would be sensible to present his words in their full context to get a fuller understanding of his position. In fact, by looking at the entire speech, there is a clear, logical trajectory leading up to his call for a "world without Zionism." One may disagree with his reasoning, but critical appraisals are infeasible without first knowing what that reasoning is.

In his speech, Ahmadinejad declares that Zionism is the West's apparatus of political oppression against Muslims. He says the "Zionist regime" was imposed on the Islamic world as a strategic bridgehead to ensure domination of the region and its assets. Palestine, he insists, is the frontline of the Islamic world's struggle with American hegemony, and its fate will have repercussions for the entire Middle East.

Ahmadinejad acknowledges that the removal of America's powerful grip on the region via the Zionists may seem unimaginable to some, but reminds the audience that, as Khomeini predicted, other seemingly invincible empires have disappeared and now only exist in history books. He then proceeds to list three such regimes that have collapsed, crumbled or vanished, all within the last 30 years:

(1) The Shah of Iran – the U.S. installed monarch

(2) The Soviet Union

(3) Iran's former arch-enemy, Iraqi dictator Saddam Hussein

In the first and third examples, Ahmadinejad prefaces their mention with Khomeini's own words foretelling that individual regime's demise. He concludes by referring to Khomeini's unfulfilled wish: "The Imam said this regime occupying Jerusalem must vanish from the page of time. This statement is very wise." This is the passage that has been isolated, twisted and distorted so famously. By measure of comparison, Ahmadinejad would seem to be calling for *regime change*, not war...

The Origin:

One may wonder: where did this false interpretation originate? Who is responsible for the translation that has sparked such worldwide controversy? The answer is surprising.

The inflammatory "wiped off the map" quote was first disseminated not by Iran's enemies, but by Iran itself. The Islamic Republic News Agency, Iran's official propaganda arm, used this phrasing in the English version of some of their news releases covering the World Without Zionism conference. International media including the BBC, Al-Jazeera, *Time* magazine and countless others picked up the IRNA quote and made headlines out of it without verifying its accuracy, and rarely referring to the source. Iran's Foreign Minister soon attempted to clarify the statement, but the quote had a life of its own. Though the IRNA wording was inaccurate and misleading, the media assumed it was true, and besides, it made great copy.

Amid heated wrangling over Iran's nuclear program, and months of continuous, unfounded accusations against Iran in an attempt to rally support for pre-emptive strikes against the country, the imperialists had just been handed the perfect raison d'être to invade. To the war hawks, it was a gift from the skies.

It should be noted that in other references to the conference, the IRNA's translation changed. For instance, "map" was replaced with "earth." In some articles it was "The Qods occupier regime should be eliminated from the surface of earth." or the similar "The Qods occup**ying** regime **must** be eliminated from the surface of earth." The inconsistency of the IRNA's translation should be evidence enough of the unreliability of the source, particularly when transcribing their news from Farsi into the English language.

The Reaction:

The mistranslated "wiped off the map" quote attributed to Iran's president has been spread worldwide, repeated thousands of times in international media, and prompted the denouncements of numerous world leaders. Virtually every major and minor media outlet has published or broadcast this false statement to the masses. Big news agencies such as The Associated Press and Reuters refer to the misquote, literally, on an almost daily basis.

Following news of Iran's remark, condemnation was swift. British Prime Minister Tony Blair expressed "revulsion" and implied that it might be necessary to attack Iran. U.N. chief Kofi Annan cancelled his scheduled trip to Iran due to the controversy. Ariel Sharon demanded that Iran be expelled from the United Nations for calling for Israel's destruction. Shimon Peres, more than once, threatened to wipe *Iran* off the map. More recently, Israel's Benjamin Netanyahu, who has warned that Iran is "preparing another holocaust for the Yahudim state" is calling for Ahmadinejad to be tried for war crimes for inciting genocide.

The artificial quote has also been subject to additional alterations. U.S. officials and media often take the liberty of dropping the "map" reference altogether, replacing it with the more acutely threatening phrase "wipe Israel off the face of the earth." Newspaper and magazine articles dutifully report Ahmadinejad has "called for the destruction of Israel." as do senior officials in the United States government.

President George W. Bush said the comments represented a "specific threat" to destroy Israel. In a March 2006 speech in Cleveland, Bush vowed he would resort to war to protect Israel from Iran, because, "the threat from Iran is, of course, their stated objective to destroy our ally Israel." Former presidential advisor Richard Clarke told Australian TV that Iran "talks openly about destroying Israel." and insists, "The president of Iran has said repeatedly that he wants to wipe Israel off the face of the earth." In an October 2006 interview with Amy Goodman, former UN Weapons Inspector Scott Ritter referred to Ahmadinejad as "the idiot that comes out and says really stupid, vile things, such as, 'It is the goal of Iran to wipe Israel off the face of the earth.'" The consensus is clear.

Confusing matters further, Mahmoud Ahmadinejad pontificates rather than give a direct answer when questioned about the statement, such as in Lally Weymouth's Washington Post interview in September 2006: (http://www.washingtonpost.com/wp-dyn/content/article/2006/09/22/AR2006092201306_pf.html)

"Q: Are you really serious when you say that Israel should be wiped off the face of the Earth?

"A: We need to look at the scene in the Middle East – 60 years of war, 60 years of displacement, 60 years of conflict, not even a day of peace. Look at the war in Lebanon, the war in Gaza – what are the reasons for these conditions? We need to address and resolve the root problem.

"Q: Your suggestion is to wipe Israel off the face of the Earth?

"A: Our suggestion is very clear:... Let the Palestinian people decide their fate in a free and fair referendum, and the result, whatever it is, should be accepted.... The people with no roots there are now ruling the land.

"Q: You've been quoted as saying that Israel should be wiped off the face of the Earth. Is that your belief?

"A: What I have said has made my position clear. If we look at a map of the Middle East from 70 years ago...

"Q: So, the answer is yes, you do believe that it should be wiped off the face of the Earth?

"A: Are you asking me yes or no? Is this a test? Do you respect the right to self-determination for the Palestinian nation? Yes or no? Is Palestine, as a nation, considered a nation with the right to live under humane conditions or not? Let's allow those rights to be enforced for these 5 million displaced people."

The exchange is typical of Ahmadinejad's interviews with the American media. Predictably, both Mike Wallace of 60 Minutes and CNN's Anderson Cooper asked if he wants to "wipe Israel off the map." As usual, the question is thrown back in the reporter's face with his standard "Don't the Palestinians have rights?, etc." retort (which is never directly answered either). Yet he *never* confirms the "map" comment to be true. This did not prevent Anderson Cooper from referring to earlier portions of his interview after a commercial break and lying, "as he said earlier, he wants Israel wiped off the map."

Even if every media outlet in the world were to retract the

mistranslated quote tomorrow, the major damage has already been done, providing the groundwork for the next phase of disinformation: complete character demonization. Ahmadinejad, we are told, is the next Hitler, a grave threat to world peace who wants to bring about a new Holocaust. According to some detractors, he not only wants to destroy Israel, but after that, he will nuke America, and then Europe! An October 2006 memo titled "Words of Hate: Iran's Escalating Threats" released by the powerful Israeli lobby group AIPAC opens with the warning, "Ahmadinejad and other top Iranian leaders are issuing increasingly belligerent statements threatening to destroy the United States, Europe and Israel." These claims not only fabricate an unsubstantiated threat, but assume far more power than he actually possesses. Alarmists would be better off monitoring the statements of the ultra-conservative Supreme Leader, Ayatollah Khamenei, who holds the most power in Iran.

As Iran's U.N. Press Officer, M.A. Mohammadi, complained to the *Washington Post* in a June 2006 letter:

"It is not amazing at all, the pick-and-choose approach of highlighting the misinterpreted remarks of Iranian President Mahmoud Ahmadinejad in October and ignoring this month's remarks by Iran's supreme leader, Ayatollah Ali Khamenei, that 'We have no problem with the world. We are not a threat whatsoever to the world, and the world knows it. We will never start a war. We have no intention of going to war with any state.'"

The Israeli government has milked every drop of the spurious quote to its supposed advantage. In her September 2006 address to the United Nations General Assembly, Israeli Foreign Minister Tzipi Livni accused Iran of working to nuke Israel and bully the world. "They speak proudly and openly of their desire to 'wipe Israel off the map.' And now, by their actions, they pursue the weapons to achieve this objective to imperil the region and threaten the world." Addressing the threat in December, a fervent Prime Minister Ehud Olmert inadvertently disclosed that his country already possesses nuclear weapons: "We have never threatened any nation with annihilation. Iran, *openly, explicitly and publicly* threatens to wipe Israel off the map. Can you say that this is the same level, when they are aspiring to have nuclear weapons, as America, France, Israel, Russia?"

Media Irresponsibility:

On December 13, 2006, more than a year after The World Without Zionism conference, two leading Israeli newspapers, the *Jerusalem Post* and *Haaretz*, published reports of a renewed threat from Ahmadinejad. The *Jerusalem Post*'s headline was Ahmadinejad: Israel will be 'wiped out', while *Haaretz* posted the title Ahmadinejad at Holocaust conference: Israel will 'soon be wiped out'.

Where did they get their information? It turns out that both papers, like most American and western media, rely heavily on write ups by news wire services such as the Associated Press and Reuters as a source for their articles. Sure enough, their sources are in fact December 12th articles by Reuter's Paul Hughes [Iran president says Israel's days are numbered], and the AP's Ali Akbar Dareini [Iran President: Israel will be wiped out].

The first five paragraphs of the *Haaretz* article, credited to "*Haaretz* Service and Agencies." are plagiarized almost 100% from the first five paragraphs of the Reuters piece. The only difference is that *Haaretz* changed "the Yahudim state" to "Israel" in the second paragraph, otherwise they are identical.

The *Jerusalem Post* article by Herb Keinon pilfers from both the Reuters and AP stories. Like *Haaretz*, it uses the following Ahmadinejad quote without attribution: ["Just as the Soviet Union was wiped out and today does not exist, so will the Zionist regime soon be wiped out," he added]. Another passage apparently relies on an IRNA report:

"The Zionist regime will be wiped out soon the same way the Soviet Union was, and humanity will achieve freedom," Ahmadinejad said at Tuesday's meeting with the conference participants in his offices, according to Iran's official news agency, IRNA.

He said elections should be held among "Yahudim, Christians and Muslims so the population of Palestine can select their government and destiny for themselves in a democratic manner."

Once again, the first sentence above was wholly plagiarized from the AP article. The second sentence was also the same, except

"He called for elections" became "He said elections should be held..."

It gets more interesting.

The quote used in the original AP article and copied in the *Jerusalem Post* article supposedly derives from the IRNA. If true, this can easily be checked.

There you will discover the actual IRNA quote was:

"As the Soviet Union disappeared, the Zionist regime will also vanish and humanity will be liberated."

Compare this to the alleged IRNA quote reported by the Associated Press:

"The Zionist regime will be wiped out soon the same way the Soviet Union was, and humanity will achieve freedom."

In the IRNA's actual report, the Zionist regime will *vanish* just as the Soviet Union *disappeared. Vanish. Disappear.* In the dishonest AP version, the Zionist regime will be "wiped out." And how will it be wiped out? *"The same way the Soviet Union was."* Rather than imply a military threat or escalation in rhetoric, this reference to Russia actually validates the intended meaning of Ahmadinejad's previous misinterpreted anti-Zionist statements.

What has just been demonstrated is irrefutable proof of media manipulation and propaganda in action. The AP deliberately alters an IRNA quote to sound more threatening. The Israeli media not only repeats the fake quote but also steals the original authors' words. The unsuspecting public reads this, forms an opinion and supports unnecessary wars of aggression, presented as self defense, based on the misinformation.

This scenario mirrors the kind of false claims that led to the illegal U.S. invasion of Iraq, a war now widely viewed as a catastrophic mistake. And yet the Bush administration and the compliant corporate media continue to marinate in propaganda and speculation about attacking Iraq's much larger and more formidable neighbor, Iran. Most of this rests on the unproven assumption that Iran is building nuclear weapons, and the lie that

Iran has vowed to physically destroy Israel. Given its scope and potentially disastrous outcome, all this amounts to what is arguably the rumor of the century.

Iran's president has written two rather philosophical letters to America. In his first letter, he pointed out that "History shows us that oppressive and cruel governments do not survive." With this statement, Ahmadinejad has also projected the outcome of his own backwards regime, which will likewise "vanish from the page of time."

My real Yahudim forefathers were in Iran since my family lost contact with them and are probably still there amongst the 35,000 Yahudim living there. So I do sympathise with the Iranians for good reason because justice calls for it. Have you ever wondered why we never hear about crimes committed against the Yahudim in Iran because they live in relative peace in a Muslim state that respects their rights? The grave of Esther is a testimony to the God of Israel and of several sages in Iran that YHWH does not hate the Iranians.

Yet we hear of countless attacks on Yahudim synagogues still in Europe today and their graves being desecrated by fascists with Hitler emblems of the swastika. This proves that Europe has more anti-Semitism than the Iranian kingdom where many live in relative peace. However the irony is also that there are Jews of Caucasian skin colour who call themselves Jews or chosen but they are not. While Christians continue to be deceived in the matter supporting the wrong people while the real Israelites amongst them the ones who were and are such as the Black Israelites those called Negro are still continued to be ignored and sidelined as sons of Ham while they are not the sons of Ham but Shem. What when YHWH raises them back then where will the Christians run to?

One has to ask if the Iranian President wanted to wipe all of Israel then surely the first people he will get rid of are the 35,000 Yahudim in Iran but they continue to live completely autonomous lives and are free to practice Torah with no state interference. Iran is also the nation that sent Yahudim back to Israel because one of the ancient kings of Iran is mentioned in scripture King Cyrus who is called YHWH's anointed (Isa 45:1).

This shows me that unfair propaganda has been created to attack Iran however we need to understand the people who are behind these things are not always sincere but only motivated by greed. What the president of Iran said if I can paraphrase is that the political Zionist government of

Israel will be removed one day and that in fact is a prophetic statement but I doubt many Christians would understand this. This is because YHWH is not going to rule the nation with secular government but Torah government and here is the proof by the prophet Isaiah.

> **Isaiah 2:2** (HTHS) And it shall come to pass in the last days, that the mountain of YHWH's house shall be established in the top of the mountains, and shall be exalted above the hills; and all nations shall flow to it.

This is not the present government running on secular values in fact it will be a future real Y'sra'elite Torah government which will rule many gentiles in Israel. So who are the gentiles in Israel today? The Muslims – which means they have a right to be in the land because they are the sons of Abraham. They will one day submit to YHWH's governance but they will not submit to the present secularists in Israel for obvious reasons since the enmity runs deep since the recreation of the political state of Israel in 1948. I do not think any people who were displaced would be happy and I can tell you our own experience of Pakistan and India. When my great grandfather died fighting the Sikhs in India when many Sikhs indiscriminately attacked him to kill our family my father was only six years old when he fled India with my grandfather.

Many Muslims, Sikhs and Hindus died in that fighting during India and Pakistan's partition in 1947 but even today emotions are evoked when those things are discussed. I however have many Sikh friends and only see that those over reactions of the Sikhs and Muslims were simply a religious zeal because one attacked the other. There were causalities on both sides but we must live with forgiveness and love and not enmity but I do know many Pakistanis who hate Indians and many Indians who hate Pakistanis so you can imagine the feelings of the Palestinian Arabs who feel that the land they had occupied at least since 637 CE and lived in it as their home has been taken from them even though there were many Yahudi families there but then Israel was not a political entity until 1948.

The present government of Israel is secular and not Torah based therefore it is not running in accordance with YHWH. This then brings us to the clear conclusion that when the Messiah returns He will setup a Torah based government and the present political Zionist government will in fact be removed. So did Mahmoud predict this that one day this regime will be removed? Yes, he did but most of you out there took that the wrong way because the media coloured his story and embellished it and most of you fell for it.

Did Ahmadinejad deny the holocaust? No. He said "If the Europeans are telling the truth in their claims that they have killed six million Yahudim in the Holocaust during the World War II - which seems they are right in their claim." It is clear from this statement that he acknowledges the guilt of Europe and wants them to find a solution for the Yahudim problem. This is not a denial of the holocaust but an acceptance of it. But to make the Iranian president look bad the Western media ran an interesting propaganda which in fact is to prepare the public for war.

I am going to tell you something so please hear me very carefully.

Israel is YHWH's time clock and the land Israel has always had a presence of some Yahudim families in it. Note, that since 637 CE there has always been a presence of some Muslims in the land also while the majority of the wealthy Turks who owned the land did not inhabit the land at all times but left their lands keeping legal title which many sold later to the returning Yahudim to Israel for high prices but Israel has had Arab nomads living there for centuries but it is made to appear that they only came after 1948 is not entirely true. This is mere propaganda which even some Christians have fallen into. Anyone who lived in the land during these centuries that is both Yahudim and Arabs were simply called Palestinians although the definition took a political terminology after the 1967 six day war.

The idea that Christians taking back Yahudim are doing a service to God is completely false and erroneous. It is actually unscriptural and many agencies are making a profit from Christians who are not wise. The Yahudim were meant to be in the world and one day to become the light to the nations when the Spirit of God moves in their midst but that would only happen if they were there in the first place but when the true gathering of the Yahudim comes about it will not be coordinated by people or by collections in churches or organisations which is a mere front for individuals for political and self aggrandizing purposes but when the real Second Exodus comes it will be by YHWH and YHWH alone. He does not need your money to take His people home so keep it.

That move will happen when the Messiah returns and not before. This is why some Torah based Yahudim groups are correct that the present state of Israel and its governance are not according to YHWH. I agree. Because Israel's governance has to be by the Law of God, it must be Torah based and not secular even for a day which we know is still yet future. This means Israel has to have the ten tribes returning to formulate a large gentile majority and a Yahudim minority in which the king will rule over many gentile people living in Israel with the Yahudim. Right now this is not the case. Note many of the exiles Hebrew Israelites people were of Negro origin so a large part of the ten tribes will likely be people of colour.

Many people who favour the political Zionist cause forget that because of them many Yahudim actually died in the holocaust since they were unwilling to help because of their own agendas at that time when both America and Great Britain were willing to accommodate escaping Yahudim from Germany but the Zionists refused to allow that to happen which caused many thousands of Yahudim to simply perish. The political Zionists have blood on their hands too so don't be so naive. Is it okay to have 100,000 Yahudim killed to establish the State as a political entity? I am not qualified to answer this question however those who died perhaps can best answer that and their families. Of course Israel needs to exist as a reality and Israel's king in this case Benjamin Netanyahu needs to have Torah as his legislation to govern Israel as this is what was commanded by YHWH since Israel cannot behave as other nations and live like heathen entities (Deut 17:18-19). Right now the gentile Netanyahu and other gentiles called themselves Jews live in the true children of Israel's land. Prepared to be removed by the hands of YHWH.

> **Deut 17:18-19** (HTHS) And it shall be, when he sits upon the throne of his kingdom, that he shall write him a copy of this Torah in a scroll out of that which is before the kohenim the Lewites: **19** And it shall be with him, and he shall read therein all the days of his life: that he may learn to fear YHWH his Elohim, to keep all the words of this Torah and these statutes, to do them:

However we know the recreation of the political state has kicked off the process of Israel's redemption and the ensuing wars and the return of the Messiah will culminate in her complete redemption.

You will be surprised to learn that it is **forbidden** for the Yahudim to go the land permanently and live there with her secular laws and it is breaking a positive commandment to do that. There are three oaths in the scriptures that were given to the Yahudim and the Babylonian Talmud backs this up that a massive exodus to Israel by human hands or by force is absolutely forbidden yet countless people are asking in Christendom to help migrate Yahudim or to donate money to do so.

Rambam a proselyte Rabbi said that it was a good deed to live in the land of Israel but at that time Israel was not a political entity so one can understand to live there under Torah yes but without Torah no. Yahudim are to stay in the nations where they have been placed until YHWH calls them out. If they are in a hostile nation then they are simply to move to another nation that is not hostile which did happen such as Yahudim leaving Germany to go to the US or to go to the Islamic kingdoms.

For Yahudim to vote in the secular Israeli government or to take part is acceptance of the secular law which is forbidden by the Bible. This is why some religious parties in Israel that are in the Knesset take part in politics only to voice concern for the Torah laws and these religious Yahudim are a minority who will not even use public government funded buses and they have their own transport system for their community and even have established their own pension systems so they are in no way participating in government funded schemes because they understand the implications of the ban through the oath I discussed earlier.

In 2004 when I went to Israel and asked Melek Yahushua whether I should move to the land permanently I was told "No" and to remain in the nations. In fact whether you believe it or not He told me that He will take me to the land Himself, which means we have to wait for Him to lead us and not a moment before. If you are in the US stay put and if you are in the UK and Europe stay put and in fact help your needy brothers in the lands of your sojourn that you are in to establish strong communities, help your Torah teachers with tithes who teach you Torah but do not go back to Israel to live there that you may not transgress a positive commandment and break the oath that our forefathers took. We are allowed to move to other nations in which we feel safe. The climate in US now has been quite racist against the Hebrew black people. Every week you hear of at least one death of a man in US due to hatred and indifference by the white population of America. Hence why it's better for those who are able to get to safer countries. I have done a teaching on this available from Rabbi Kefa from our website www.african-israel.com.

If you want to go to any country then select a suitable nation in Africa because they will be first in the March back to Y'sra'el.

The real Black Yahudim being in the four corners of the world are a prophecy fulfilled and also they are to shine the light of Torah to the world that is why their presence is much needed as a divine will. The Yahudim wherever they live will become a benefit to those nations and in turn the gentiles can increase them.

Now do you see why the real black Yahudim are being killed in the land and racism is very high against them by the European Zionists who are not the chosen? These deaths are unnecessary and are a warning to all those who want to live there before the return of the Messiah which will signal the end redemption of Israel. All the land disputes will be resolved then and not a moment before.

> **Ezek 22:25** (KJV) There is a conspiracy of her prophets in the midst there, like a roaring lion ravening the prey; they have devoured souls; they have taken the treasure and precious things; they have made her many widows in the midst there.

All the political Zionist puppet prophets in Israel are nothing but liars and because of their lies many women are without husbands today and have become widows because they have been killed by the radicals.

Then we must ask how YHWH will fulfil this prophecy that only He will lead them while we have at least five to six million Yahudim there in Israel. This is indeed very easy. In the future there will be a big war and half of Jerusalem will be taken, at that time Israelis will flee the land and many foreign nations will take the Yahudim back such as the United States and Europe. This is when Israel will be emptied but not completely. After this event when the Messiah returns then all the Yahudim will be taken by the hand of the Messiah and we await this scenario and you can be sure this is how it will be fulfilled. How do we know this? Many teachers of prophecy were saying that the Yahudim will run to Petra and stay in Jordan?

> **Isa 2:10** (HTHS) Enter into the rock, and hide yourself in the dust, for fear of YHWH, and for the esteem of his majesty.

This is unfortunately tied to the false idea of a pre-tribulation rapture or mid tribulation rapture. No such thing will occur. For further reading read Micah 2:12 and Rev 12:6-17.

However since YHWH is their refuge he will take the real Yahudim back to the nations and then bring them back in great numbers then we will find a complete fulfilment of the prophecy. As I suggested many European Jews would end up leaving Israel to live abroad since they do not even belong in the land or if they remain many of them will be killed outright so be warned.

If you would like to dig further then I will give you a reference for the Talmud Ketubot 110b-111a, which you can check up. I will let you search out the scripture references but if you get stuck I will help you find them but for now I do not give them to the idolatrous nations who do not obey the Torah. I do not want you to have trouble finding these references but

I will help you with the Talmud discussion and here it is and you can follow it through since it will lead you to the references in scripture also.

> Ketubot 110b - 111a, from Shir HaShirim
>
> In the Babylonian Diaspora right after the destruction of the First Temple, Rabbi Ze'ira asked Rabbi Yehudah if he is permitted to return to Eretz Israel.
>
> Rabbi Yehudah answered: Whoever ascends from Babylon to Eretz Israel transgresses a positive commandment. Only God decides about the end of the Babylonian Exile. Hence, He will give us a sign. It is absolutely forbidden to make up our own minds and rush back to Eretz Israel.

Now you can decide if you want to follow the whims and desires of Christians and go back to the land to be killed or maimed or some misguided people in Israel who support the present state of Israel and its anti-Torah government with Zionists gentiles.

Since the returning Yahudim have technically broken the oaths they are hunted like Gazelles and Deers and I hope this is absolutely clear in the present that this is the oath which then becomes a curse upon those who break it. I do not want to say too much on the subject.

If you think I just made all that up then here is the ruling of the Gemara on breaking of the oaths. Note any political Zionism is anti-Torah and anti-God. In fact the political Zionist's caused many deaths in the holocaust because of their twisted agenda at least 100,000 Yahudim perished. Some Rabbi's such as Teitelbaum blame the Zionists for the holocaust and I can see the reasons for that.

> God said to the Hebrews: "If you abide by the oath, it will be well and good for you, but if not, I will permit your **flesh to be hunted by the idolaters as the gazelles and as the hinds of the field**". (Underline mine)

The idolater is a reference to the radical Islamists. You cannot go back to the land until the Messiah returns and takes you there. Some Rabbis understand that if you are persecuted in the nations that you can go back to the land of Israel but to strictly live by Torah and not secular government but it is still preferable to live outside the land and that is what upholds the oath. You are allowed to visit the land each year even in your exile as many times as you wish without any restrictions

Note this is not to confuse with that I do not agree with the land of Israel, I do, and I say that Israel is the time clock of Elohim but I agree that Israel should not have a secular government but Torah based one and until YHWH calls Israel she is only delaying her redemption with political parties that do nothing for the land of Israel and her people. The people must strive for Torah governance and remove themselves from the influence of nations and their agendas because as long as they remain liberal this will not be possible.

If you have read my book Islam, Peace or Beast and World War III part one then you will have a pretty accurate picture of where we are heading if not I suggest you get those to fill any gaps because they will help you decide your plans for yourself and your children of where and what you should be doing in the coming days, months and years. The Bible is full of prophetic insight and if you follow scripture and stick to YHWH's voice His Torah then you cannot go wrong with your eternal destiny. I pray this book will help you to do just that. If you need to contact me for any clarification or further questions you can write to me by e-mail to shimoun63@yahoo.com or Phone Rabbi Kefa in the US 1-210-827-3907. I suggest for you to get a more accurate picture of the Bible you get the latest translated Hebraic Study Bible from www.forever-israel.com international which will help you study and understand many key issues. It is called the Hidden Truths Hebraic Scrolls Complete or the Tanak and Brit Ha Chadasha (NT)

May the Master Yahushua guide and bless/increase those of you who obey His Torah.

Rabbi Simon Altaf Hakohen

For groundbreaking articles… www.forever-israel.com.

We suggest you visit our website to see the following Titles:
www.forever-israel.com

Beyth Yahushua – the Son of Tzadok, the Son of Dawud

Would you like to know the identity of Yahushua's family the man you call Jesus? Did He have brothers and sisters, did He get married, and are not Rabbis meant to marry?

Is it true if Mary Magdalene was His wife and if not then what relationship did she have with him?

Who was Nicodemus and what relationship did Yahushua, have with Nicodemus? Who was the wider family of Yahushua?

For far too long He has been portrayed as the wandering man with no belongings and no family and living outside his home with women offering him money and food. This picture is both misleading and deceptive.

Do you want to know the powerful family of Yahushua that was a threat to Rome?

Who were Mark, Luke, and Matthew? Was Luke a gentile or a Hebrew priest?

What about the genealogy of Luke and Matthew in which the two fathers of Yahushua mentioned are Heli or Jacob in Matthew chapter 1:16 and Luke chapter 3:23 respectively?

This book will give you new insights and the rich history of Yahushua.

Islam, Peace or Beast
Have you ever wondered why radical Muslims are blowing up buildings, bombings planes and creating havoc? We illustrate in this book the reality of radical Islam and the end of days that are upon us. Why are our governments reluctant to tell us the truth we uncover many details. Does the Bible reference Middle-Eastern nations or European nations, how many verses can you spot for Europe? Are Muslims just maligned or what we see in Iraq today is what was spoken about in Isaiah 13 and Isaiah 14? The jihad crazed mind, Rev 17, the beast that arose out of the desert, the beheadings now on a TV in front of you myth or reality.

Does the prophet Ezekiel confirm the end is with Islamists or Europeans? Your eyes are about to be opened on a story that began back in Genesis 4000 years ago.

World War III – Unmasking the End-Times Beast
Who is the anti-Messiah, what countries are aligned with him and many of your other questions answered. All revealed in this book. Which might be the ten nations of the anti-Messiah? What did the prophets say on these events? Is the anti-Messiah a Jew? Where is Babylon and the daughter of Babylon in 2015. The true epic battle for Jerusalem. What part will the United States and United Kingdom play in the End of Days. See how accurate Rabbi Simon predicts the coming together of these nations. What are the ships of Kittim, who is Ararat, Minni and Ashkenaz? Who are the two thirds of people that will be killed?

World War III – Salvation of the Jews

- How will the salvation of the Jews come about, will they convert to Christianity?
- Will the 3rd Temple be built before the coming of the Messiah? Where is the real site of the Third Temple? Analyzed and explained with the correct hermeneutics.
- Will we have a war with Iran and when? Considering the pundits have been wrong since the last 7 years and only Rabbi Simon has been on track up to this time. What signs will absolutely indicate impending war with Iran calculated and revealed.
- When will the Messiah come, what signs should we be looking for, is it on a Jubilee year?
- Will America win the war in Afghanistan? Yes and No answer with details.
- Who is the prince of Ezekiel and why is he making sin sacrifices. Can one call these educational? Read the correct answers...
- Should we support the Jewish Aliyah to Israel?

Rabbi Simon is the only Rabbi to look at the thorny issues that no one has addressed to date while many people mostly run with popular churchy opinions coloured by bad theology by picking and choosing verses in isolation. Is modern Zionism biblical? Is Israel right to take over territories occupied by Palestinians today? Should people be selling up homes to go and live in Israel? All these thorny questions and even more answered in this book the sequel to the popular prophecy book World War III - Unmasking the End-Times Beast.

Dear Muslim – Meet YHWH the Elohim of Abraham
Truth explained, best seller step by step detailing and unveiling Islam! This book is designed for that friend, son or daughter who is about to convert into Islam but needs to read this first. This is the <u>one</u> stop to saving their soul. Don't procrastinate, get it today so that they may see what is the truth before they cause themselves to be confounded and duped into something totally not true.

The Feasts of YHWH, the Elohim of Israel
Have you ever asked why the feasts were given to Israel as a people? What is the meaning of the festivals and what about their purpose which is all explained in this detailed book that delves into this? Why are we to obey the feasts forever and if we do not then we could potentially lose our place in the kingdom entry! Well no one said that before but now you will see and experience an exhilarating experience of knowing what it is like to be there. How does it feel to be up all night to celebrate the festival of Shavuot (Pentecost), what does it mean and many other details.

Testament of Abraham
Now it's time to hear Abraham's story from his own mouth what happened, how did he become God's friend. What other missing information that we are not told about is made available. Without Abraham there will be no Judaism, no Islam and no Christianity.

He is the pivotal point upon which all three religious text claim right but who does Abraham really belong to?

What is Truth?

Have you wondered what truth is and how we measure it? How do we arrive at the conclusion that what you have is truth? How do you know that the religion you have been following for so many years is the original faith? Can we examine Atheism and say why it is or is not true. We examine these things.

Yeshua or Isa

If you want to witness to your Muslim friends or relatives about the truth of Yahushua and the Holy Bible, this is a must have book.

Hidden Truths Hebraic Scrolls Tanak 7th Edition Brit Ha Chadasha (NT)

An excellent translation of the New Testament Scriptures to edify and to teach you correctly the words of the disciples of the Master Yahushua and many important meanings of the texts. What did the Master say and what did he mean. What about the difficult writings of Paul, elaborated and explained in a manner that you will be truly enlightened.

Hidden Truths Hebraic Scrolls Tanak 7th Edition

The Bible more myths busted. Packed absolutely full of information - no Hebrew roots Bible even comes close this is guaranteed and these scrolls are the difference between night and day, see for yourself!!! The politically incorrect guide to the Elohim of Israel and the real chosen people of YHWH. Are you willing to listen to what YHWH has said about our world and how He is going to restore all things back including His real chosen people hidden to this day?

Many texts uncovered and explained in great details accurately and many corrections made to the many faulty translations out there making this a real eye-opener text.

- ➔ Was Chava (Eve) the only woman in the garden? We reveal a deep held secret.
- ➔ Where did the demons come from?
- ➔ Ezekiel refers to some of Israel's evil deeds in Egypt explicitly uncovered which are glossed over in the King James Version.
- ➔ Who are the Real Hebrews of the Bible, which people does the land of Y'sra'el really belong to? Time to do away with the deception.
- ➔ Did Abraham keep the Sabbath? We show you when and where.
- ➔ But I thought Keturah was Hagar, another error of Judaism corrected.
- ➔ But I thought Keturah was married to Abraham after Sarah's death, no not really. A very bad textual translation.
- ➔ Who was Balaam, a profit for cash as are many pastors and Bishops today doing the same thing running and chasing after the Almighty dollar?
- ➔ Who were Abraham's ancestors, Africa or Europeans?
- ➔ Why did Isaac marry at forty years of age, what happened to his first wife? Rebecca was not his only wife, an error and ignorance of Christendom exposed?
- ➔ Where is Noah's ark likely to be? Not Ararat in Turkey or Iran another error.
- ➔ Who are the four wives of Abraham and who is the real firstborn? Not Ishmael and not even Isaac. Was Isaac his only begotten son another error?
- ➔ All the modification of modern Judaism of the scribes has been undone to give you what was the real text including the original conversation of the Serpent with Chava (Gen 3) unedited plus Abraham's conversation unedited at last in Genesis 18.

The legendary Rabbi Simon Altaf Hakohen guarantees that this will teach you to take the best out there and open their eyes in prophecy, historical argument and theology. He will personally mentor you through the texts of the Torah, the prophets. Does any Bible seller offer this extent of training? We do. And Rabbi Simon is available at the end of an e-mail or just a telephone call away for questions that you have all this time.

Sefer Yashar (The Book of Jasher)
The book of Yashar has been translated from the original sources and with added commentary, corrected names of Elohim with the sacred names and with other missing text from the Hebrew. This will add to the gaps in your knowledge from the book of Genesis such as the following:

- What did the wicked do before the flood?
- Who were Abraham's African ancestors?
- Did Abraham have two wives?
- What relationship did Abraham have with Eli'ezer?
- Did Isaac wait forty years to be married?
- Why did Sarah die so suddenly?
- Did Moses marry in Egypt?
- Moses, what colour? White or Black.
- Many other questions now answered.

Seferim Chanoch (The Books of Enoch)
The books of Enoch details the fall, the names of the angels, what happened in the beginning and what was the result of those fallen angels. Where are they now and what will happen to them. He also reveals the birth of Noach and some very important details around this about the African ancestry of the patriarchs. And many other important details to complete your knowledge.

Yahushua, The Black Messiah

Have you been lied to about the true identity of Yahushua known popularly as Jesus of Nazareth? Have you been shown pictures of the son of the pope Alexander, the Borgia Cesare and may have believed that this Caucasian hybrid was Yahushua whose image was used in all the Western world in the 16th century? What ethnicity was Yahushua the Messiah and what race of people did He belong to? Is it important that we know His ethnicity? What colour was Moses, King David and King Solomon? We examine and look at the massive fraud perpetrated upon the western nations by their leaders to hide the real identity of the true Hebrew Israelite people and race which are being restored in these Last Days. Yahushua said everything will be restored and that includes His and His people's ethnicity and colour. Would you like to know because it affects your eternity, your destiny and His true message then get this book now. HIs New Covenant is what will give you Salvation or remove you from eternal life!!

Hebrew Wisdom – Kabbalah in the Brit Ha Chadasha
The book's purpose is to illustrate basic principles of Kabbalah and to reveal some of the Kabbalah symbolisms. We look at the Sefirots what they mean and how they apply to some of the teachings. We also look at the first chapter in Genesis and examine some of the symbols there. We examine the name of Elohim in Exodus 3:14 and see what it means.

The Apocrypha (With Pirke Avot 'Ethics of The Fathers')
Read the fifteen books of the Apocrypha to get an understanding of the events both of the exile and of Israel's early history. Read Ethics of the Fathers to understand rabbinic wisdom and some important elements of the story of Genesis. The tests, the trials and the miracles of the Temples. Without these books the story in the bible is incomplete and has gaps which these books will fill up and give you a more complete understanding.

Forever-Israel Siddur transliterated Hebrew with English (Daily life prayers 7th Edition)

Many times we wonder what prayers should we do when we go to bed, when we leave our home in the morning and how do we pray daily? What prayer should I do if I have a ritual bath? What prayer is for affixing a Mezuzah? Each year you wonder how to do the Passover Aggadah and what is the procedure. This book also covers women's niddah laws to give you understanding into women's ritual purity. Unlike other prayer books Rabbi Simon Altaf actually bothers to explain small details that are important and often ignored. This is one book you should not be without. The festival readings and the 72 names of God are included in the text.

World War III, The Second Exodus, Y'sra'el's return journey home

How will the genetic Hebrews be taken back to the land? Are the present day Jews in Y'sra'el of ancient stock? Is there any prophecy of foreigners invading Y'sra'el and inhabiting the land? How will Elohim have war with Amalek and wipe them out and who is Amalek today? Why is the Church so confused about bible prophecy?

How will the end come and why is the world hiding the identity of the true Y'sra'elites? Will there be a rapture or marching back on foot? What happens if we die in our exile? And many more questions answered. The time has come to expose the errors of others.

What Else Have They Kept From Us?

This book is as the result of an e-mail conversation with a lady who asked me some questions and one of her questions upon my answer was "What else have they kept from us?" This was the question that led to this book because instead of answering people with small sections of answers I decided the time had come that a book had to be written to answer and address everything as it happened from the start to the end so that many may see that the deception is real and it's a deep cunning deception which starts from your TV screens, in your newspapers followed by wherever you go in your daily life.

How would a person know that they are being deceived if they do not know what to look for? Its like a Ten Pound note well if you saw the original then you have something to compare the false note with but what if you were <u>never</u> presented with the original and always had the fake in your pocket then you will likely think the fake is real and this is how it is with Christianity today that is simply mixing paganism with truth. A false Ten pound note or a bad tender which will give you no value when you redeem it as I uncover it in the pages of this book. Who was Yahushua, the real Hebrews and Israel.

Patriarchal Marriage, Y'sra'el's Right-Ruling Way of Life, Methods and Practice

How did the Y'sra'elites live? What form of marriage did they practice and how did they practice it? This book is about to show you what was God's design from the beginning and how the Y'sra'elites lived within God's required parameters. Today these things appear mythological but here we show you the methods and ways of how this lifestyle was practiced and is being restored in these last days, while the much touted gentile monogamy is wrecking lives destroying families and society around us. How many marriages are breaking down as a result of the wrong model and how many children are living fatherless lives, while women live husbandless and unfulfilled lives. This book will show you why the Greek and Roman monogamy model with a husband and a wife and a bit on the side does not work. While Elohim's model of plural marriage is an everlasting model that not only works but saves many children from losing their father's and women from losing good husbands.

The Scroll of Yahubel (Jubilees)
The information that is missing in the Torah has been put in here to aid us in understanding the book of Genesis more. There are gaps in Genesis with what happened with Noakh? What was going on in Moses's time? This scroll allows us to piece together that information that is so important for our understanding. True names edition with many corrections made.

Who am I?
A Children's book to help the black Hebrew children with identity and direction in life. Many Hebrew children while looking for identity easily stray. While they search for love they end up in gangs to prove themselves and search for that missing something. When they do not find love in their homes due to broken homes often venturing out with devastating consequences, getting involved in criminal activities to prove themselves ruining their lives. This book's purpose is to help these children and even adults find themselves to teach them who they are and to find sound direction in life to secure you to the God of our ancestors where you belong. This will help change many lives.

Hidden Truths Hebraic Scrolls Compendium Guide Chumash Torah - For those who have the Hidden-Truths Hebraic Scrolls this is a must buy to give you a deeper understanding under the text and its meaning where the footnotes are expounded upon further in various books of the scrolls. To learn the secrets of the Torah. All the Parshas expounded for further understanding. It also contains all the parsha notes.

Hebrew Characters, The Power to have prayers answered

Have you ever tried praying and find that either your prayers take very long time to answer or they don't get answered at all? In frustration you ask other friends to pray for you in hope that you may get an answer from God soon. I have given considerable thought about the condition of our people and how many languish in poverty, in situations where they seek for help because they are given false dogmas, put in religious bondage and slavery of the mind and heart.

Many times they make their own lives harder because they have spent so much time in the nations that they just want to live like the gentiles and not Hebrew as they are unaware how to benefit themselves that await them. I know it can be a lonely road at times. Our Abbah in the heavens feels our pain while we live in exile He sends the Shekinah to be with us. He longs for us to return back to the contracts that we may receive all the increases and benefits that are only meant for us.

However we pass our life by with this that and the other person who gives us no joy but we think maybe if we carry on suffering things will change for the better but things NEVER change. This book was written to help for a time such as this to better the lives of our people. To empower them with the right petitions to give them benefits and increases in employment, love, marriage and sickness. This will help you break the spells of witchcraft, dealing with jealous people around you and personal anger issues. This will help you deal with demonic presences in your homes. This will show you how to receive a timely answer to all your prayers. I have used these methods for my students all over the world which have proven successful for them and have greatly benefited them. It takes many generations for a right-ruling priest to be born in our generations. How many generations our people have suffered the scourge of the curses for not obeying the Torah? Many are still suffering. The Most High is going to raise his priests one by one until we get our restoration complete. Rabbi Simon is of the priestly family born to help his people.

The Kohen is meant to be a benefit to the people of Y'sra'el and is one of the person's that has been given the authority to stand between the heavenly court and the earthly realm. Christian clergy has been lying to you for so long that you don't know what is good for you anymore. The Melekzadek priest's job is not to stand between the heaven and earth as you have been wrongly taught, his job is to be a King and serve justice on the earth with the Torah. While the Christian clergy teaches everyone can be a Melekzadek this is not the truth. Only the Kings of Israel can right hold that title, it's not for anyone else.
There is only one everlasting priesthood and that is the Lewitical one. This book has been written by a Lewitical priest of Beyth of Tzadok, its time you reap the benefits so decide wisely. Even if you are a gentile looking to become part of Israel by conversion the opportunity is open to you to obey the Torah and join us.
I want you all to benefit and to receive what rightly belongs to you. I could have sold this book for $100 a piece because everything in this manual would forever change your life once you put it in practice but I decided not to do that as my purpose was to help my people and not hinder them, now the rest is up to you if you want to take the next step.

Now that I know I am a Hebrew
You don't just wake up one day and say You are a Hebrew. Being Hebrew brings many processes that need to be completed before you are finally cleaned up as the Abbah desires to fulfil your responsibilities. This book is in the hope to help many of our people who are Hebrews and desiring the change to rid them of idolatry and clean up to present to the Abbah a sacrifice with sweet aroma so that they may serve Him faithfully according to His desire! Are you willing to make the sacrifices required to follow the God of Israel?

Religious Confusion and the Everlasting Path to the Torah

Everyone claims their religion is the truth or you will go to hell. The Torah makes only one claim that God is interested in our world affairs.

All those that are confused about which religion to follow there is only one voice of God and that voice is found in the Torah of Moses revealed in the Messiah Yahushua. For your eternal rest and peace in your life choose the Torah. This book helps you to make the wise choice to help your life. Everything around you is compromised and the entire man made religions claim to truth is nothing but smokes and mirrors to cheat people out of their eternal destiny. Turn back to the Torah to find your eternal future and hope.

www.ingramcontent.com/pod-product-compliance
Lightning Source LLC
Chambersburg PA
CBHW020732160426
43192CB00006B/203

9780982508008